TISS-MAT

Management Aptitude Test

Latest Edition
Practice Kit

20 Tests
20 Mock Test

Based On Real Exam Pattern

✓ Thoroughly Revised and Updated

✓ Detailed Analysis of all MCQs

Title : TISS-MAT Management Aptitude Test
Author Name : Mr. Rohit Manglik
Published By : EduGorilla Community Pvt. Ltd.
Publishers Address : 12/651, First Floor Opp. Arvindo Park, Near Jama Masjid, Indira Nagar, Lucknow, Uttar Pradesh-226016, India

Copyright EduGorilla

ISBN : 978-81-94874-71-3

Second Edition

Disclaimer EduGorilla

Compiled and created by EduGorilla Community Pvt. Ltd

Printed By EduGorilla Community Pvt. Ltd.

ROHIT MANGLIK
CEO, EduGorilla

Editor's Note

Dear Applicants,

People say *"Success comes to those who work hard."* But I've seen people working hard for their exams day in and day out for marginal success. While others succeed in their examinations by putting in just half the work. So are they God Gifted? No! I believe that it's because they work *smart* and not just *hard*. Similarly, for your exams, you should strategize your preparation so as to increase the likelihood of success. Well with EduGorilla get ready to increase your *chances of selection* in your exam by *16x*.

EduGorilla helps you in not only working *hard* but also working in a *smart and strategic* manner. With EduGorilla's preparation package, you get a chance to make your exam preparation easy, and a fun learning path towards selection. Finding the right path to your preparations can be difficult if you don't know in which direction to head. Don't worry, we have you covered! EduGorilla will be your guide to success in your journey. With our Preparation Package, you can prepare strategically and beat the exam in just one attempt.

EduGorilla's Preparation Package includes-

- **Test Series**
- **Books**

Our preparation package is handcrafted as per the latest changes, expert opinions, and students' discretion. Thus, enabling you to get through each stage of the selection process for your exam.

Our Books are designed by the teachers and experts of the respective exam with a combined 150+ years of experience; to provide you with easy, efficient, and effective learning. Our books are smart, in the sense that not only do they give you the answers to the questions but also provide similar questions for practice.

EduGorilla's competent Test Series gives you real-time experience and confidence through which you can clear your offline or online exam in just one attempt. We currently host 83,000+ mock tests for 1,440+ competitive and academic exams.

Thus, EduGorilla misses no chance to assist you in your preparation and covers all stages of the exam, so that you don't have to look anywhere else.

We provide complete preparation packages for defense, banking, teaching, and other National & State-Level exams. Hence, it doesn't matter which exam you aspire to because you will reach your success.

ALL THE BEST !
Let EduGorilla be your Guide to Success.

Rohit Manglik,
Founder and CEO, EduGorilla

INTRODUCTION

EduGorilla focuses on guiding students to succeed in their examinations. With that in mind, our book, titled "TISS-MAT : Management Aptitude Test", has been drafted through the collective efforts of our distinguished experts with 150+ years of combined experience. This book consists of questions that are created following the latest changes in the syllabus and exam pattern. We compiled the book on the basis of questions that are most likely to appear in the TISS-MAT. Through EduGorilla's "TISS-MAT : Management Aptitude Test" your chances of success will increase 16x.

EduGorilla does this through our Complete Preparation Package. This package consists of well-conceptualized and structured content in the form of questions that are tailor-made according to your needs and will help you practice for exams in a smart way by pinpointing all the necessary information. It also provides hints and solutions, along with a smart answer sheet for your self-evaluation. You can assess your shortcomings and work accordingly on areas that may require more of your attention.

EduGorilla promises to help you succeed in your examination and accomplish your dream goals. We believe in our aspirants and see them at the top of the merit list. And the first step towards the top is to start preparing with us. EduGorilla's "TISS-MAT : Management Aptitude Test" includes the following attributes.

- Well-Researched Content
- Top-Notch Quality
- Detailed Answers and Analysis
- Smart Answer Sheet
- Exam Relevant Questions

Therefore, EduGorilla fortifies your preparation and makes it durable enough to help you stand tall and beat the examination.

TISS-MAT

Scan QR code for Eligibility, Exam Pattern, Syllabus and more.

Book ID: 0638

TABLE OF CONTENTS

Mock Test 01

Comprehension

Ques (1-5):Direction: Read the following passage carefully and answer the question given below it.

Most of the competitive examinations conducted for admission for higher education or job recruitments are objective in nature. They have several advantages over the subjective ones, for both the examining authorities and the examinees. The multiple choice questions (MCQs) are the predominant type of objective questions. For each question a number of alternative answers, usually four, coded as (a), (b), and so on are given, one of which would be the correct or the 'most fitting' answer and the rest distractors. The examinee chooses and indicates the 'correct' answer. The evaluation is done electronically with utmost precision. The subjective type involves elaborate answering and its evaluation involves human elements, and therefore, sometimes, subject to vagaries. Thus the objective type of examining has the advantages of almost error-free evaluation, efficient answering by examinees who may have good subjective knowledge but no language proficiency and considerable saving in time for evaluation.

However, the question paper preparation of objective type requires more care and talent. First, the standard of the questions must suit the level of the candidates tested. Next, while some of the questions could be straight forward, from basic concepts learnt from textbooks or classes, some should be application oriented and based on a little extensions of those basic concepts. Such questions will help identify better talent in a group, which is an important aim of competitive examinations. All the answer codes must have almost equal probability of being the correct answer and the correct answer must be randomly distributed. (Some say that the choice (c) is often the correct answer code.). The concept of negative marking for wrong answers is not acceptable to some of us. They feel that wise guessing could be allowed and should not be discouraged with penalty if it goes wrong. It should be noted that wise guessing is already allowed, as it is one of the methods of narrowing down to the correct answer after eliminating the wrong answers. If by this you are not narrowing down to the correct answer, then your guess is not wise but wild, which should be discouraged.

The implication of wild guesses can be brought out with an example of a candidate A taking an objective test. Suppose A does not even open the question booklet, but goes on marking one particular answer code, say (b), for all the 100 questions of the test, which may take less than five minutes. If there are four multiple choices, (b) would be the correct answer choice for about 25 questions, in all probability, getting him 25 marks out of the total marks of 100. Say now, B, a serious student who would have sincerely attempted might have got much less; how to tackle this situation? A should get only zero which he deserves. The purpose of examinations, particularly competitive ones, is to correctly assess the relative merits of candidates, which is made possible by the negative marking system. Awarding of any concessions to anyone is a matter that can be taken up at a later stage.

Q.1 Why objective evaluation is prefered over the one which is done subjectively?

A. Objective evaluation is almost error-free
B. Technology used builds precision in marking
C. The subjective types are bound to have human error
D. Both A and C

Q.2 What does the author mean by the implication of wild guesses?

A. Wild guessing is a bad habit
B. Guessing an answer shows lack of merit
C. Those who get selected by luck are not good people
D. A wild guess in exams can costs dearly

Q.3 What of the following is the nearest in meaning to "IMPLICATIONS" ?

A. Suggestion **B.** Innuendo
C. Indication **D.** All of them

Q.4 Which of the following statements is incorrect according to the passage?

A. Preparing objective type questions requires more skills
B. In several tests, scheme of negative marking is being adopted
C. Answering "most fitting" answer is in itself is arbitrary
D. Purpose of examinations is to assess the relative merits of candidates

Q.5 Other than the right option, "_______" has been used to describe rest of the options. Identify that word from the passage

A. Attention-grabber **B.** Diversion
C. Distractors **D.** Gimmick

Ques (6-7):Direction: Read the following passage carefully and answer the question given below it. Certain parts are given in bold to answer some of the question based on the passage.

The task which Gandhiji undertook was not only the achievement of political freedom but also the establishment of a social order based on truth and non violence, unity and peace, equality and universal brotherhood, and maximum freedom for all. This unfinished part of his experiment was perhaps more difficult to achieve than the achievement of political freedom. Political struggle involved fight against a foreign power and all one do was either join it or wish it's success. In establishing social order of this pattern, there was lively possibility of a conflict arising between groups and classes, of our own people. Experience shows that man values his possessions even more than his life because in the former he sees the means for perpetuation and survival of his descendants even after his body is reduced to ashes. A new order cannot be established without radically changing the mind and attitude of men towards property and at some stage or the other, the 'haves' have to yield place to 'have-nots'. We have seen, in our time, attempts to achieve a kind of egalitarian society and a picture of it after it was achieved. But this was done, by and large, through the use of physical force.

In the ultimate analysis, it is difficult, if not impossible to say that the instinct to possess has been **rooted out** or that it will not reappear in an even worse form under a different **guise**. It may even be that, like a has kept confined within containers under great pressure, or water held by a big fan, once a barrier breaks the reaction will one day sweep back with a violence equal in extent and intensity to what was used to establish and maintain the outward egalitarian form. This
enforced egalitarianism consists, in its own bosom, the seed of its own destruction. The root cause of class conflict is possessiveness or the acquisitive instance. So long as the ideal that is to be achieved is one of securing the maximum material satisfaction, possessiveness can neither be suppressed nor eliminated but will grow on what it feeds. Nor will it Will cease to be such – it is possessiveness, still, whether it is confined to only a few it is shared by many. If **egalitarianism** bis to be ensured, it has to be based on not on the possession of the maximum material goods by a few or by all but on voluntary, enlightened renunciation of those goods which cannot be shared by others or can be enjoyed only at the expense of theirs. This calls for substitution of spiritual values that is sometimes equated with progress these days, neither spells peace nor progress. Mahatma Gandhi has shown us how the acquisitive instinct inherent in man could be transmuted by the adoption of the **ideal of trusteeship** by which the wealthy people would be the trustees of trusts that looked after the welfare of the people in general.

Q.6 What can you infer from the phrase "root out"?

A. To destroy something
B. Instill something
C. Find and remove something/ someone
D. To flatten something

Q.7 Choose the most appropriate title for the passage:

A. Material values v/s Spiritual values
B. Class conflicts in an egalitarian society
C. The Gandhiji's vision of social order
D. The renunciation of possessive instinct

Ques (8-10):Direction: Read the following passage carefully and answer the question given below it. Certain parts are given in bold to answer some of the question based on the passage.

The task which Gandhiji undertook was not only the achievement of political freedom but also the establishment of a social order based on truth and non violence, unity and peace, equality and universal brotherhood, and maximum freedom for all. This unfinished part of his experiment was perhaps more difficult to achieve than the achievement of political freedom. Political struggle involved fight against a foreign power and all one do was either join it or wish it's success. In establishing social order of this pattern, there was lively possibility of a conflict arising between groups and classes, of our own people. Experience shows that man values his possessions even more than his life because in the former he sees the means for perpetuation and survival of his descendants even after his body is reduced to ashes. A new order cannot be established without radically changing the mind and attitude of men towards property and at some stage or the other, the 'haves' have to yield place to 'have-nots'. We have seen, in our time, attempts to achieve a kind of egalitarian society and a picture of it after it was achieved. But this was done, by and large, through the use of physical force.

In the ultimate analysis, it is difficult, if not impossible to say that the instinct to possess has been **rooted out** or that it will not reappear in an even worse form under a different **guise**. It may even be that, like a has kept confined within containers under great pressure, or water held by a big fan, once a barrier breaks the reaction will one day sweep back with a violence equal in extent and intensity to what was used to establish and maintain the outward egalitarian form. This
enforced egalitarianism consists, in its own bosom, the seed of its own destruction. The root cause of class conflict is possessiveness or the acquisitive instance. So long as the ideal that is to be achieved is one of securing the maximum material satisfaction, possessiveness can neither be suppressed nor eliminated but will grow on what it feeds. Nor will it Will cease to be such – it is possessiveness, still, whether it is confined to only a few it is shared by many. If **egalitarianism** bis to be ensured, it has to be based on not on the possession of the maximum material goods by a few or by all but on voluntary, enlightened renunciation of those goods which cannot be shared by others or can be enjoyed only at the expense of theirs. This calls for substitution of spiritual values that is sometimes equated with progress these days, neither spells peace nor progress. Mahatma Gandhi has shown us how the acquisitive instinct inherent in man could be transmuted by the adoption of the **ideal of trusteeship** by which the wealthy people would be the trustees of trusts that looked after the welfare of the people in general.

Q.8 Select the most appropriate option to complete the given sentence.

Gandhi aimed at:

A. Achieving political freedom
B. Establishing a non violent society
C. Universal brotherhood
D. A,B and C

Q.9 Egalitarianism means:

A. Suppression
B. Social and political equality
C. Violence
D. Inequality

Q.10 Which one of the following is the most similar in meaning to the word "GUISE" ?

A. Illusion
B. Disappear
C. Appearance
D. Reprove

Management Data Interpretation

Ques (11-13): The following table shows the profit (figures given in INR crore) earned by top four hotel groups for last five financial years.

	Raj	Sheela	CTI	Milton
$2009-10$	238	121	239	70
$2010-11$	285	144	237	77
$2011-12$	265	149	270	87
$2012-13$	299	179	319	99
$2013-14$	330	201	388	131

Q.11 The average profit earned by Sheela group of hotels for the given period is how much percentage more than that earned by Milton group of hotels?

A. 66% **B.** 71% **C.** 75% **D.** 62%

Q.12 In $2012-13$ what's the percentage share of Raj group of hotels among the given four groups?

A. 32.2% **B.** 36.1% **C.** 34.6% **D.** 33.4%

Q.13 What is the highest percentage increase in the profit of Raj group with respect to that of the previous year?

A. 20% **B.** 18% **C.** 16% **D.** 13%

Ques (14-16):Direction: Study the chart and answer the following question:

The following pie-chart shows the percentage of different grades achieved by students on the final exam in physics.

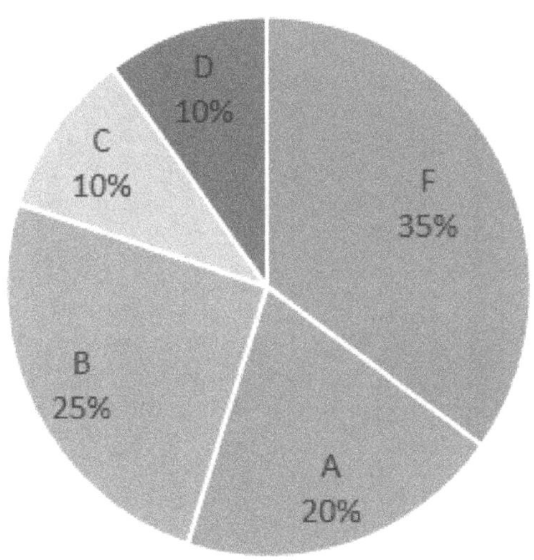

Q.14 If 250 students took the exam, how many students get D grade?

A. 35 **B.** 25 **C.** 10 **D.** 29

Q.15 If 500 students give the exam, how many students get C grade?

A. 50 **B.** 20 **C.** 35 **D.** 10

Q.16 What percent of the students who failed the exam would have had to pass it, in order for percent of students passing the exam to be at least 77% out of 500?

A. 15% **B.** 21% **C.** 23% **D.** 27%

Ques (17-19):Direction: Study the chart given below and answer the following question:

The line graph given below shows the speed of Alex at different time.

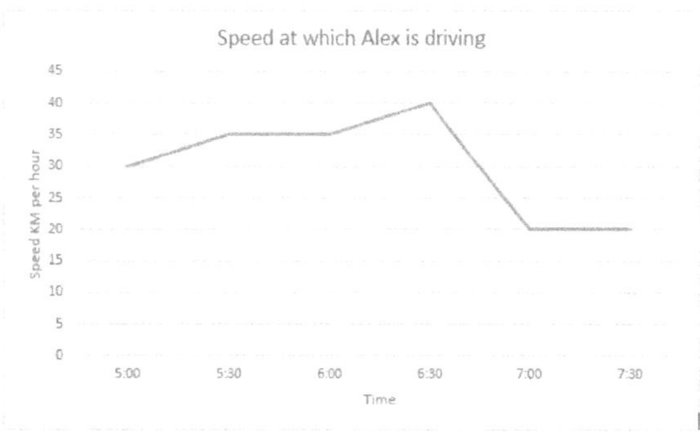

Q.17 How far, in km, did Alex drive between $5:30$ and $6:00$?

A. 20 **B.** $17\frac{1}{2}$ **C.** 35 **D.** $12\frac{1}{2}$

Q.18 What was Alex's average speed, in $km/hour$ between $5:30$ to $6:30$?

A. 25.25 **B.** 35.5 **C.** 42.5 **D.** 36.25

Q.19 For what percent of time Alex driving at $35km/hour$ or faster?

A. 35 **B.** 25 **C.** 27 **D.** 60

Ques (20-22):Direction: Study the chart given below and answer the following question:

The line graph given below shows the profit of two companies A and B across multiple years.

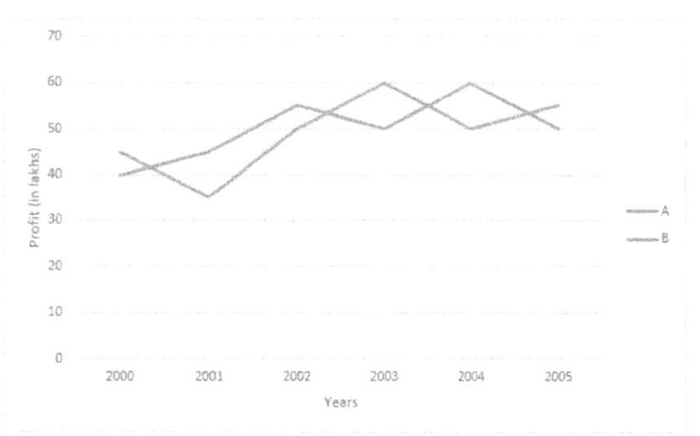

Q.20 Firm A spent $35,00,000$ in the year 2002. What is the income of Firm A in that year?

A. 15,42,500 **B.** 20,00,000
C. 15,25,000 **D.** 90,00,000

Q.21 If the expenditure of both the firms A and B in the year 2004 was equivalent, then what was the ratio between the income of Firm A to Firm B?

A. 15:6 **B.** 6:15 **C.** 6:5 **D.** 16:5

Q.22 In which of the following years was the maximum percentage of growth/decline with respect to the previous years in case of Company B?

A. $2000-2001$ **B.** $2001-2002$
C. $2002-2003$ **D.** $2003-2004$

Ques (23-25):Direction: Study the chart given below and answer the following question:

The following bar graph shows the price per share of two stocks A and B on June 5 of 6 years.

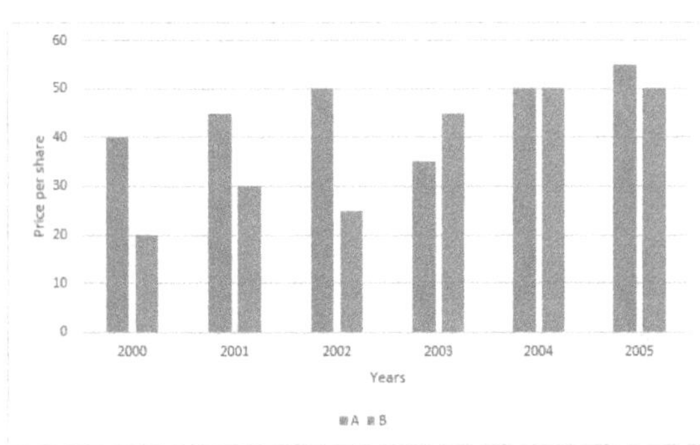

Q.23 What is the difference, in dollars, of a share of stock A, between the highest and lowest value?

A. Rs. 10 **B.** Rs. 15 **C.** Rs. 20 **D.** Rs. 25

Q.24 In which year, there was the greatest difference between the price of the share of the stock A and a share of stock B?

A. 2003 **B.** 2004 **C.** 2002 **D.** 2005

Q.25 In which year, the ratio of the value of a share of stock A to the value of a share of stock B is the greatest?

A. 2002 **B.** 2003 **C.** 2004 **D.** 2005

Business Awareness

Q.26 Name the first Indian businessman who found place in the cover story of Forbes magazine:

A. Azim Hasham Premji
B. Narayan Murthy
C. Dr Reddy
D. Anil Ambani

Q.27 Which Payments Bank becoming the first bank to offer cash backs on deposits?

A. Postal Payments Bank
B. Airtel Payments Bank
C. Aditya Birla Payments Bank
D. Paytm Payments Bank

Q.28 Rahul Dravid is associated with the advertising campaign of which bank?

A. Bank of Baroda **B.** Bank of India
C. HDFC **D.** HSBC

Q.29 Name the Brand that advertises itself with the slogan 'The Vision Of Sound'?

A. Samsung TVs **B.** Thomson TVs
C. Sansui TVs **D.** BPL TVs

Q.30 Which company uses tagline "Drive your way" ?

A. Yamaha **B.** Toyota **C.** Hyundai **D.** Erickson

Q.31 Grand Vitara XV-7 is a vehicle launched by:

A. Maruti Suzuki **B.** Hyundai
C. GM **D.** Ford

Q.32 Which news paper has the motto - Journalism of Courage?

A. The Indian Express
B. The Guardian
C. The Washington Post
D. The Hindustan Times

Q.33 Sagem, which launched mobile phones in India, is a company from?

A. China **B.** Korea **C.** France **D.** Italy

Q.34 Taj Hotels has entered into a marketing alliance with The Shilla Hotels & Resorts of Korea. Shilla Hotels is affiliated to which industrial group?

A. Samsung **B.** Daewoo **C.** LG **D.** Hyundai

Q.35 HRM is _____.

A. A staff function
B. A line function
C. A staff function, line function and accounting function
D. All of the above

// Smart Answer Sheet //

Correct Indicates percentage of students who answered questions correctly.

Skipped Indicates percentage of students who skipped questions.

Q.	Ans.	Correct / Skipped
1	D	45.26 % / 3.02 %
2	D	28.02 % / 21.12 %
3	D	24.14 % / 25.43 %
4	C	34.05 % / 26.73 %
5	C	41.81 % / 27.16 %
6	C	40.52 % / 30.17 %
7	C	27.16 % / 32.32 %
8	D	49.57 % / 32.76 %
9	B	46.55 % / 33.62 %
10	C	33.19 % / 34.05 %
11	B	25.0 % / 21.12 %
12	D	25.43 % / 28.02 %
13	A	21.55 % / 29.74 %
14	B	50.43 % / 29.74 %
15	A	49.57 % / 30.6 %
16	C	18.1 % / 32.33 %
17	B	34.91 % / 31.04 %
18	D	23.28 % / 33.19 %
19	D	15.52 % / 33.19 %
20	D	17.67 % / 34.49 %
21	C	28.88 % / 36.21 %
22	B	30.17 % / 37.93 %
23	C	27.59 % / 37.93 %
24	C	40.95 % / 39.65 %
25	A	27.59 % / 37.5 %
26	A	38.36 % / 19.4 %
27	D	40.52 % / 20.26 %
28	A	34.91 % / 22.42 %
29	A	34.05 % / 21.98 %
30	C	32.76 % / 22.41 %
31	A	38.36 % / 22.42 %
32	A	33.62 % / 21.98 %
33	C	18.53 % / 23.28 %
34	A	21.12 % / 23.28 %
35	A	21.55 % / 22.42 %

Performance Analysis	
Avg. Score (%)	28.57%
Toppers Score (%)	100.0%
Your Score	

//Hints and Solutions//

1. As mentioned in the passage, 'The subjective type involves elaborate answering and its evaluation involves human elements, and therefore, sometimes, subject to vagaries. Thus the objective type of examining has the advantages of almost error-free evaluation, efficient answering by examinees who may have good subjective knowledge but no language proficiency and considerable saving in time for evaluation.'

Both A and C are mentioned in the starting paragraph. No explicit mention of option B.

Hence, the correct option is (D).

2. By the implication of wild guesses the author means that a wild guess in exams can costs dearly as by probability he will be at risk of getting negative marks.

Hence, the correct option is (D).

3. Implication - the conclusion that can be drawn from something although it is not explicitly stated.

Suggestion - a plan or idea that somebody mentions for somebody else to discuss and consider.

Innuendo - a remark that suggests something but does not refer to it directly, or this type of remark in general.

Indication - something that shows something; a sign.

So all of them have meaning nearest to implications.

Hence, the correct option is (D).

4. There is no such mention in the passage about 'Answering "most fitting" answer is in itself is arbitrary'.

Hence, the correct option is (C).

5. As mentioned in the sentence 'one of which would be the correct or the 'most fitting' answer and the rest distractors', the word distractors has been used to describe rest of the options.

Hence, the correct option is (C).

6. Root out means to find and remove something/someone.

Hence, the correct option is (C).

7. On evaluating the passage we can conclude that the most appropriate title for the passage will be 'the Gandhiji's vision of social order'.

Hence, the correct option is (C).

8. According to the passage Gandhi aimed at:

- Achieving political freedom
- Establishing a non violent society
- Universal brotherhood

Hence, the correct option is (D).

9. Egalitarianism – a doctrine that all are people and deserve equal rights and opportunities.

So out of the given options the meaning of egalitarianism is social and political equality.

Hence, the correct option is (B).

10. Guise – an external form, appearance typically concealing the true nature of something.

So out of the given options appearance has the most similar meaning to guise.

Hence, the correct option is (C).

11. Total profit earned by Sheela group of Hotels $= 121 + 144 + 149 + 179 + 201 = 794$

Total profit earned by Milton group of Hotels $= 70 + 77 + 87 + 99 + 131 = 464$

Average profit earned by Sheela group of Hotels $= \frac{794}{5}$

$= 158.8$

Average profit earned by Milton group of Hotels $= \frac{464}{5}$

$= 92.8$

Difference between average profit earned by Sheela group of Hotels and Milton group of Hotels

$= 158.8 - 92.8$

$= 66$

The percentage by which the average profit earned by Sheela group of hotels for the given period is more than that earned by Milton group of hotels

$= \frac{66}{92.8} \times 100 = 71.12\%$

Hence, the correct option is (B).

12. Raj group in $2012 - 13 = 299$
And all four hotels together in $2012 - 13 = 299 + 179 + 319 + 99 = 896$
So, the ratio is $\frac{299}{896} = \frac{1}{3}$ (almost)

Percentage of $\frac{1}{3}$
$= 33.33\%$

Hence, the correct option is (D).

13. For Raj group the highest increase is for $2009 - 10$ to $2010 - 11$
Where the increase is $285 - 238 = 47$ on 238
So, the percentage increase is $47 \times \frac{100}{238}$
$= 19.74\%$

Hence, the correct option is (A).

14. Given:

Percentage of $D\% = 10\%$
Number of student who took exam $= 250$

Student who got grade $D = 10\%$ of 250

$\Rightarrow 250 \times \frac{10}{100} = 25$

Hence, the correct option is (B).

15. Given:

Percentage of $C\% = 10\%$
Number of student who took exam $= 500$

Student who got grade $C = 10\%$ of 500

$\Rightarrow 500 \times \frac{10}{100} = 50$

Hence, the correct option is (A).

16. Number of passed students $= 500 \times \frac{77}{100} = 385$
Thus for the passing rate to have been at least 77%, no more than 115 students should fail.

Which is 23% of 500.

Hence, the correct option is (C).

17. Since Alex is driving at constant speed $35\ km/hour$ during
$5:30$ to $6:00$
Thus in half hour he drove
$\frac{1}{2} \times 35$
$= 17\frac{1}{2} km$

Hence, the correct option is (B).

18. From the graph we see that clearly from $5:30$ to $6:00$ Alex average speed was clearly $35\ km/hour$,

And from $6:00$ to $6:30$ Alex speed steadily increased from 35 to $40 km/hour$.
So, during $6:00$ to $6:30$ hour his average speed was:
$\frac{35+40}{2} = \frac{75}{2} = 37.5 km/hour$
Thus in the given hour his average speed was:
$\frac{37.5+35}{2} = 36.25 km/hr$.

Hence, the correct option is (D).

19. If we convert the total time and the highlighted time into minutes we will get 1.5 hours $= 90$ minutes and 2.5 hours $= 150$ minutes.

If we derive the percentage from this we get , $\frac{90}{150} \times 100 = 60$

Hence, the correct option is (D).

20. Profit of Firm A in 2002 is $55,00,000$
Income $=$ Profit $+$ Expenditure
$= 35,00,000 + 55,00,000$
$= 90,00,000$

Hence, the correct option is (D).

21. Let X be the expenditure of the Firm A, since expenditure of the firms A and B are equivalent
Income of Firm $A = X + 60,00,000$
Income of Firm $B = X + 50,00,000$
$X + 60,00,000 : X + 50,00,000$
$\Rightarrow$ ratio is $6:5$

Hence, the correct option is (C).

22. Profit in $2001 = 350000$
Profit in $2002 = 500000$
Decline $= 500000 - 350000 = 150000$
$= \frac{150000}{350000} \times 100 = 43\%(\text{ approx })$

Hence, the correct option is (B).

23. According to the bar graph, the highest value of the share of stock A was Rs. 55 in 2005 and the lowest value the share of stock A was Rs. 35 in 2003.
Thus,
Difference $55 - 35 =$ Rs. 20

Hence, the correct option is (C).

24. In 2000 difference between price of the share of stock A and B as price of A is Rs. 40 and price of B is Rs. 20.

Difference is $40 - 20 =$ Rs. 20

In 2001 difference between price of the share of stock A and B as price of A is Rs. 45 and price of B is Rs. 30.

Difference is $45 - 30 =$ Rs. 15

In 2002 difference between price of the share of stock A and B as price of A is Rs. 50 and price of B is Rs. 25.

Difference is $50 - 25 =$ Rs. 25

In 2003 difference between price of the share of stock A and B as price of A is Rs. 35 and price of B is Rs. 45.

Difference is $45 - 35 =$ Rs. 10

In 2004 difference between price of the share of stock A and B as price of A is Rs. 50 and price of B is Rs. 50.

Difference is $50 - 50 =$ Rs. 0

In 2005 difference between price of the share of stock A and B as price of A is Rs. 55 and price of B is Rs. 50.

Difference is $55 - 50 =$ Rs. 5

So on seeing all the values we can conclude that the greatest difference between price of the share of stock A and B as price of A was in 2002.

Hence, the correct option is (C).

25. According to the bar graph,
The period from 2003 to 2005 the values of the shares of two stocks are very close, so we neglect these years.
Now, there is a greatest difference between the shares of stock A and B in 2002,

Which is $50:25$ where price of share of stock of $A=$ Rs. 50 and price of share of stock of $B=$ Rs. 25
$\Rightarrow 2:1$

So the ratio of the value of a share of stock A to the value of a share of stock B is the greatest in 2002.

Hence, the correct option is (A).

26. Azim Hasham Premji was the first Indian businessman who found place in the cover story of Forbes magazine.
Azim Hashim Premji (born 24 July 1945) is an Indian business tycoon, investor, engineer, and philanthropist, who was the chairman of Wipro Limited.
Hence, the correct option is (A).

27. Paytm Payments Bank becoming the first bank to offer cash backs on deposits.

Payments Bank is a new bank model visualised by the Reserve Bank of India. As a Payments Bank, Paytm can now accept customer deposits upto Rs. 1 lakh per customer in a savings or current account and offer other banking services like Debit Cards, Online Banking and Mobile Banking.

Payments Banks can not offer financial products of their own, but partner with other banks.

Hence, the correct option is (D).

28. Rahul Dravid is associated with the advertising campaign of Bank of Baroda.
Bank of Baroda (BOB) is an Indian multinational, public sector banking and financial services company. It is the third largest public sector bank in India, with 131 million customers, a total business of US$218 billion, and a global presence of 100 overseas offices.
Hence, the correct option is (A).

29. Samsung TVs advertises itself with the slogan 'The Vision Of Sound'.

The Samsung Group is a South Korean multinational conglomerate headquartered in Samsung Town, Seoul. It comprises numerous affiliated businesses, most of them united under the Samsung brand

Hence, the correct option is (A).

30. Hyundai Company uses the tagline "Drive your way".

The Hyundai Motor Company (commonly known as Hyundai) is a South Korean multinational automotive manufacturer headquartered in Seoul. Hyundai Motor Company was founded in 1967 and, along with its 32.8 percent owned subsidiary, Kia Motors, and its 100 percent owned luxury subsidiary, Genesis Motor, and electric vehicle subsidiary, Ioniq, altogether comprise the Hyundai Motor Group.

Hence, the correct option is (C).

31. Grand Vitara XV-7 is a vehicle launched by Maruti Suzuki.
Maruti Suzuki India Limited, formerly known as Maruti Udyog Limited, is an Indian automobile manufacturer headquartered in New Delhi. It is a subsidiary of the Japanese automotive manufacturer Suzuki Motor Corporation.
Hence, the correct option is (A).

32. The Indian Express has the motto - Journalism of Courage.

The Indian Express is the daily English newspaper published in India. It was founded by Shri Ramnath Goenka in 1932.

Hence, the correct option is (A).

33. Sagem, which launched mobile phones in India, is a company from France.
SAGEM (Société d'Applications Générales de l'Électricité et de la Mécanique, translated as "Company of General Applications of Electricity and Mechanics") was a major French company involved in defense electronics, consumer electronics and communication systems.
Hence, the correct option is (C).

34. Shilla Hotels is affiliated to Samsung.

Hotel Shilla started operations in March 1979 at the direction of Lee Byung-chull, founder of the Samsung Group. Before 1979, it was the state guest house of Republic of Korea under the Park Chung-hee government. Now, it has been expanding into the commissioned management of fitness facilities as well as into the restaurant business.

Hence, the correct option is (A).

35. HRM is a staff function.

A "staff function" supports the organization with specialized advisory and support functions. For example, human resources, accounting, public relations and the legal department are generally considered to be staff functions.

Hence, the correct option is (A).

Mock Test 02

Comprehension

Ques (1-6):Direction: Read the following passage carefully and answer the question given below it. Certain parts are given in bold to answer some of the question based on the passage.

Sometimes to upend entrenched power structures, a revolution is required. Naming and shaming powerful men in the #Metoo campaign is in many ways a revolutionary act. The truth about most was known, spoken in whispers, but not to their face. But now that **omerta has been broken** by some **intrepid** women , there's a **palpable** sense of power and possibility.

Revolutions are by definition anarchic, as they are aimed against those who make and enforce the rules. So it has been with #MeToo. Men are named, sometimes anonymously, and the naming itself requires punitive action to be taken against them. There isn't really any room for discussion on context or degree of culpability. Some have raised questions about due process, and the response has been, somewhat reasonably, that due process has failed. And it is true, arguing for due process when due process has failed feels a bit like batting for status quo. So let it be said, #MeToo despite its limitations is unreservedly a good development.However, the question is, what next? The #MeToo movement is more than just outing powerful men, it is about shifting the balance of power between men and women, transferring the punitive aspects — shame, denial of work opportunities — from the victim to the perpetrator. It is about ending impunity embedded in our social construct by shaping new social mores. This is and has to be a collective effort, and it is important for the #MeToo movement to have these discussions.

Let the burden of shame now be shifted to where it is supposed to- the perpetrators and not the women; the victims. It's the woman who has to hide from the world. And by and large, due to this very fact prevailing in Indian society that many women ultimately choose to leave their jobs, or seek employment elsewhere, when they confront inappropriate behaviour from their colleagues.

Another very important aspect which should be taken care of is that of equality, where there's no inhibitions, no sense of caution. Women need healthy **camaraderie** in place of needless caution. Respect, not condescension. They would like colleagues to engage with them, not be patronising. And the fact that they are still having to demand these is telling.

Q.1 Against whom the writer suggests are revolutions usually aimed at ?

A. The guilty men

B. Perpetrators

C. Against the government agencies

D. Those who make and enforce laws

Q.2 Which of the following statements is not true according to the passage?

A. Just naming and shaming the perpetrators does not account for culpability

B. Due process has failed leading to crimes

C. Sexual harassment is anything that makes a woman uncomfortable

D. The campaign has broken the power structures

Q.3 Which of the following options does the author suggests while talking about transferring the punitive aspects?

A. shame

B. denial of work opportunities

C. respect

D. Both A and B

Q.4 Which of the following is most similar in meaning to "PALPABLE" ?

A. Enraged **B.** Disgusted

C. Nefarious **D.** Noticeable

Q.5 What kind of environment does the writer advocate for women in conclusion of the passage?

A. Workplace with maximum security

B. Men need not patronise women

C. Healthy camaraderie instead of needless caution

D. Both B and C

Q.6 Which of the following is the most similar in meaning to the word "PATRONISING" ?

A. Scorn **B.** Snub

C. Condescend **D.** Indulge

Ques (7-8):Direction: Read the following passage carefully and answer the question given below it. Certain parts are given in bold to answer some of the question based on the passage.

While adopting a technology, Indians have made changes to their attitudes and societal norms but often also made the technology work around their instincts. One area where the law of the jungle seems to prevail is the road, especially in cities. As a rule, typically, two-wheelers and cars don't consider lanes important. We don't want to wait our turn but keep jumping lanes and **wading** around obstacles. We seem to be possessed by a primal urge to get ahead of others even if it means the driver of the car or the two-wheeler rider on the other lane has to jam hard on his brakes.

Over the next 15 years, however, Indian driving is likely to be disrupted by electric vehicles that the Indian government seems keen on introducing, without transitioning to hybrids. Far less polluting and carbon-emitting, the electric car, however, poses a challenge to Indian driving practices. The motor is much quieter than the engine and the transmission system has fewer parts too. "All one hears is wind, tyre and road noise, which is minimal in city driving," says Mahesh Babu, CEO of Mahindra Electric. Imagine thousands of cars moving around, quietly, on our roads. Electric motors are among the **perkiest** prime movers. After starting, they can very quickly ramp up to full speed, unlike the internal combustion engine that needs to idle and takes time to increase speed. "Instant torque and quick acceleration," sums up Mr. Babu. Maximum torque is available for a range of speeds too.

Another crucial, efficiency-boosting attribute of the electric car will be regenerative braking. It is a cute application of an old physics law where the electric motor powering the car can reverse its role, becoming a generator and charging the battery. The generator load is the resistance that provides braking torque and it can be varied if you want to just bring down the speed, not stop the car altogether.Electric cars present a unique opportunity for Indian drivers. Instead of **tamping down** the technology, we can instead change our habits — be mindful of lanes, wait our turn, be polite and respectful of others and their needs, and make our driving smoother, as well as make best use of regenerative braking.

Q.7 What can you infer from the phrase "TAMPING DOWN"?

A. To lead to an accident

B. Crush someone

C. Toning of rules

D. Reduce importance of something

Q.8 Which one of the following is the most similar in meaning to the word "PERKIEST"?

A. Beneficial **B.** Bouncy

C. Productive **D.** Lively

Ques (9-10):Direction: Read the following passage carefully and answer the question given below it. Certain parts are given in bold to answer some of the question based on the passage.

While adopting a technology, Indians have made changes to their attitudes and societal norms but often also made the technology work around their instincts. One area where the law of the jungle seems to prevail is the road, especially in cities. As a rule, typically, two-wheelers and cars don't consider lanes important. We don't want to wait our turn but keep jumping lanes and **wading** around obstacles. We seem to be possessed by a primal urge to get ahead of others even if it means the driver of the car or the two-wheeler rider on the other lane has to jam hard on his brakes.

Over the next 15 years, however, Indian driving is likely to be disrupted by electric vehicles that the Indian government seems keen on introducing, without transitioning to hybrids. Far less polluting and carbon-emitting, the electric car, however, poses a challenge to Indian driving practices. The motor is much quieter than the engine and the transmission system has fewer parts too. "All one hears is wind, tyre and road noise, which is minimal in city driving," says Mahesh Babu, CEO of Mahindra Electric. Imagine thousands of cars moving around, quietly, on our roads. Electric motors are among the **perkiest** prime movers. After starting, they can very quickly ramp up to full speed, unlike the internal combustion engine that needs to idle and takes time to increase speed. "Instant torque and quick acceleration," sums up Mr. Babu. Maximum torque is available for a range of speeds too.

Another crucial, efficiency-boosting attribute of the electric car will be regenerative braking. It is a cute application of an old physics law where the electric motor powering the car can reverse its role, becoming a generator and charging the battery. The generator load is the resistance that provides braking torque and it can be varied if you want to just bring down the speed, not stop the car altogether.Electric cars present a unique opportunity for Indian drivers. Instead of **tamping down** the technology, we can instead change our habits — be mindful of lanes, wait our turn, be polite and respectful of others and their needs, and make our driving smoother, as well as make best use of regenerative braking.

Q.9 How do Indians adopt new technologies?

A. With full consciousness

B. Use it with utmost care and using it productively

C. Refrain from sharing it

D. Mould it according to our habits

Q.10 Which one of the following is most similar in meaning to "WADING"?

A. Sidelining **B.** Trudge

C. Cascading **D.** Amplify

Management Data Interpretation

Ques (11-15):Direction: Study the following graph carefully to answer the given question.

The graph shows time (in minutes) taken by various pipes to fill a cistern.

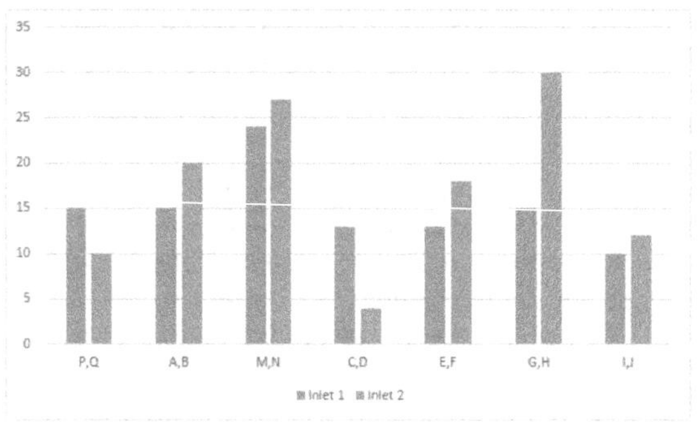

Q.11 A large cistern can be filled by two pipes P and Q. How many minutes will it take to fill the Cistern from an empty state if Q is used for half the time and P and Q fill it together for the other half?

A. 6.5 minutes **B.** 7.5 minutes

C. 8.5 minutes **D.** 9.5 minutes

Q.12 Two pipes M and N can fill a tank. If both the pipes are opened simultaneously, after how much time should N be closed so that the tank is full in 8 minutes?

A. 14 minutes **B.** 12 minutes

C. 15 minutes **D.** 18 minutes

Q.13 Three pipe E, F, and R can fill a tank. If Pipe R alone can fill a tank in 24 minutes then the pipe R is closed 12 minutes before the tank is filled. In what time the tank is full?

A. $8\frac{5}{13}$ **B.** $8\frac{4}{13}$ **C.** $7\frac{4}{13}$ **D.** $8\frac{6}{13}$

Q.14 Two pipes C and D can fill a cistern. If they are opened on alternate minutes and if pipe C is opened first, in how many minutes will the tank be full?

A. 4 minutes **B.** 5 minutes
C. 2 minutes **D.** 6 minutes

Q.15 Two pipes, A and B are opened simultaneously and it is found that due to the leakage in the bottom, $\frac{17}{7}$ minutes are taken extra to fill the tank. If the tank is full, in what approximate time would the leak empty it?

A. 27 minutes **B.** 32 minutes
C. 36 minutes **D.** 39 minutes

Ques (16-20):Direction: Study the following graph carefully and answer the following question given below.

The two graphs given below show the total and the difference of number of boys and girls in various schools respectively.

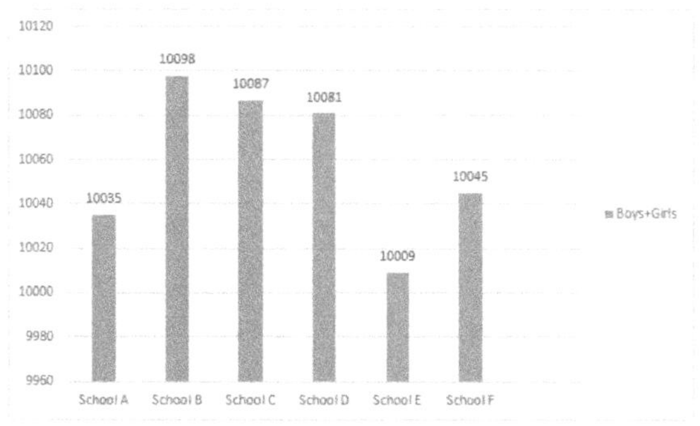

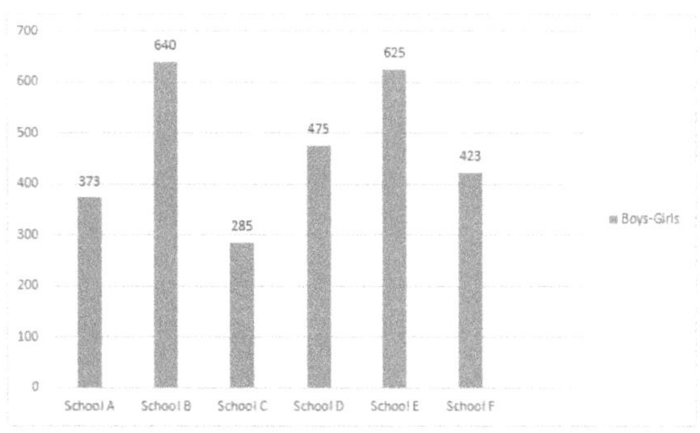

Q.16 What is the difference between Number of Girls in School A and Number of Girls in School B?

A. 100 **B.** 101 **C.** 102 **D.** 103

Q.17 Girls in School C forms approximately what percent of the total number students in that School?

A. 45.5% **B.** 47.5% **C.** 48.5% **D.** 49.5%

Q.18 What is the ratio of Sum of Boys in School D and Girls in School E together to the Sum of Girls in School D and Boys in School E together is?

A. $997:1012$ **B.** $997:1012$
C. $1000:1011$ **D.** $1000:1013$

Q.19 How many number of Boys are there in School F?

A. 5134 **B.** 5234 **C.** 5334 **D.** 5444

Q.20 In which of the following School least no of Girls are present?

A. School A **B.** School B
C. School C **D.** School E

Ques (21-25):Direction: Study the Pie Chart and answer the following question

The following pie chart shows the percentage of cakes sold throughout the week.

Cakes on Everyday day $=$ No of Vanilla Cakes $+$ No of Chocolate Cakes

Total cakes sold in the week $= 8400$

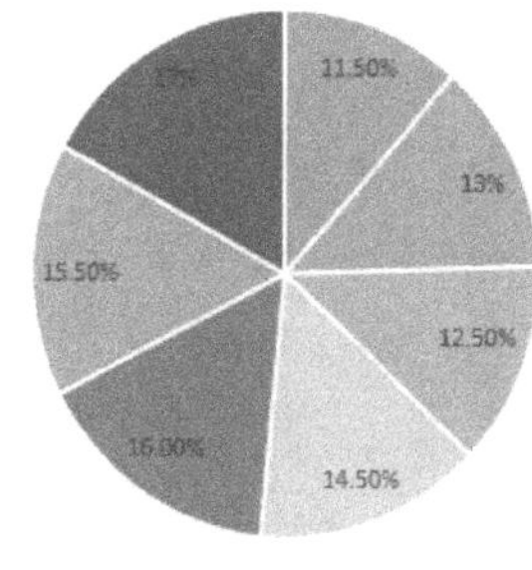

Q.21 The ratio of Number of Vanilla Cakes Sold to Chocolate Cakes Sold is $2:1$ of the total cakes sold on Monday and the ratio of the number of Vanilla Cakes Sold to Chocolate Cakes Sold is $3:2$ in the total Cakes sold on Wednesday. Then difference of Vanilla Cakes Sold on Monday and Vanilla Cakes sold on Wednesday is?

A. 13 **B.** 14 **C.** 15 **D.** 16

Q.22 If the ratio of Vanilla Cakes Sold on Thursday to Vanilla Cakes sold on Saturday is $3:4$, Number of Chocolate Cakes Sold on Thursday is equal to Number of Chocolate on Saturday then Number of Chocolate Cakes sold on Saturday is equal to total number of Cakes sold on which day?

A. Monday **B.** Tuesday
C. Wednesday **D.** Thursday

Q.23 If the average number of Vanilla Cakes Sold on Friday and Sunday are 858 and Number of Chocolate Cakes Sold on Sunday are 72 more than Number of Chocolate Cakes sold on Friday then Number of Chocolate Cakes sold on Friday is?

A. 482 **B.** 492 **C.** 498 **D.** 512

Q.24 Ratio of Vanilla Cakes Sold to Chocolate Cakes Sold is $46:45$ on Tuesday then how many number of Vanilla Cakes are Sold on that day?

A. 540 **B.** 546 **C.** 552 **D.** 562

Q.25 If the ratio of Vanilla Cakes sold to Chocolate Cakes sold on Monday is $2:1$ and the ratio of Selling Price of Vanilla Cake to Chocolate Cake is the $1:4$, total amount earned by him on Monday is Rs. 9660 then what is the rate of One Vanilla Cake?

A. Rs 4 **B.** Rs 5 **C.** Rs 10 **D.** Rs 20

Business Awareness

Q.26 Who owns the rights for Pizza Hut, Cream Bell and Costa Coffee in India?

A. Ravi Jaipuria **B.** Ashok Chauhan
C. Anu Agha **D.** Nikhil Meswani

Q.27 Which company has recently introduced 'Dura Technology' in building cars?

A. Ford **B.** Mitsubshi
C. GM **D.** Maruti-Suzuki

Q.28 China's TCL Communication has a joint venture agreement with which European company for manufacturing mobile handsets?

A. Siemens **B.** Nokia
C. Alcatel **D.** None of these

Q.29 Brand Name 'YKK' is related to:

A. Cars **B.** Cellular Phones
C. Zip **D.** Shoe polish

Q.30 Inputs to the selection process include all but__________.

A. Job analysis **B.** Supervision
C. HR planning **D.** Job applicants

Q.31 In which of the following method of recruitment, employees are encouraged to recommend the names of their friends working in other organisations for possible vacancy in the near future.

A. Job posting **B.** Gate hiring
C. Campus recruitment **D.** Employee referrals

Q.32 Job posting is__________.

A. Posting of an employee
B. A method of Recruitment
C. Is an appraisal technique
D. An internet recruitment

Q.33 Health insurance, retirement pension, payment for overtime, etc., are ________.

A. Base pay **B.** Variable pay
C. Benefits **D.** All of these

Q.34 __________ means the total receipts from sales divided by the number of unit sold.

A. Average revenue
B. Total revenue
C. Marginal revenue
D. Incremental revenue

Q.35 Which of the following is a macroeconomic concept?

A. Business cycle **B.** National income
C. Government policy **D.** All of the above

// Smart Answer Sheet //

Correct Indicates percentage of students who answered questions correctly.

Skipped Indicates percentage of students who skipped questions.

Q.	Ans.	Correct	Skipped
1	D	84.75 %	13.02 %
2	A	32.63 %	67.28 %
3	D	50.56 %	34.56 %
4	D	17.56 %	76.32 %
5	D	10.41 %	87.38 %
6	C	50.79 %	45.32 %
7	D	60.24 %	38.77 %
8	D	44.98 %	51.27 %
9	D	82.66 %	14.87 %
10	B	26.23 %	70.89 %
11	B	50.79 %	32.49 %
12	D	16.79 %	79.18 %
13	B	12.61 %	67.53 %
14	D	59.15 %	30.87 %
15	D	25.99 %	71.11 %
16	C	41.35 %	43.43 %
17	C	84.57 %	12.33 %
18	A	61.76 %	37.01 %
19	B	86.57 %	13.06 %
20	D	40.6 %	47.48 %
21	B	27.6 %	71.24 %
22	A	15.04 %	74.24 %
23	B	21.89 %	71.59 %
24	C	55.24 %	41.48 %
25	B	10.9 %	76.01 %
26	A	64.52 %	30.46 %
27	A	52.43 %	44.18 %
28	C	14.18 %	78.75 %
29	C	30.21 %	69.01 %
30	B	57.76 %	32.87 %
31	D	26.02 %	73.49 %
32	B	58.74 %	40.2 %
33	C	64.94 %	30.97 %
34	A	58.22 %	30.17 %
35	D	76.02 %	11.78 %

Performance Analysis	
Avg. Score (%)	40.0%
Toppers Score (%)	62.86%
Your Score	

//Hints and Solutions//

1. According to the sentence 'Revolutions are by definition anarchic, as they are aimed against those who make and enforce the rules' the writer suggests are revolutions usually aimed at those who make and enforce laws.

Hence, the correct option is (D).

2. According to the passage 'just naming and shaming the perpetrators does not account for culpability' is not true as it is not mentioned anywhere in the passage.

Hence, the correct option is (A).

3. According to the sentence 'transferring the punitive aspects — shame, denial of work opportunities' we can say that both shame and denial of work opportunities are suggested by the author while talking about transferring the punitive aspects.

Hence, the correct option is (D).

4. Palpable means so intense as to seem almost tangible.

So out of the given options noticeable is the most similar meaning to palpable.

Hence, the correct option is (D).

5. The writer advocates environment for women in conclusion of the passage:

- which has healthy camaraderie instead of needless caution
- where men need not patronise women

Hence, the correct option is (D).

6. Patronise means to treat with an apparent kindness which betrays a feeling of superiority.

So out of the given options condescend is the most similar meaning to patronising as condescend means to behave towards somebody in a way that shows that you think you are better or more important than him/her.

Hence, the correct option is (C).

7. Tamping down means to reduce the importance/significance of anything

Hence, the correct option is (D).

8. Perkiest - cheerful and lively.

Beneficial - having a good or useful effect.

Bouncy - full of energy.

Productive - yielding positive results.

Lively - full of energy, interest, excitement.

So, out of the given options lively is the most similar in meaning to perkiest.

Hence, the correct option is (D).

9. Indians adopt new technologies as we mould it according to our habits.

Hence, the correct option is (D).

10. Wading is to walk with difficulty through fairly deep water, mud, etc.

Trudge is to walk with slow, heavy steps, for example because you are very tired.

So trudge is the most similar in meaning to wading.

Hence, the correct option is (B).

11. P takes 15 minutes to fill the cistern alone.

Part of cistern filled by P in 1 minute $=\frac{1}{15}$

Q takes 10 minutes to fill the cistern alone.

Part of cistern filled by Q in 1 minute $=\frac{1}{16}$

Part filled by P and Q together $=\frac{1}{15}+\frac{1}{10}=\frac{1}{6}$

Part filled by $Q=\frac{1}{10}$

Let the total time required to fill the tank be $2x$.

So, according to question Q alone and P and Q together will work for x minutes each.

Work done by Q alone in x minutes $=\frac{x}{10}$

Work done by P and Q together in x minutes $=\frac{x}{6}$

So,

$$\frac{x}{6}+\frac{x}{10}=1$$

On solving this we get,

$$x=\frac{15}{4}$$

Now the total time is $2x$,

$\Rightarrow 2x=\frac{15}{2}=7.5$ minutes.

Hence, the correct option is (B).

12. Time taken by $M(x)=24$ minutes

Time taken by $N(y)=27$ minutes

Total time $(t)=8$ minutes

Time at which N should be closed $=y\left(1-\left(\frac{t}{x}\right)\right)$

$=27\left(1-\left(\frac{8}{24}\right)\right)$

$=18$ minutes.

Hence, the correct option is (D).

13. Time taken by $E=12$ minutes

Time taken by $F = 18$ minutes

Time taken by $R = 24$ minutes

Let T is the time taken by the pipes to fill the tank.

Work done in 1 min by $E = \frac{1}{12}$

Work done in 1 min by $F = \frac{1}{18}$

Work done in 1 min by $R = \frac{1}{24}$

So, according to the question,

$$\left(\frac{1}{12}+\frac{1}{18}+\frac{1}{24}\right) \times (T-12) + \left(\frac{1}{12}+\frac{1}{18}\right) \times 12 = 1$$

On solving this we get,

$$T = \frac{108}{13} = 8\frac{4}{13}$$

Hence, the correct option is (B).

14. Pipe C can fill in 12 minutes.
Pipe D can fill in 4 minutes.

Work done in 1 minute by $C = \frac{1}{12}$

Work done in 1 minute by $D = \frac{1}{4}$

So, For every two minutes,

$\frac{1}{12}+\frac{1}{4}=\frac{1}{3}$ Part filled

So, if $\frac{1}{3}$ part is filled in 2 minutes.

Total time taken to fill the cistern $= 6$ minutes.

Hence, the correct option is (D).

15. Pipe A can fill in 15 minutes.

Pipe B can fill in 20 minutes.

Work done in 1 minute by $A = \frac{1}{15}$

Work done in 1 minute by $B = \frac{1}{20}$

Work done in 1 minute by A and B together $= \frac{1}{15}+\frac{1}{20}$

$\Rightarrow \frac{7}{20}$

So, the total time taken by both pipes before the leak was developed

$= \frac{60}{7}$ minutes.

Now, leaks is developed which will take T time to empty the tank

So, $\left(\frac{1}{15}+\frac{1}{20}-\frac{1}{T}\right) = \frac{1}{11}$

Solve for T,

We will get $\frac{660}{17}$ minutes

$= 39$ minutes (approx.)

Hence, the correct option is (D).

16. In School A:
Total of boys and girls
$\text{Boys} + \text{Girls} = 10035$......(i)
Difference of boys and girls
$\text{Boys} - \text{Girls} = 373$......(ii)
On solving (i) and (ii) we get,
$\text{Girls} = 4831$
In School B:
Total of boys and girls
$\text{Boys} + \text{Girls} = 10098$......(iii)
Difference of boys and girls
$\text{Boys} - \text{Girls} = 640$......(iv)
On solving (iii) and (iv) we get,
$\text{Girls} = 4729$
Difference of number of girls in school A and school B,
$= 4831 - 4729$
$= 102$
Hence, the correct option is (C).

17. In school C:
Total of boys and girls
$\text{Boys} + \text{Girls} = 10087$......(i)
Difference of boys and girls
$\text{Boys} - \text{Girls} = 285$......(ii)
On solving (i) and (ii) we get,
$\text{Girls} = 4901$
$\%$ of girls in school $C = \frac{4901}{10087}$
$= 48.58\%$
Hence, the correct option is (C).

18. In School D:
Total of boys and girls
$\text{Boys} + \text{Girls} = 10081$......(i)
Difference of boys and girls
$\text{Boys} - \text{Girls} = 475$......(ii)
On solving (i) and (ii) we get,
$\text{Boys} = 5278$
$\text{Girls} = 4803$
In School E:
Total of boys and girls
$\text{Boys} + \text{Girls} = 10009$......(iii)
Difference of boys and girls
$\text{Boys} - \text{Girls} = 625$......(iv)
On solving (iii) and (iv) we get,
$\text{Boys} = 5317$
$\text{Girls} = 4692$
So, as per question

Ratio $= (5278 + 4692):(4803 + 5317)$
$9970:10120$
$997:1012$
Hence, the correct option is (A).

19. In school F:
Total of boys and girls
$\text{Boys} + \text{Girls} = 10045$......(i)
Difference of boys and girls
$\text{Boys} - \text{Girls} = 423$......(ii)
On solving (i) and (ii) we get,
$\text{Boys} = 5234$
Hence, the correct option is (B).

20. In School A:
Total of boys and girls
$\text{Boys} + \text{Girls} = 10035$......(i)
Difference of boys and girls
$\text{Boys} - \text{Girls} = 373$......(ii)
On solving (i) and (ii) we get,
$\text{Girls} = 4831$
In School B:
Total of boys and girls
$\text{Boys} + \text{Girls} = 10098$......(iii)
Difference of boys and girls
$\text{Boys} - \text{Girls} = 640$......(iv)
On solving (iii) and (iv) we get,
$\text{Girls} = 4729$
In school C
Total of boys and girls
$\text{Boys} + \text{Girls} = 10087$......(v)
Difference of boys and girls
$\text{Boys} - \text{Girls} = 285$......(vi)
On solving (v) and (vi) we get,
$\text{Girls} = 4901$
In School D:
Total of boys and girls
$\text{Boys} + \text{Girls} = 10081$......(vii)
Difference of boys and girls
$\text{Boys} - \text{Girls} = 475$......(viii)
On solving (vii) and (viii) we get,
$\text{Girls} = 4803$
In School E:
Total of boys and girls
$\text{Boys} + \text{Girls} = 10009$......(ix)
Difference of boys and girls
$\text{Boys} - \text{Girls} = 625$......(x)
On solving (ix) and (x) we get,
$\text{Girls} = 4692$
In school F:
Total of boys and girls
$\text{Boys} + \text{Girls} = 10045$......(xi)
Difference of boys and girls
$\text{Boys} - \text{Girls} = 423$......(xii)
On solving (xi) and (xii) we get,
$\text{Girls} = 4811$
From above calculations:
School $A: 4831$
School $B: 4729$
School $C: 4901$
School $D: 4803$
School $E: 4692$
Hence, the correct option is (D).

21. Percentage of cake sold on monday $= 11.5\%$

Monday Cakes sold $= 8400 \times 11.5\% = 966$
Ratio of Vanilla cakes: Chocolate cakes $= 2:1$
Number of Vanilla cakes sold on Monday $= \frac{2}{3} \times 966$

$= 644$

Percentage of cake sold on wednesday $= 12.5\%$

Monday Cakes sold $= 8400 \times 12.5\% = 1050$

Ratio of Vanilla cakes: Chocolate cakes $= 3:2$

Number of Vanilla cakes sold on Wednesday $= \frac{3}{5} \times 1050$
$= 630$

Difference of Vanilla cakes sold on Monday and Wednesday

$= 644 - 630$

$= 14$

Hence, the correct option is (B).

22. Percentage of cakes sold on Thursday $= 14.5\%$

Total cakes sold on Thursday $= 8400 \times 14.5\% = 1218$

Percentage of cakes sold on Saturday $= 15.5\%$

Total cakes sold on Saturday $= 8400 \times 15.5\% = 1302$

As per question, Number of Chocolate Cakes Sold on Thursday is equal to Number of Chocolate on Saturday.

So, the difference of number of vanilla cakes on Thursday and Saturday is the same as the difference of total number of cakes on Thursday and Saturday.

Let the number of vanilla cakes on Thursday be V_1.

And the number of vanilla cakes on Saturday be V_2.

So, Difference of number of vanilla cakes on Thursday and Saturday

$V_1 - V_2 = 1302 - 1218$

$V_1 - V_2 = 84$......(i)

It is also given that ratio of vanilla cakes in Thursday and Saturday

$V_1 : V_2 = 3:4$......(ii)

On solving (i) and (ii) we get,

$V_1 = 252$ and $V_2 = 336$

Total number of vanilla cakes on Saturday $= 336$

Total number of chocolate cakes on Saturday $= 1302 - 336$

$= 966$

Percentage of cakes on Monday $= 11.5\%$

Total number of cakes on Monday $= 84 \times 11.5\%$

$= 966$

So, the number of chocolate cakes sold on Saturday is equal to total number of cakes sold on on Monday.

Hence, the correct option is (A).

23. Percentage of cakes sold on Friday $= 16\%$

Total cakes sold on Friday $= 8400 \times 16\% = 1344$

Percentage of cakes sold on Sunday $= 17\%$

Total cakes sold on Sunday $= 8400 \times 17\% = 1428$

Let the number of vanilla cakes on Friday be V_1

Let the number of vanilla cakes on Sunday be V_2

Let the number of chocolate cakes on Friday be C_1

Let the number of chocolate cakes on Sunday be C_2

As per question,

$\frac{V_1+V_2}{2} = 858$

$V_1 + V_2 = 1716$......(i)

Total cakes on Friday and Saturday

$= 1344 + 1428$

$= 2772$

So,

$2772 = V_1 + V_2 + C_1 + C_2$

Using (i) we get,

$2772 = 1716 + C_1 + C2$

$C_1 + C_2 = 1056$......(ii)

Also given in question,

$C_2 - C_1 = 72$......(iii)

On solving (ii) and (iii) we get,

$C_1 = 492$

Hence, the correct option is (B).

24. Percentage of cakes sold on Tuesday $= 13\%$

Total cakes sold on Friday $= 8400 \times 13\% = 1092$

Given that ratio of vanilla cake to chocolate cake on Tuesday $= 46:45$

Number of vanilla cakes on Tuesday

$= \frac{46}{91} \times 1092$

$= 552$

Hence, the correct option is (C).

25. Percentage of cakes sold on Monday $= 11.50\%$

Total cakes sold on Monday $= 8400 \times 11.50\% = 966$

Given that ratio of vanilla cake to chocolate cake on Monday $= 2:1$

Number of vanilla cakes on Monday

$= \frac{2}{3} \times 966$

$= 644$

Number of chocolate cakes on Monday

$= \frac{1}{3} \times 966$

$= 322$

Let the Selling price of vanilla cake be P_1 and chocolate cake be P_2

It is also given in question that $P_1 : P_2 = 1:4$......(i)

Total cost of 644 vanilla cakes $= 644P_1$

Total cost of 322 chocolate cakes $= 322P_2$

As per question,

$644P_1 + 322P_2 = 9660$......(ii)

On solving (i) and (ii) we get,

$P_1 = 5$

Hence, the correct option is (B).

26. Ravi Jaipuria owns the rights for Pizza Hut, Cream Bell and Costa Coffee in India.

Ravi Jaipuria is an Indian billionaire and chairman of RJ Corp. He owns fast-food outfit Devyani International.

Hence, the correct option is (A).

27. Ford has recently introduced 'Dura Technology' in building cars.

Ford Motor Company, commonly known as Ford, is an American multinational automaker that has its main headquarters in

Dearborn, Michigan, a suburb of Detroit. It was founded by Henry Ford and incorporated on June 16, 1903.

Hence, the correct option is (A).

28. China's TCL Communication has a joint venture agreement with European company Alcatel for manufacturing mobile handsets.

In April 2004, TCL and Alcatel announced the creation of a mobile phone manufacturing joint venture: Alcatel Mobile Phones. TCL injected 55 million euros in the venture in return for a 55 per cent shareholding.

Hence, the correct option is (C).

29. Brand Name 'YKK' is related to zip.

YKK stands for Yoshida Kogyo Kabushikikaisha. In 1934 Tadao Yoshida founded Yoshida Industries Limited).

Hence, the correct option is (C).

30. Inputs to the selection process include all but supervision. Supervision is the act or function of overseeing something or somebody.
A person who performs supervision is a "supervisor", but does not always have the formal title of supervisor. A person who is getting supervision is the "supervisee".

Hence, the correct option is (B).

31. In employee referrals method of recruitment, employees are encouraged to recommend the names of their friends working in other organisations for possible vacancy in the near future.

Employee referral is a structured program that companies and organizations use to find talented people by asking their existing employees to recommend candidates from their existing networks.

Hence, the correct option is (D).

32. Job posting is an internet recruitment.

Job postings are the primary means through which companies recruit new applicants for available positions.

Hence, the correct option is (B).

33. Health insurance, retirement pension, payment for overtime, etc., are benefits.

Benefits are any perks offered to employees in addition to salary. The most common benefits are medical, disability, and life insurance; retirement benefits; paid time off; and fringe benefits.

Hence, the correct option is (C).

34. Average revenue means the total receipts from sales divided by the number of unit sold.

Hence, the correct option is (A).

35. All of the above are macroeconomic concept.

Macroeconomics is a branch of economics that studies how an overall economy—the market or other systems that operate on a large scale—behaves. Macroeconomics studies economy-wide phenomena such as inflation, price levels, rate of economic growth, national income, gross domestic product (GDP), and changes in unemployment.

Hence, the correct option is (D).

Mock Test 03

Comprehension

Ques (1-5):Direction: Read the following passage carefully and answer the question given below.

Philosophy of Education is a label applied to the study of the purpose, process, nature, and ideals of education. It can be considered a branch of both philosophy and education. Education can be defined as the teaching and learning of specific skills, and the imparting of knowledge, judgment, and wisdom, and is something broader than the societal institution of education we often speak of.

Many educationalists consider it a weak and woolly field, too far removed from the practical applications of the real world to be useful. But philosophers dating back to Plato and the Ancient Greeks have given the area much thought and emphasis, and there is little doubt that their work has helped shape the practice of education over the millennia.

Plato is the earliest important educational thinker, and education is an essential element in "The Republic" (his most important work on philosophy and political theory, written around 360 B.C.). In it, he advocates some rather extreme methods: removing children from their mothers' care and raising them as wards of the state, and differentiating children suitable to the various castes, the highest receiving the most education, so that they could act as guardians of the city and care for the less able. He believed that education should be holistic, including facts, skills, physical discipline, music, and art. Plato believed that talent and intelligence are not distributed genetically and thus is be found in children born to all classes, although his proposed system of selective public education for an educated minority of the population does not really follow a democratic model.

Aristotle considered human nature, habit, and reason to be equally important forces to be cultivated in education, the ultimate aim of which should be to produce good and virtuous citizens. He proposed that teachers lead their students systematically, and that repetition be used as a key tool to develop good habits, unlike Socrates' emphasis on questioning his listeners to bring out their own ideas. He emphasized the balancing of the theoretical and practical aspects of subjects taught, among which he explicitly mentions reading, writing, mathematics, music, physical education, literature, history, and a wide range of sciences, as well as play, which he also considered important.

During the Medieval period, the idea of Perennialism was first formulated by St. Thomas Aquinas in his work "De Magistro". Perennialism holds that one should teach those things deemed to be of everlasting importance to all people everywhere, namely principles and reasoning, not just facts (which are apt to change over time), and that one should teach first about people, not machines or techniques. It was originally religious in nature, and it was only much later that a theory of secular perennialism developed.

During the Renaissance, the French skeptic Michel de Montaigne (1533 – 1592) was one of the first to critically look at education. Unusually for his time, Montaigne was willing to question the conventional wisdom of the period, calling into question the whole edifice of the educational system, and the implicit assumption that university-educated philosophers were necessarily wiser than uneducated farmworkers, for example.

Q.1 What is the difference between the approaches of Socrates and Aristotle?

A. Aristotle felt the need for repetition to develop good habits in students; Socrates felt that students need to be constantly questioned.

B. Aristotle felt the need for rote-learning; Socrates emphasized dialogic learning.

C. There was no difference.

D. Aristotle emphasized the importance of paying attention to human nature; Socrates emphasized science.

Q.2 Why do educationists consider philosophy a 'weak and woolly' field?

A. It is not practically applicable

B. Its theoretical concepts are easily understood

C. It is irrelevant for education

D. None of the above

Q.3 What do you understand by the term 'Perennialism', in the context of the given comprehension passage?

A. It refers to something which is of ceaseless importance

B. It refers to something which is quite unnecessary

C. It refers to something which is abstract and theoretical

D. It refers to something which existed in the past and no longer exists now

Q.4 Were Plato's beliefs about education democratic?

A. No, he believed that only the rich have the right to acquire education

B. Yes

C. No, he believed that only a select few are meant to attend schools

D. No, he believed that all pupils are not talented

Q.5 Why did Aquinas propose a model of education which did not lay much emphasis on facts?

A. Facts are not important

B. Facts do not lead to holistic education

C. Facts change with the changing times

D. Facts are frozen in time

Ques (6-10):Direction: Read the following passage carefully and answer the question given below it.

With all the information surrounding the official discovery of the Higgs boson, it can be difficult to appreciate how this innovation can impact the average person. However, to understand why the so-called "God particle" is so crucial, and why so many scientists are celebrating, you must understand where it came from.

The Higgs boson is often called "the God particle" because it's said to be what caused the "Big Bang" that created our universe many years ago. The nickname caught on so quickly (even though scientists and clergy alike do not care for it) partly because it's a great explanation of what it's supposed to do -- the Higgs boson is what joins everything and gives it matter.

So, when scientists from the European Organization for Nuclear Research (CERN) working with the Large Hadron Collider in Geneva, Switzerland, finally confirmed the discovery of the Higgs boson, physicists where thrilled. This information was announced in a statement by the Geneva-based CERN, and at physics convention on the same day.

The finding did not come easily, and since 2008 CERN has been putting together the $10 billion Large Hadron Collider to specifically create high-energy collisions to prove that the Higgs boson exists.

The particle, a boson, was first found last July and many thought that it might not be the correct boson, but once scientists finished recent testing an affirmative judgment was made. They were on the right track.

"The preliminary results with the full 2012 data set are magnificent and to me it is clear that we are dealing with a Higgs boson though we still have a long way to go to know what kind of Higgs boson it is," said CMS spokesperson Joe Incandela in a statement. CMS -- short for Compact Muon Solenoid experiment -- is one of the two teams working with CERN to make this discover, the other is ATLAS.

This discovery is huge to the scientific community because it gives validity to The Standard Model of Physics, which is the authoritative theory for particle physics. The only element or particle that is part of the Standard model and hasn't been discovered is the Higgs boson, until now.

The confirmation was crucial because the model dictates how the basic pieces of matter act together. If it was proved incorrect, or that the there was no Higgs boson, the way modern scientists look at particle physics would be completely altered, therefore changing many of the current technological assumptions.

With this discovery, there is the ability to have huge implications in scientific advances, and it is said to be a big contender for the Nobel Prize this year.To show how much of an impact a discovery like this can have on our lives, Kyle Cranmer, an assistant professor of Physics at New York University, suggests looking at how early 20th century physicists were trying to understand the atom, and from there developed quantum mechanics.

"Quantum mechanics is about as esoteric as it gets, and it's the subject of several philosophy of science books focusing on determinism and physical reality, but it was also led to the invention of the transistor, the key ingredient for all modern electronics," said Cranmer in an email to CBS News. "Quantum mechanics also led to the invention of the laser and other medical technologies like MRI's, PET scans. The list goes on and on, and none of these practical applications were anticipated by those that developed quantum mechanics."

Q.6 Why is the Higgs boson often called 'the God particle'?

A. Because it has many practical applications in every major field and it is compared to something that only God can create

B. Because the scientists after centuries of research has discovered this particle as the final outcome

C. Because it's said to be what caused the 'Big Bang' that created our universe many years ago

D. Because it is said the this particle can explain both the theory of gravity and that of quantum mechanics

Q.7 Why is the discovery of the Higgs boson considered huge to the scientific community?

A. Because CERN has put together the $10 billion Large Hadron Collider to specifically create high-energy collisions to prove that the Higgs boson exists

B. Because it gives validity to The Standard Model of Physics, which is the authoritative theory for particle physics

C. Because the only element or particle that is part of the Standard model and hasn't been discovered is the Higgs boson, until now

D. Because the model dictates how the basic pieces of matter act together

Q.8 What could have been the repercussion, had it been proved that the Higgs boson doesn't exist?

A. The way modern scientists look at particle physics would be completely altered, therefore changing many of the current technological assumptions

B. The scientist would never be able to validate The Standard Model of Physics, which is the authoritative theory for particle physics

C. Human beings could never gauge how the basic pieces of matter act together

D. The scientists behind the discovery of the Higgs boson would not win the Nobel Prize this year

Q.9 Why does Kyle Cranmer compare the discovery of the Higgs boson to the development of quantum mechanics?

A. To justify why the scientists behind the discovery of the Higgs boson should win the Nobel Prize this year

B. To demonstrate how many of the current technological assumptions depended on the discovery of the Higgs boson

C. To show how much of an impact the discovery of the Higgs boson can have on human lives

D. To state why the failure of the experiment could alter the way modern scientists look at particle physics

Q.10 Which of the following were the outcomes of quantum mechanics, according to the passage?

i. Laser

ii. Transistors

iii. Digital Cameras

iv. LEDs

A. ii and iii **B.** i, ii and iii

C. iii and iv **D.** i and ii

Management Data Interpretation

Ques (11-15):Direction: Study the following table chart carefully and answer the question given beside.

The table given below shows the percentage of appeared and qualified candidates in a competitive examination from different institutes.

Institutes	Appeared Candidates $= 24000$	Qualified Candidates $= 4000$
	Percentage of appeared candidates	Percentage of qualified candidates
A	25%	18%
B	10%	12%
C	15%	18%
D	12%	16%
E	18%	20%
F	20%	16%

Q.11 What is the ratio of the qualified candidates from institutes D, E and F together to the appeared candidates from institutes A, B and C together?

A. 11:17 **B.** 12:67 **C.** 19:75 **D.** 13:75

Q.12 What percentage of the candidates from institute C has been declared qualified out of the total candidates appeared from this institute?

A. 30% **B.** 25% **C.** 40% **D.** 20%

Q.13 What is the percentage of students who qualified from the institute C and D together with respect to those who appeared from the institute C and D together?

A. 24.98% **B.** 30.98% **C.** 20.98% **D.** 31.98%

Q.14 Which institute has the highest percentage of candidates qualified with respect to those appeared?

A. A **B.** D **C.** C **D.** E

Q.15 What is the ratio of qualified candidates from institute B to the appeared candidates from institute F?

A. 1:10 **B.** 2:11 **C.** 3:14 **D.** 4:17

Ques (16-20):Direction: Study the following table chart carefully and answer the question given below.

The chart shows the number of employees in various department in 5 companies.

	ABC Group	JMD	BCGI	Younker	Zelman
TECHNICAL	200	350	270	70	120
OPERATIONS	175	200	150	340	180
H.R	50	30	25	35	20
FINANCE	300	50		100	75
			120		

Q.16 Find the ratio of employees of Technical, Operations and Finance between BCGI and Younker companies.

A. 18:17 **B.** 17:16 **C.** 19:21 **D.** 32:33

Q.17 What percentage of total employees are in Operations department for all companies?

A. 36.53% **B.** 35.23% **C.** 37.42% **D.** 29.82%

Q.18 Find the average number of employees from the Technical department hired by all companies taken together.

A. 200 **B.** 205

C. 198 **D.** None of these

Q.19 What is the percentage of technical and operations employees in BCGI as compared to operations and H.R employees in Younker?

A. 12% **B.** 108%

C. 114% **D.** None of these

Q.20 What is the percentage of H.R employees in Zelman?

A. 7% **B.** 5.06% **C.** 4.98% **D.** 5.6%

Ques (21-22):Direction: Study the table chart carefully and answer the question given below.

Person	No. of days they worked	Percentage of work done to complete the project
A	8	20%
B	3	10%
C	6	25%
D	15	30%
E	6	15%

Q.21 A and B started doing the work. After 10 days they both left, and C joined the work. He completed his part of work. Now the remaining work was completed by F in 16 days. In how many days can F complete whole work?

A. 30 days **B.** 96 days **C.** 48 days **D.** 24 days

Q.22 G who can complete whole work in 30 days replaced A and did A's part of work. He left and then B also worked for same number of days as G. If remaining work was completed by M who can do complete work in one-fourth the number of days in which E can complete the work, then in how many days was the whole work completed?

A. 22 days **B.** 14 days **C.** 21 days **D.** 18 days

Ques (23-25):Direction : Study the chart and answer the question the pie chart given here represents the domestic expenditure of a family in percent if the total monthly income of the family is Rs. 33,650

Expenditure of Family

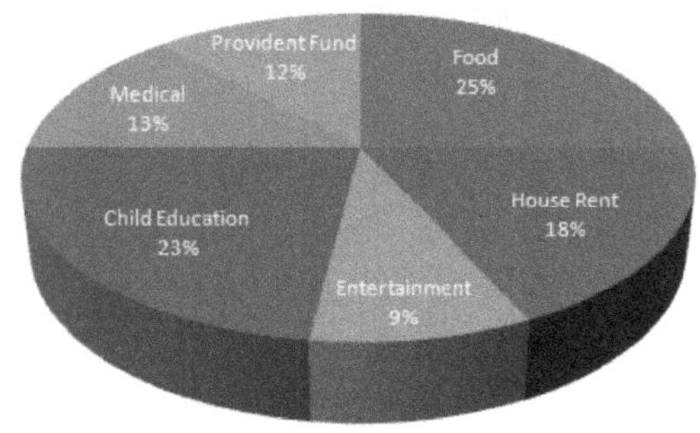

Q.23 The annual savings in the form of provident fund would be:

A. Rs. 48456 **B.** Rs. 48540
C. Rs. 44856 **D.** Rs. 45480

Q.24 After provident fund deductions and payment of house rent, the total monthly income of the family remains:

A. Rs. 23545 **B.** Rs. 24435
C. Rs. 23555 **D.** Rs. 25355

Q.25 The total amount per month, the family spends on food and entertainment combined together, is:

A. Rs. 11432 **B.** Rs. 11441
C. Rs. 12315 **D.** Rs. 12443

Business Awareness

Q.26 Central Board of Direct Taxes (CBDT) signed a Memorandum of Understanding for data sharing with which organisation?

A. Central Board of Indirect Taxes and Customs
B. Director General of Foreign Trade
C. Employee Provident Fund Organisation
D. Securities Exchange Board of India

Q.27 Which payment application has launched India's first numberless card of the country?

A. Payzapp **B.** FamPay
C. FreeCharge **D.** PayTm

Q.28 Which Mutual Fund House manages the Bharat Bond Exchange Traded Fund (ETF)?

A. SBI Mutual Fund
B. ICICI Prudential Mutual Fund
C. Edelweiss Mutual Fund
D. Kotak Mahindra Mutual Fund

Q.29 Asian Development Bank (ADB) recently signed a USD 177 million loan agreement with India to upgrade road connectivity of which state?

A. Madhya Pradesh **B.** Andhra Pradesh
C. Maharashtra **D.** West Bengal

Q.30 Which Indian technology company announced a strategic partnership with Avaloq, to provide wealth management services?

A. Wipro **B.** Infosys
C. HCL **D.** Tech Mahindra

Q.31 The Indian Government has imposed safeguard duty on which product till July 2021, to protect domestic manufacturers?

A. Medical devices **B.** Solar cells
C. Textile **D.** Electronics

Q.32 Which Indian organisation has entered the list of world's top 100 companies on the Fortune Global 500 list?

A. Reliance Industries **B.** HDFC
C. State Bank of India **D.** Adani Ports

Q.33 Ashima Goyal, Jayanth R Varma and Shashanka Bhide were recently appointed as the members of which committee?

A. Finance Commission
B. Monetary Policy Committee
C. Appointments Committee of the Cabinet
D. Bank Board Bureau

Q.34 Singapore based GIC and TPG Capital have acquired stake in which Indian company?

A. Byju's **B.** Reliance Retail
C. Shoppers Stop **D.** Future Retail

Q.35 What is that describes the duties of the job, authority relationship, skills requirement, conditions of work etc.

A. Job analysis **B.** Job enlargement
C. Job enrichment **D.** Job evaluation

// Smart Answer Sheet //

Correct — Indicates percentage of students who answered questions correctly.

Skipped — Indicates percentage of students who skipped questions.

Q.	Ans.	Correct	Skipped
1	A	63.95 %	31.53 %
2	A	76.43 %	19.37 %
3	A	88.57 %	10.01 %
4	B	60.49 %	35.32 %
5	C	41.15 %	44.81 %
6	C	82.1 %	10.55 %
7	B	89.45 %	10.26 %

Q.	Ans.	Correct	Skipped
8	A	66.01 %	31.34 %
9	C	46.62 %	42.9 %
10	D	66.83 %	31.12 %
11	D	69.0 %	30.41 %
12	D	50.27 %	44.33 %
13	C	64.01 %	31.06 %
14	B	12.67 %	71.91 %

Q.	Ans.	Correct	Skipped
15	A	49.64 %	48.69 %
16	A	87.03 %	10.75 %
17	A	58.61 %	31.46 %
18	D	78.74 %	15.03 %
19	D	62.52 %	35.84 %
20	B	54.2 %	35.38 %
21	B	18.12 %	72.93 %

Q.	Ans.	Correct	Skipped
22	D	78.87 %	10.1 %
23	A	61.49 %	32.86 %
24	C	48.54 %	45.89 %
25	B	81.48 %	16.0 %
26	A	52.9 %	38.06 %
27	B	77.92 %	19.46 %
28	C	17.71 %	74.19 %

Q.	Ans.	Correct	Skipped
29	C	65.29 %	30.67 %
30	B	43.91 %	39.07 %
31	B	63.88 %	35.01 %
32	A	84.81 %	11.7 %
33	B	14.01 %	79.34 %
34	B	69.43 %	30.2 %
35	A	64.85 %	35.09 %

Performance Analysis	
Avg. Score (%)	31.43%
Toppers Score (%)	60.0%
Your Score	

//Hints and Solutions//

1. According to the passage, Aristotle felt the need for repetition to develop good habits in students as mentioned in 'Aristotle considered human nature, habit, and reason to be equally important forces to be cultivated in education, the ultimate aim of which should be to produce good and virtuous citizens'.

Socrates felt that students need to be constantly questioned because their approaches were different as mentioned in 'Aristotle considered human nature, habit, and reason to be equally important forces to be cultivated in education, the ultimate aim of which should be to produce good and virtuous citizens'.

Hence, the correct option is (A).

2. According to the passage, Educationists consider philosophy a 'weak and woolly' field is not practically applicable as mentioned in 'Many educationalists consider it a weak and woolly field, too far removed from the practical applications of the real world to be useful'.

Hence, the correct option is (A).

3. According to the passage, 'Perennialism' refers to something which is of ceaseless importance because the term comes from the root word 'perennial' – which means ceaseless.

Hence, the correct option is (A).

4. According to the passage, Plato's beliefs about education were democratic.

It is mentioned in sentence 'Plato believed that talent and intelligence are not distributed genetically and thus is be found in children born to all classes, although his proposed system of selective public education for an educated minority of the population does not really follow a democratic model'.

Hence, the correct option is (B).

5. According to the passage, Aquinas proposed a model of education which did not lay much emphasis on facts as facts do change with the changing times, it is mentioned in 'Perennialism holds that one should teach those things deemed to be of everlasting importance to all people everywhere, namely principles and reasoning, not just facts' .

Hence, the correct option is (C).

6. According to the passage, Higgs boson often called 'the God particle' because it's said to be what caused the 'Big Bang' that created our universe many years ago.

It is mentioned as it is in the 1st line of the 2nd paragraph.

Hence, the correct option is (C).

7. According to the passage, the discovery of the Higgs boson considered huge to the scientific community because it gives validity to The Standard Model of Physics, which is the authoritative theory for particle physics. It is mentioned in 'This discovery is huge to the scientific community because it gives validity to The Standard Model of Physics, which is the authoritative theory for particle physics'.

Hence, the correct option is (B).

8. According to the passage, had it been proved that the Higgs boson doesn't exist then the way modern scientists look at particle physics would be completely altered, therefore changing many of the current technological assumptions. It is mentioned in 'If it was proved incorrect, or that the there was no Higgs boson, the way modern scientists look at particle physics would be completely altered, therefore changing many of the current technological assumptions'.

Hence, the correct option is (A).

9. According to the passage, Kyle Cranmer compare the discovery of the Higgs boson to the development of quantum mechanics to show how much of an impact the discovery of the Higgs boson can have on human lives. It is mentioned in 'To show how much of an impact a discovery like this can have on our lives, Kyle Cranmer, an assistant professor of Physics at New York University, suggests looking at how early 20th century physicists were trying to understand the atom, and from there developed quantum mechanics'.

Hence, the correct option is (C).

10. According to the passage, Laser and Transistors were the outcomes of quantum mechanics, according to the passage.

It is mentioned in lines 'but it was also led to the invention of the transistor, the key ingredient for all modern electronics' and 'Quantum mechanics also led to the invention of the laser and other medical technologies like MRI's, PET scans'.

Hence, the correct option is (D).

11. Qualified candidates from D, E and $F = (16 + 20 + 16)\%$ of 4000

$= 2080$

Appeared candidates from A, B and $C = (25 + 10 + 15)\%$ of 24000

$= 12000$

Required ratio $= \frac{2080}{12000}$

$= 13:75$

Hence, the correct option is (D).

12. Qualified candidates from institute $C = 18\%$ of 4000

$= 720$

Appeared candidates from institute $C = 15\%$ of 24000 $= 3600$

Required $\% = \frac{720}{3600} \times 100$

$= 20\%$

Hence, the correct option is (D).

13. Qualified candidates from C and D together $= \{18 + 16\}\%$ of 4000

$= 1360$

Appeared candidates from C and D together $= \{15 + 12\}\%$ of 24000

$= 6480$

Required $\% = \frac{1360}{6480} \times 100$

$= 20.98\%$

Hence, the correct option is (C).

14. Percentage of candidates qualified with respect to those appeared,

$A = \frac{18\% \times 4000}{25\% \times 24000} \times 100$

$= \frac{18 \times 4}{25 \times 24} \times 100$

$B = \frac{12\% \times 4000}{10\% \times 24000} \times 100$

$= \frac{12 \times 4}{10 \times 24} \times 100$

$C = \frac{18\% \times 4000}{15\% \times 24000} \times 100$

$= \frac{18 \times 4}{15 \times 24} \times 100$

$D = \frac{16\% \times 4000}{12\% \times 24000} \times 100$

$= \frac{16 \times 4}{12 \times 24} \times 100$

$E = \frac{20\% \times 4000}{18\% \times 24000} \times 100$

$= \frac{20 \times 4}{18 \times 24} \times 100$

$F = \frac{16\% \times 4000}{20\% \times 24000} \times 100$

$= \frac{16 \times 4}{20 \times 24} \times 100$

In these values $\frac{4}{24}$ can be discarded because it is common in comparison. So,

$A = \frac{18}{25} \times 100$

$B = \frac{12}{10} \times 100$

$C = \frac{18}{15} \times 100$

$D = \frac{16}{12} \times 100$

$E = \frac{200}{18} \times 100$

$F = \frac{16}{20} \times 100$

Here, A and F are less than 100% , so they are removed without solving.

$B = 120\%, C = 1.2, D = 133.33\%, E = 110\%$

D has the highest percentage of qualified candidates with respect to those appeared.

Hence, the correct option is (B).

15. Qualified candidates from institute $B = 12\%$ of 4000

Appeared candidates from institute from institute $F = 20\%$ of 24000

Required ratio $= \frac{12\% \times 4000}{20\% \times 24000}$

$= 1:10$

Hence, the correct option is (A).

16. Employees In BCGI in required department $= 270 + 150 + 120$

$= 540$

Employees In Younker in required department $= 70 + 340 + 100$

$= 510$

Required ratio $= 540:510$

$= 18:17$

Hence, the correct option is (A).

17. Employees In operations $= 175 + 200 + 150 + 340 + 180$

$= 1045$

Total employees in 5 companies

$= 200 + 350 + 270 + 70 + 120 + 175 + 200 + 150 + 340 + 180 + 50 + 30 + 25 + 35 + 20 + 300 + 50 + 120 + 100 + 75$

$= 2860$

Required percentage $= \frac{1045}{2860} \times 100$

$= 36.53\%$

Hence, the correct option is (A).

18. Total technical employees hired by 5 companies $= 200 + 350 + 270 + 70 + 120$

$= 1010$

Average $= \frac{1010}{5}$

$= 202$

Hence, the correct option is (D).

19. Technical and operations employees in BCGI $= 270 + 150$

$= 420$

Operation and H.R employee in Younker $= 340 + 35$

$= 375$

Required $\% = \frac{420}{375} \times 100$

$= 112\%$

Hence, the correct option is (D).

20. Total employee in Zelman $= 120 + 180 + 20 + 75$

$= 395$

Total HR in Zelman $= 20$

Required $\% = \frac{20}{395} \times 100$

$= 5.06\%$
Hence, the correct option is (B).

21. A does 20% work in 8 days.
So, 100% work in $100 \times \frac{8}{20}$
$= 40$ days
B does 10% work in 3 days
So,
100% work in $100 \times \frac{3}{10}$
$= 30$ days
1 day work of A and B together is:-
So, $\frac{1}{40} + \frac{1}{30} = \frac{7}{120}$
So in 10 days they completed $\frac{7}{12}$ part of the work
Now,
C completed $25\% = \frac{1}{4}$ of work
So now remaining work $= 1 - \left(\frac{7}{12} + \frac{1}{4}\right)$
$= \frac{1}{6}$
F complete $\frac{1}{6}$ work in 16 days,

So, he does complete work in 96 days.

Hence, the correct option is (B).

22. A's part of work $= 20\%$
$= \frac{1}{5}$
So, G does whole work in 30 days,
$\Rightarrow \frac{1}{5}$ work in $\frac{1}{5} \times 30 = 6$ days
Now,
B also worked for 6 days.
B can complete 10% of work in 3 days.
So, B can complete the whole work in,

$= 100 \times \frac{3}{10}$
$= 30$ days
So, in 6 days,
B completed $\frac{6}{30} = \frac{1}{5}$ of work
Now, remaining work
$= 1 - \left(\frac{1}{5} + \frac{1}{5}\right) = \frac{3}{5}$
Now, E can complete 15% of work in 6 days.
So, E can complete the whole work in taken time
$= 100 \times \frac{6}{15}$
$= 40$ days

M can complete the work in $\frac{1}{4}^{\text{th}}$ of number of days of E.
$= \frac{1}{4} \times 40$
$= 10$ days

So, M completed $\frac{3}{5}$ work in taken time
$= \frac{3}{5} \times 10$
$= 6$ days
So, total number of days $= 6 + 6 + 6$
$= 18$

Hence, the correct option is (D).

23. $\%$ of Provident fund $= 12\%$

Annual provident fund saving $= 12\%$ of Rs. 33650×12
$= \frac{(12 \times 33650 \times 12)}{100}$
$=$ Rs, 48456

Hence, the correct option is (A).

24. $\%$ of Provident fund $= 12\%$

$\%$ of House rent $= 18\%$

Remaining income after provident fund deductions and payment of house rent $= [100 - 12 - 18]\%$ of Rs. 33650,

$=$Rs. $\frac{(70 \times 33650)}{100}$
$=$Rs. 23555
Hence, the correct option is (C).

25. $\%$ of Food $= 25\%$

$\%$ of Entertainment $= 9\%$

Spent on food and entertainment
$= 34\%$ of Rs. 33650
$= \frac{(34 \times 33650)}{100}$
$=$Rs. 11441
Hence, the correct option is (B).

26. A Memorandum of Understanding (MoU) was recently signed between the Central Board of Direct Taxes (CBDT) and the Central Board of Indirect Taxes and Customs (CBIC) for data exchange between the two organisations.
This MoU succeeds the agreement signed between them in the year 2015. During the event, a Data Exchange Steering Group has also been constituted that will meet periodically to review the data exchange status.
Hence, the correct option is (A).

27. One of the country's digital payment applications, Fampay has recently launched the country's first numberless card, targeted at teenagers.
Using these numberless debit cards, minors can make online and offline payments without opening a bank account. The card has no numbers on it and all the details are saved on the FamPay application.
Hence, the correct option is (B).

28. Edelweiss Asset Management Company manages the Bharat Bond Exchange Traded Fund (ETF). It has formally launched the second series of the ETF.

During December 2019, it had launched the first series. With this tranche, the fund house seeks to raise up to Rs 14,000 crore from retail and institutional investors. Bharat Bond ETFs invest in AAA-rated papers of public sector companies (CPSEs and PSEs).

Hence, the correct option is (C).

29. The Asian Development Bank (ADB) recently signed a USD 177 million loan agreement with the Government of India to upgrade 450 kilometers (km) of state highways and major district roads in the state of Maharashtra.
The project is expected to improve road connectivity between rural areas and urban centres in the state and enable rural communities to access markets and employment opportunities. The project will also develop a road safety audit framework and strengthen road safety measures.
Hence, the correct option is (C).

30. Indian Technology major Infosys announced a strategic partnership with Switzerland -based software company Avaloq, to provide wealth management services through digital platforms. Avaloq is a wealth management software and digital technology provider. As per the agreement, Infosys will be a strategic implementation partner for Avaloq's wealth management suite of solutions. This partnership will focus on providing industry-based wealth management solutions to their clients.
Hence, the correct option is (B).

31. The Indian Government has imposed safeguard duty on solar cells for one more year till July 2021 to protect domestic manufacturers.
This move will also discourage cheap imports from countries like China. Directorate General of Trade Remedies (DGTR), the investigative arm of the Commerce Ministry had recommended to the Department of Revenue for this imposition of duty.
Hence, the correct option is (B).

32. Mukesh Ambani led Reliance Industries has gone 10 places ahead in the Fortune Global 500 list and entered into the world's top 100 companies.
As per the recent 2020 ranking released by Fortune, Reliance has been ranked at 96th place globally. This is the highest rank ever of any Indian company on the Fortune Global 500 list. Indian Oil Corporation (IOC) slipped to 151st rank, Oil and Natural Gas Corporation (ONGC) is ranked 190th while State Bank of India (SBI) is at 221st rank.
Hence, the correct option is (A).

33. The Union Government has recently appointed economists Ashima Goyal, Jayanth R Varma and Shashanka Bhide as members of the Monetary Policy Committee (MPC) of the Reserve Bank of India (RBI).
The Appointments Committee of the Cabinet (ACC), headed by the prime minister, approved the names. The new members will replace Chetan Ghate, Pami Dua and Ravindra Dholakia. The RBI had earlier postponed the last meeting of the MPC.

Hence, the correct option is (B).

34. Singapore based sovereign wealth fund GIC and global private equity firm TPG Capital have invested a total of Rs. 7,350 crores in Reliance Retail.
Reliance Retail Ventures has attracted more than USD 2 billion in investments from global investors, over the past few months. GIC will invest for a 1.22 percent stake while TPG Capital Management will invest for a 0.41 percent equity stake.
Hence, the correct option is (B).

35. Job analysis describes the duties of the job, authority relationship, skills requirement, conditions of work etc. Job analysis is the process of gathering and analyzing information about the content and the human requirements of jobs, as well as, the context in which jobs are performed. This process is used to determine placement of jobs.
Hence, the correct option is (A).

Mock Test 04

Comprehension

Ques (1-6):Direction: Read the following passage carefully and answer the question that follows.

Bill Gates is a lot luckier than you might realise. He may be a very talented man who worked his way up from geek to the top spot on the list of the world's richest people. But his extreme success perhaps tells us more about the importance of circumstances beyond his control than it does about how skill and perseverance are rewarded.

We often fall for the idea that the exceptional performers are the most skilled or talented. But this is flawed. Exceptional performances tend to occur in exceptional circumstances. Top performers are often the luckiest people, who have benefited from being at the right place and right time. They are what we call outliers, whose performances may be examples set apart from the system that everyone else works within.

Many treat Gates, and other highly successful people like him, as deserving of huge attention and reward, as people from whom we could learn a lot about how to succeed. But assuming life's "winners" got there from performance alone is likely to lead to disappointment. Even if you could imitate everything Gates did, you would not be able to replicate his initial good fortune.

For example, Gates's upper-class background and private education enabled him to gain extra programming experience when less than 0.01% of his generation then had access to computers. His mother's social connection with IBM's chairman enabled him to gain a contract from the then-leading PC company that was crucial for establishing his software empire.

This is important because most customers who used IBM computers were forced to learn how to use Microsoft's software that came along with it. This created an inertia in Microsoft's favour. The next software these customers chose was more likely to be Microsoft's, not because their software was necessarily the best, but because most people were too busy to learn how to use anything else.

Microsoft's success and market share may differ from the rest by several orders of magnitude, but the difference was really enabled by Gate's early fortune, reinforced by a strong success-breeds-success dynamic. Of course, Gates's talent and effort played important roles in the extreme success of Microsoft. But that's not enough for creating such an outlier. Talent and effort are likely to be less important than circumstances in the sense that he could not have been so successful without the latter.

One might argue that many exceptional performers still gained their exceptional skill through hard work, exceptional motivation or "grit", so they do not deserve to receive lower reward and praise. Some have even suggested that there is a magic number for greatness, a ten-year or 10,000-hour rule. Many professionals and experts did acquire their exceptional skill through persistent, deliberate practices. In fact, Gates' 10,000 hours learning computer programming as a teenager has been highlighted as one of the reasons for his success.

But detailed analyses of the case studies of experts often suggest that certain situational factors beyond the control of these exceptional performers also play an important role. For example, three national champions in table tennis came from the same street in a small suburb of one town in England.

This wasn't a coincidence or because there was nothing else to do but practise ping pong. It turns out that a famous table tennis coach, Peter Charters, happened to retire in this particular suburb. Many kids who lived on the same street as the retired coach were attracted to this sport because of him and three of them, after following the "10,000-hour rule", performed exceptionally well, including winning the national championship.

Their talent and efforts were, of course, essential for realising their exceptional performances. But without their early luck (having a reliable, high-quality coach and supportive families), simply practicing 10,000 hours without adequate feedback wouldn't likely lead a randomly picked child to become a national champion.

We could also imagine a child with superior talent in table tennis suffering from early bad luck, such as not having a capable coach or being in a country where being an athlete was not considered to be a promising career. Then they might never have a chance to realise their potential. The implication is that the more exceptional a performance is, the fewer meaningful, applicable lessons we can actually learn from the "winner".

When it comes to moderate performance, it seems much more likely that our intuition about success is correct. Conventional wisdom, such as "the harder I work the luckier I get" or "chance favours the prepared mind", makes perfect sense when talking about someone moving from poor to good performance. Going from good to great, however, is a different story.

Being in the right place (succeeding in a context where early outcome has an enduring impact) at the right time (having early luck) can be so important that it overwhelms merits. With this in mind there's a good case that we shouldn't just reward or imitate life's winners and expect to have similar success. But there is a case that the winners should consider imitating the likes of Gates (who became a philanthropist) or Warren Buffett (who argues that richer Americans should pay higher taxes) who have chosen to use their wealth and success to do good things. The winners who appreciate their luck and do not take it all deserve more of our respect.

Q.1 Which of the following statements best sum up the author's view of Bill Gates and his success?

A. Bill Gates' genius has been much hyped by sensationalists who misguide young people into believing that they can emulate his success.

B. Bill Gates is more of an opportunist than he is talented, as he simply happened to be in the right place at the right time.

C. Bill Gates is no doubt hardworking and intelligent, but his good fortune is what put him in the right circumstances to make use of his qualities.

D. Bill Gates was exceptionally lucky from the start and that has gone a long way in contributing to his success.

Q.2 Which of the following examples best represent an outlier, as described in the passage?

A. A young boy belonging to a poor family studies very hard on his own, and manages to crack one of the toughest competitive examinations in the country. He then takes admission in one of the top B-schools, and later gets a placement in one of the top companies of the country.

B. A student is new to a college. He falls behind in studies during the first semester due to stress and inability to adjust to a new place. Due to his poor academic performance, he is labelled as an idiot, one who would never be able to have a successful career. At the end of the year, when the results of the entire class are announced, it is found that the student excelled across several subjects, and performed reasonably well in the rest.

C. Elections are being held in a college for the post of sports captain. Student A is expected to win this election, as he has represented his college in several sports competitions, and won trophies. Student B has also won awards in sports competitions on behalf of his college, but is not liked by most students for being rude and ill-mannered. On the day the results are announced, surprisingly, it is found that Student B was elected for the post.

D. A student is new to a college. He falls behind in studies during the first semester due to stress and inability to adjust to a new place. Due to his poor academic performance, he is labelled as an idiot, one who would never be able to have a successful career. Dejected by his treatment, he drops out of college. He works on developing a new computer program, the first of its kind, that soon becomes popular, and he becomes rich and famous.

Q.3 Which of the following best describes the tone of the passage?

A. Critical
B. Pessimistic
C. Cautionary
D. Advisory

Q.4 Which of the following questions cannot be answered on the basis of the information given in the passage?

A. What are the conditions that must be fulfilled in order to be characterised as an outlier?

B. Why must one not imitate the behaviour of life's winners?

C. What kind of life's winners are more deserving of our respect?

D. What were the factors at the start of Gates' career that enabled him to make use of his talent and become successful?

Q.5 It can be understood from the passage that the author believes which of the following statements?

A. Just like Bill Gates, Warren Buffet is also an outlier whose success was caused more by situational factors.

B. One must not imitate Bill Gates or Warren Buffet in any of their behaviour.

C. One should respect and imitate the generous and good acts done by people like Gates and Buffet, who have spent their wealth productively.

D. One should only respect winners who acknowledge the role luck played in their success, and Bill Gates is not one of them.

Q.6 It can be understood that the main purpose of the author in the third paragraph is to:

A. To clear the misconception that winners are not deserving of huge attention and reward as their success was not caused by performance alone.

B. To clear the misconception that simply imitating winners will not lead to success as their success is not due to performance alone.

C. To clear that misconception that one can achieve success by imitating Bill Gates.

D. To clear the misconception that there were factors other than Gates' talent that led him towards success.

Ques (7-10):Direction: Read the following passage carefully and answer the question that follows.

After many years of practising Buddhism in Thailand, my experience expands beyond the immediate community in Sri Racha. In recent years as I have visited the White Dragon Temple, the social unrest in Thailand has crept into the religious aspect of my trips.

Religion exists as an innate piece of the landscape that etches itself into the small details of Thailand. It occupies both a very physical presence within the community and also a mental one. According to the Office of National Buddhism, 40,717 Buddhist temples exist in Thailand. Of these temples, a large portion resides in Bangkok, Thailand's capital.

Aside from being an important tourist element, Buddhism plays an important part in the lives of Thai people - an estimated 94% of all Thai people practice Buddhism in the country according to a Central Intelligence Agency report. Time and time again, there have been movements - in 1997, 2007, and 2014 - to concretize Buddhism as the nation's official religion. The Thai Constitutional Drafting Committee (CDC) has, however, remained neutral in the relationship between the state and religion.

Though the government's ideological stance on religion is decidedly impartial, significant ripples exist in this seemingly placid surface, and religion morphs into a central focal point in many instances, whether the Thai government takes an intimate position on it or not. Faith remains a link to the personal lives of common citizens and royalty alike. King Bhumibol's funeral on October 14, 2016 featured traditional Buddhist funeral rites with the ritualistic bathing of the king's body and the chanting of orange-robed monks. Adding to this ceremonious burial, his body resided in the Temple of the Emerald Buddha so that people could pay their respects to the revered king, who provided stability for his country for 70 years. Though the king in Thailand did not hold any true, legislative power, he was a reverential symbol for the people of the country. His majesty's death occurred at a moment of tension in the country as a number of attacks rocked Thailand and has only caused this pressure to spill-over. Religion is something that connects people in Thailand yet, at the same time, can be a divisive element as is evident from attacks that have occurred in the nation over the last few years.

In the span of less than a day between August 11th and 12th of 2016, 11 bombings hit five provinces in Thailand, killing at least four Thai nationals and injuring 36. These bombings occurred almost a year after one of the most devastating attacks in Thai history in Bangkok, which killed 20 people and wounded 125 more. What's more, these attacks coincided with the Queen Sirikit's birthday. On August 17, 2015, Uighur militants splintered the Thai state as they bombed the Erawan Shrine. Though the motives for the attack were more aimed at the states' repatriation of Uighur refugees, the targeting of the temple was calculated: not only is the area around the shrine a densely populated area but also, it is frequented by many tourists. These acts of terrorism that assail the kingdom have left many Thais scared and unsure in a time, without a unifying leader. Known epithetically as the "land of smiles," Thailand has had little to smile about of late.

In light of this tumultuous time in the nation's history, religious institutions like the White Dragon Temple became integral in steadying the country's course. Through the diligent service that the temple provides for the community, it is a rallying point for many frightened Thais. See Knok, the central spiritual leader in the temple, and his followers have proved to be a "stabilizing element in the wake of the King's death," especially in Sri Racha, by continuing with their public works projects - providing educational help, burial services, food distribution, and a variety of other support structures. These actions from local community leaders have started to mend the fractures that occur on a national level.

I returned to Thailand in August of 2016, during the bombings in the southern provinces of the country. On one day during this visit, I bagged fruit and food for followers and local community members alike. The cadence of shifting palates of food and thump of vegetables into bags kept time with my human tempo. With each bag I loaded onto the palates, I could measure the burden on the community of Sri Racha lift slightly. In the glimmering eyes of the young men that I worked with, I could see the brightness of Thailand's future. Beneath me, I could feel the flexing and contracting of a nation, not torn by conflict but ready to rebuild and strive onward if only for a moment.

Q.7 What is the main purpose behind the author's words when he says: "Known epithetically as the "land of smiles," Thailand has had little to smile about of late"?

A. To point out the hardships that have plagued Thailand.

B. To point out the hypocrisy of the Thai society as they do not live up to their name - 'the land of smiles'.

C. To bring out the irony of the situation where a country known for its smiles and happiness, has unhappy circumstances rather than happy ones.

D. To explain the origin of the epithet that Thailand is known by, and to suggest that it no longer holds true for the country.

Q.8 Which of the following statement(s) is/ are confirmed from the facts provided in the passage?

I. The lack of a strong and unifying political leader in Thailand has made the country stagger further when it comes to dealing with the recent acts of terrorism that have struck the country.

II. The recent terrorist attacks in Thailand are an example of how religion can play a major role in bringing people of a common culture together in difficult times.

III. Efforts to make Buddhism as the official religion of Thailand have so far not panned out, as the government does not let religion interfere with state matters.

A. Only I **B.** Only I and II
C. Only II and III **D.** Only I and III

Q.9 Which of the following best sums up the final note on which the author ends the passage?

A. Thailand still has hopes of a good future and can overcome its hardships if the people of the country work collectively towards rebuilding the country.

B. Thailand can optimistically hope for a brighter tomorrow provided it somehow manages not to disintegrate in the light of the conflict that seeks to tear it asunder.

C. The society of Thailand must take the initiative to fight back all threats if it is to hope for a brighter future.

D. It is the youth of Thailand which will ultimately contribute to the rebuilding of the country and make the future shine again.

Q.10 Which of the following can be said to be the central idea of the sixth paragraph?

A. The role of the government in rebuilding the country after terrorist threats.

B. The role of the local people in rebuilding the country after terrorist threats.

C. The role of the religious institutions in rebuilding the country after terrorist threats.

D. The role of the White Dragon Temple in rebuilding the country after terrorist threats.

Management Data Interpretation

Ques (11-15):Direction: Study the table given below and answer the question that follows.

Foreign Tourist Arrivals and Foreign Exchange Earnings in India

Year	Foreign Tourist Arrivals (in lakhs)	Estimated foreign Exchange earnings (in million US $)
1996 – 97	23.34	2878
1997 – 98	23.71	2914
1998 – 99	23.97	2993
1999 – 00	25.05	3036
2000 –	26.99	3168

01		
2001 – 02	24.25	2910
2002 – 03	24.70	3029
2003 – 04	29.25	3833

Q.11 The decline in the number of tourists in the year $2001-02$ from the preceding year was

A. 2 lakhs **B.** 2.5 lakhs
C. 2.74 lakhs **D.** 3 lakhs

Q.12 What was the average foreign exchange earning per tourist in the year $1999-2000$?

A. $ 1212 **B.** $ 12 **C.** $ 1.2 **D.** $ 120

Q.13 What percent reduction of foreign exchange earnings took place in the year $2001-02$ compared with the preceding year?

A. 6.5 **B.** 7.1 **C.** 7.9 **D.** 8.1

Q.14 What has been the per cent growth in tourist arrivals from $1999-2000$ to $2003-2004$?

A. 16.75 **B.** 15.75 **C.** 18.75 **D.** 4.2

Q.15 How many US dollars were earned in the period $1996-97$ to $1998-99$, as a result of foreign tourists?

A. $ 878 million **B.** $ 87.8 million
C. $ 8.7 million **D.** $ 8785 million

Ques (16-18):Direction: Study the following table chart carefully and answer the questions given beside

The following table represents the distance (in km) travelled by five persons in seven different days of a week.

Persons	Sunday	Monday	Tuesday	Wednesday	Thursday	Friday	Saturday
A	700	550	840	460	880	380	820
B	500	450	630	540	350	440	840
C	650	800	480	280	680	460	780
D	400	620	720	620	300	520	760
E	250	520	650	740	340	380	560

Q.16 Distance travelled by B in all the days together is what percent of the distance travelled by C in all the days together?

A. 64.24% **B.** 78.23%
C. 88.65% **D.** None of these

Q.17 If the speed of B on Monday is $60\ km/h$ and speed of D on Saturday is $80\ km/h$. Find the respective ratio of time taken by B and D.

A. 19:15 **B.** 13:17 **C.** 17:13 **D.** 15:19

Q.18 Find the difference between total distance travelled by C on Sunday, Monday and Tuesday together and total distance travelled by E on Thursday, Friday and Saturday together.

A. 540 km **B.** 650 km **C.** 720 km **D.** 830 km

Ques (19-23):Direction: The line graphs given below show the sale of three brands of soft drinks (bottles in millions) in the period $1998-2003$. Refer to the graphs to answer the question that follows.

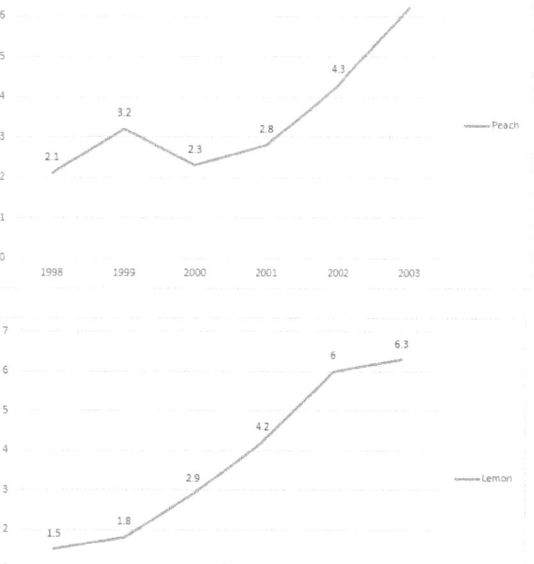

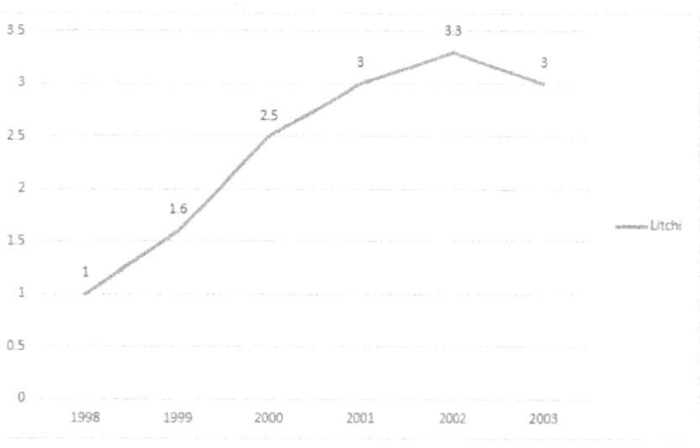

Q.19 From the graph over the given period, which drink in which year has shown the highest percentage growth in sale over the previous year?

A. Peach, 1999 **B.** Lemon, 2001
C. Peach, 2002 **D.** Lemon, 2000

Q.20 In the year 2004, Peach records 40% growth in sale while Lemon sale grows by over 25% over the previous year. What is the difference in the sale of these brands in year 2004?

A. 2.1 million bottles **B.** 0.8 million bottles

C. 1.6 million bottles **D.** 2.4 million bottles

Q.21 In the year 2004, the ratio of the sale of the three drinks happens to be same as that in 1998. What should be the approximate total sale of drinks of the three brands in the year 2004, if the sale of Litchi increased by 10% over the previous year?

A. 15 million **B.** 8 million
C. 10 million **D.** 5 million

Q.22 Each case contains 24 bottles and average selling price per bottle is Rs. 9. If the three brands of drinks command a market share of 80%, then what was the total industry size in year 2003?

A. Rs. 17.5 crores **B.** Rs. 20 crores
C. Rs. 420 crores **D.** Rs. 560 crores

Q.23 Each case contains 24 bottles and average selling price per bottle is Rs. 9. If there is an excise duty of Rs. 16 per case, what is the total excise duty collected in the year 2003 from the three products?

A. 2.8 crores **B.** 1.03 crores
C. 2.32 crores **D.** 2.7 crores

Ques (24-25):Direction : Study the following table chart carefully and answer the questions given beside.

The following table represents the number of employees in five different organisations in 2012,2013, 2014 and 2015.

Organization	2012	2013	2014	2015
P	5000	8800	3600	6200
Q	4800	10200	12100	8300
R	5500	6500	8800	4250
S	8000	4800	9000	5650
T	7600	7200	8400	3880

Q.24 Find the Total number of employees in all the organisations in 2013.

A. 35450 **B.** 32200 **C.** 37500 **D.** 36560

Q.25 Number of employees in organization P in 2013 and 2014 together is what percent of number of employees in organization R in 2014 and 2015 together?

A. 80.01% **B.** 95.01% **C.** 91.01% **D.** 88.52%

Business Awareness

Q.26 As per the Sexual Harassment of Women at Workplace Act which of the following act is not termed as Sexual Harassment?

A. A demand or request for a sexual favour
B. Sexually coloured remarks
C. Bad Physical contact
D. Meeting in the cabin of the office

Q.27 The number of subordinates a superior can effectively handle is called:

A. Organizing people **B.** Span of control
C. Direction **D.** Coordination

Q.28 A ____ is a company's plan for how it will balance its internal strengths and weaknesses with external opportunities and threats in order to maintain a competitive advantage.

A. SWOT analysis **B.** Mission statement
C. Strategy **D.** Tactic

Q.29 One of the following companies does have business interest in both oil and shipping sectors. Identify this.

A. Essar Group **B.** ONGC
C. Reliance Group **D.** Tata Group

Q.30 Brazil-based bus body maker Marcopolo has entered into a Joint venture with which Indian Company to manufacture fully-built buses and coaches?

A. Eicher **B.** Ashok Leyland
C. Tata Motors **D.** Swaraz Mazda

Q.31 Which organisation conducted a virtual meet with Germany, to promote export of fresh fruits and vegetables from India?

A. ECGC **B.** EXIM Bank
C. APEDA **D.** NABARD

Q.32 Which Indian Bank has partnered with Defence Forces for providing customised banking services?

A. State Bank of India
B. Bank of Baroda
C. Punjab National Bank
D. Canara Bank

Q.33 When will India's New Foreign Trade Policy will come into effect?

A. February 1, 2021 **B.** March 1, 2021
C. April 1, 2021 **D.** September 1, 2021

Q.34 Which of the following companies is also present in other sectors like FMCG, Electrical equipment, apart from IT?

A. Patni Computers **B.** Wipro
C. Infosys **D.** Polaris

Q.35 Which regulating body has amended the regulations on transferring of assets by liquidator of a stressed firm?

A. RBI **B.** SEBI **C.** IBBI **D.** NCLT

// Smart Answer Sheet //

Correct — Indicates percentage of students who answered questions correctly.

Skipped — Indicates percentage of students who skipped questions.

Q.	Ans.	Correct	Skipped
1	C	51.56 %	47.72 %
2	D	30.73 %	67.58 %
3	D	11.99 %	69.69 %
4	A	44.62 %	52.06 %
5	C	59.24 %	37.58 %
6	B	25.02 %	71.21 %
7	C	32.25 %	67.38 %
8	D	49.95 %	32.08 %
9	A	30.88 %	68.87 %
10	C	66.97 %	31.07 %
11	C	81.81 %	17.34 %
12	A	69.25 %	30.73 %
13	D	66.71 %	30.11 %
14	A	48.54 %	34.93 %
15	D	84.64 %	14.0 %
16	D	12.4 %	83.68 %
17	D	59.38 %	40.04 %
18	B	62.94 %	33.49 %
19	D	22.93 %	69.62 %
20	B	64.25 %	35.05 %
21	A	28.75 %	68.66 %
22	A	21.06 %	67.25 %
23	B	49.59 %	39.24 %
24	C	83.84 %	12.15 %
25	B	45.63 %	51.06 %
26	D	85.08 %	11.9 %
27	B	69.61 %	30.39 %
28	C	63.06 %	32.27 %
29	A	19.17 %	71.67 %
30	C	57.97 %	35.91 %
31	C	19.64 %	75.08 %
32	B	61.11 %	37.89 %
33	C	57.08 %	37.72 %
34	B	85.11 %	12.94 %
35	C	41.96 %	46.78 %

Performance Analysis	
Avg. Score (%)	48.57%
Toppers Score (%)	74.29%
Your Score	

//Hints and Solutions//

1. C is the right answer, as it best sums up the view the author has of Gates as mentioned in the sentence 'even if you could imitate everything Gates did, you would not be able to replicate his initial good fortune'.

A is incorrect as the passage makes no mention of the fact the young people are misguided, he simply seeks to clear a misconception.

B is incorrect as the author does acknowledge Gates' talent, and does not call him an opportunist.

D is incorrect as it attributes all of his success to luck, and makes no mention of his own qualities.

Hence, the correct option is (C).

2. D presents the outlier as we can infer that most college dropouts do not go on to have rich or successful careers.

An outlier, as described in the passage is one 'whose performances may be examples set apart from the system that everyone else works within.' This would mean someone with extraordinary talent, one who excels in a position, where others might fail.

The character in option A does show talent and skill, but is not that extraordinary, as it shows the normal good outcome of hard work. Moreover, once the boy cracked the examination, everything else was bound to follow.

B is incorrect as this is not very extraordinary or surprising, as we are given factors that led to his poor performance; this implies that the student himself was not lacking in hard work or intellect.

C is incorrect as it presents a surprising situation, but is not extraordinary enough on the part of the student, with respect to his talent or skill.

Hence, the correct option is (D).

3. D is the right answer, as the author seeks to advise the readers to not imitate outliers, or reward them with too much of praise.

A is incorrect as the author does not criticise anyone or anything. He acknowledges Gates' talent, while subtly suggesting that there were factors other than his talent that were at play.

B is incorrect as the author does not speak in a pessimistic or negative way about anything.

C is incorrect as this would be too strong a word to describe the author's tone. The author offers suggestion and advice rather than a warning.

Hence, the correct option is (D).

4. A is the right answer, as the passage only tells us what outliers are, not the conditions that must be fulfilled in order to be characterised as one.

B is incorrect as this question is answered throughout the passage: 'Being in the right place (succeeding in a context where early outcome has an enduring impact) at the right time (having early luck) can be so important that it overwhelms merits. With this in mind there's a good case that we shouldn't just reward or imitate life's winners and expect to have similar success.'

C is incorrect as this question is answered in the last few lines: 'The winners who appreciate their luck and do not take it all deserve more of our respect.'

D is incorrect as this question is answered in the first few paragraphs: ', Gates's upper-class background and private education enabled him to gain extra programming experience when less than 0.01% of his generation then had access to computers. His mother's social connection with IBM's chairman enabled him to gain a contract from the then-leading PC company that was crucial for establishing his software empire.'

Hence, the correct option is (A).

5. 'But there is a case that the winners should consider imitating the likes of Gates (who became a philanthropist) or Warren Buffett (who argues that richer Americans should pay higher taxes) who have chosen to use their wealth and success to do good things.' These lines make it clear that the author believes the statement given in option C.

A is incorrect as the author neither mentions nor implies this.

B is incorrect as the author does say that there is a case that winners should imitate Gates in his generous acts and how he has used his wealth and success for good things.

D is incorrect as countered by the following lines: 'But there is a case that the winners should consider imitating the likes of Gates (who became a philanthropist) or Warren Buffett (who argues that richer Americans should pay higher taxes) who have chosen to use their wealth and success to do good things.' These lines also make it clear that the author believes the statement given in option C.

Hence, the correct option is (C).

6. B is the right answer, as the author seeks to clear the misconception that success cannot be achieved simply by imitating life's winners, as they did not succeed through performance alone.

A is incorrect as the author does not directly say or imply that attention and respect should not be given to winners. Rather he focuses more on the suggestion that one must not fall into the trap of imitating them and expecting similar returns.

C is incorrect as the passage talks of all winners, not only Gates, although it does talk of him as an example.

D is incorrect as this is his primary purpose in later paragraphs, not the third one.

Hence, the correct option is (B).

7. C is the right answer, as it best sums up the main purpose that the author has in mind while using these words.

A is incorrect as although the author does narrate the hardships that have plagued Thailand of late, this sentence makes a conclusion rather than specifically talk of the hardships.

B is incorrect as the author does not talk of hypocrisy of the Thai people; he does not in any way hold them responsible for not living up to their name. Instead, by means of examples in the next paragraph, he seeks to delicately suggest that it is ironical and contrary to expectation that a country known for its smiles is facing circumstances that would disable its people to remain happy or smile.

D is incorrect as although it is partially correct - the author does claim that the epithet no longer holds true for Thailand, he does not give us the origins of this epithet.

Hence, the correct option is (C).

8. Only I and III are the correct statements.

I is confirmed from the information given in the fifth paragraph, which tells us that the acts of terrorism have left the Thai people unsure and scared, especially since there is no unifying leader as mentioned in lines 'These acts of terrorism that assail the kingdom have left many Thais scared and unsure in a time, without a unifying leader'.

III is confirmed from the information provided in the third paragraph which tells us that there have been movements to make Buddhism the official religion; however, the state has remained neutral in the relationship between the state and religion, from which we infer that this is the reason why those movements have not been successful as mentioned in sentence 'there have been movements - in 1997, 2007, and 2014 - to concretize Buddhism as the nation's official religion'.

II cannot be confirmed from the passage; on the contrary, it is contradicted by the information given in the fourth paragraph which tells us that the recent terrorism acts show how religion can play a divisive role. D is the right answer, as only I and III are correct.

Hence, the correct option is (D).

9. A is the right answer, as it best sums up the final note on which the author ends the passage.

B is incorrect as the author asserts that he does not see Thailand torn by conflict, rather he sees it actively fighting to secure its future, so the possibility of disintegration, as mentioned in B does not exist.

C is incorrect as the author says that the country is already fighting back, not that it should fight back.

D is incorrect as the author does not single out a specific section of the society that would rebuild the country.

Hence, the correct option is (A).

10. C is correct as it describes the role played by religious institutions in rebuilding the country after the unfortunate terrorist attacks.

A is incorrect as the paragraph does not talk of the government's role.

B is incorrect as the paragraph does not talk about the role played by local people, rather we can say that it talks about the role of local community leaders.

D is incorrect as it is too specific and restricts itself to the White Dragon Temple, while the paragraph only seeks to illustrate the role played by religious institutions by means of giving an example of one such institution.

Hence, the correct option is (C).

11. Foreign tourist arrival in $2000-01=26.99$ lakhs

Foreign tourist arrival in $2001-02=24.25$ lakhs

Decline in number of tourists $=(26.99-24.25)$ lakhs

$=2.74$ lakhs

Hence, the correct option is (C).

12. Foreign tourist arrival in $1999-2000=25.05$ lakhs $=25.05\times10^5$

Foreign Exchange Earnings in $1999-2000=3036$ million

$=3036\times10^6$

Average foreign exchange earning per tourist $=\frac{3036\times10^6}{25.05\times10^5}$

$=\$\ 1212$ approx.

Hence, the correct option is (A).

13. Foreign exchange earnings in $2001-02=2910$ million

Foreign exchange earnings in $2000-01=3168$ million

So,

Reduction of foreign exchange earnings took place in the year $2001-02$ compared with the preceding year $=(3168-2910)$ million

Percentage reduction in foreign exchange earnings $=\frac{3168-2910}{3168}\times100$

$=\frac{258}{3168}\times100$

$=8.14\%$

$=8.1\%$

Hence, the correct option is (D).

14. Foreign Tourist Arrivals in $1999-00=25.05$ lakhs

Foreign Tourist Arrivals in $2003-04=29.25$ lakhs

So,

Growth of Foreign tourist arrivals took place in the year $2003-04$ compared with $1999-00=(29.25-25.05)$ lakhs

Percentage growth in Foreign tourist arrivals $=\frac{29.25-25.05}{25.05}\times100$

$=\frac{4.2}{25.05}\times100$

$=16.76\%$

Hence, the correct option is (A).

15. Foreign Exchange Earnings in $1996-97 = \$\ 2878$ million

Foreign Exchange Earnings in $1997-98 = \$\ 2914$ million

Foreign Exchange Earnings in $1998-99 = \$\ 2993$ million

Total earning in the given period $= \$\ (2878 + 2914 + 2993)$ million

$= \$\ 8785$ million

Hence, the correct option is (D).

16. Distance travelled by B on Sunday $= 500\ km$
Distance travelled by B on Monday $= 450\ km$
Distance travelled by B on Tuesday $= 630\ km$
Distance travelled by B on Wednesday $= 540\ km$
Distance travelled by B on Thursday $= 350\ km$
Distance travelled by B on Friday $= 440\ km$
Distance travelled by B on Saturday $= 840\ km$
Distance travelled by B in all the days together
$= (500 + 450 + 630 + 540 + 350 + 440 + 840)\ km$
$= 3750\ km$
Distance travelled by C on Sunday $= 650\ km$
Distance travelled by C on Monday $= 800\ km$
Distance travelled by C on Tuesday $= 480\ km$
Distance travelled by C on Wednesday $= 280\ km$
Distance travelled by C on Thursday $= 680\ km$
Distance travelled by C on Friday $= 460\ km$
Distance travelled by C on Saturday $= 780\ km$
Distance travelled by C in all the days together
$= (650 + 800 + 480 + 280 + 680 + 460 + 780)\ km$
$= 4130\ km$
Required $\% = \frac{3750}{4130} \times 100$
$= 90.79\%$

Hence, the correct option is (D).

17. Distance travelled by B on Monday $= 450\ km$

Speed of B on Monday $= 60\ km/hr$

Distance travelled by D on Saturday $= 760\ km$

Speed of D on Saturday $= 80\ km/hr$

We know,

$$\text{Speed} = \frac{\text{Distance}}{\text{Time}}$$

Time taken by B on Monday $= \frac{450}{60}$ hours

$= 7.5$ hours

Time taken by D on Saturday $= \frac{760}{80}$ hours

$= 9.5$ hours

Respective ratio $= 75:95$

$= 15:19$

Hence, the correct option is (D).

18. Distance travelled by C on Sunday $= 650\ km$

Distance travelled by C on Monday $= 800\ km$

Distance travelled by C on Tuesday $= 480\ km$

Distance travelled by E on Thursday $= 340\ km$

Distance travelled by E on Friday $= 380\ km$

Distance travelled by E on Saturday $= 560\ km$

Total distance travelled by C on Sunday, Monday and Tuesday together $= (650 + 800 + 480)\ km$

$= 1930\ km$
Total distance travelled by E on Thursday, Friday and Saturday together $= (340 + 380 + 560)\ km$

$= 1280\ km$
Required difference $= (1930 - 1280)\ km$

$= 650\ km$

Hence, the correct option is (B).

19. Sale of Peach brand in $1998 = 2.1$ million
Sale of Peach brand in $1999 = 3.2$ million
Sale of Peach brand in $2000 = 2.3$ million
Sale of Peach brand in $2001 = 2.8$ million
Sale of Peach brand in $2002 = 4.3$ million
Sale of Peach brand in $2003 = 6.2$ million
Sale of Lemon brand in $1998 = 1.5$ million
Sale of Lemon brand in $1999 = 1.8$ million
Sale of Lemon brand in $2000 = 2.9$ million
Sale of Lemon brand in $2001 = 4.2$ million
Sale of Lemon brand in $2002 = 6$ million
Sale of Lemon brand in $2003 = 6.3$ million
Sale of Litchi brand in $1998 = 1$ million
Sale of Litchi brand in $1999 = 1.6$ million
Sale of Litchi brand in $2000 = 2.5$ million
Sale of Litchi brand in $2001 = 3$ million
Sale of Litchi brand in $2002 = 3.3$ million
Sale of Litchi brand in $2003 = 3$ million
Growth of Peach in $1999 = (3.2 - 2.1)$ million
Growth $\% = \frac{3.2-2.1}{2.1} \times 100 = 52.38\%$
Growth of Peach in $2001 = (2.8 - 2.3)$ million

Growth $\% = \frac{2.8-2.3}{2.3} \times 100 = 21.74\%$
Growth of Peach in $2002 = (4.3 - 2.8)$ million
Growth $\% = \frac{4.3-2.8}{2.8} \times 100 = 53.57\%$
Growth of Peach in $2003 = (6.2 - 4.3)$ million
Growth $\% = \frac{6.2-4.3}{4.3} \times 100 = 44.19\%$
Growth of Lemon in $1999 = (1.8 - 1.5)$ million
Growth $\% = \frac{1.8-1.5}{1.5} \times 100 = 20\%$
Growth of Lemon in $2000 = (2.9 - 1.8)$ million
Growth $\% = \frac{2.9-1.8}{1.8} \times 100 = 61.11\%$
Growth of Lemon in $2001 = (4.2 - 2.9)$ million
Growth $\% = \frac{4.2-2.9}{2.9} \times 100 = 44.83\%$
Growth of Lemon in $2002 = (6 - 4.2)$ million
Growth $\% = \frac{6-4.2}{4.2} \times 100 = 42.86\%$
Growth of Lemon in $2003 = (6.3 - 6)$ million
Growth $\% = \frac{6.3-6}{6} \times 100 = 5\%$
Growth of Litchi in $1999 = (1.6 - 1)$ million
Growth $\% = \frac{1.6-1}{1} \times 100 = 60\%$
Growth of Litchi in $2000 = (2.5 - 1.6)$ million
Growth $\% = \frac{2.5-1.6}{1.6} \times 100 = 56.25\%$
Growth of Litchi in $2001 = (3 - 2.5)$ million
Growth $\% = \frac{3-2.5}{2.5} \times 100 = 20\%$
Growth of Litchi in $2002 = (3.3 - 3)$ million
Growth $\% = \frac{3.3-3}{3} \times 100 = 10\%$
From the calculations shown above we can conclude that in 2000 Lemon drink has shown the maximum growth.

Hence, the correct option is (D).

20. Sale of Peach brand in $2003 = 6.2$ million
Growth in $2004 = 40\%$
Sale of Peach brand in $2004 = 6.2 \times \frac{140}{100}$ million
$\Rightarrow 8.68$ million
Sale of Lemon brand in $2003 = 6.3$ million
Growth in $2004 = 25\%$
Sale of Lemon brand in $2004 = 6.3 \times \frac{125}{100}$ million
$\Rightarrow 7.87$ million
Difference in the sale of these brands in year in 2002
$= (8.68 - 7.87)$ million
$= 0.81$ million

Hence, the correct option is (B).

21. Sale of Peach brand in $1998 = 2.1$ million
Sale of Lemon brand in $1998 = 1.5$ million
Sale of Litchi brand in $1998 = 1$ million
Sale of Peach brand in $2003 = 6.2$ million
Sale of Lemon brand in $2003 = 6.3$ million
Sale of Litchi brand in $2003 = 3$ million
Growth of Litchi brand in $2004 = 10\%$
Sale of Litchi brand in $2004 = 3 \times \frac{110}{100}$ million
$\Rightarrow 3.3$ million
Ratio of all the three brands in $1998 = 2.1: 1.5: 1$
Thus, total sale of drinks in $2004 = (2.1 + 1.5 + 1) \times 3.3$
$\Rightarrow 15.18$ million

Hence, the correct option is (A).

22. Sale of Peach brand in $2003 = 6.2$ million
Sale of Lemon brand in $2003 = 6.3$ million
Sale of Litchi brand in $2003 = 3$ million
Total sale in $2003 = 6.2 + 6.3 + 3$ million
$\Rightarrow 15.5$ million
Given Price per bottle $=$ Rs. 9
Total Selling Price of three brands $=$ Rs. $15.5 \times 10^6 \times 9$
$\Rightarrow$ Rs. 139500000
Since these 3 brands constitute only 80% of total market.
Thus, total industry size $= 139500000 \times \frac{100}{80}$
$\Rightarrow$ Rs. $174{,}375{,}000$
$\Rightarrow$ Rs. 17.5 crores (approx.)

Hence, the correct option is (A).

23. Sale of Peach brand in $2003 = 6.2$ million
Sale of Lemon brand in $2003 = 6.3$ million
Sale of Litchi brand in $2003 = 3$ million
Total sale in $2003 = (6.2 + 6.3 + 3)$ million
$\Rightarrow 15.5$ million
Total bottles in a case $= 24$
Total number of cases $= \frac{15.5 \times 10^6}{24}$
Excise Duty per case $=$ Rs. 16
Total excise (in crores) $= \frac{15.5 \times 10^6}{24} \times \frac{16}{10^7}$
$\Rightarrow 1.03$ crores

Hence, the correct option is (B).

24. Total employees in organisation P in $2013 = 8800$
Total employees in organisation Q in $2013 = 10200$
Total employees in organisation R in $2013 = 6500$
Total employees in organisation S in $2013 = 4800$
Total employees in organisation T in $2013 = 7200$
Total number of employees in all the organisation in 2013
$= 8800 + 10200 + 6500 + 4800 + 7200$
$= 37500$

Hence, the correct option is (C).

25. Number of employees in organization P in 2013 and 2014 together $= 8800 + 3600 = 12400$

Number of employees in organization R in 2014 and 2015 together $= 8800 + 4250 = 13050$

Reqd. $\% = \frac{12400}{13050} \times 100 = 95.01\%$

Hence, the correct option is (B).

26. Meeting in the cabin of the office can't be termed as sexual harassment because it is part of official work. These activities come under sexual Harassment:-

a) Improper Physical touch

b) A demand or request for a sexual favour

c) Sexually coloured remarks

d) Showing pornography

e) Lewd comment

f) Any other unwelcome physical verbal or non-verbal behaviour of sexual nature.

Hence, the correct option is (D).

27. The number of subordinates a superior can effectively handle is called **Span of control**.

As an example, a manager with five direct reports has a span of control of five. The span of control determines the level of interactions and responsibilities associated with employees and managers.

Hence, the correct option is (B).

28. A **strategy** is a company's plan for how it will balance its internal strengths and weaknesses with external opportunities and threats in order to maintain a competitive advantage. Strategy is a general plan to achieve one or more long-term or overall goals under conditions of uncertainty.

Hence, the correct option is (C).

29. Essar Group have business interest in both oil and shipping sectors.

Essar Group, is an Indian multinational conglomerate and construction company, founded by Shashi Ruia and Ravi Ruia, in 1969. Essar Global Fund Limited (EGFL) controls a number of assets across the core sectors of Energy (Oil Refining, Oil & Gas Exploration & Production, Power), Infrastructure (Ports, Projects), Metals & Mining, and Services (Shipping, Oilfield Services, IT). EGFL holds near 100% stake in all its investments.

Hence, the correct option is (A).

30. Tata Motors, India's largest automobile company, and Marcopolo, the Brazil-based global leader in body-building for buses and coaches, announced a joint venture company in India to manufacture and assemble fully-built buses and coaches.

Hence, the correct option is (C).

31. Agricultural and Processed Food Products Export Development Authority (APEDA) had organised a virtual meeting with importers of Germany to promote export of fresh fruits and vegetables from India. The event was organised in collaboration with Indian Embassy in Germany and German Agribusiness Alliance.
APEDA is an apex body under the Ministry of Commerce and Industry which regulates export of agricultural products in India.

Hence, the correct option is (C).

32. Leading Public sector lender Bank of Baroda (BoB) has signed a memorandum of understanding (MoU) with Indian Navy and Indian Coast Guard.
Under the MoU, the bank is to offer customised services along with a several facilities to the account holders. The bank has also renewed its MoU with the Indian Army to offer customised banking services through 'Baroda Military Salary Package'.

Hence, the correct option is (B).

33. The new Foreign Trade Policy of India, is set to take effect from 1st April 2021. The policy will be in effect for 5 years from 2021 to 2026.
It aims to make India a leader in international trade. It is also known that the District Export Hubs initiative will form an important component of the new Foreign Trade Policy.

Hence, the correct option is (C).

34. Wipro is also present in other sectors like FMCG, Electrical equipment, apart from IT.

Wipro Limited is an Indian multinational corporation that provides information technology, consulting and business process services. It is headquartered in Bangalore, Karnataka, India. In 2013, Wipro separated its non-IT businesses and formed the privately owned Wipro Enterprises.

Hence, the correct option is (B).

35. The Insolvency and Bankruptcy Board of India (IBBI) has recently amended regulations to fast-track the resolution process. Under the new regulations, the liquidator of a stressed firm can assign or transfer an asset, which is not readily realisable, to any person after consulting consultation committee of stakeholders. With NCLT's approval, they may also distribute the undisposed of assets amongst stakeholders.

Hence, the correct option is (C).

Mock Test 05

Comprehension

Ques (1-3):Direction: Read the given passage carefully and answer the question that follows.

The research suggests a radically different view, in which learning of a child's first language does not rely on an innate grammar module. Instead the new research shows that young children use various types of thinking that may not be specific to language at all such as the ability to classify the world into categories (people or objects, for instance) and to understand the relations among things. These capabilities, coupled with a unique human ability to grasp what others intend to communicate, allow language to happen.

The new findings indicate that if researchers truly want to understand how children, and others, learn languages, they need to look outside of Chomsky's theory for guidance. This conclusion is important because the study of language plays a central role in diverse disciplines from poetry to artificial intelligence to linguistics itself; misguided methods lead to questionable results. Further, language is used by humans in ways no animal can match; if you understand what language is, you comprehend a little bit more about human nature.

Chomsky's first version of his theory, put forward in the mid-20th century, meshed with two emerging trends in Western intellectual life. First, he posited that the languages people use to communicate in everyday life behaved like mathematically based languages of the newly emerging field of computer science. His research looked for the underlying computational structure of language and proposed a set of procedures that would create "well-formed" sentences. The revolutionary idea was that a computer like program could produce sentences real people thought were grammatical. That program could also purportedly explain as well the way people generated their sentences. This way of talking about language resonated with many scholars eager to embrace a computational approach to everything.

As Chomsky was developing his computational theories, he was simultaneously proposing that they were rooted in human biology. In the second half of the 20th century, it was becoming ever clearer that our unique evolutionary history was responsible for many aspects of our unique human psychology, and so the theory resonated on that level as well. His universal grammar was put forward as an innate component of the human mind—and it promised to reveal the deep biological underpinnings of the world's 6,000-plus human languages. The most powerful, not to mention the most beautiful, theories in science reveal hidden unity underneath surface diversity, and so this theory held immediate appeal.

But evidence has overtaken Chomsky's theory, which has been inching toward a slow death for years. It is dying so slowly because, as physicist Max Planck once noted, older scholars tend to hang on to the old ways: "Science progresses one funeral at a time."

Q.1 According to the passage which of the following is true regarding Chomsky's theory for guidance?

A. The children use various types of thinking that may not be specific to language.

B. The learning of a child's first language does not rely on an innate grammar module.

C. The study of language plays a central role in diverse disciplines.

D. While learning misguided methods lead to questionable results.

Q.2 Why does the author use the term "Science progresses one funeral at a time."?

A. The term means science grows slowly.

B. The new invention is made only when we have an old invention.

C. With every one new innovation the old innovation is outdated.

D. No science is complete without a new invention.

Q.3 Which of the following shows why the old theories are deceasing?

A. Chomsky's first version of his theory, put forward in the mid-20th century, meshed with two emerging trends in Western intellectual life.

B. As Chomsky was developing his computational theories, he was simultaneously proposing that they were rooted in human biology.

C. The new theory of language plays a central role in diverse disciplines from poetry to artificial intelligence.

D. The new findings indicate that if researchers truly want to understand how children, and others, learn languages, they need to look outside of Chomsky's theory for guidance.

Ques (4-6):Direction: Read the given passage carefully and answer the question that follows.

Today, in order to deal successfully with economic vagaries and stiff competition, organisations must establish and maintain an environment that supports the open exchange and exploration of ideas, leading to fuller participation, greater innovation, and better decisions. But for this to happen, they must first stop viewing disagreement or conflict as negative. Conflicting ideas should not be snubbed or discouraged but allowed to undergo a thorough process of development. Some amount of positive or healthy conflict is essential to encourage lateral thinking and innovation. In the office setting, people come from different backgrounds and therefore bring different perspectives to the table.

It is important to recognise that when differences exist conflict is inevitable. The challenge however is to turn conflict into a constructive force. Disagreements often lead to an examination of different options. Better decisions emerge only when there is an attempt to break the status quo and explore new horizons. Though it is clearly evident that without conflict there can be no innovation, pitched battles aimed at outwitting opponents should be discouraged at all costs. A balanced stance that dissociates ego from the outcome of the conflict alone can help achieve success.

In order to turn conflict into a productive force the good side of the conflict must be highlighted. When people accept that conflicts are inevitable they understand that differences are natural and important. By focusing on improving relationships within each group and between various groups, organisations can promote meaningful dialogues that lead to successful resolution of conflicts.

This will obviously result in a win-win for all. While the employees walk away from conflict feeling happy and satisfied, the organisations gain the much-needed competitive edge in the bargain.

Q.4 It can be understood from the passage that organisations must:

(1) promote healthy conflicts that allow good ideas to grow.

(2) potray conflicts as hindrances to progress.

(3) dissuade employees from resorting to conflicts as they always have a negative impact.

(4) must ensure that conflicts do not give way to internecine rivalries.

A. Only (1) **B.** (1) and (2)

C. (1), (3) and (4) **D.** (1) and (4)

Q.5 According to the passage, constructive conflicts lead to all the following EXCEPT:

A. Out of the box thinking

B. Heated altercations

C. Good interpersonal relations

D. Better solutions

Q.6 Identify the statement that is NOT true according to the passage.

A. Conflicting ideas should not be brushed off by the organisations

B. A pragmatic approach to resolving conflicts will mutually benefit all the parties concerned

C. Disagreements in an office setting are quite normal as people come from different backgrounds

D. Organisations must encourage internal competitiveness and safeguard individual interests of the employees

Ques (7-10):Direction: Read the given passage carefully and answer the question that follows.

Around the World in Eighty Days is an adventure novel by the French writer Jules Verne, first published in French in 1872. Around the World in Eighty Days is a rip-roaring adventure story set, in the first place, in Victorian England, but which ranges throughout the world following its protagonist Phileus Fogg. Written with a cosmopolitan and open view of the world, and with a boy's own spirit of adventure, Around the World in Eighty Days is a brilliant exponent of its genre.

Vivid in its descriptions, and putting forwards Fogg, a cold, brittle man, who slowly shows that he does have a heart as the apogee of what it is to be an Englishman, Around the World in Eighty Days both wonderfully captures a spirit of adventure that was bubbling around the turn of the century, and a book impossible to put down.

The story begins in London where the reader is introduced to an incredibly precise and controlled man by the name of Fogg. Fogg lives happily, although a little mysteriously, for no-one knows the true origin of his wealth. He goes to his gentleman's club every day and it is there that he accepts a wager to travel around the world in eighty days

He packs his things and, along with his manservant, Passe-partout he sets out on his journey.

Early on in his voyage, a police inspector begins to trail him, because he believes Fogg is a bank robber. After getting a reasonably uneventful start, difficulties emerge in India when Fogg realities that a train line he was hoping to take has not be entirely finished. So, he takes an elephant instead.

This diversion is fortunate in one way, for Fogg meets and saves an Indian woman from a marriage to which she did not consent. On his journey Fogg will fall in love with Aouda and, on his return to England will make her his wife. In the interim, however, Fogg faces a number of challenges, including losing Passe-partout to a Yokohama circus and being attacked by Native Indians in the American Midwest who carry off the perennially unfortunate Passe-partout.

During this incident, Fogg shows his humanity by going off personally to save his manservant, despite the fact that this could well cost him his bet. Finally, Fogg manages to get back onto British soil (albeit by leading a mutiny aboard a French steamer) and seemingly in enough time to win his bet.

At this point, the police Inspector arrests him, delaying him just too long to make his bet. He returns home saddened by his failure, but brightened by the fact that Aouda has agreed to marry him. When Passe-partout is sent to arrange the wedding, he realizes that it is a day earlier than they think (by traveling East across the International date line they have gained a day), and so Fogg wins his bet.

Unlike many of his more science-based fiction, Jules Verne's Around the World in Eighty Days is interested in the capabilities of technology in his own time, and the things that human beings can achieve armed only with a sense of adventure and an exploratory spirit. It is also a brilliant dissection of what it is to be English in the time of empire.

Fogg is a brilliantly drawn character, a man who is stiff upper-lipped and precise in all his habits. However, as the novel goes on the very icy man begins to thaw. He begins to place the importance of friendship and love above his usual concerns of reserve and punctuality. In the end, he is willing to lose his bet in order to personally help a friend, and he doesn't care about defeat because he has won the hand of the woman he loves.

Q.7 Which of the following statements can be inferred from the passage?

A. A classic story, peopled with people who would be long remembered, it is a breath-taking roller-coaster ride around the world and a touching view of an older and better time.

B. A story that shows us that nothing is impossible to do in the world only if we have proper technology.

C. The movie is not an original concept it is copied from six sources.

D. The main actor in the movie is actually a very strong headed, and is callousness.

Q.8 According to the passage which of the following is true regarding the movie?

A. Around the World in Eighty Days is a classic adventure novel by the French writer Jules Verne, published in 1873

B. The movie is considered as an adventure movie with a motive

C. Around the World in Eighty Days was written during difficult times, both for France and for Verne

D. The title Around the World in Eighty Days is not original about six sources have been suggested as the origins of the story

Q.9 Which of the following shows why was the bet accepted?

A. To prove the gentlemen club that he can win the bet.

B. To prove that he is not a cold, brittle man.

C. Fogg had own spirit of adventure and wanted to complete his book.

D. To see the world in just 80 days and to share his experience to the world.

Q.10 Which of the following best describes a paradox mentioned in the passage?

A. Although it perhaps doesn't have the great literary merit of some of the other novels written around the same time, but Around the World in Eighty Days certainly makes up for it through its vivid descriptions and the vitality of its characters.

B. He goes to his gentleman's club every day and it is there that he accepts a wager to travel around the world in eighty days

C. After getting a reasonably uneventful start, difficulties emerge in India when Fogg realities that a train line he was hoping to take has not be entirely finished.

D. He returns home saddened by his failure, but brightened by the fact that Aouda has agreed to marry him.

Management Data Interpretation

Ques (11-15):Direction : Study the following table chart carefully and answer the questions given beside.

The following table represents Maximum marks of five subjects and marks obtained by five students in five subjects.

Students	Physics (Out of 75)	Mathematics (Out of 100)	Chemistry (Out of 75)	Biology (Out of 75)	English (Out of 120)
Ragini	56	65	45	38	95
Rohan	60	52	62	55	88
Sohan	50	78	70	58	88
Mohini	55	82	65	66	110
Mohan	42	96	64	72	104

Q.11 Marks obtained by Ragini in Chemistry and Biology together is what percent of the marks obtained by Mohini in Physics and Mathematics together?

A. 66.23% **B.** 60.58% **C.** 58.34% **D.** 54.32%

Q.12 Find the respective ratio of the marks obtained by all the students in Mathematics and marks obtained by all the students in Chemistry.

A. 293:351 **B.** 373:306
C. 351:293 **D.** 306:373

Q.13 Find the overall percentage of Sohan in all the subjects.

A. 62.7% **B.** 58.4% **C.** 77.3% **D.** 79.1%

Q.14 Find the difference between percentage of marks obtained by Mohan in English and that of Rohan in Physics.

A. 6.67% **B.** 4.59% **C.** 5.53% **D.** 3.12%

Q.15 Find the sum of marks obtained by Rohan in all the subjects.

A. 515 **B.** 427 **C.** 611 **D.** 317

Ques (16-20):Direction : Study the following bar graphs carefully and answer the question given below.

Below graph shows the City wise Population in thousands.

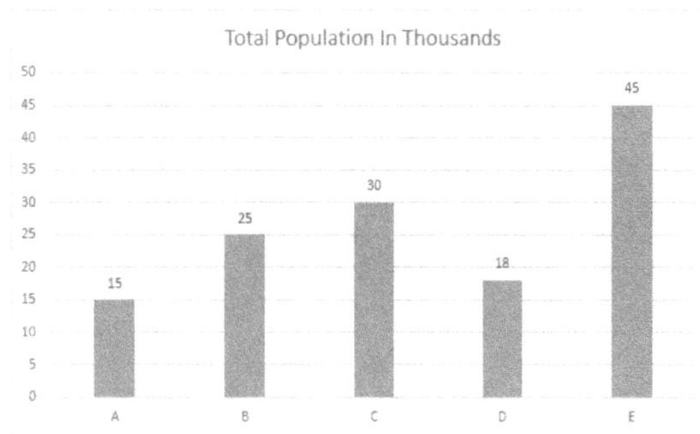

Below graph shows percentage of Male population out of total population of that particular City.

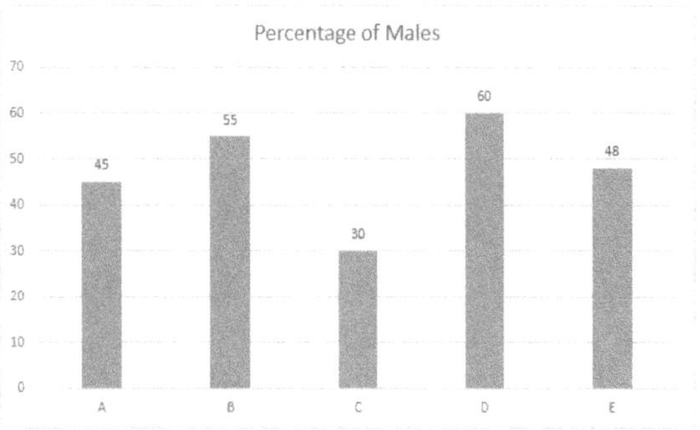

Q.16 What is the ratio of Number of Males of City C to that of City E ?

A. 5:12 **B.** 4:7 **C.** 1:5 **D.** 2:7

Q.17 What is the approximate average number of Males from City A, B and D ?

A. 10966 **B.** 10433 **C.** 11533 **D.** 12677

Q.18 Number of Females in City C is what percent more or less than number of males in City D ?

A. 55.55% **B.** 66.67% **C.** 47.44% **D.** 94.44%

Q.19 Population of City F is 25% more than population of City E. If the ratio of Males to Females in F is $7:8$, then Females of City F is what percent of Females of City A ?

A. 343.43% **B.** 437.63%
C. 369.69% **D.** 363.63%

Q.20 If 70% Male and 30% Female population in City B are literate, then what is the total number of illiterate persons in City B ?

A. 12000 **B.** 13000 **C.** 12750 **D.** 14250

Ques (21-25):Direction: Study the following pie chart carefully and answer the question given below.

Pie-chart given below shows investment (in terms of percentage) out of total investment of five different persons.

Total Investment = Rs. 160,000

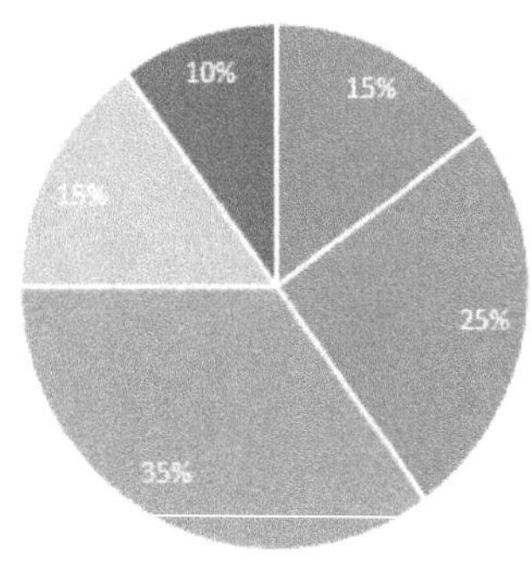

Q.21 Bhanu and Hemant started a business together. Bhanu left the business 9 months after starting of business but Hemant continued for the entire year. Find the difference between profit shares of Bhanu and Hemant if total profit at the end of the year is Rs. 15400 ?

A. Rs. 4200 **B.** Rs. 4500 **C.** Rs. 4800 **D.** Rs. 3600

Q.22 Abir and Dharam started a business together but after 6 months Abir is replaced by Hemant. Dharam left the business 2 months after Abir while Hemant worked for total ' x ' months. Out of total profit of Rs. 13050 , Abir got Rs. 6750, and then find the value of $'x'$?

A. 3 **B.** 6 **C.** 5 **D.** 4

Q.23 Abir, Sanjay and Chandru started a business together. Sanjay invested Rs. 4000 more than amount invested by Chandru. Sanjay left the business after 6 months of starting of business. After 2 months more, Chandru left the business. Out of the annual profit if Abir and Chandru together got Rs. 8736, then find total annual profit?

A. Rs. 12200 **B.** Rs. 13300
C. Rs. 11400 **D.** None of these

Q.24 Find the average of the investment of Abir, Bhanu, Dharam and Hemant together?

A. Rs. 40000 **B.** Rs. 34000
C. Rs. 24000 **D.** Rs. 45000

Q.25 The investment of Chandru is how much percent more/less than the investment of Dharam?

A. 50% more **B.** 33.33% more
C. 33.33% less **D.** 50% less

Business Awareness

Q.26 Which of the following BPO companies is wholly-owned subsidiary of Polaris Consulting and Services?

A. Spectramind **B.** Drogeon
C. WNS **D.** Optimus

Q.27 When the demand of a commodity also depends upon prices of the substitutes & complementaries or relative prices then it is called:

A. Income-Demand **B.** Price-demand
C. Cross-Demand **D.** None

Q.28 'Khazanah' is the state-owned investment holding arm of which country?

A. Malaysia **B.** Japan
C. Singapore **D.** Mauritius

Q.29 Which Indian was recently named as Chairman of the World Economic Forum's IT Governors community?

A. Abidali Neemuchwala
B. C. Vijayakumar
C. Rajesh Gopinathan
D. Rishad Premji

Q.30 Sun life of Canada is operating in India in alliance with:

A. Bermans **B.** Sahara Group
C. Thapars **D.** Aditya Birla Group

Q.31 Which automobile firm is set to acquire the automotive business of Ford India?

A. Mahindra & Mahindra
B. Tata Motors
C. Hyundai
D. Kia Motors

Q.32 Which global financial institution is set to grant $450 million loan to India for Atal Bhujal Yojana (ABHY)?

A. Asian Development Bank
B. World Bank
C. Asian Infrastructure Investment Bank
D. New Development Bank

Q.33 Which of the following Stock exchanges is called "Big Board"?

A. Nasdaq
B. London Stock Exchange
C. Mumbai Stock Exchange
D. New York Stock Exchange

Q.34 HRP stands for:

A. Human Resource Project
B. Human Resource Planning
C. Human Recruitment Planning
D. Human Recruitment Procedure

Q.35 How can high potential employees be developed for future positions?

A. Internal training
B. Increasing pal skill
C. Managing employee
D. Allowing them to do further studies

// Smart Answer Sheet //

Correct Indicates percentage of students who answered questions correctly.

Skipped Indicates percentage of students who skipped questions.

Q.	Ans.	Correct	Skipped
1	B	48.16 %	46.64 %
2	C	84.1 %	11.4 %
3	D	57.82 %	36.88 %
4	D	23.03 %	67.07 %
5	B	56.37 %	36.26 %
6	D	22.19 %	75.25 %
7	A	87.68 %	10.14 %
8	B	79.79 %	18.56 %
9	C	40.64 %	36.79 %
10	D	76.32 %	17.3 %
11	B	81.81 %	17.53 %
12	B	58.97 %	33.74 %
13	C	82.65 %	16.63 %
14	A	56.49 %	39.12 %
15	D	76.24 %	23.7 %
16	A	40.29 %	43.4 %
17	B	59.01 %	39.14 %
18	D	27.58 %	72.0 %
19	D	17.44 %	73.38 %
20	A	29.05 %	67.44 %
21	A	29.33 %	69.79 %
22	D	26.85 %	72.91 %
23	D	58.54 %	34.1 %
24	B	52.62 %	41.24 %
25	A	59.77 %	36.26 %
26	D	64.66 %	30.87 %
27	C	84.09 %	14.55 %
28	A	16.43 %	67.5 %
29	B	20.72 %	75.26 %
30	D	59.31 %	38.17 %
31	A	63.93 %	32.48 %
32	B	59.31 %	36.18 %
33	D	78.94 %	12.72 %
34	B	76.74 %	14.43 %
35	A	61.5 %	33.78 %

Performance Analysis	
Avg. Score (%)	45.71%
Toppers Score (%)	71.43%
Your Score	

//Hints and Solutions//

1. Option (B) is correct because the first line of the passage indicates this as mentioned in 'in which learning of a child's first language does not rely on an innate grammar module'.

Option (A) is incorrect because this is true as per the new research and not according to the Chomsky's theory for guidance as mentioned in 'Instead the new research shows that young children use various types of thinking that may not be specific to language at all such as the ability to classify the world into categories (people or objects, for instance) and to understand the relations among things'.

Option (C) is incorrect because this is true as per the new research and not according to the Chomsky's theory for guidance as mentioned in 'This conclusion is important because the study of language plays a central role in diverse disciplines from poetry to artificial intelligence to linguistics itself; misguided methods lead to questionable results'.

Option (D) is incorrect because his is true as per the new research and not according to the Chomsky's theory for guidance as mentioned in 'This conclusion is important because the study of language plays a central role in diverse disciplines from poetry to artificial intelligence to linguistics itself; misguided methods lead to questionable results'.

Hence, the correct option is (B).

2. Option (C) is correct because "evidence has overtaken Chomsky's theory, which has been inching toward a slow death for years. It is dying so slowly because, as physicist Max Planck once noted, older scholars tend to hang on to the old ways" these lines give a better idea that the above answer is correct.

Option (A) is incorrect because it is not the appropriate meaning for the term.

Option (B) is incorrect because it is not the appropriate meaning for the term.

Option (D) is incorrect because it is not the appropriate meaning for the term.

Hence, the correct option is (C).

3. Option (D) is correct because it clearly mentions that due to the new theories the old theories lose their importance.

Option (A) is incorrect because it does not shows that the old theories are deceasing.

Option (B) is incorrect because it does not shows that the old theories are deceasing.

Option (C) is incorrect because it is related to new theories.

Hence, the correct option is (D).

4. Only (1) and (4) reflect what is said in the passage.

(1) can be inferred from the passage, it is understood that organisations must portray conflicts as normal and stop viewing them as negative since healthy conflicts lead to creation of new ideas as mentioned in 'Though it is clearly evident that without conflict there can be no innovation'.

(4) can be inferred from the line 'By focusing on improving relationships within each group and between various groups, organisations can promote meaningful dialogues that lead to successful resolution of conflicts'.

Hence, the correct option is (C).

5. 'Altercations' means disagreement. 'Heated altercations' are unproductive and healthy conflicts don't lead to those. So, (B) is the exception.

'Today, in order to deal successfully with economic vagaries and stiff competition, organisations must establish and maintain an environment that supports the open exchange and exploration of ideas, leading to fuller participation, greater innovation, and better decisions' renders (D) is true.

Sentence 3 of the first paragraph 'positive conflict essential to encourage lateral thinking' suggest (A) is true.

'On improving relationships within each group and between various groups, organisations can promote meaningful dialogues that lead to successful resolution of conflicts' suggests (C) is true.

Hence, the correct option is (B).

6. Choice (D) is not true because the passage says that 'internal competitiveness' does not help in turning conflict to a constructive force and safeguarding individual interests hampers team spirit.

The sentence 'Conflicting ideas should not be snubbed or discouraged but allowed to undergo a thorough process of development' suggests choice (A) is true.

The sentence 'This will obviously result in a win-win for all' corroborates (B).

The sentence 'In the office setting, people come from different backgrounds and therefore bring different perspectives to the table' suggests that choice (C) is true.

Hence, the correct option is (D).

7. Option (A) is correct because the author in the above passage mentioned and it can also be understood the way a man goes around the entire world in just 80 days by facing all the difficulties still wins the bet this was possible only because of his will power and optimistic attitude.

Option (B) is incorrect because the use of technology is wrongly written.

Option (C) is incorrect because this cannot be inferred from the above passage.

Option (D) is incorrect because this cannot be inferred from the above passage as he is shown to have humanity as mentioned in 'Fogg shows his humanity by going off personally to save his manservant'.

Hence, the correct option is (A).

8. Option (B) is correct because the passage starts with these lines.

Option (A) is incorrect because no information is provided in the passage.

Option (C) is incorrect because no information is provided in the passage.

Option (D) is incorrect because it is invalid answer.

Hence, the correct option is (B).

9. Option (C) is correct because the same line is mentioned above in the passage as "a spirit of adventure that was bubbling around the turn of the century, and a book impossible to put down".

Option (A) is incorrect because it is not mentioned above.

Option (B) is incorrect because it is invalid answer.

Option (D) is incorrect because it is invalid answer as it is not mentioned above.

Hence, the correct option is (C).

10. Option (D) is correct because paradox can be seen in the sentence.

Option (A) is incorrect because though a paradox can be seen in the sentence but it is not from the passage above.

Option (B) is incorrect because no paradox can be seen in the sentence.

Option (C) is incorrect because no paradox can be seen in the sentence.

Hence, the correct option is (D).

11. Marks obtained by Ragini in Chemistry and Biology together $= 45 + 38$
$= 83$
Marks obtained by Mohini in Physics and Mathematics together
$= 55 + 82$
$= 137$
Required $\% = \frac{83}{137} \times 100$
$= 60.58\%$

Hence, the correct option is (B).

12. Marks obtained by all the students in Mathematics $= 65 + 52 + 78 + 82 + 96$
$= 373$
Marks obtained by all the students in Chemistry $= 45 + 62 + 70 + 65 + 64$
$= 306$
Required ratio $= 373:306$

Hence, the correct option is (B).

13. Total marks in all the subjects $= 75 + 100 + 75 + 75 + 120$
$= 445$
Marks obtained by Sohan in all the subjects $= 50 + 78 + 70 + 58 + 88$
$= 344$

Required $\% = \frac{344}{445} \times 100$
$= 77.3\%$

Hence, the correct option is (C).

14. Percentage of marks obtained by Mohan in English
$= \frac{104}{120} \times 100$
$= 86.67\%$
Percentage of marks obtained by Rohan in Physics $= \frac{60}{75} \times 100$
$= 80\%$
Required difference $= (86.67 - 80)\%$
$= 6.67\%$

Hence, the correct option is (A).

15. Sum of marks obtained by Rohan in all the subjects $= 60 + 52 + 62 + 55 + 88 = 317$

Hence, the correct option is (D).

16. Population of City $C = 30000$

Percentage of Males in City $C = 30\%$

Number of Males in City $C = 30000 \times \frac{30}{100}$
$= 9000$

Population of City $E = 45000$

Percentage of Males in City $E = 48\%$

Number of Males in City $E = 45000 \times \frac{48}{100}$
$= 21600$

Required Ratio $= \frac{9000}{21600}$
$= 5:12$

Hence, the correct option is (A).

17. Population of City $A = 15000$

Percentage of Males in City $A = 45\%$

Number of Males in City $A = 15000 \times \frac{45}{100}$
$= 6750$

Population of City $B = 25000$

Percentage of Males in City $B = 55\%$

Number of Males in City $B = 25000 \times \frac{55}{100}$
$= 13750$

Population of City $D = 18000$

Percentage of Males in City $D = 60\%$

Number of Males in City $D = 18{,}000 \times \frac{60}{100}$

$= 10800$

Average $= \frac{6750+13750+10800}{3}$

$= 10433.33$

$= 1043$ (approx.)

Hence, the correct option is (B).

18. Population of City $C = 30000$

Percentage of Males in City $C = 30\%$

So, Percentage of females in City $C = 70\%$

Number of Females in city $C = 30000 \times \frac{70}{100}$

$= 21000$

Population of City $D = 18000$

Percentage of Males in City $D = 60\%$

Number of males in City $D = 18000 \times \frac{60}{100}$

$= 10800$

Difference $= 21000 - 10800$

$= 10200$

Required $\% = \frac{10200}{10800} \times 100$

$= 94.44\%$

Hence, the correct option is (D).

19. Population of City $E = 45000$

Given that the Population of City F is 25% more than that of City E.

So, Population of City $F = 45{,}000 \times \frac{125}{100}$

$= 56{,}250$

Also given that,

Ratio of Male to Females in F is $7:8$

Females in City $F = 56250 \times \frac{8}{15}$

$= 30000$

Population of City $A = 15000$

Percentage of Males in City $A = 45\%$

Percentage of Females in City $A = 55\%$

Females of City $A = 15000 \times \frac{55}{100}$

$= 8250$

Required $\% = \frac{30000}{8250} \times 100$

$= 363.63\%$

Hence, the correct option is (D).

20. Population of City $B = 25000$

Percentage of Males in City $B = 55\%$

Male Population of City $B = 25000 \times \frac{55}{100}$

$= 13750$

Literate Males $= 70\%$

Number of Literate Males $= 13750 \times \frac{70}{100}$

$= 9625$

Percentage of Females in City $B = 45\%$

Female Population of City $B = 25000 \times \frac{45}{100}$

$= 11250$

Literate Females $= 30\%$

Number of Literate Females $= 11250 \times \frac{30}{100}$

$= 3375$

Total Literate Persons $= 9625 + 3375$

$= 13000$

Total Illiterate Persons $= 25000 - 13000$

$= 12000$

Hence, the correct option is (A).

21. Investment of Bhanu $= 35\%$ of 160000

$=$ Rs. 56000

Investment of Hemant $= 15\%$ of 160000

$=$ Rs. 24000

Ratio of their investment $= 56000:24000$

$= 7:3$

Ratio of their time $= 9:12$

$= 3:4$

Ratio of their profit share $= \frac{7\times3}{3\times4}$

$= 7:4$

Sun of ratios i.e. 11 corresponds to 15400

1 corresponds to $= \frac{15400}{11}$

$= 1400$

Difference between their profit share = ratio difference

$= 7 - 4$

$= 3$

So, 3 will correspond to $= 1400 \times 3$

$=$ Rs. 4200

Hence, the correct option is (A).

22. Investment of Abir $= 25\%$ of 160000

$= \text{Rs. } 40000$

Investment of Hemant $= 15\%$ of 160000

$= \text{Rs. } 24000$

Investment of Dharam $= 10\%$ of 160000

$= \text{Rs. } 16000$

Ratio of their investments $= 40000:24000:16000$

$= 5:3:2$

Ratio of their time period $= 6:x:8$

Ratio of the profit share $= 5(6):3(x):2(8)$

$= 30:3x:16$

Abir's profit share $= \text{Rs. } 6750$

So,

$\Rightarrow \frac{30}{30+3x+16} = \frac{6750}{13050}$

$\Rightarrow \frac{30}{46+3x} = \frac{6750}{13050}$

On solving this we get,

$x = 4$

Hence, the correct option is (D).

23. Total investment $= 160000$

Investment of Abir $= 25\%$ of 160000

$= \text{Rs. } 40000$

Investment of Sanjay $= \text{Rs. } [(15\% \text{ of } 160000 + 4000]$

$= \text{Rs. } 28000$

Investment of Chandru= 15% of 160000

$= \text{Rs. } 24000$

Ratio of their investment $= 40000:28000:24000$

$= 10:7:6$

Ratio of their time period $= 12:6:8 = 6:3:4$

Ratio of their profit share $= 10 \times 6:7 \times 3:6 \times 4$

$= 60:21:24$

$\Rightarrow 20:7:8$

Profit share of Abir and Chandru $= \text{Rs. } 8736$

$= 20 + 8$

$= 28$

28 corresponds to 8736

1 will correspond to $= \frac{8736}{28}$

Total Profit share $= 20 + 7 + 8$

$= 35$

35 will correspond to $= \frac{8736 \times 35}{28}$

$= \text{Rs. } 10920$

Hence, the correct option is (D).

24. Investment of Abir $= 25\%$ of 160000

Investment of Bhanu $= 35\%$ of 160000

Investment of Dharam $= 10\%$ of 160000

Investment of Hemant $= 15\%$ of 160000

Average of their investment

$= \{25 + 35 + 10 + 15\} \times \frac{160000}{4 \times 100}$

$\Rightarrow 85 \times \frac{160000}{400}$

$= \text{Rs. } 34000$

Hence, the correct option is (B).

25. The investment of Chandru $= 15\%$ of 160000

$= \text{Rs. } 24000$

The investment of Dharam $= 10\%$ of 160000

$= \text{Rs. } 16000$

Difference $= 24000 - 16000$

$= 8000$

Required $\% = \frac{8000}{16000} \times 100$

$= 50\%$ more

26. Optimus is wholly-owned subsidiary of Polaris Consulting and Services.

Polaris Consulting & Services (Polaris) is one of the leading Digital Transformation companies in the world with particular emphasis on the Financial Services industry.

Hence, the correct option is (D).

27. When the demand of a commodity also depends upon prices of the substitutes & complementaries or relative prices then it is called Cross-Demand.

Cross-Demand refers to change in the quantity demanded of a good when the price of a related good changes.

Hence, the correct option is (C).

28. 'Khazanah' is the state-owned investment holding arm of Malaysia.

Khazanah Nasional Berhad is the sovereign wealth fund of the Government of Malaysia, entrusted with growing the nation's long-term wealth via distinct commercial and strategic objectives.

Hence, the correct option is (A).

29. The Head of the IT Industry at the World Economic Forum, Eric White announced that C. Vijayakumar, the President & CEO of HCL Technologies, would be the chairman of the World Economic Forum's IT Governors community.

The announcement was made during the 50th annual meeting of WEF in Davos. The IT Governors community of WEF convenes CEOs of the world's top Information Technology firms for tackling the issues in the field and solving them together. The community, under Vijayakumar will focus on the industry's concerns including Talent re-skilling, Data governance and Security.

Hence, the correct option is (B).

30. Sun life of Canada is operating in India in alliance with Aditya Birla Group.

Birla Sun Life Asset Management now known as the Aditya Birla Sun Life Mutual Fund (ABSLAMC), is an investment managing company registered under the Securities and Exchange Board of India. It is a joint venture between Sun Life and the Aditya Birla Group of India.

Established in 1994, BSLAMC has been a joint venture between the Aditya Birla Group and Sun Life since 1999.

With more than $34 billion U.S. in assets under management as of 2017, Aditya Birla Sun Life Asset Management Company is one of the largest asset managers in India.

Hence, the correct option is (D).

31. The Competition Commission of India (CCI) has recently approved the formation of Joint Venture (JV) between Mahindra & Mahindra and Ford Motor and the transfer of automotive business of Ford India to the JV.
The new venture to be formed would acquire the automotive business of Ford India Pvt Ltd (FIPL), which is a wholly-owned subsidiary of Ford Motor company. The automotive business includes manufacturing plants of Ford India in Chennai and Sanand (Gujarat).

Hence, the correct option is (A).

32. The Indian government and the World Bank recently signed a USD 450 million loan agreement to support the national programme Atal Bhujal Yojana (ABHY).
The National programme was launched with an objective of arresting the groundwater depletion and strengthening groundwater institutions. The World Bank-supported programme will be implemented in the states of Gujarat, Maharashtra, Haryana, Karnataka, Rajasthan, Madhya Pradesh, and Uttar Pradesh and cover 78 districts.

Hence, the correct option is (B).

33. Big Board is a nickname for the New York Stock Exchange (NYSE), located at 11 Wall Street, New York City, New York. The New York Stock Exchange, or Big Board, is the oldest stock exchange in the United States.

Hence, the correct option is (D).

34. HRP stands for Human Resource Planning.

Human Resource Planning (HRP) is the continuous process of systematic planning ahead to achieve optimum use of an organization's most valuable asset quality employees.

Hence, the correct option is (B).

35. High potential employees can be developed for future positions by internal training.

Successful internal training identifies the exact skills and knowledge that participants need to succeed in their jobs. It also prepares employees for success in their next job. Internal training is presented in the language and terminology that participants understand and can relate to.

Hence, the correct option is (A).

Mock Test 06

Comprehension

Ques (1-5):Direction: Read the following passage carefully and answer the question given below it.

In the 16th century, an age of great marine and terrestrial exploration, Ferdinand Magellan led the first expedition to sail around the world. As a young Portuguese noble, he served the king of Portugal, but he became involved in the quagmire of political intrigue at court and lost the king's favour. After he was dismissed from service by the king of Portugal, he offered to serve the future Emperor Charles V of Spain.

A papal decree of 1493 had assigned all land in the New World west of 50 degrees W longitude to Spain and all the land east of that line to Portugal. Magellan offered to prove that the East Indies fell under Spanish authority. On September 20, 1519, Magellan set sail from Spain with five ships. More than a year later, one of these ships was exploring the topography of South America in search of a water route across the continent. This ship sank, but the remaining four ships searched along the southern peninsula of South America. Finally, they found the passage they sought near 50 degrees S latitude. Magellan named this passage the Strait of All Saints, but today it is known as the Strait of Magellan.

One ship deserted while in this passage and returned to Spain, so fewer sailors were privileged to gaze at that first panorama of the Pacific Ocean. Those who remained crossed the meridian now known as the International Date Line in the early spring of 1521 after 98 days on the Pacific Ocean. During those long days at sea, many of Magellan's men died of starvation and disease.

Later, Magellan became involved in an insular conflict in the Philippines and was killed in a tribal battle. Only one ship and 17 sailors under the command of the Basque navigator Elcano survived to complete the westward journey to Spain and thus prove once and for all that the world is round, with no precipice at the edge.

Q.1 The 16th century was an age of great _____ exploration.

A. cosmic **B.** land
C. mental **D.** common man

Q.2 Magellan lost the favour of the king of Portugal when he became involved in a political _______.

A. entanglement **B.** discussion
C. negotiation **D.** problem

Q.3 The Pope divided New World lands between Spain and Portugal according to their location on one side or the other of an imaginary geographical line 50 degrees west of Greenwich that extends in a ________ direction.

A. north and south **B.** crosswise
C. easterly **D.** south east

Q.4 One of Magellan's ships explored the ________ of South America for a passage across the continent.

A. coastline **B.** mountain range
C. physical features **D.** islands

Q.5 Four of the ships sought a passage along a southern _____.

A. coast
B. inland
C. body of land with water on three sides
D. border

Ques (6-10):Direction: Read the following passage carefully and answer the question given below it.

Marie Curie was one of the most accomplished scientists in history. Together with her husband, Pierre, she discovered radium, an element widely used for treating cancer and studied uranium and other radioactive substances. Pierre and Marie's amicable collaboration later helped to unlock the secrets of the atom.

Marie was born in 1867 in Warsaw, Poland, where her father was a professor of physics. At an early age, she displayed a brilliant mind and a blithe personality. Her great exuberance for learning prompted her to continue with her studies after high school. She became disgruntled, however, when she learned that the university in Warsaw was closed to women. Determined to receive a higher education, she defiantly left Poland and in 1891 entered the Sorbonne, a French university, where she earned her master's degree and a doctorate in physics.

Marie was fortunate to have studied at the Sorbonne with some of the greatest scientists of her day, one of whom was Pierre Curie. Marie and Pierre were married in 1895 and spent many productive years working together in the physics laboratory. A short time after they discovered radium, Pierre was killed by a horse-drawn wagon in 1906. Marie was stunned by this horrible misfortune and endured heartbreaking anguish. Despondently she recalled their close relationship and the joy that they had shared in scientific research. The fact that she had two young daughters to raise by herself greatly increased her distress.

Curie's feeling of desolation finally began to fade when she was asked to succeed her husband as a physics professor at the Sorbonne. She was the first woman to be given a professorship at the world-famous university. In 1911 she received the Nobel Prize in chemistry for isolating radium. Although Marie Curie eventually suffered a fatal illness from her long exposure to radium, she never became disillusioned about her work. Regardless of the consequences, she had dedicated herself to science and to revealing the mysteries of the physical world.

Q.6 The Curies' ________ collaboration helped to unlock the secrets of the atom.

A. friendly **B.** competitive

C. courteous **D.** industrious

Q.7 Marie had a bright mind and a _____ personality.
A. strong **B.** lighthearted
C. humorous **D.** strange

Q.8 When she learned that she could not attend the university in Warsaw, she felt ________.
A. hopeless **B.** annoyed
C. depressed **D.** worried

Q.9 Marie ________ by leaving Poland and travelling to France to enter the Sorbonne.
A. challenged authority
B. showed intelligence
C. behaved
D. was distressed

Q.10 ________ she remembered their joy together.
A. Dejectedly **B.** Worried
C. Tearfully **D.** Happily

Management Data Interpretation

Ques (11-15):Direction: Study the following graph carefully and answer the questions given below:

Distribution of candidates who were enrolled for MBA entrance exam and the candidates (out of those enrolled) who passed the exam in different institutes:

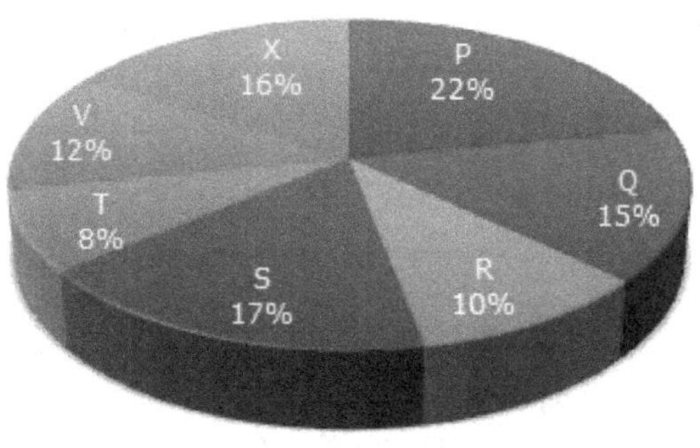

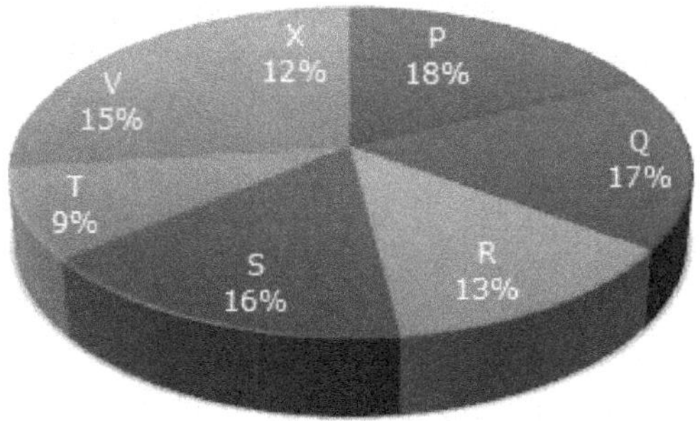

Q.11 What percentage of candidates passed the Exam from institute T out of the total number of candidates enrolled from the same institute?
A. 50% **B.** 62.5% **C.** 75% **D.** 80%

Q.12 Which institute has the highest percentage of candidates passed to the candidates enrolled?
A. Q **B.** R **C.** V **D.** T

Q.13 The number of candidates passed from institutes S and P together exceeds the number of candidates enrolled from institutes T and R together by-
A. 228 **B.** 279 **C.** 399 **D.** 407

Q.14 What is the percentage of candidates passed to the candidates enrolled for institutes Q and R together?
A. 68% **B.** 80% **C.** 74% **D.** 65%

Q.15 What is the ratio of candidates passed to the candidates enrolled from institute P?
A. 9:11 **B.** 14:17 **C.** 6:11 **D.** 9:17

Ques (16-20):Direction: Study the following graph carefully and answer the questions given below:

Two different finance companies declare a fixed annual rate of interest on the amounts invested with them by investors. The rate of interest offered by these companies may differ from year to year depending on the variation in the economy of the country and the banks rate of interest. The annual rate of interest offered by the two Companies P and Q over the years is shown by the line graph provided below.

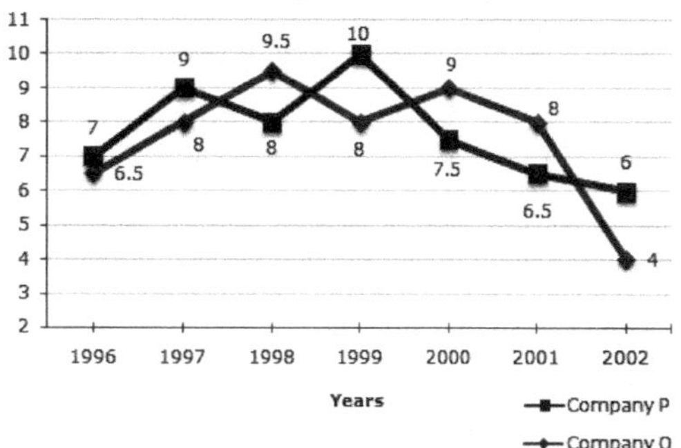

Q.16 A sum of Rs. 4.75 lakhs was invested in Company Q in 1999 for one year. How much more interest would have been earned if the sum was invested in Company P?
A. Rs. 19000 **B.** Rs. 14250
C. Rs. 11750 **D.** Rs. 9500

Q.17 If two different amounts in the ratio $8:9$ are invested in Companies P and Q respectively in 2002, then the amounts received after one year as interests from Companies P and Q are respectively in the ratio?
A. 2:3 **B.** 3:4 **C.** 6:7 **D.** 4:3

Q.18 In 2000, a part of Rs. 30 lakhs was invested in Company P and the rest was invested in Company Q for one year. The total interest received was Rs. 2.43 lakhs. What was the amount invested in Company P?

A. Rs. 9 lakhs **B.** Rs. 11 lakhs
C. Rs. 12 lakhs **D.** Rs. 18 lakhs

Q.19 An investor invested a sum of Rs. 12 lakhs in Company P in 1998. The total amount received after one year was re-invested in the same Company for one more year. The total appreciation received by the investor on his investment was?

A. Rs. 296200 **B.** Rs. 242200
C. Rs. 225600 **D.** Rs. 216000

Q.20 An investor invested Rs. 5 lakhs in Company Q in 1996. After one year, the entire amount along with the interest was transferred as an investment to Company P in 1997 for one year. What amount will be received from Company P, by the investor?

A. Rs. 594550 **B.** Rs. 580425
C. Rs. 577800 **D.** Rs. 577500

Ques (21-25): The following table gives the sales of batteries manufactured by a company over the years.

Year	Types of batteries					Total
	$4AH$	$7AH$	$32AH$	$35AH$	$55AH$	
1992	75	144	114	102	108	543
1993	90	126	102	84	126	528
1994	96	114	75	105	135	525
1995	105	90	150	90	75	510
1996	90	75	135	75	90	465
1997	105	60	165	45	120	495
1998	115	85	160	100	145	605

Q.21 What was the approximate percentage increase in the sales of $55AH$ batteries in 1998 compared to that in 1992?

A. 28% **B.** 31% **C.** 33% **D.** 34%

Q.22 The total sales of all the seven years are the maximum for which battery?

A. $4AH$ **B.** $7AH$ **C.** $32AH$ **D.** $35AH$

Q.23 What is the difference in the number of $35AH$ batteries sold in 1993 and 1997?

A. 24000 **B.** 28000 **C.** 35000 **D.** 39000

Q.24 The percentage of $4AH$ batteries sold to the total number of batteries sold was maximum in the year?

A. 1994 **B.** 1995 **C.** 1996 **D.** 1997

Q.25 In case of which battery there was a continuous decrease in sales from 1992 to 1997?

A. $4AH$ **B.** $7AH$ **C.** $32AH$ **D.** $35AH$

Business Awareness

Q.26

1. A recent survey (by Bloomberg) shows that the USA has fallen behind emerging markets in Brazil, China and India as the preferred place to invest. Why is it so?
2. The unstable economic situation of the USA which the global investors feel is not likely to improve in the near future.
3. Global investors are finding Brazil, China and India more amenable to foreign investment.

Select the correct answer using the code given below

A. Only 1 **B.** only 2
C. Both 1 and 2 **D.** Neither 1 nor 2

Q.27 India's market regulator SEBI is on course to relax investment norms for sovereign wealth funds, the investment vehicles which are directly controlled by the government of a country. The main reason behind this move is

A. The desire of the Government of India to attract more foreign investment.
B. Pressure by foreign Governments on India to execute specific mutual agreements on financial services.
C. SEBI's desire to create a more level playing field for foreign investors.
D. RBI's relevant directives to SEBI.

Q.28 Which of the following statements are correct?

1. The global economy relied on oil for much of the 20th century as a portable and indispensable fuel.
2. The immense wealth associated with oil generates political struggles to control it.
3. The history of petroleum is also the history of war and struggle.
4. Nowhere is this more obviously the case of war and struggle than in West Asia and Central America.

Select the correct answer using the codes given below

A. 1, 2, 3 and 4 **B.** 2 and 4
C. 1 and 3 **D.** 1, 2 and 3

Q.29 Consider the following statements about the Sinking Fund

1. It is a method of repayment of public debt.
2. It is created by the government out of budgetary revenues every year.

Winch of the statements given above is/are contacted?

A. Only 1 **B.** Only 2

C. Both 1 and 2 **D.** Neither 1 nor 2

Q.30 Match the following

List I (Five Year Plan)	List II (Emphasis)
A. First	1. Food security and women empowerment
B. Second	2. Heavy industries
C. Fifth	3. Agriculture and community development
D. Ninth	4. Removal of poverty

A. 1,2,4,3 **B.** 1,4,2,3 **C.** 3,2,4,1 **D.** 3,4,2,1

Q.31 Which of the following demographic issues represents a challenge for human resource managers?

A. Increasingly diverse workforce
B. Aging workforce
C. Increasing use of contingent workers
D. All of the above

Q.32 The ________ programme once installed must be continued on a permanent basis.

A. job evaluation
B. training & Development
C. recruitment
D. all of the above

Q.33 The first of May in 1927 was for the first time celebrated as 'Labour Day' at

A. Calcutta **B.** Bombay
C. Madras **D.** Ahmedabad

Q.34 A worker who has been employed in an office for more than a year but dismissed by his employer without any appropriate reason. This matter must be addressed under the ____

A. Industrial Disputes Act, 1947
B. Minimum Wages Act, 1948
C. The Payment of Wages Act, 1936
D. None of the Above

Q.35 The Ahmedabad Textile Labour Association is an example of

A. Craft Union **B.** Staff Union
C. Industrial Union **D.** General Union

// Smart Answer Sheet //

Correct — Indicates percentage of students who answered questions correctly.

Skipped — Indicates percentage of students who skipped questions.

Q.	Ans.	Correct	Skipped
1	B	59.54 %	30.14 %
2	A	79.08 %	18.92 %
3	A	85.11 %	11.45 %
4	C	17.49 %	77.52 %
5	C	59.3 %	34.4 %
6	A	57.17 %	42.55 %
7	B	40.72 %	32.17 %
8	B	62.38 %	32.1 %
9	A	78.05 %	18.7 %
10	A	56.87 %	33.36 %
11	C	65.68 %	33.99 %
12	B	83.13 %	15.69 %
13	C	55.83 %	39.31 %
14	B	79.93 %	10.91 %
15	C	19.01 %	69.17 %
16	D	42.63 %	37.7 %
17	D	68.87 %	30.46 %
18	D	80.21 %	15.38 %
19	C	49.51 %	40.36 %
20	B	82.31 %	10.18 %
21	D	89.27 %	10.59 %
22	C	23.11 %	76.77 %
23	D	53.94 %	34.42 %
24	D	45.29 %	46.54 %
25	B	27.14 %	69.24 %
26	C	18.65 %	71.0 %
27	A	45.33 %	51.05 %
28	A	47.81 %	38.23 %
29	A	83.39 %	13.09 %
30	C	45.22 %	54.2 %
31	D	62.08 %	37.41 %
32	A	88.15 %	11.8 %
33	B	81.32 %	17.67 %
34	A	61.81 %	33.57 %
35	C	44.98 %	49.97 %

Performance Analysis	
Avg. Score (%)	60.0%
Toppers Score (%)	65.71%
Your Score	

//Hints and Solutions//

1. The 16th century was an age of great **terrestrial** exploration.

"Terrestrial" means land. No choice here offers a synonym for "marine," e.g. nautical/naval/water/seagoing, and no other choices match either marine or terrestrial.

Hence, the correct option is (B).

2. Magellan lost the favour of the king of Portugal when he became involved in a political **quagmire**.

"Quagmire" means literally a bog or marsh, and figuratively an involved situation difficult to escape; entanglement is a synonym, more specifically similar than the other choices.

Hence, the correct option is (A).

3. The Pope divided New World lands between Spain and Portugal according to their location on one side or the other of an imaginary geographical line 50 degrees west of Greenwich that extends in a **longitudes** direction.

Longitudes are imaginary geographical lines running north and south. Latitudes run east and west. The other choices do not equal either latitude or longitude in direction.

Hence, the correct option is (A).

4. One of Magellan's ships explored the **topography** of South America for a passage across the continent.

Topography means the physical features of a landmass. It does not mean coastline (A), mountain range (B), or islands (D).

Hence, the correct option is (C).

5. Four of the ships sought a passage along a southern **peninsula**.

A peninsula is a piece of land connected to the mainland by an isthmus and projecting into the ocean such that it is surrounded on three sides by water. A peninsula is not a coast (A), it is not found inland (B), and it is not a border (D).

Hence, the correct option is (C).

6. The Curies' **amicable** collaboration helped to unlock the secrets of the atom.

"Amicable" means friendly. It does not mean competitive (B), i.e. oppositional, ambitious, or aggressive; courteous (C), i.e. polite; industrious (D), their collaboration was in physics, but moreover, the passage specifically describes their collaboration as "amicable."

Hence, the correct option is (A).

7. Marie had a bright mind and a **blithe** personality.

"Blithe" means light-hearted. It does not mean strong (A), humorous (B), or funny; strange (D).

Hence, the correct option is (B).

8. When she learned that she could not attend the university in Warsaw, she felt **disgruntled**.

"Disgruntled" means annoyed. It does not mean hopeless (A), depressed (C), or worried (D).

Hence, the correct option is (B).

9. Marie challenged authority by going to study at the Sorbonne because Warsaw's university did not admit women. The passage indicates this challenge by describing her "defiantly" leaving Poland for France; i.e., she was defying authority. The passage does not indicate she "showed intelligence" (B), "behaved" (C), or was "distressed" (D) or upset by her move.

Hence, the correct option is (A).

10. Despondently she remembered their joy together.

A synonym for "despondently" is "dejectedly," meaning sadly, with despair or depression. The passage indicates this by describing Curie's emotional state as one of "heartbreaking anguish" over her husband's sudden accidental death. She is not described in this passage as worried (B) by her memories or recalling them tearfully (C), happily (D).

Hence, the correct option is (A).

11. Required percentage $= \left(\frac{9\% \text{ of } 5700}{8\% \text{ of } 8550} \times 100\right)\% = \left(\frac{9 \times 5700}{8 \times 8550} \times 100\right)\% = 75\%$

Out of the total number of enrolled candidates 75% of candidates passed the exam from institute T.

Hence, the correct option is (C).

12. The percentage of candidates passed to candidates enrolled can be determined for each institute as under:

(i) $P = \left[\left(\frac{18\% \text{ of } 5700}{22\% \text{ of } 8550}\right) \times 100\right]\% = \left[\frac{18 \times 5700}{22 \times 8550} \times 100\right]\% = 54.55\%$

(ii) $Q = \left[\left(\frac{17\% \text{ of } 5700}{15\% \text{ of } 8550}\right) \times 100\right]\% = 75.56\%$

(iii) $R = \left[\left(\frac{13\% \text{ of } 5700}{10\% \text{ of } 8550}\right) \times 100\right]\% = 86.67\%$

(iv) $S = \left[\left(\frac{16\% \text{ of } 5700}{17\% \text{ of } 8550}\right) \times 100\right]\% = 62.75\%$

(v) $T = \left[\left(\frac{9\% \text{ of } 5700}{8\% \text{ of } 8550}\right) \times 100\right]\% = 75\%$

(vi) $V = \left[\left(\frac{15\% \text{ of } 5700}{12\% \text{ of } 8550}\right) \times 100\right]\% = 83.33\%$

(vii) $X = \left[\left(\frac{12\% \text{ of } 5700}{16\% \text{ of } 8550}\right) \times 100\right]\% = 50\%$

Highest of these is 86.67% corresponding to institute R.

Hence, the correct option is (B).

13. Difference between number of candidates passed from institute S and P

$=[(16\% + 18\%) \text{ of } 5700] - [(8\% + 10\%) \text{ of } 8550]$

$=[(34\% \text{ of } 5700) - (18\% \text{ of } 8550)]$

$= (1938 - 1539)$
$= 399$
The number of candidates enrolled from institute T and R together by 399.
Hence, the correct option is (C).

14. Candidates passed from institutes Q and R together $=$ $[(13\% + 17\%)$ of $5700]$
$= 30\%$ of 5700
Candidates enrolled from institutes Q and R together $=$ $[(15\% + 10\%)$ of $8550]$
$= 25\%$ of 8550
$\therefore$ Required Percentage $= \left(\frac{30\% \text{ of } 5700}{25\% \text{ of } 8550} \times 100\right)\%$

$= \left(\frac{30 \times 5700}{25 \times 8550} \times 100\right)\%$
$= 80\%$

Hence, the correct option is (B).

15. Required ratio $= \left(\frac{18\% \text{ of } 5700}{22\% \text{ of } 8550}\right) = \left(\frac{18 \times 5700}{22 \times 8550}\right) = \frac{6}{11}$

The ratio of candidates passed to the candidates enrolled from institute P is $6:11$.

Hence, the correct option is (C).

16. Given,
Sum invested in company Q in $1999 = 4.75$ lakhs
Interest rate of company P in year $1999 = 8\%$
Difference between company Q and P
$=$ Rs. $[(10\%$ of $4.75) - (8\%$ of $4.75)]$ lakhs
$=$ Rs. $(2$ of $4.75)$ lakhs
$=$ Rs. 0.095 lakhs
$=$ Rs. 9500
Hence, the correct option is (D).

17. Let the amounts invested in 2002 in Companies P and Q be Rs. $8x$ and Rs. $9x$ respectively.
Then, interest received after one year from Company $P =$ Rs. $(6\%$ of $8x)$
$=$ Rs. $\frac{48}{100}x$
and interest received after one year from Company $Q =$ Rs. $(4\%$ of $9x)$
Rs. $\frac{36}{100}x$

Required ratio $= \frac{\left(\frac{48}{100}x\right)}{\left(\frac{36}{100}x\right)} = \frac{4}{3}$
The amounts received after one year as interests from Companies P and Q are in the ratio $4:3$.
Hence, the correct option is (D).

18. Let Rs. x lakhs be invested in Company P in 2000, the amount invested in Company Q in $2000 =$ Rs. $(30 - x)$ lakhs.

Total interest received from the two Companies after 1 year
$=$ Rs. $[(7.5\%$ of $x) + \{9\%$ of $(30 - x)\}]$ lakhs
$=$ Rs. $\left[2.7 - \left(\frac{1.5x}{100}\right)\right]$lakhs
$\therefore \left[2.7 - \left(\frac{1.5x}{100}\right)\right] = 2.43$
$\Rightarrow x = 18$
The amount invested in Company P is Rs. 18 lakhs.
Hence, the correct option is (D).

19. Amount received from Company P after one year (i.e., in 1999) on investing Rs. 12 lakhs in it

$=$ Rs. $[12 + (8\%$ of $12)]$ lakhs

$=$ Rs. 12.96 lakhs

Amount received from Company P after one year on investing Rs. 12.96 lakhs in the year 1999

$=$ Rs. $[12.96 + (10\%$ of $12.96)]$ lakhs

$=$ Rs. 14.256

Appreciation received on investment during the period of two years

$=$ Rs. $(14.256 - 12)$ lakhs

$=$ Rs. 2.256 lakhs

$=$ Rs. 225600

Hence, the correct option is (C).

20. Amount received from Company Q after one year on investment of Rs. 5 lakhs in the year 1996
$=$ Rs. $[5 + (6.5\%$ of $5)]$ lakhs
$=$ Rs. 5.325 lakhs
Amount received from Company P after one year on an investment of Rs. 5.325 lakhs in the year 1997
$=$ Rs. $[5.325 + (9\%$ of $5.325)]$ lakhs
$=$ Rs. 5.80425 lakhs
Rs. 580425 will be received from Company P, by the investor.

Hence, the correct option is (B).

21. Required percentage $= \left[\frac{(145-108)}{108} \times 100\right]\%$
$= 34.26\%$
$\approx 34\%$ sales will increase of $55AH$ batteries in 1998 compared to 1992.
Hence, the correct option is (D).

22. The total sales (in thousands) of all the seven years for various batteries are-
For $4AH = 75 + 90 + 96 + 105 + 90 + 105 + 115 = 676$
For $7AH = 144 + 126 + 114 + 90 + 75 + 60 + 85 = 694$

For $32AH = 114 + 102 + 75 + 150 + 135 + 165 + 160 = 901$

For $35AH = 102 + 84 + 105 + 90 + 75 + 45 + 100 = 601$

For $55AH = 108 + 126 + 135 + 75 + 90 + 120 + 145 = 799$

Clearly, sales are maximum in case of $32AH$ batteries.
Hence, the correct option is (C).

23. Given,
Sale of $35AH$ batteries in year $1993 = 84$
Sale of $35AH$ batteries in year $1997 = 45$
Required difference $= [(84 - 45) \times 1000] = 39000$
Hence, the correct option is (D).

24. The percentages of sales of $4AH$ batteries to total sales in different years are-

For $1992 = \left(\frac{75}{543} \times 100\right)\% = 13.81\%$

For $1993 = \left(\frac{90}{528} \times 100\right)\% = 17.05\%$

For $1994 = \left(\frac{96}{525} \times 100\right)\% = 18.29\%$

For $1995 = \left(\frac{105}{510} \times 100\right)\% = 20.59\%$

For $1996 = \left(\frac{96}{465} \times 100\right)\% = 19.35\%$

For $1997 = \left(\frac{105}{495} \times 100\right)\% = 21.21\%$

For $1998 = \left(\frac{115}{605} \times 100\right)\% = 19.01\%$

Clearly, the percentage is maximum in 1997.

Hence, the correct option is (D).

25. From the table, it is clear that the sales of $7AH$ batteries have been decreasing continuously from 1992 to 1997.

Hence, the correct option is (B).

26. Both 1 and 2 – According to Bloomberg LP, an American company, the economy of the USA has fallen. Instead, Brazil, India, China have emerged as investor-friendly nations.

Hence, the correct option is (C).

27. Market regulator Sebi (Securities and Exchange Board of India) was on course to relax investment norms for sovereign wealth funds, the investment vehicles which are directly controlled by the government of a country, from 10% to 20% that applied to foreign institutional investors (FIIs). The reason behind the move was to attract foreign investment in India.

Hence, the correct option is (A).

28. The global economy relied on oil for much of the 20th century as a portable and indispensable fuel. The immense wealth associated with oil generates political struggles to control it, and the history of petroleum is also the history of war and struggle

Hence, the correct option is (A).

29. A sinking fund is a fund created by the government and gradually accumulated every year by setting aside a part of current public revenue in such a way that it would be sufficient to pay off the funded debt at the time of maturity. Under this method, the aggregate burden of public debt is least felt, as the burden of taxing the people to repay the debt is spread evenly over the period of the accumulation of the fund. The preferable alternative for the government is to raise a new loan and credit the proceeds of the sinking fund. It is a separate fund established by the government.

Hence, the correct option is (A).

30.

- First Five Year Plan (1951-56) – Agriculture and community development
- Second Five Year Plan (1956-61) – Heavy Industry
- Fifth Five Year Plan (1974-79) – Removal of Poverty
- Ninth Five Year Plan (1997-2002) – Food Security and woman empowerment

Hence, the correct option is (C).

31. Following demographic issues represents a challenge for human resource managers-

- Increasingly diverse workforce
- Aging workforce
- Increasing use of contingent workers

Hence, the correct option is (D).

32. Job evaluation is the process of establishing the value or worth of jobs in a job hierarchy and compares the relative intrinsic value or worth of jobs within an organization. Once this programme installed must be continued on a permanent basis.

Hence, the correct option is (A).

33. In India, while some media reports suggest that the Labour Day was first observed in Madras (now Chennai) in 1923, organised by the Labour Kisan Party, it was in 1927 that for the first time it was officially observed as is mentioned in Foner's book.

In the book, it is mentioned that an appeal by the All-India Trade Union Congress at its Delhi session in 1927 triggered demonstrations in Calcutta (now Kolkata), Madras and Bombay.

Hence, the correct option is (B).

34. A worker who has been employed for more than a year can only be dismissed on the permission of the appropriate government office/concerned authority. This worker must be given valid reasons before dismissal under the Industrial Disputes Act, 1947.

Hence, the correct option is (A).

35. In the year 1918 father of the nation Mahatma Gandhi along with Anasuya Sarabhai and Shankerlal Banker founded the Ahmadabad textile labor association which is an example of the Industrial Union.

Hence, the correct option is (C).

Mock Test 07

Comprehension

Ques (1-5):Direction: Read the following passage carefully and answer the question that follows.

Mount Vesuvius, a volcano located between the ancient Italian cities of Pompeii and Herculaneum, has received much attention because of its frequent and destructive eruptions. The most famous of these eruptions occurred in 79 A.D.

The volcano had been inactive for centuries. There was little warning of the coming eruption, although one account unearthed by archaeologists says that a hard rain and a strong wind had disturbed the celestial calm during the preceding night. Early the next morning, the volcano poured a huge river of molten rock down upon Herculaneum, completely burying the city and filling the harbor with coagulated lava.

Meanwhile, on the other side of the mountain, cinders, stone, and ash rained down on Pompeii. Sparks from the burning ash ignited the combustible rooftops quickly. Large portions of the city were destroyed in the conflagration. Fire, however, was not the only cause of destruction. Poisonous sulfuric gases saturated the air. These heavy gases were not buoyant in the atmosphere and therefore sank toward the earth and suffocated people.

Over the years, excavations of Pompeii and Herculaneum have revealed a great deal about the behavior of the volcano. By analyzing data, much as a zoologist dissects an animal specimen, scientists have concluded that the eruption changed large portions of the area's geography. For instance, it turned the Sarno River from its course and raised the level of the beach along the Bay of Naples. Meteorologists studying these events have also concluded that Vesuvius caused a huge tidal wave that affected the world's climate.

In addition to making these investigations, archaeologists have been able to study the skeletons of victims by using distilled water to wash away the volcanic ash. By strengthening the brittle bones with acrylic paint, scientists have been able to examine the skeletons and draw conclusions about the diet and habits of the residents. Finally, the excavations at both Pompeii and Herculaneum have yielded many examples of classical art, such as jewelry made of bronze, which is an alloy of copper and tin. The eruption of Mount Vesuvius and its tragic consequences have provided everyone with a wealth of data about the effects that volcanoes can have on the surrounding area. Today, volcanologists can locate and predict eruptions, saving lives, and preventing the destruction of other cities and cultures.

Q.1 The poisonous gases were not _______ in the air.

A. able to float **B.** visible
C. able to evaporate **D.** invisible

Q.2 Scientists analyzed data about Vesuvius in the same way that a zoologist _______ a specimen.

A. describes in detail
B. studies by cutting apart
C. photographs
D. chart

Q.3 _______ have concluded that the volcanic eruption caused a tidal wave.

A. scientists who study oceans
B. scientists who study atmospheric conditions
C. scientists who study ash
D. scientists who study animal behaviour

Q.4 Scientists have used _______ water to wash away volcanic ash from the skeletons of victims.

A. bottled **B.** volcanic **C.** purified **D.** sea

Q.5 Herculaneum and its harbour were buried under_______ lava.

A. liquid **B.** solid **C.** flowing **D.** gas

Ques (6-10):Direction: Read the following passage carefully and answer the question that follows.

The conflict had existed between Spain and England since the 1570s. England wanted a share of the wealth that Spain had been taking from the lands it had claimed in the Americas.

Elizabeth I, Queen of England, encouraged her staunch admiral of the navy, Sir Francis Drake, to raid Spanish ships and towns. Though these raids were on a small scale, Drake achieved dramatic success, adding gold and silver to England's treasury and diminishing Spain's supremacy.

Religious differences also caused conflict between the two countries. Whereas Spain was Roman Catholic, most of England had become Protestant. King Philip II of Spain wanted to claim the throne and make England a Catholic country again. To satisfy his ambition and also to retaliate against England's theft of his gold and silver, King Philip began to build his fleet of warships, the Spanish Armada, in January 1586.

Philip intended his fleet to be indestructible. In addition to building new warships, he marshaled 130 sailing vessels of all types and recruited more than 19,000 robust soldiers and 8,000 sailors. Although some of his ships lacked guns and others lacked ammunition, Philip was convinced that his Armada could withstand any battle with England.

The martial Armada set sail from Lisbon, Portugal, on May 9, 1588, but bad weather forced it back to port. The voyage resumed on July 22 after the weather became more stable.

The Spanish fleet met the smaller, faster, and more maneuverable English ships in battle off the coast of Plymouth, England, first on July 31 and again on August 2. The two battles left Spain vulnerable, having lost several ships and with its ammunition depleted. On August 7, while the Armada lay at anchor on the French side of the Strait of Dover, England sent eight burning ships into the midst of the Spanish fleet to set it on fire. Blocked on one side, the Spanish ships could only drift away, their crews in panic and disorder. Before the Armada could regroup, the English attacked again on August 8.

Although the Spaniards made a valiant effort to fight back, the fleet suffered extensive damage. During the eight hours of battle, the Armada drifted perilously close to the rocky coastline. At the moment when it seemed that the Spanish ships would be driven onto the English shore, the wind shifted, and the Armada drifted out into the North Sea. The Spaniards recognized the superiority of the English fleet and returned home, defeated.

Q.6 King Philip recruited many _____ soldiers and sailors.

A. warlike **B.** strong
C. accomplished **D.** timid

Q.7 The _____ Armada set sail on May 9, 1588.

A. complete **B.** warlike
C. independent **D.** isolated

Q.8 The two battles left the Spanish fleet ________.

A. open to change **B.** triumphant
C. open to attack **D.** defeated

Q.9 The Armada was _____ on one side.

A. closed off **B.** damaged
C. alone **D.** circled

Q.10 Sir Francis Drake added wealth to the treasury and diminished Spain's______

A. unlimited power **B.** unrestricted growth
C. territory **D.** treaties

Management Data Interpretation

Ques (11-15):Direction: The following pie-charts show the distribution of students of graduate and post-graduate levels in seven different institutes in a town.

Distribution of students at the graduate and post-graduate levels in seven institutes:

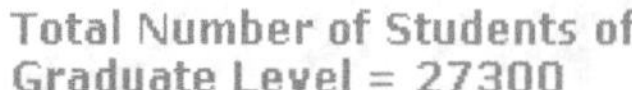

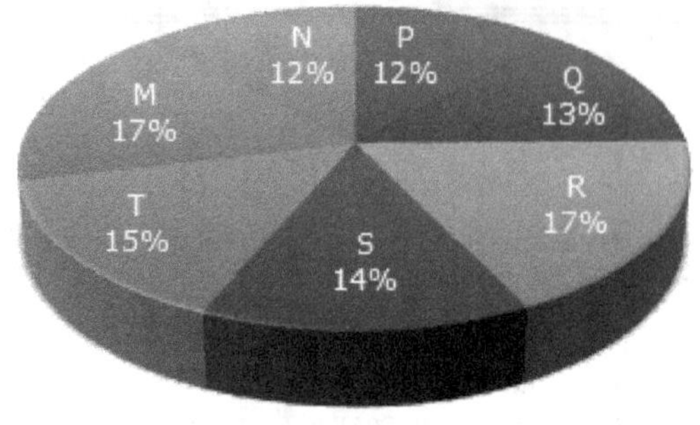

Total Number of Students of Post-Graduate Level = 24700

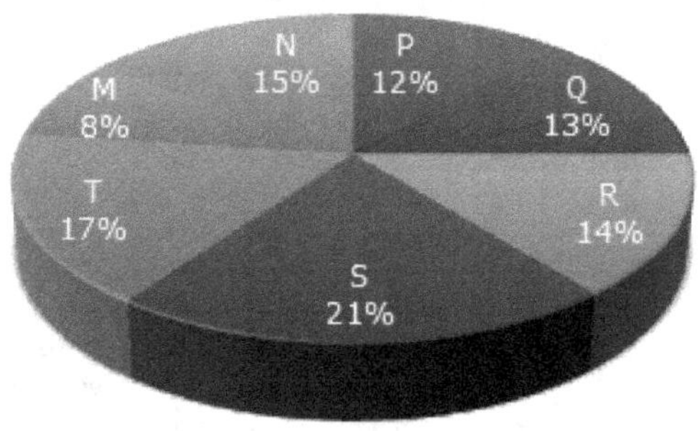

Q.11 What is the total number of graduate and post-graduate level students is institute R?

A. 8320 **B.** 7916 **C.** 9116 **D.** 8099

Q.12 What is the ratio between the number of students studying at post-graduate and graduate levels respectively from institute S?

A. 14:19 **B.** 19:21 **C.** 17:21 **D.** 19:14

Q.13 How many students of institutes of M and S are studying at the graduate level?

A. 7516 **B.** 8463 **C.** 9127 **D.** 9404

Q.14 What are the ratio between the number of students studying at post-graduate level from institutes S and the number of students studying at the graduate level from institute Q?

A. 13:19 **B.** 21:13 **C.** 13:8 **D.** 19:13

Q.15 Total number of students studying at post-graduate level from institutes N and P is

A. 5601 **B.** 5944 **C.** 6669 **D.** 8372

Ques (16-20):Direction: The following line graph gives the percentage of the number of candidates who qualified an examination out of the total number of candidates who appeared for the examination over a period of seven years from 1994 to 2000.

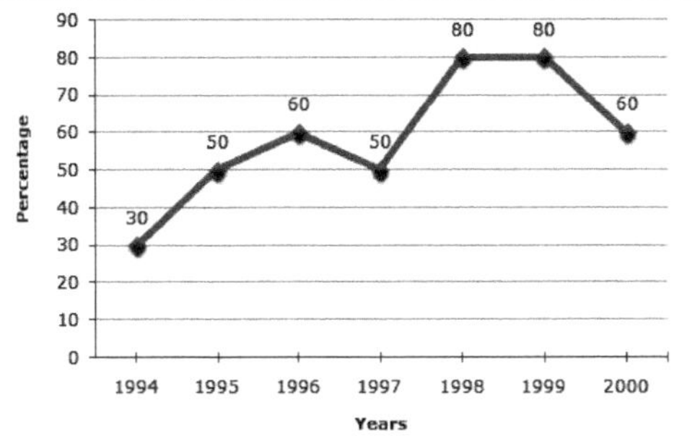

Q.16 The difference between the percentage of candidates qualified to appeared was maximum in which of the following pairs of years?

A. 1994 and 1995 **B.** 1997 and 1998
C. 1998 and 1999 **D.** 1999 and 2000

Q.17 In which pair of years was the number of candidates qualified, the same?

A. 1995 and 1997 **B.** 1995 and 2000
C. 1998 and 1999 **D.** Data inadequate

Q.18 If the number of candidates qualified in 1998 was 21200, what did the number of candidates appear in 1998?

A. 32000 **B.** 28500 **C.** 26500 **D.** 25000

Q.19 If the total number of candidates appeared in 1996 and 1997 together was 47400, then the total number of candidates qualified in these two years together was?

A. 34700 **B.** 32100
C. 31500 **D.** Data inadequate

Q.20 The total number of candidates qualified in 1999 and 2000 together was 33500 and the number of candidates appeared in 1999 was 26500. What was the number of candidates in 2000?

A. 24500 **B.** 22000 **C.** 20500 **D.** 19000

Ques (21-25): A school has four sections A, B, C, D of Class IX students.

The results of half-yearly and annual examinations are shown in the table given below.

Result	Number of students			
	Section A	Section B	Section C	Section D
Students failed in both Exams	28	23	17	27
Students failed in half-yearly but passed in Annual Exams	14	12	8	13
Students passed in half-yearly but failed in Annual Exams	6	17	9	15
Students passed in both Exams	64	55	46	76

Q.21 If the number of students passing an examination be considered a criterion for comparison of the difficulty level of two examinations, which of the following statements is true in this context?

A. Half yearly examinations were more difficult.
B. Annual examinations were more difficult.
C. Both the examinations had almost the same difficulty level.
D. The two examinations cannot be compared for difficulty level.

Q.22 How many students are there in Class IX in the school?

A. 336 **B.** 189 **C.** 335 **D.** 430

Q.23 Which section has the maximum pass percentage in at least one of the two examinations?

A. A Section **B.** B Section
C. C Section **D.** D Section

Q.24 Which section has the maximum success rate in the annual examination?

A. A Section **B.** B Section
C. C Section **D.** D Section

Q.25 Which section has the minimum failure rate in the half-yearly examination?

A. A Section **B.** B Section
C. C Section **D.** D Section

Business Awareness

Q.26 _______suggests Human Resource Strategy in itself may not be effective.

A. Peter Drucker **B.** Tony Groundy
C. John Zimmerman **D.** Anonymous

Q.27 _______ is the simple act of comparison & learning for organisational improvement.

A. Benchmarking **B.** Feedback
C. Ranking **D.** Job evaluation

Q.28 Choose the wrongly matched pair of CEO?

A. ICICI - K.V.Kamath
B. Cadbury India - Mathew Cadbury
C. Reliance Petrochemical - Anil Ambani
D. HDFC -Deepak Parekh

Q.29 Which of these is not a producer of steel?

A. SAIL

B. TISCO

C. Jindal Steel & Power Limited (JSPL)

D. TELCO

Q.30 Who among the following presented the first budget (interim) of Independent India?

A. Manmohan Singh

B. Jawaharlal Nehru

C. R. K. Shanmukham Chetty

D. N.D. Tiwari

Q.31 In which evaluation method, the evaluator is asked to describe the strong and weak aspects of the employee's behaviour.

A. Graphic rating scale

B. Aircraft Engine

C. Essay evaluation

D. Management by Objective

Q.32 Oil refinery and sugar mill are classified under which industries?

A. Primary

B. Secondary

C. Tertiary

D. None of the above

Q.33 Which of the following cannot be classified as an auxiliary to trade?

A. Mining

B. Insurance

C. Warehouse

D. Transport

Q.34 Human Resource Management aims to maximize employees as well as Organizational

A. Effectiveness

B. Economy

C. Efficiency

D. Performativity

Q.35 The total effect of a price change of a commodity is

A. Substitution effect plus price effect

B. Substitution effect plus income effect

C. Substitution effect plus the demonstration effect

D. Substitution effect minus income effect

// Smart Answer Sheet //

Correct Indicates percentage of students who answered questions correctly.

Skipped Indicates percentage of students who skipped questions.

Q.	Ans.	Correct / Skipped	Q.	Ans.	Correct / Skipped	Q.	Ans.	Correct / Skipped	Q.	Ans.	Correct / Skipped	Q.	Ans.	Correct / Skipped
1	A	49.94 % / 30.66 %	8	C	60.21 % / 31.79 %	15	C	81.36 % / 11.13 %	22	D	43.4 % / 40.08 %	29	D	47.31 % / 47.58 %
2	B	62.58 % / 36.06 %	9	A	44.64 % / 53.62 %	16	B	85.7 % / 10.69 %	23	D	43.3 % / 46.05 %	30	C	53.6 % / 35.25 %
3	B	51.75 % / 44.8 %	10	A	55.88 % / 42.52 %	17	D	81.62 % / 15.8 %	24	A	46.25 % / 49.88 %	31	C	78.18 % / 19.0 %
4	C	54.43 % / 33.22 %	11	D	40.77 % / 45.92 %	18	C	60.4 % / 32.37 %	25	D	54.64 % / 40.19 %	32	B	48.6 % / 31.91 %
5	B	59.52 % / 36.45 %	12	D	84.12 % / 12.08 %	19	D	85.17 % / 14.31 %	26	B	79.87 % / 19.99 %	33	A	46.68 % / 49.05 %
6	B	41.42 % / 42.7 %	13	B	81.46 % / 14.74 %	20	C	42.57 % / 42.11 %	27	A	48.7 % / 44.36 %	34	A	52.07 % / 31.49 %
7	B	83.39 % / 15.3 %	14	D	78.27 % / 19.87 %	21	C	61.94 % / 31.96 %	28	C	54.34 % / 39.83 %	35	B	85.65 % / 10.21 %

Performance Analysis	
Avg. Score (%)	60.0%
Toppers Score (%)	60.0%
Your Score	

//Hints and Solutions//

1. "Buoyant" means able to float. The passage indicates this by indicating that the gases, therefore, sank toward the earth and suffocated people. Buoyant does not mean visible (B) or possible to see. Able to float/buoyant does not mean able to evaporate (C). Evaporation means turning to vapor, which only liquids can do. Gases are already vapors. Buoyant does not mean invisible (D) or unseen.
Hence, the correct option is (A).

2. "Dissect" means to cut apart for study. It does not mean to describe in detail (A), to photograph (C), or to chart (D) a specimen.
Hence, the correct option is (B).

3. Meteorologists are scientists who study atmospheric conditions, particularly weather. Scientists who study oceans (A) are oceanographers, i.e. marine scientists. Scientists who study ash (C) do not exist as members of a separate discipline. Climate scientists and many others concerned with its effects study volcanic ash. Scientists who study animal behaviour (D) are ethologists or animal behaviourists and do not study ash.
Hence, the correct option is (B).

4. Distilled water is purified water. Distilled water is not equivalent to bottled (A), volcanic (B), sea (D).
Hence, the correct option is (C).

5. "Coagulated" means solidified. Liquid (A) is an opposite of solid. Flowing (C) assumes a liquid, not solid, state. Gas (D) is another opposite of solid. (Three states of matter, like volcanic material, are liquid, solid, and gaseous.)
Hence, the correct option is (B).

6. "Robust" means strong. It does not mean warlike (A), accomplished (C), or competent, timid (D).
Hence, the correct option is (B).

7. "Martial" means warlike or war-related. It does not mean complete (A), independent (C), or isolated (D).
Hence, the correct option is (B).

8. "Vulnerable" means open to attack or susceptible to harm. It does not mean open to change (A) or receptive, triumphant (B) or victorious, defeated (D).
Hence, the correct option is (C).

9. The passage indicates the Armada was "blocked" on one side, i.e. closed off rather than damaged (B) (it was damaged extensively, not on one side); alone (C) or circled (D), i.e. surrounded, neither of which can be done on only one side.

Hence, the correct option is (A).

10. "Supremacy" means unlimited power, not unrestricted growth (B). The passage states that Drake diminished Spain's supremacy, but does not specifically mention diminishing its territory (C). Drake's raids enriched England and reduced Spain's power; no mention is made of eliminating any treaties (D).
Hence, the correct option is (A).

11. Required number $=(17\%$ of $27300)+(14\%$ of $24700)$

$=4641+3458$

$=8099$

Hence, the correct option is (D).

12. Required ratio $=\frac{(21\% \text{ of } 24700)}{(14\% \text{ of } 27300)}$

$=\frac{(21\times24700)}{14\times27300}$

$=\frac{19}{14}$

Hence, the correct option is (D).

13. Students of institute M at graduate level $=17\%$ of $27300=4641$
Students of institute S at graduate level $=14\%$ of $27300=3822$
$\therefore$ Total number of students at graduate in institutes M and $S=(4641+3822)$
$=8463$
Hence, the correct option is (B).

14. Required ratio $=\frac{(21\% \text{ of } 24700)}{(13\% \text{ of } 27300)}$

$=\frac{(21\times24700)}{13\times27300}$

$=\frac{19}{13}$

Hence, the correct option is (D).

15. Required number $=(15\%$ of $24700)+(12\%$ of $24700)$
$=3705+2964$
$=6669$
Hence, the correct option is (C).

16. The differences between the percentages of candidates qualified to appeared for the given pairs of years are-

For 1994 and $1995=50-30=20$

For 1998 and $1999=80-80=0$

For 1994 and $1997=50-30=20$

For 1997 and $1998=80-50=30$

For 1999 and $2000=80-60=20$

Thus, the maximum difference is between the years 1997 and 1998.
Hence, the correct option is (B).

17. The graph gives the data for the percentage of candidates qualified to appeared and unless the absolute values of the number of candidates qualified or candidates appeared are know we cannot compare the absolute values for any two years.

So, the data is inadequate to solve this question.
Hence, the correct option is (D).

18. The number of candidates appeared in 1998 be x.

Then, 80% of $x = 21200$

$\Rightarrow x = \frac{21200 \times 100}{80} = 26500$ (required number).

Hence, the correct option is (C).

19. The total number of candidates qualified in 1996 and 1997 together, cannot be determined until we know at least, the number of candidates appeared in any one of the two years 1996 or 1997 or the percentage of candidates qualified to appear in 1996 and 1997 together.

So, the data is inadequate.
Hence, the correct option is (D).

20. The number of candidates qualified in $1999 = (80\%$ of $26500) = 21200$

$\therefore$ Number of candidates qualified in $2000 = (33500 - 21200) = 12300$

Let the number of candidates appeared in 2000 be x.

Then, 60% of $x = 12300$

$\Rightarrow x = \left(\frac{12300 \times 100}{60}\right) = 20500$

Hence, the correct option is (C).

21. Number of students who passed half-yearly exams in the school
$=$ (Number of students passed in half-yearly but failed in annual exams) $+$ (Number of students passed in both exams)
$= (6 + 17 + 9 + 15) + (64 + 55 + 46 + 76)$
$= 288$
Also, Number of students who passed annual exams in the school
$=$ (Number of students failed in half-yearly but passed in annual exams) $+$ (Number of students passed in both exams)
$= (14 + 12 + 8 + 13) + (64 + 55 + 46 + 76)$
$= 288$
Since, the number of students passed in half-yearly $=$ the number of students passed in annual exams. Therefore, it can be inferred that both the examinations had almost the same difficulty level.
Thus, Statements (A), (B), and (D) are false and Statement (C) is true.
Hence, the correct option is (C).

22. Since the classification of the students on the basis of their results and sections form independent groups, so the total number of students in the class
$= (28 + 23 + 17 + 27 + 14 + 12 + 8 + 13 + 6 + 17 + 9 + 15 + 64 + 55 + 46 + 76)$
$= 430$
Hence, the correct option is (D).

23. Pass percentages in at least one of the two examinations for different sections are-

Section $A = \left[\frac{(14+6+64)}{(28+14+6+64)} \times 100\right]\% = \left[\frac{84}{112} \times 100\right]\% = 75\%$

Section $B = \left[\frac{(12+17+55)}{(23+12+17+55)} \times 100\right]\% = \left[\frac{84}{107} \times 100\right]\% = 78.5\%$

Section $C = \left[\frac{(8+9+46)}{(17+8+9+46)} \times 100\right]\% = \left[\frac{63}{80} \times 100\right]\% = 78.75\%$

Section $D = \left[\frac{(13+15+76)}{(27+13+15+76)} \times 100\right]\% = \left[\frac{104}{131} \times 100\right]\% = 79.39\%$

Clearly, the pass percentage is maximum for Section D.
Hence, the correct option is (D).

24. Total number of students passed in annual exams in a section
$= [$ (No. of students failed in half-yearly but passed in annual exams) $+($ No. of students passed in both exams) $]$ in that section

$\therefore$ Success rate in annual exams in Section A

$= \left[\frac{\text{No. of students of Section A passed in annual exams}}{\text{Total number of students in Section } A} \times 100\right]\%$

$= \left[\frac{(14+64)}{(28+14+6+64)} \times 100\right]\%$

$= \left[\frac{78}{112} \times 100\right]\%$

$= 69.64\%$

Similarly, the success rate in annual exams in-

Section $B = \left[\frac{(12+55)}{(23+12+17+55)} \times 100\right]\% = \left[\frac{67}{107} \times 100\right]\% = 62.62\%$

Section $C = \left[\frac{(8+46)}{(17+8+9+46)} \times 100\right]\% = \left[\frac{54}{80} \times 100\right]\% = 67.5\%$

Section $D = \left[\frac{(13+76)}{(27+13+15+76)} \times 100\right]\% = \left[\frac{89}{131} \times 100\right]\% = 67.94\%$

Hence, the correct option is (A).

25. Total number of failures in half-yearly exams in a section
$= [$ (Number of students failed in both exams) $+$ (Number of students failed in half-yearly but passed in Annual exams) $]$ in that section

$\therefore$ Failure rate in half-yearly exams in Section A

$= \left[\frac{\text{Number of students of Section A failed in half-yearly}}{\text{Total number of students in Section A}} \times 100\right]\%$

$= \left[\frac{(28+14)}{(28+14+6+64)} \times 100\right]\%$

$= \left[\frac{42}{112} \times 100\right]\%$

$= 37.5\%$

Similarly, the failure rate in half-yearly exams in-

Section

$B = \left[\frac{(23+12)}{(23+12+17+55)} \times 100\right]\% = \left[\frac{35}{107} \times 100\right]\% = 32.71\%$

Section

$C = \left[\frac{(17+8)}{(17+8+9+46)} \times 100\right]\% = \left[\frac{25}{80} \times 100\right]\% = 31.25\%$

Section

$D = \left[\frac{(27+13)}{(27+13+15+76)} \times 100\right]\% = \left[\frac{40}{131} \times 100\right]\% = 30.53\%$

Hence, the correct option is (D).

26. Tony Groundy suggests Human Resource Strategy in itself may not be effective. HR Strategy (Human Resource Strategy) is a designation for a long-term plan created to achieve objectives in the field of human resource and human capital management and development in the organization. Human Resource strategy is one of the outputs of strategic management in the field of human resources management.
Hence, the correct option is (B).

27. Benchmarking is a simple act of comparison & learning for organisational improvement. Benchmarking is the process of identifying "best practice" in relation to both products (including) and the processes by which those products are created and delivered. The search for "best practice" can taker place both inside a particular industry and also in other industries.

Hence, the correct option is (A).

28. Mukesh D Ambani is the CEO of Reliance Petrochemical Limited.

Therefore, Reliance Petrochemical - Anil Ambani is the wrongly matched pair.

Hence, the correct option is (C).

29. TELCO is not a producer of steel. SAIL, TISCO, Jindal Steel & Power Limited (JSPL) are producers of steel.

A telephone company, also known as a TELCO, telephone service provider, or telecommunications operator, is a kind of communications service provider (CSP), more precisely a telecommunications service provider (TSP), that provides telecommunications services such as telephony and data communications access.

Steel Authority of India Limited (SAIL) is a Government steel-making company in India. SAIL produces iron and steel at five integrated plants and three special steel plants.

Formerly known as Tata Iron and Steel Company Limited (TISCO), Tata Steel is among the top steel-producing companies in the world with an annual crude steel capacity of 34 million tonnes per annum.

Jindal Steel & Power Limited (JSPL), a part of the USD 22 billion diversified O. P. Jindal Group, is a leading Indian Steel manufacturer and Power producer.

Hence, the correct option is (D).

30. The first budget (interim) of Independent India presented by R K Shanmukham Chetty on November 26, 1947. That budget was an interim Budget. It was only a review of the economy and no new taxes were proposed as the budget day for 1948-49 was just 95 days away.

Hence, the correct option is (C).

31. In the essay evaluation method, the evaluator is asked to describe the strong and weak aspects of the employee's behaviour. In the essay method approach, the appraiser prepares a written statement about the employee being appraised. The statement usually concentrates on describing specific strengths and weaknesses in job performance.

Hence, the correct option is (C).

32. The secondary sector of the economy involves the transformation of raw materials into goods. An oil refinery and a sugar factory are categorized as secondary industries as their raw materials (crude oil and sugarcane) are processed into finished goods (oil and sugar).

Hence, the correct option is (B).

33. The activities which are meant to assist trade are known as Auxiliaries to trade. They are generally referred to as services as they assist industry and trade like insurance, warehousing, transportation etc. While mining is the process of extraction of valuable minerals from the earth.
Hence, the correct option is (A).

34. Human Resource Management aims to maximize employees as well as Organizational Effectiveness. Pushing responsibility to lower levels of the organization, making processes smoother and more efficient, and teaching managers to empowering employees to take risks and find new solutions-all have an immense impact on the speed and efficiency of the organization. These are the primary focus of Human Resources.
Hence, the correct option is (A).

35. The total effect of a price change of a commodity is the substitution effect plus income effect. The income effect is the change in consumption patterns due to a change in purchasing power. This occurs with income increases, price changes, and even currency fluctuations. Since income is not good in and of itself (it can only be exchanged for goods and services), price decreases increase purchasing power.
Hence, the correct option is (B).

Mock Test 08

Comprehension

Ques (1-5):Directions: Read the passage carefully and answer the question given below :

For generations, companies have been selling fair skin to young Indian women, promising better marriage and employment prospects. However, over the last few years, men have become a favoured target audience. This followed the realization that the Indian alpha male, denied a choice in male-specific grooming products, had been using women's fairness creams all along. Until the mid-2000s, deodorants and shaving creams were the only grooming products advertised for men. But India's largest consumer goods companies sensed an opportunity and launched a slew of fairness products for male consumers.

In India, as in other parts of the world, light skin is the culturally accepted and endorsed form of beauty, and children absorb this message at a young age. According to a 2015 research report by Nielsen, urban Indian men believe that fair skin can improve professional prospects. The cultural pressure to look fair, argues Kiran Khalap, branding expert and founder at communications consultancy Chlorophyll, is something inherent in our society, not manufactured by companies. "And it is certainly not restricted to India: China and Japan have had skin-whitening products for centuries, well before they met Western 'white' people," he said. However, there is a growing awareness among consumers that companies are exploiting their insecurities, and critics have taken some of the biggest fairness brands, and the celebrities who endorse them, to task for their casual discrimination.

Earlier this month, Bollywood actor Abhay Deol took to Facebook to trounce his fellow actors who earn millions from endorsing fairness creams. This comes a few years after actress Nandita Das launched the "Dark is Beautiful" campaign to encourage Indians to embrace a wider definition of beauty. These efforts are slowly making a difference, increasing awareness, and encouraging consumers to take pride in their natural skin tones. That means Indian companies will eventually have to change their approach. "My sense is that brands will wake up to the new reality, and you will see propositions reworked around clearer skin (and) glow, rather than pure fairness," Leo Burnett's Sinha said.

Rajesh Krishnamurthy, business head for the consumer product division at The Himalaya Drug Company, believes that over time the men's grooming category will evolve to include a wider range of products, including those for normal skin, just like in the women's skincare category. "Companies are increasingly realizing that you cannot continue to bullshit consumers anymore; these are educated young men who will question what you sell to them," said Shantanu Deshpande, co-founder, and CEO of the male-grooming startup Bombay Shaving Company.

Q.1 With reference to the passage, why exactly was "Dark is Beautiful" campaign initiated?

A. To motivate Indians to ditch their liking for the fair skin and accept their inherent beauty.

B. To throw light on the sinister intentions of fairness brands.

C. To make sure that Indians do not fall prey to misleading beauty product advertisements.

D. To encourage Indians to be sympathetic towards people with other skin tones.

Q.2 What were the findings of the 2015 research report by Nielsen?

A. Indian urban men presumed that being fair enhanced their professional opportunities.

B. Indian urban men believed that being fair would give them better marriage and employment contracts.

C. Indian urban men would eventually question the logic behind male-grooming product advertisements.

D. Indian urban men do not endorse the concept of fairness helping them in their personal and professional life.

Q.3 Choose a similar word in meaning to the word "trounce"

A. Vacillation　　**B.** Temerity

C. Lambaste　　**D.** Nefarious

Q.4 What is the tone of the passage?
[SSC Sub Inspector (CPO), 2018], [SSC Sub Inspector (CPO), 2017]

A. Didactic　　**B.** Skeptical

C. Descriptive　　**D.** Satirical

Q.5 What is the central idea of the passage?

A. Though people endorsed skin fairness products, they are now realizing that they are being taken for a ride by such products.

B. Only men ardently use whitening creams to boost their personality.

C. The brand marketing of fairness product companies are evolving to appease the target audience of India.

D. Brands are frivolous when it comes to the campaigning of their beauty products.

Ques (6-10):Direction: Read the following passage carefully and answer the question that follows.

On August 22, 1939, Adolf Hitler summoned his top military generals to Obersalzberg, where he delivered a speech explaining his plans for war, first with Poland, then with the rest of Europe. Despite resistance from those both inside and outside Germany, Hitler felt exceedingly confident that he could defy the will of the international community and conquer vast amounts of land. In his speech at Obersalzberg, he laid out numerous factors he believed would contribute to the success of his war plans.

Chief among Hitler's sources of confidence in Germany's brazen war plans was German military quickness. Hitler said, "Our strength lies in our quickness." On the advice of Colonel-

General von Brauchitsch, Hitler believed Poland could be captured in a few weeks, an astonishingly short amount of time given the recent history of trench warfare and the long history of protracted European military engagements that resulted in minimal land gains and high casualty counts.

Hitler's confidence in the ability of the German military to inflict considerable brutality further strengthened his determination to pursue an exceedingly ambitious plan of territorial aggrandizement. He said, "I shall shoot everyone who utters one word of criticism" and noted that "the goal to be obtained in the war is not that of reaching certain lines but of physically demolishing the opponent." In this vein, Hitler ordered his military to "be hard, be without mercy, [and] act more quickly and brutally than others...for it scares the others off." Hitler believed that enemies, not used to this type of brutality, would surrender quickly.

In addition to speed and brutality, Hitler believed that, in the end, history would overlook his inhumane conduct. To support this view, which turned out to be anything but prescient, Hitler invoked a Pollyannaish view of Asian leader Genghis Kahn. In Hitler's eyes, Kahn "sent millions of women and children into death knowingly and with a light heart," yet "history sees in him only the great founder of States."

Although Hitler brimmed with confidence and experienced initial yet widely-expected success in Poland and then in Denmark, he overlooked important considerations. In many ways, Hitler made the same mistake Napoleon Bonaparte made years earlier. Hitler believed he could advance further and conquer Britain, yet, like Napoleon, Hitler did not adequately foresee the insurmountable barrier posed by Britain's island status. Despite the damage inflicted at the hands of the German Luftwaffe during the Battle of Britain (1940), British forces eventually won this important battle. Nevertheless, Hitler pressed on and, in an even more fateful decision that carried echoes of a Napoleonic tactical misstep, invaded the USSR where his forces suffered the decisive defeat of World War II at Stalingrad in 1943. In the end, Hitler's reputation in history proved to be as brutal and decisive as the battle plans and philosophy he announced at Obersalzberg.

Q.6 According to the passage, Hitler's confidence in his military strategy stemmed from its:

A. Surprise invasions
B. Emphasis on unconventional warfare
C. Reliance on air supremacy
D. Swift brutality

Q.7 The author of the passage is primarily concerned with explaining:

A. The logistics of Hitler's war strategy and the mechanics of its failure
B. The philosophy of Hitler's war strategy and the world's reaction
C. Why Hitler believed his war plans would succeed and why they eventually failed
D. Hitler's plans and their failure with an eye to pre-1900 history

Q.8 Which of the following best characterizes the author's view of the relationship between Hitler and Napoleon?

A. Governed with similar styles
B. Fought military conflicts with similar ideologies
C. In general, shared a legacy as overly ambitious leaders
D. At a high-level, some similarities in military missteps existed

Q.9 According to the passage, what best describes the author's understanding of why Hitler's military campaign eventually failed?

A. Failed to demoralize opponents
B. Overlooked important tactical and geographic considerations
C. Underestimated international resolve
D. Fell behind technological advancements of European enemies

Q.10 According to the passage, Hitler's confidence in the war plans announced at Obersalzberg stemmed from all of the following EXCEPT:

A. The speed of the German military
B. The brutality of the German military
C. The plan to stifle dissent
D. The history of overlooking European military brutality

Management Data Interpretation

Ques (11-15):Direction: Study the following pie-diagrams carefully and answer the question given below it:

Percentage Composition of Human Body

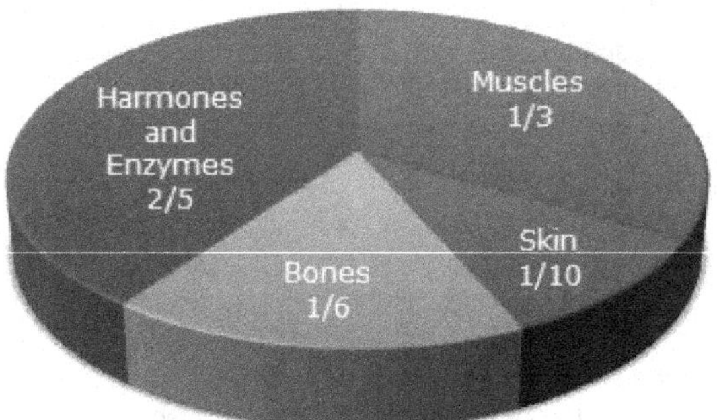

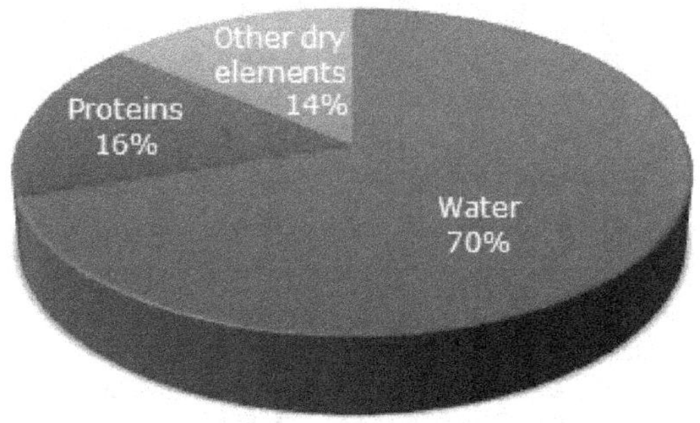

Q.11 What percent of the total weight of the human body is equivalent to the weight of the proteins in the skin in the human body?

A. 0.016 **B.** 1.6

C. 0.16 **D.** Data inadequate

Q.12 What will be the quantity of water in the body of a person weighing 50 kg?

A. 20 kg **B.** 35 kg **C.** 41 kg **D.** 42.5 kg

Q.13 What is the ratio of the distribution of proteins in the muscles to that of the distribution of proteins in the bones?

A. 1:18 **B.** 1:2 **C.** 2:1 **D.** 18:1

Q.14 To show the distribution of proteins and other dry elements in the human body, the arc of the circle should subtend at the centre an angle of:

A. 54° **B.** 126° **C.** 108° **D.** 252°

Q.15 In the human body, what part is made of neither bones nor skin?

A. $\frac{1}{40}$ **B.** $\frac{3}{80}$

C. $\frac{2}{5}$ **D.** None of these

Ques (16-20):Direction: Study the following line graph which gives the number of students who joined and left the school in the beginning of the year for six years, from 1996 to 2001.

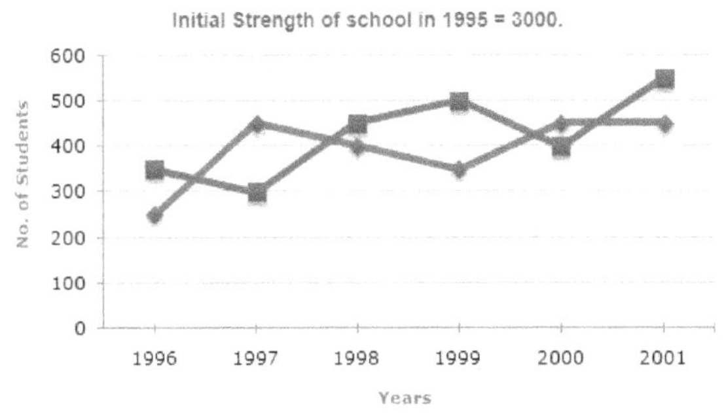

Q.16 The number of students studying in the school during 1999 was?'

A. 2950 **B.** 3000 **C.** 3100 **D.** 3150

Q.17 The strength of school increased/decreased from 1997 to 1998 by approximately what percent?

A. 1.2% **B.** 1.7% **C.** 2.1% **D.** 2.4%

Q.18 The number of students studying in the school in 1998 was what percent of the number of students studying in the school in 2001?

A. 92.13% **B.** 93.75% **C.** 96.88% **D.** 97.25%

Q.19 During which of the following pairs of years, the strength of the school was the same?

A. 1999 and 2001 **B.** 1998 and 2000

C. 1997 and 1998 **D.** 1996 and 2000

Q.20 Among the given years, the largest number of students joined the school in the year?

A. 1996 **B.** 1998 **C.** 2001 **D.** 2000

Ques (21-25):Direction: Study the following table and answer the questions.

Subject	Marks out of 50				
	40 **and above**	30 **and above**	20 **and above**	10 **and above**	0 **and above**
Physics	9	32	80	92	100
Chemistry	4	21	66	81	100
Average (Aggregate)	7	27	73	87	100

Q.21 What is the difference between the number of students passed with 30 as cut-off marks in Chemistry and those passed with 30 as cut-off marks in aggregate?

A. 3 **B.** 4 **C.** 5 **D.** 6

Q.22 If at least 60% marks in Physics are required for pursuing higher studies in Physics, how many students will be eligible to pursue higher studies in Physics?

A. 27 **B.** 32 **C.** 34 **D.** 41

Q.23 The percentage of a number of students getting at least 60% marks in Chemistry over those getting at least 40% marks in aggregate, is approximate?

A. 21% **B.** 27% **C.** 29% **D.** 31%

Q.24 The number of students scoring less than 40% marks in aggregate is?

A. 13 **B.** 19 **C.** 20 **D.** 27

Q.25 If it is known that at least 23 students were eligible for a Symposium on Chemistry, then the minimum qualifying marks in Chemistry for eligibility to Symposium would lie in the range?

A. 40 – 45 **B.** 30 – 40

C. 20 – 30 **D.** Below 20

Business Awareness

Q.26 Who is the author of the famous Management book "The Seven Habits of Highly Effective People"?

A. Peter Drucker **B.** Steve Covey

C. Henry Ford **D.** David Ogilvy

Q.27 Which newspaper has the motto - Journalism of Courage?

A. The Hindustan Times

B. The Washington Post

C. The Indian Express

D. The Guardian

Q.28 Devaluation is said to occur when the exchange rate is _____.

A. Decreased **B.** Increased

C. Kept constant **D.** None of these

Q.29 With reference to the Exchange rate, consider the following statements:

1. Managed floating exchange rate system is a mixture of a flexible exchange rate system and a fixed rate system.

2. In dirty floating, central banks intervene to buy and sell foreign currencies in an attempt to moderate exchange rate movements whenever they feel that such actions are appropriate.

Select the correct answer using the code given below.

A. 1 only **B.** 2 only
C. Both 1 and 2 **D.** Neither 1 nor 2

Q.30 Business means:

A. Commerce
B. Industry and commerce
C. Trade and commerce
D. Selling and buying of goods

Q.31 Which Company took over Hindustan Zinc Limited (HZL)?

A. Binani Zinc **B.** Reliance
C. Gujrat Ambuja **D.** Sterlite

Q.32 What is the corporate entity of the ISRO?

A. Space Sanchar Nigam Ltd
B. Antrix Corporation
C. Nakshatra Nigam Ltd
D. Mahajagatik Pradhikaran

Q.33 A valid definition of a business purpose is to _____.

A. Create a customer
B. Maximize profits
C. Serve society
D. Increase the wealth of the firm

Q.34 Memorandum of Association of a firm contains ______.

A. Rules regarding the internal management of the company
B. Rules regarding the constitution and activities of the company
C. Rules regarding external management
D. Rules regarding the constitution

Q.35 Successful managers are

A. Efficient & effective
B. Strict to employees
C. Wrong Policymakers
D. Wrong decision-makers

// Smart Answer Sheet //

Correct Indicates percentage of students who answered questions correctly.

Skipped Indicates percentage of students who skipped questions.

Q.	Ans.	Correct	Skipped
1	A	77.31 %	11.5 %
2	A	61.47 %	33.81 %
3	C	82.18 %	14.38 %
4	C	53.64 %	45.3 %
5	A	82.26 %	12.56 %
6	D	84.88 %	13.46 %
7	C	48.06 %	34.05 %
8	D	55.75 %	43.87 %
9	B	65.1 %	33.09 %
10	D	64.16 %	30.27 %
11	B	42.82 %	47.29 %
12	B	25.44 %	70.47 %
13	C	67.55 %	32.03 %
14	C	81.76 %	11.98 %
15	D	82.39 %	11.03 %
16	D	81.04 %	10.5 %
17	B	19.59 %	67.47 %
18	B	81.57 %	14.6 %
19	D	62.81 %	36.62 %
20	C	43.24 %	47.46 %
21	D	50.3 %	31.01 %
22	B	81.08 %	10.16 %
23	C	41.39 %	40.89 %
24	D	48.84 %	38.19 %
25	C	67.86 %	31.27 %
26	B	43.47 %	43.85 %
27	C	59.47 %	31.44 %
28	B	67.35 %	30.52 %
29	C	56.12 %	30.62 %
30	B	81.84 %	12.11 %
31	D	47.0 %	52.34 %
32	B	45.01 %	47.4 %
33	A	83.44 %	16.3 %
34	B	58.87 %	35.39 %
35	A	52.65 %	33.01 %

Performance Analysis	
Avg. Score (%)	51.43%
Toppers Score (%)	74.29%
Your Score	

//Hints and Solutions//

1. The passage mentions- "This comes a few years after actress Nandita Das launched the "Dark is Beautiful" campaign to encourage Indians to embrace a wider definition of beauty." points at option (A) which mirrors the context of this statement.

Option (B) can be eliminated as it is extreme and not true with respect to the notion of the campaign.

Option (C) can be ruled out as it is not the reason behind the campaign.

Option (D) can be eliminated as it contradicts the fundamental idea of the campaign.

Hence, the correct option is (A).

2. Option (A) is corroborated by the sentence "According to a 2015 research report by Nielsen, urban Indian men believe that fair skin can improve professional prospects."

As per the passage, all the other options are incorrect.

Hence, the correct option is (A).

3. The word "trounce" means 'to express sharp disapproval or criticism of someone'.

Option (A) can be eliminated as "vacillation" means 'indecision', it is unrelated in meaning to the given word.

Option (B) can be eliminated as "temerity" means 'excessive confidence or boldness', it is unrelated in meaning to the given word.

Option (C) is apt as "lambaste" means 'to criticize someone harshly' and is synonymous with the given word.

Option (D) can be eliminated as "nefarious" means 'wicked or criminal' it is unrelated to the given word.

Hence, the correct option is (C).

4. The passage talks about the reign of fairness products prevalent mainly in India. The author points out how fairness companies have used the cultural notion of light skin being a scale to judge beauty. The author then describes the partiality of Indians towards fair skin which is gradually diminishing due to growing awareness among consumers who endorse beauty products.

A didactic tone implies that the author is trying to teach/introduce a new concept to the readers.

A skeptical tone implies that the author has a dismissive attitude towards the contents of the passage.

A descriptive tone is used when the author is examining and explaining a particular situation.

A satirical tone is used by the author when he wants to deliver a message in an indirect form or by using a prop.

Hence, the correct option is (C).

5. The passage essentially talks about how we Indians are drawn towards the fairness syndrome and how this stance is changing thanks to the awareness among people that beauty companies are a farce and that natural skin tone is better rather than becoming fair. This is evident in option (A).

Option (B) can be eliminated as it points at men being overtly fond of fairness products leaving the fact that even women obsess over such products.

Option (C) can be ruled out as it talks only about brand marketing and does not take anything else into consideration.

Option (D) can be ruled out as there is no inkling towards the brands being frivolous.

Hence, the correct option is (A).

6. Beginning in the second paragraph, the author explains why Hitler felt confident in his military strategy:

2nd Paragraph: "Chief among Hitler's sources of confidence in Germany's brazen war plans was German military quickness. Hitler said, 'Our strength lies in our quickness.'"

3rd Paragraph: The military's ability "to inflict considerable brutality".

4th Paragraph: History would overlook brutality.

Aggregating together the points from above, we can conclude that Hitler's confidence in his military strategy came from: (1) speed (2) brutality.

This summarizes the two main sources of confidence.

Hence, the correct option is (D).

7. In order to understand the main thrust of the passage, examine the logical flow and main points of the passage.

1st Paragraph: Introduction
2nd Paragraph: Hitler's Sources of Confidence
3rd Paragraph: Hitler's Sources of Confidence
4th Paragraph: Hitler's Sources of Confidence
5th Paragraph: Brief Explanation of Hitler's Failure

This encapsulates the author's main points and line of argument.

Hence, the correct option is (C).

8. The passage of interest is:

"In many ways, Hitler made the same mistake Napoleon Bonaparte made years earlier. Hitler believed he could conquer Britain, yet, like Napoleon, Hitler did not adequately foresee the insurmountable barrier posed by Britain's island status. Hitler pressed on and, in an even more fateful decision that carried echoes of a Napoleonic tactical misstep, invaded the USSR".

This answer matches the author's assertion (shown in the quote above) that both Napoleon and Hitler made mistakes in dealing with Britain.

Hence, the correct option is (D).

9. The part of the passage that is of special interest is:

"He overlooked important considerations. Hitler believed he could advance further and conquer Britain, yet, like Napoleon, Hitler did not adequately foresee the insurmountable barrier posed by Britain's island status. Hitler pressed on and, in an even more fateful decision that carried echoes of a Napoleonic tactical misstep, invaded the USSR where his forces suffered the decisive defeat of World War II".

This passage indicates that Hitler made mistakes in overlooking geographical considerations (i.e., "Britain's island status") and tactical considerations (i.e., "echoes of a Napoleonic tactical misstep").

This answer matches the author's explanation, given in the final paragraph.

Hence, the correct option is (B).

10. The passage never mentions that history overlooked the brutality of a European military. Instead, the passage cites Hitler's recollection of history's positive outlook on "Asian leader Genghis Kahn".

Hence, the correct option is (D).

11. Let, the bodyweight be x kg.

Then, weight of skin protein in the body $= [16\%$ of $\left(\frac{1}{10}\right.$ of $\left.x\right)]$ kg

$= \left(\frac{16}{1000}x\right)$ kg

$\therefore$ Required percentage $= \left[\frac{\left(\frac{16x}{1000}\right)}{x} \times 100\right]\% = 1.6\%$

Hence, the correct option is (B).

12. According to the question,

Quantity of water in the body of a person weighing 50 kg $=$ $(70\%$ of $50)$ kg

$= 35$ kg

Hence, the correct option is (B).

13. Distribution of proteins in the muscles $= 16\%$ of $\frac{1}{3}$

Distribution of proteins in bones $= 16\%$ of $\frac{1}{6}$

Required ratio $= \frac{16\% \text{ of} \frac{1}{3}}{16\% \text{ of} \frac{1}{6}}$

$= \frac{6}{3} = \frac{2}{1}$

$= 2:1$

Hence, the correct option is (C).

14. Percentage of proteins and other dry elements in the body $= (16\% + 14\%)$

$= 30\%$

Therefore, Central angle corresponding to proteins and other dry elements together $= 30\%$ of $360°$

$= 108°$

Hence, the correct option is (C).

15. Part of the body made of bones $= \frac{1}{6}$

Part of the body made of skin $= \frac{1}{10}$

Part of the body made of neither bones nor skin

$= 1 - \left(\frac{1}{6} + \frac{1}{10}\right)$

$= \frac{11}{15}$

Hence, the correct option is (D).

16. Given,

Number of students in $1995 = 3000$

Number of students in $1996 = 3000 - 250 + 350 = 3100$

Number of students in $1997 = 3100 - 450 + 300 = 2950$

Number of students in $1998 = 2950 - 400 + 450 = 3000$

Number of students in $1999 = 3000 - 350 + 500 = 3150$

Hence, the correct option is (D).

17. Important data noted from the given graph:

In 1996: Number of students left $= 250$ and a number of students joined $= 350$.

In 1997: Number of students left $= 450$ and a number of students joined $= 300$.

In 1998: Number of students left $= 400$ and number of students joined $= 450$.

In 1999: Number of students left $= 350$ and number of students joined $= 500$.

In 2000: Number of students left $= 450$ and number of students joined $= 400$.

In 2001: Number of students left $= 450$ and number of students joined $= 550$.

Therefore, the numbers of students studying in the school (i.e., strength of the school) in various years:

In $1995 = 3000$ (given)

In $1996 = 3000 - 250 + 350 = 3100$

In $1997 = 3100 - 450 + 300 = 2950$.

In $1998 = 2950 - 400 + 450 = 3000$

In $1999 = 3000 - 350 + 500 = 3150$

In $2000 = 3150 - 450 + 400 = 3100$

In $2001 = 3100 - 450 + 550 = 3200$

Percentage increase in the strength of the school from 1997 to $1998 = \left[\frac{(3000-2950}{2950} \times 100\right]\%$

$= 1.69\% \approx 1.7\%$

Hence, the correct option is (B).

18. Given,

Number of students in $1995 = 3000$

Number of students in $1996 = 3000 - 250 + 350 = 3100$

Number of students in $1997 = 3100 - 450 + 300 = 2950$

Number of students in $1998 = 2950 - 400 + 450 = 3000$

Number of students studying in the school in $2001 = 3200$

Therefore, Required percentage $= \left(\frac{3000}{3200} \times 100\right)\% = 93.75\%$

Hence, the correct option is (B).

19. Important data noted from the given graph :

In 1996: Number of students left $= 250$ and a number of students joined $= 350$.

In 1997: Number of students left $= 450$ and a number of students joined $= 300$.

In 1998: Number of students left $= 400$ and number of students joined $= 450$.

In 1999: Number of students left $= 350$ and a number of students joined $= 500$.

In 2000: Number of students left $= 450$ and a number of students joined $= 400$.

In 2001: Number of students left $= 450$ and a number of students joined $= 550$.

Therefore, the numbers of students studying in the school (i.e., the strength of the school) in various years :

In $1995 = 3000$ (given)

In $1996 = 3000 - 250 + 350 = 3100$

In $1997 = 3100 - 450 + 300 = 2950$

In $1998 = 2950 - 400 + 450 = 3000$

In $1999 = 3000 - 350 + 500 = 3150$

In $2000 = 3150 - 450 + 400 = 3100$

In $2001 = 3100 - 450 + 550 = 3200$

As calculated above, in the years 1996 and 2000 the strength of the school was the same i.e., 3100.

Hence, the correct option is (D).

20. Important data noted from the given graph:

In 1996: Number of students left $= 250$ and a number of students joined $= 350$.

In 1997: Number of students left $= 450$ and a number of students joined $= 300$.

In 1998 : Number of students left $= 400$ and number of students joined $= 450$.

In 1999: Number of students left $= 350$ and a number of students joined $= 500$.

In 2000: Number of students left $= 450$ and a number of students joined $= 400$.

In 2001: Number of students left $= 450$ and a number of students joined $= 550$.

Therefore, the numbers of students studying in the school (i.e., the strength of the school) in various years:

In $1995 = 3000$ (given)

In $1996 = 3000 - 250 + 350 = 3100$

In $1997 = 3100 - 450 + 300 = 2950$

In $1998 = 2950 - 400 + 450 = 3000$

In $1999 = 3000 - 350 + 500 = 3150$

In $2000 = 3150 - 450 + 400 = 3100$

In $2001 = 3100 - 450 + 550 = 3200$

As calculated above, the largest number of students (i.e., 550) joined the school in the year 2001.

Hence, the correct option is (C).

21. Required difference $=$ (Number of students scoring 30 and above marks in Chemistry) $-$ (Number of students scoring 30 and above marks in aggregate)

$= 27 - 21$

$= 6$

Hence, the correct option is (D).

22. We have 60% of $50=\left(\frac{60}{100}\times 50\right)=30$

$\therefore$ Required number $=$ Number of students scoring 30 and above marks in Physics $=32$

Hence, the correct option is (B).

23. Number of students getting at least 60% marks in Chemistry $=$ Number of students getting 30 and above marks in Chemistry

$=21$

Number of students getting at least 40% marks in aggregate $=$ Number of students getting 20 and above marks in aggregate

$=73$

Required percentage $=\left(\frac{21}{73}\times 100\right)\%$

$=28.77\%$

$\approx 29\%$

Hence, the correct option is (C).

24. We have 40% of $50=\left(\frac{40}{100}\times 50\right)=20$

$\therefore$ Required number = Number of students scoring less than 20 marks in aggreagate

$=100$ - Number of students scoring 20 and above marks in aggregate

$=100-73$

$=27$

Hence, the correct option is (D).

25. Since 66 students get 20 and above marks in Chemistry and out of this 21 students get 30 and above marks, therefore to select top 35 students in Chemistry, the qualifying marks should lie in the range $20-30$.

Hence, the correct option is (C).

26. "The Seven Habits of Highly Effective People" first published in 1989, is a business and self-help book written by Stephen Covey. Covey presents an approach to being effective in attaining goals by aligning oneself to what he calls "true north" principles based on a character ethic that he presents as universal and timeless.
Hence, the correct option is (B).

27. The Indian Express is the daily English newspaper published in India. It was founded by Shri Ramnath Goenka in 1932. It is one of the few impartial newspapers which represents the voice of the people and the oppressed. It questions the authority and power and its motto or tagline is 'Journalism of Courage.'
Hence, the correct option is (C).

28. Devaluation is said to occur when the exchange rate is increased by social action under a pegged exchange rate system. The opposite of devaluation is a revaluation. Or, the government may choose to leave the exchange rate unchanged and deal with the BoP problem by the use of the monetary and fiscal policy.

Hence, the correct option is (B).

29. Without any formal international agreement, the world has moved on to what can be best described as a managed floating exchange rate system. It is a mixture of a flexible exchange rate system (the floating part) and a fixed rate system (the managed part).

Under this system, also called dirty floating, central banks intervene to buy and sell foreign currencies in an attempt to moderate exchange rate movements whenever they feel that such actions are appropriate. Official reserve transactions are, therefore, not equal to zero.
Hence, the correct option is (C).

30. Business means Industry and commerce. The industry is an economic activity, concerned with the procurement and processing of raw materials into finished products, that reach the customer. Commerce is a business activity, wherein exchange for goods and services for value, is done on a large scale.

Hence, the correct option is (B).

31. Sterlite Opportunities and Ventures Limited (SOVL) was merged with Sterlite Industries India Ltd in April 2011. Sterlite Industries merged with Sesa Goa Ltd to form Sesa Sterlite Limited in August 2013. Sesa Sterlite was renamed Vedanta Limited in April 2015. Hindustan Zinc is now a direct subsidiary of Vedanta Limited. Hindustan Zinc Limited (HZL) is an Indian integrated mining and resources producer of zinc, lead, silver, and cadmium.
Hence, the correct option is (D).

32. Antrix Corporation Limited (ACL), Bengaluru is a wholly owned Government of India Company under the administrative control of the Department of Space. Antrix Corporation Limited was incorporated as a private limited company owned by Government of India in September 1992 as a Marketing arm of ISRO for promotion and commercial exploitation of space products, technical consultancy services and transfer of technologies developed by Indian Space Research Organisation.
Hence, the correct option is (B).

33. A valid definition of a business purpose is to create a customer. The customer is the foundation of a business and keeps it in existence. The customer alone gives employment. And it is to supply the customer that society entrusts wealth-producing resources to the business enterprise.
Hence, the correct option is (A).

34. Memorandum of Association of a firm contains rules regarding the constitution and activities of the company. Memorandum of Association (MoA) is a legal document that specifies the scope of business activities of the company and information about the shareholding of the company. The MoA is a document prepared for the company registration procedure.
Hence, the correct option is (B).

35. Successful managers are efficient & effective. In management, operating inefficient and ineffective ways is a key to good

performance and to successfully reaching the goals set for the business. While efficiency and effectiveness are similarly desirable characteristics of business behavior, either one is often seen as attainable only at the expense of the other.
Hence, the correct option is (A).

Mock Test 09

Comprehension

Ques (1-5):Direction: Read the following passage carefully and answer the question that follows.

Marketing executives in television work with a relatively stable advertising medium. In many ways, the television ads aired today are similar to those aired two decades ago. Most television ads still feature actors, still run 30 or 60 seconds, and still show a product. However, the differing dynamics of the Internet pose unique challenges to advertisers, forcing them to adapt their practices and techniques on a regular basis.

In the early days of Internet marketing, online advertisers employed banner and pop-up ads to attract customers. These techniques reached large audiences, generated many sales leads, and came at a low cost. However, a small number of Internet users began to consider these advertising techniques intrusive and annoying. Yet because marketing strategies relying heavily on banners and pop-ups produced results, companies invested growing amounts of money into purchasing these ad types in hopes of capturing market share in the burgeoning online economy. As consumers become more sophisticated, frustration with these online advertising techniques grew. Independent programmers began to develop tools that blocked banner and pop-up ads. The popularity of these tools exploded when the search engine Google, at the time an increasingly popular website fighting to solidify its place on the Internet with giants Microsoft and Yahoo, offered free software enabling users to block pop-up ads. The backlash against banner ads grew as new web browsers provided users the ability to block image-based ads such as banner ads. Although banner and pop-up ads still exist, they are far less prominent than during the early days of the Internet.

A major development in online marketing came with the introduction of pay-per-click ads. Unlike banner or pop-up ads, which originally required companies to pay every time a website visitor saw an ad, pay-per-click ads allowed companies to pay only when an interested potential customer clicked on an ad. More importantly, however, these ads circumvented the pop-up and banner blockers. As a result of these advantages and the incredible growth in the use of search engines, which provide excellent venues for pay-per-click advertising, companies began turning to pay-per-click marketing in droves. However, as with the banner and pop-up ads that preceded them, pay-per-click ads came with their drawbacks. When companies began pouring billions of dollars into this emerging medium, online advertising specialists started to notice the presence of what would later be called click fraud: representatives of a company with no interest in the product advertised by a competitor click on the competitor's ads simply to increase the marketing cost of the competitor. Click fraud grew so rapidly that marketers sought to diversify their online positions away from pay-per-click marketing through new mediums.

Although pay-per-click advertising remains a common and effective advertising tool, marketers adapted yet again to the changing dynamics of the Internet by adopting new techniques such as pay-per-performance advertising, search engine optimization, and affiliate marketing. As the pace of the Internet's evolution increases, it seems all the more likely that advertising successfully on the Internet will require a strategy that shuns constancy and embraces change.

Q.1 The author implies what about the future of pay-per-performance advertising?

A. Although it improves on pay-per-click advertising, it is still vulnerable to click fraud.

B. It will one day become extinct as Internet users discover drawbacks with it.

C. Internet users will develop free software to block its effectiveness.

D. It will eventually become less popular with advertisers as the Internet evolves and drawbacks emerge.

Q.2 Which of the following most accurately states the main idea of the passage?

A. Although pay-per-click advertising remains a wide-spread and effective online advertising medium, its popularity is likely to diminish as the Internet evolves.

B. Internet advertising is not well received by Internet users, causing independent programmers to subvert advertisers.

C. Unlike television, the Internet has experienced dramatic changes in short periods of time.

D. Unlike television, the Internet has evolved rapidly, forcing online marketers to develop new advertising strategies and mediums.

Q.3 According to the passage, which of the following best describes the current status of pop-up ads?

A. Widely used

B. Less popular now than at earlier times

C. A frequent target of click fraud

D. Non-existent due to pop-up blockers

Q.4 According to the passage, which of the following best describes the practice of click fraud?

A. Clicking on the banner advertisements of rival companies

B. Using software to block advertisements

C. Utilizing search engine optimization to visit the pages of competitors

D. Clicking on the pay-per-click ads of competitors

Q.5 According to the passage, the largest point at which the television and Internet differ as an advertising medium is:

A. The type of individual each medium reaches

B. Whether the medium is interactive

C. The pace at which the medium evolves

D. The cost of advertising with each medium

Ques (6-10):Direction: Read the following passage carefully and answer the question that follows.

On the surface, the conquest of the Aztec empire by Herman Cortes is one of the most amazing military accomplishments in history. With a small fighting force numbering in the hundreds, Cortes led the Spanish explorers into victory against an Aztec population that many believe topped 21 million. In light of such a seemingly impossible victory, the obvious question is: how did a small group of foreign fighters manage to topple one of the world's strongest, wealthiest, and most successful military empires?

Several factors led to Cortes' success. First, the Spanish exploited animosity toward the Aztecs among rival groups and convinced thousands of locals to fight. In one account of a battle, it is recorded that at least 200,000 natives fought with Cortes. Next, the Spanish possessed superior military equipment in the form of European cannons, guns, and crossbows, leading to effective and efficient disposal of Aztec defenses. For example, Spanish cannons quickly defeated large Aztec walls that had protected the empire against big and less technically advanced armies.

Despite the Spanish advantages, the Aztecs probably could have succeeded in defending their capital city of Tenochtitlan had they leveraged their incredible population base to increase their army's size and ensured that no rogue cities would ally with Cortes. In order to accomplish this later goal, Aztec leader Motecuhzoma needed to send envoys to neighboring cities telling their inhabitants about the horrors of Spanish conquest and the inevitability of Spanish betrayal.

In addition, the Aztecs should have exploited the fact that the battle was taking place on their territory. No reason existed for the Aztecs to consent to a conventional battle, which heavily favored the Spanish. Motecuhzoma's forces should have thought outside the box and allowed Cortes into the city, only to subsequently use hundreds of thousands of fighters to prevent escape and proceed in surprise "door-to-door" combat. With this type of battle, the Aztecs would have largely thwarted Spanish technological supremacy. However, in the end, the superior weaponry of the Spanish, the pent-up resentment of Aztec rivals, the failure of Aztec diplomacy, and the lack of an unconventional Aztec war plan led to one of the most surprising military outcomes in the past one thousand years.

Q.6 Which of the following best characterizes the main point the author is trying to convey in the passage?

A. Aztec failure to fight an unconventional war led to an unnecessary defeat

B. Spanish victory was neither as impressive nor as surprising as it may first appear

C. Resentment toward the Aztecs led to their demise

D. Herman Cortes masterminded an amazing military accomplishment

Q.7 The passage is sequentially organized in which of the following ways?

A. Introduce an enigma, explain the reasons for the enigma, discuss the inevitability of the enigma

B. Define a problem, explain the sources of the problem, offer a solution to the problem

C. Introduce a mystery, offer an explanation for the mystery, provide an alternative explanation for the mystery

D. Introduce a mystery, offer an explanation for the mystery, provide an alternative explanation for the mystery

Q.8 The author implies which of the following about the Aztec view toward an unconventional military confrontation of the Spanish?

A. The Aztecs did not consider it

B. The Aztecs considered it, but rejected it out of beliefs about how battles ought to be fought,

C. The Aztecs considered this, but it was too late

D. The Aztecs were certain a victory could be achieved via traditional combat

Q.9 According to the passage, all of the following led to Cortes' success EXCEPT:

A. Advanced crossbows

B. Nimble military force

C. Local Spanish allies

D. Local tribal friction

Q.10 Which of the following best characterizes the author's view about the inevitability of Aztec demise at the hands of the Spanish?

A. Absolutely Inevitable

B. Likely Inevitable

C. Ambivalent

D. Likely Not Inevitable

Management Data Interpretation

Ques (11-15):Direction: Study the following graph and the table and answer the questions given below.

Data of different states regarding population of states in the year 1998.

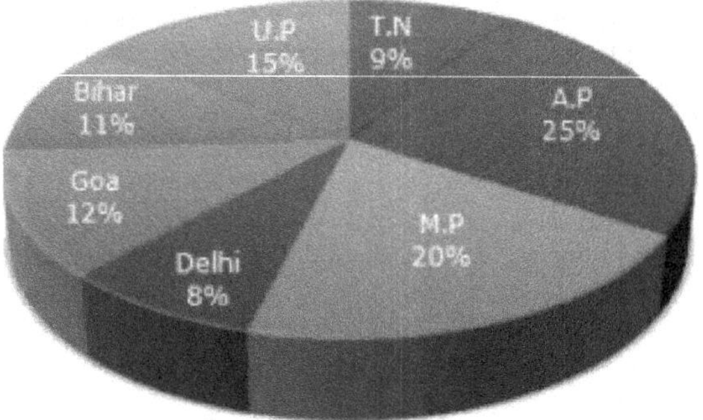

Total population of the given States $= 3276000$.

States	Sex and Literacy wise Population Ratio			
	Sex		Literacy	
	M	F	Literate	Illiterate
A.P	5	3	2	7
M.P	3	1	1	4
Delhi	2	3	2	1
Goa	3	5	3	2
Bihar	3	4	4	1

U.P.	3	2	7	2
T.N.	3	4	9	4

Q.11 What will be the percentage of the total number of males in U.P., M.P. and Goa together to the total population of all the given states?

A. 25% **B.** 27.5% **C.** 28.5% **D.** 31.5%

Q.12 What was the total number of illiterate people in A.P. and M.P. in 1998?

A. 876040 **B.** 932170 **C.** 981550 **D.** 1161160

Q.13 What is the ratio of the number of females in T.N. to the number of females in Delhi?

A. 7:5 **B.** 9:7 **C.** 13:11 **D.** 15:14

Q.14 What was the number of males in U.P. in the year 1998?

A. 254650 **B.** 294840 **C.** 321470 **D.** 341200

Q.15 If in the year 1998, there was an increase of 10% in the population of U.P. and 12% in the population of M.P. compared to the previous year, then what was the ratio of populations of U.P. and M.P. in 1997?

A. 42:55 **B.** 48:55 **C.** 7:11 **D.** 4:5

Ques (16-20):Direction: In a school, the periodical examination are held every second month. In a session during April 2001 - March 2002, a student of Class IX appeared for each of the periodical exams. The aggregate marks obtained by him in each periodical exam are represented in the line-graph given below.

Marks Obtained by the student in Six Periodical Held in Every Two Months During the Year in the Session 2001 – 2002.

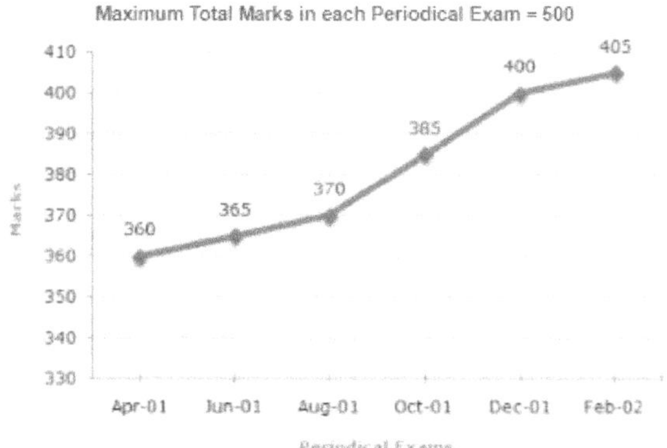

Q.16 In which periodical exams did the student obtain the highest percentage increase in marks over the previous periodical exams?

A. June, 01 **B.** August, 01
C. Oct, 01 **D.** Dec, 01

Q.17 The total number of marks obtained in February 02 is what per cent of the total marks obtained in April 01?

A. 110% **B.** 112.5% **C.** 115% **D.** 116.5%

Q.18 What is the percentage of marks obtained by the student in the periodical exams of August, 01 and Oct, 01 taken together?

A. 73.25% **B.** 75.5% **C.** 77% **D.** 78.75%

Q.19 What are the average marks obtained by the student in all the periodical exams during the last session?

A. 373 **B.** 379 **C.** 381 **D.** 385

Q.20 In which periodical exams there is a fall in the percentage of marks as compared to the previous periodical exams?

A. None **B.** June, 01 **C.** Oct, 01 **D.** Feb, 02

Ques (21-25):Direction: Study the following table and answer the questions based on it.

Number of Candidates Appeared, Qualified and Selected in a Competitive Examination from Five States Delhi, H.P, U.P, Punjab and Haryana Over the Years 1994 to 1998.

Year	Delhi			H.P			U.P			Punjab			Haryana		
	App	Qual	Sel	App	Qual	Sel	App	Qual	Sel	App	Qual	Sel	App	Qual	Sel
1997	8000	850	94	7800	810	82	7500	720	78	8200	680	85	6400	700	75
1998	4800	500	48	7500	800	65	5600	620	85	6800	600	70	7100	650	75
1999	7500	640	82	7400	560	70	4800	400	48	6500	525	65	5200	350	55
2000	9500	850	90	8800	920	86	7000	650	70	7800	720	84	6400	540	60
2001	9000	800	70	7200	850	75	8500	950	80	5700	485	60	4500	600	75

Q.21 For which state the average number of candidates selected over the years is the maximum?

A. Delhi **B.** H.P **C.** U.P **D.** Punjab

Q.22 The percentage of candidates qualified from Punjab over those appeared from Punjab is highest in the year?

A. 1997 **B.** 1998 **C.** 1999 **D.** 2000

Q.23 In the year 1997, which state had the lowest percentage of candidates selected over the candidates appeared?

A. Delhi **B.** H.P **C.** U.P **D.** Punjab

Q.24 The number of candidates selected from Haryana during the period under review is approximately what percent of the number selected from Delhi during this period?

A. 79.5% **B.** 81% **C.** 84.5% **D.** 88.5

Q.25 The percentage of candidates selected from U.P over those qualified from U.P is highest in the year?

A. 1997 **B.** 1998 **C.** 1999 **D.** 2001

Business Awareness

Q.26 Which of the following is the most important objective of Human Resource Management (HRM)?

A. Minimize the role of humans by replacing them with machines
B. Teach humans how to deal with stress in the workplace
C. Ensure people are kept busy in the organization
D. Proper utilization of available skilled workforce

Q.27 Which of the following is not a part of the Planning function of Human Resource Management (HRM)?

A. Establish goals
B. Develop rules and procedures
C. Establish departments/divisions
D. Develop forecasting methods

Q.28 In the production approach of calculating GDP, how do we calculate GDP at market prices?

A. Value-added at basic prices + taxes on goods and services – subsidies on goods and services
B. Total National Income + Sales Taxes + Depreciation + Net Foreign Factor Income
C. Value-added at basic prices - taxes on goods and services + subsidies on goods and services.
D. Consumption (C) + Investment (I) + Government Spending (G) + Net Exports

Q.29 Which of the following is/are true about the National Productivity Council of India?

I. It is an autonomous, multipartite, non-profit organization under the Department of Commerce, Ministry of Commerce & Industry.

II. It has equal representation from employers' & workers' organizations and the Government.

III. The National Productivity Week's theme for 2018 was "Industry 4.0 Leapfrog Opportunity for India ".

A. Only I **B.** Only II
C. Only I and II **D.** Only II and III

Q.30 The agreement of partnership ______.

A. must be oral
B. must be in writing
C. can be either oral or in writing
D. must be in writing on a stamp paper

Q.31 Which of the following is NOT a goal of Human Resource Management (HRM)?

A. Integration of HRM with the corporate strategy of the Organization
B. Producing the desired human behavior that helps to achieve Organisations goals
C. Creation of a flexible environment that can easily adopt change
D. To endure proper delivery of products

Q.32 Which of the following approach emphasizes the "effect of psychological and social factors on employees" performance?

A. Scientific approach
B. Rational approach
C. Human relations approach
D. Systematic approach

Q.33 As per Budget 2018-19, The Government has exempted the profits of Farmer Producer Companies (FPC) from tax for a period of _______ years?

A. 4 years **B.** 2 years **C.** 5 years **D.** 7 years

Q.34 Business means _______.

A. commerce
B. industry and commerce
C. trade and commerce
D. selling and buying of goods

Q.35 The primary aim of co-operative is to _______.

A. earn more profits **B.** serve the members
C. raise production **D.** raise more money

// Smart Answer Sheet //

Correct — Indicates percentage of students who answered questions correctly.

Skipped — Indicates percentage of students who skipped questions.

Q.	Ans.	Correct	Skipped
1	D	68.21 %	30.21 %
2	D	50.23 %	48.07 %
3	B	55.01 %	39.85 %
4	D	45.59 %	40.55 %
5	C	46.13 %	33.87 %
6	B	44.28 %	42.73 %
7	A	63.98 %	30.19 %
8	A	42.7 %	44.29 %
9	B	40.8 %	36.45 %
10	D	56.07 %	33.06 %
11	C	89.89 %	10.02 %
12	D	69.47 %	30.29 %
13	D	88.79 %	10.99 %
14	B	79.18 %	10.48 %
15	A	60.23 %	30.95 %
16	C	41.39 %	56.89 %
17	B	87.53 %	10.82 %
18	B	82.16 %	17.1 %
19	C	79.78 %	18.2 %
20	A	87.87 %	11.91 %
21	A	18.31 %	72.03 %
22	D	55.58 %	38.7 %
23	D	51.12 %	31.23 %
24	D	86.85 %	11.02 %
25	B	66.6 %	32.49 %
26	D	48.47 %	40.0 %
27	C	69.73 %	30.12 %
28	A	52.72 %	33.04 %
29	D	59.54 %	38.11 %
30	C	46.85 %	45.05 %
31	D	50.48 %	47.76 %
32	C	45.19 %	41.97 %
33	C	45.04 %	49.94 %
34	B	77.61 %	11.62 %
35	B	86.83 %	10.22 %

Performance Analysis	
Avg. Score (%)	57.14%
Toppers Score (%)	65.71%
Your Score	

//Hints and Solutions//

1. The central theme of the passage is that the Internet is evolving rapidly and current advertising mediums will eventually be replaced (albeit not completely) by new mediums. Just after mentioning pay-per-performance advertising, the author concludes by saying "As the pace of the Internet's evolution increases, it seems all the more likely that advertising successfully on the Internet will require a strategy that shuns constancy and embraces change."

(A) There is no mention of click-fraud applying to pay-per-performance advertising. Since click-fraud does not apply to all online advertising methods and no description of pay-per-performance advertising is given, it is not possible to infer that click-fraud applies to pay-per-performance advertising.

(B) The passage never asserts that Internet ad strategies become "extinct." Rather it asserts that they dwindle in popularity as Internet users adapt and the ad strategies become less effective.

(C) Developing software to block ads referred to the problem with pop-up and banner advertisements. The article never implied that this problem existed with all Internet advertising strategies.

(D) Since the main point of the article is that the Internet evolves and online advertising strategies change, it is reasonable to conclude that pay-per-performance advertising will have a similar fate as the other advertising strategies mentioned in the passage: declining popularity over time.

Hence, the correct option is (D).

2. This statement encapsulates the author's point in each paragraph: the evolution of the Internet is forcing advertisers to change their strategies rapidly. The phrase "unlike the television" ties into the introductory point.

(A) While the passage does make these statements about pay-per-click advertising, the passage only discusses pay-per-click advertising in one paragraph. This answer represents an example that the author uses to further the main point of the passage. But, it is not the main point itself.

(B) Although the changing of Internet marketing strategies is a constant theme, nowhere does the article focus as its main point on the efforts of independent programmers. Instead, the passage focuses on the efforts of advertisers to adapt to changes. Moreover, this answer fails to make sense of the introduction and conclusion.

(C) Although this statement is true, it is far too broad. The central theme of the passage (given in the sentence "forcing them to adapt their practices and techniques on a regular basis") is not reflected in this answer, which omits any reference to marketing and advertising strategies.

(D) This statement encapsulates the author's point in each paragraph: the evolution of the Internet is forcing advertisers to change their strategies rapidly. The phrase "unlike the television" ties into the introductory point.

Hence, the correct option is (D).

3. The crucial sentence in the passage is: "Although banner and pop-up ads still exist, they are far less prominent than during the early days of the Internet."

(A) There is no support for this in the passage. It is implicitly contradicted by the words "far less prominent."

(B) This answer reflects the statement in the passage.

(C) Pay-per-click advertising is a target of "click fraud," not banner ads, which suffered from blocking programs.

(D) The passage states that pop-ups "still exist."

Hence, the correct option is (B).

4. The pertinent sentence from the passage is: "pay-per-click ads came with their drawbacks. When companies began pouring billions of dollars into this emerging medium, online advertising specialists started to notice the presence of what would later be called "click fraud": representatives of a company with no interest in the product a competitor advertised clicked on the competitor's ads simply to increase the marketing cost of the competitor."

(A) Click-fraud pertains to pay-per-click advertising, not banner advertising.

(B) This answer describes pop-up blockers, not click fraud.

(C) Click-fraud pertains to pay-per-click advertising, not search engine optimization.

(D) This matches the description of click-fraud in the passage.

Hence, the correct option is (D).

5. The key sentences are at the beginning, where television and the Internet are compared: "In many ways, the television ads aired today are similar to those aired two decades ago. Most television ads still feature actors, still run 30 or 60 seconds, and still show a product. However, the differing dynamics of the Internet pose unique challenges to advertisers, forcing them to adapt their practices and techniques on a regular basis."

(A) There is no mention of the type of individual.

(B) Although there is a difference in whether the medium is interactive, this is never mentioned in the text.

(C) This key difference is an important theme in the passage and is mentioned in the beginning.

(D) The article never mentions cost.

Hence, the correct option is (C).

6. In order to ascertain the main point that the author is trying to make, it is important to examine the logical flow of the passage.

1st Paragraph: Explain a seemingly amazing accomplishment and ask whether it really is as impressive as it first appears.

2nd Paragraph: Explain factors that made the impressive accomplishment not as impressive.

3rd Paragraph: Explain how the seemingly amazing accomplishment didn't have to turn out the way it did.

4th Paragraph: Explain how the seemingly amazing accomplishment didn't have to turn out the way it did.

(A) The Aztec failure to fight in an unconventional manner is discussed only in the last paragraph and is mentioned only to make a larger point: the fall of the Aztec was not as impressive as it originally appeared.

(B) This encapsulates the logical flow and main points of the passage.

(C) This topic is only discussed during part of the second paragraph and is mentioned only to make a larger point: the fall of the Aztec was not as impressive as it originally appeared.

(D) The main point of the passage is to challenge this common belief and point out that it was not as amazing as is often asserted.

Hence, the correct option is (B).

7. In order to see the sequential ordering, break down the logical flow of the passage.

1st Paragraph: Introduce something that looks very impressive on the surface and ask how it happened.

2nd Paragraph: Offer several factors that help explain what seemed so impressive and unbelievable.

3rd Paragraph: Provide several ways that the seemingly unbelievable was not inevitable.

4th Paragraph: Continue with paragraph 3. Conclude by noting that the seemingly unbelievable and unexplainable was both explainable and not inevitable.

To summarize the sequential organization:

Introduce an enigma ("how did a small group of foreign fighters manage to topple one of the world's strongest, wealthiest, and most successful military empires?")

Explain reasons for the enigma (2nd paragraph)

Discuss the inevitability of the enigma (3rd and 4th paragraphs)

(A) This matches the sequential order explained above.

(B) The third and fourth paragraphs are not offering a solution to a problem but rather discussing the inevitability of an outcome.

(C) The third and fourth paragraphs are not providing an alternative explanation for the mystery but rather discussing the inevitability of the mystery.

(D) The third and fourth paragraphs are not providing an alternative answer to the question but rather discussing the inevitability of the mystery.

Hence, the correct option is (A).

8. The author never mentions that the Aztecs had a view toward an unconventional military conflict with the Spanish. The topic is mentioned only as the author notes that the Aztecs should have pursued this type of confrontation with the Spanish. Further, when the author did mention unconventional combat, he prefaced it with the statement: "Motecuhzoma's forces should have thought outside the box." Based upon these facts, our best inference is that the Aztecs did not ever consider an unconventional military confrontation with Cortes.

(A) This seems to be implied in the author's suggestion that "Motecuhzoma's forces should have thought outside the box."

(B) The passage never mentions nor implies that the Aztecs considered an unconventional military confrontation with the Spanish.

(C) The passage never mentions nor implies that the Aztecs considered an unconventional military confrontation with the Spanish.

(D) The passage never mentions nor implies that the Aztecs were certain they could achieve victory in a traditional means.

Hence, the correct option is (A).

9. (A) The passage mentions this as a source of success: "the Spanish possessed superior military equipment in the form of European cannons, guns, and crossbows".

(B) Although the passage mentions that Cortes' army was small, it implies this as a weakness. The passage never states that the military was nimble nor does it mention this as a source of success.

(C) The passage mentions this as a source of success: "In one account of a battle, it is recorded that at least 200,000 natives fought with Cortes."

(D) The passage mentions this as a source of success: "animosity toward the Aztecs among rival groups".

Hence, the correct option is (B).

10. The relevant portion of the passage is: "Despite the Spanish advantages, the Aztecs probably could have succeeded in defending their capital city of Tenochtitlan."

(A) This does not match with the passage: "the Aztecs probably could have succeeded in defending their capital".

(B) This does not match with the passage: "the Aztecs probably could have succeeded in defending their capital".

(C) This does not match with the passage: "the Aztecs probably could have succeeded in defending their capital".

(D) This does match with the passage: "the Aztecs probably could have succeeded in defending their capital".

Hence, the correct option is (D).

11. Number of males in U.P $=[\frac{3}{5}$ of $(15\%$ of $N)] = \frac{3}{5} \times \frac{15}{100} \times N = 9 \times \frac{N}{100}$

Where, total population of given state $(N) = 3276000$.

Number of males in M.P. $= [\frac{3}{4}$ of $(20\%$ of $N)] = \frac{3}{4} \times \frac{20}{100} \times N = 15 \times \frac{N}{100}$

Number of males in Goa $= [\frac{3}{8}$ of $(12\%$ of $N)] = \frac{3}{8} \times \frac{12}{100} \times N = 4.5 \times \frac{N}{100}$

$\therefore$ Total number of males in these three states $=$

$(9 + 15 + 4.5) \times \frac{N}{100}$

$= \left(28.5 \times \frac{N}{100}\right)$

∴ Required Percentage $= \left[\frac{\left(28.5\times\frac{N}{100}\right)}{N} \times 100\right] \% =$

28.5%

Hence, the correct option is (C).

12. No. of illiterate people in A.P. $= [\frac{7}{9}$ of $(25\%$ of $3276000] = 637000$

No. of illiterate people in M.P. $= [\frac{4}{5}$ of $(20\%$ of $3276000] = 524160$

∴ Total number $= (637000 + 524160) = 1161160$

Hence, the correct option is (D).

13. Required ratio $= \frac{\frac{4}{7}\text{ of } (9\% \text{ of } 3276000)}{\frac{3}{5}\text{ of } (8\% \text{ of } 3276000)}$

$= \frac{\left(\frac{4}{7}\times9\right)}{\left(\frac{3}{5}\times8\right)}$

$= \left(\frac{4}{7} \times 9 \times \frac{5}{3} \times \frac{1}{8}\right)$

$= \frac{15}{14}$

Hence, the correct option is (D).

14. Number of males in U.P. $= [\frac{3}{5}$ of $(15\%$ of $3276000)]$

$= \frac{3}{5} \times \frac{15}{100} \times 3726000$

$= 294840$

Hence, the correct option is (B).

15. Let x be the population of U.P. in 1997 . Then,

Population of U.P. in $1998 = 110\%$ of $x = \frac{110}{100} \times x$

Also, let y be the population of M.P. in 1997. Then,

Population of M.P. in $1998 = 112\%$ of $y = \frac{112}{100} \times y$

Ratio of populations of U.P. and M.P. in $1998 = \frac{\left(\frac{110}{100}\times x\right)}{\left(\frac{112}{100}\times y\right)} =$

$\frac{110x}{112y}$

From the pie-chart, this ratio is $\frac{15}{20}$.

$\therefore \frac{110x}{112y} = \frac{15}{20}$

$\Rightarrow \frac{x}{y} = \frac{15}{20} \times \frac{112}{110} = \frac{42}{55}$

Thus, ratio of populations of U.P. and M.P. in $1997 = x : y = 42 : 55$

Hence, the correct option is (A).

16. Percentage increase in marks in various periodical exams compared to the previous exams are-

For Jun $01 = \left[\frac{(365-360)}{360} \times 100\right] \% = 1.39\%$

For Aug $01 = \left[\frac{(370-365)}{365} \times 100\right] \% = 1.37\%$

For Oct $01 = \left[\frac{(385-370)}{370} \times 100\right] \% = 4.05\%$

For Dec $01 = \left[\frac{(400-385)}{385} \times 100\right] \% = 3.90\%$

For Feb $02 = \left[\frac{(404-400)}{400} \times 100\right] \% = 1.25\%$

Clearly, the highest percentage increase in marks is on Oct 01.

Hence, the correct option is (C).

17. Required percentage $= \left(\frac{405}{360} \times 100\right) \%$

$= 112.5\%$

Hence, the correct option is (B).

18. Required percentage $= \left[\frac{(370+385)}{(500+500)} \times 100\right] \%$

$= \left(\frac{755}{1000} \times 100\right) \%$

$= 75.5\%$

Hence, the correct option is (B).

19. Average marks obtained in all the periodical exams $= \frac{1}{6} \times [360 + 365 + 370 + 385 + 400 + 405]$

$= 380.83$

≈ 381

Hence, the correct option is (C).

20. As is clear from the graph, the total marks obtained in periodical exams, go on increasing. Since the maximum marks for all the periodical exams are the same; it implies that the percentage of marks also goes on increasing.

Thus, in none of the periodical exams, there is a fall in the percentage of marks compared to the previous exam.

Hence, the correct option is (A).

21. The average number of candidates selected over the given period for various states are-

For Delhi $= \frac{94+48+82+90+70}{5} = \frac{384}{5} = 76.8$

For H.P. $= \frac{82+65+70+86+75}{5} = \frac{378}{5} = 75.6$

For U.P. $= \frac{78+85+48+70+80}{5} = \frac{361}{5} = 72.2$

For Punjab $= \frac{85+70+65+84+60}{5} = \frac{364}{5} = 72.8$

For Haryana $= \frac{75+75+55+60+75}{5} = \frac{340}{5} = 68$

Clearly, this average is maximum for Delhi.
Hence, the correct option is (A).

22. The percentages of candidates qualified from Punjab over those appeared from Punjab during different years are-

For $1997 = \left(\frac{680}{8200} \times 100\right)\% = 8.29\%$

For $1998 = \left(\frac{600}{6800} \times 100\right)\% = 8.82\%$

For $1999 = \left(\frac{525}{6500} \times 100\right)\% = 8.08\%$

For $2000 = \left(\frac{720}{7800} \times 100\right)\% = 9.23\%$

For $2001 = \left(\frac{485}{5700} \times 100\right)\% = 8.51\%$

Clearly, this percentage is highest for the year 2000.
Hence, the correct option is (D).

23. The percentages of candidates selected over the candidates appeared in 1997, for various states are-

(i) For Delhi $= \left(\frac{94}{8000} \times 100\right)\% = 1.175\%$

(ii) For H.P. $= \left(\frac{82}{7800} \times 100\right)\% = 1.051\%$

(iii) For U.P. $= \left(\frac{78}{7500} \times 100\right)\% = 1.040\%$

(iv) For Punjab $\left(\frac{85}{8200} \times 100\right)\% = 1.037\%$

(v) For Haryana $\left(\frac{75}{6400} \times 100\right)\% = 1.172\%$

Clearly, this percentage is the lowest for Punjab.
Hence, the correct option is (D).

24. Required percentage $= \left[\frac{(75+75+55+60+75)}{(94+48+82+90+70)} \times 100\right]\%$

$= \left[\frac{340}{384} \times 100\right]\%$

$= 88.54\%$

$\approx 88.5\%$

Hence, the correct option is (D).

25. The percentages of candidates selected from U.P. over those qualified from U.P. during different years are-

For $1997 = \left(\frac{78}{720} \times 100\right)\% = 10.83\%$

For $1998 = \left(\frac{85}{620} \times 100\right)\% = 13.71\%$

For $1999 = \left(\frac{48}{400} \times 100\right)\% = 12\%$

For $2000 = \left(\frac{70}{650} \times 100\right)\% = 10.77\%$

For $2001 = \left(\frac{80}{950} \times 100\right)\% = 8.42\%$

Clearly, this percentage is highest for the year 1998.
Hence, the correct option is (B).

26. Human refers to the skilled workforce in an organization.

Resource refers to limited availability or scarcity.

Management refers to how to optimize and make the best use of such limited or scarce resources so as to meet the organization's goals and objectives.

Therefore, Human Resource Management (HRM) is meant for the proper utilization of available skilled workforce and also to make efficient use of existing human resources in the organization.

This is the most important objective of HRM.

Hence, the correct option is (D).

27. Planning is the first and basic function of management and everything depends upon planning as it is a process of thinking about things before they happen and making preparations in advance to deal with them.

Planning consists of the following-

(A) Establishing goals and objectives to be achieved.

(B) Developing rules and procedures which have to be followed by the employees.

(D) Determining plans and forecasting techniques as a part of human resource planning to avoid any shortfall of the workforce.

Option (C) is a function of organizing and is the correct answer.

Hence, the correct option is (C).

28. The production approach adds up the value-added at basic prices of all industries, for example, agriculture, manufacturing, construction, retailing, banking, health services. Value added is the value of goods or services that have been produced minus the value of the goods and services needed to produce them. The production approach adds up the value-added at basic prices. To this are added taxes on goods or services, while subsidies on goods or services are subtracted in order to calculate GDP at market prices.
Hence, the correct option is (A).

29. NPC is a national-level autonomous organization under the Department of Industrial Policy & Promotion (DIPP), Ministry of Commerce & Industry to promote productivity culture in India. It was established as a registered society on 12th February 1958 by the Government to stimulate and promote productivity and quality consciousness across all sectors in the country.

It is a tri-partite non-profit organization (NGO) with equal representation from the government, employers, and workers' organizations. It also has representatives from technical and professional institutions including members from local productivity councils and the chamber of commerce on its Governing Body.

It also implements the productivity promotion schemes of the Government and carries out programs of Tokyo-based Asian Productivity Organization (APO), an inter-governmental body of which India is a founder member.

The National Productivity Council is observing National Productivity Day today, and National Productivity Week till 18th February. It is the 60th Anniversary of the National Productivity Council and is being celebrated as Diamond Jubilee Year. "Industry 4.0 Leapfrog Opportunity for India " has been selected as the theme for the National Productivity Week -2018.

Only II and III are correct.

Hence, the correct option is (D).

30. A partnership is an agreement between two or more persons who decided to do business and share its profits and losses. To have a legal relationship between the partners, the partnership agreement becomes the basis. The agreement can be in written form or oral form. An oral agreement is equally valid.
Hence, the correct option is (C).

31. To endure proper delivery of products is NOT a goal of HRM. The primary objective of HRM is to ensure the availability of a competent and willing workforce to an organization. Beyond this, there are other objectives, too. Specifically, HRM objectives are four folds- societal, organizational, functional, and personal.
Hence, the correct option is (D).

32. The human relations approach emphasizes the' effect of psychological and social factors on employees' performance. According to Human Relations Approach, management is the Study of the behavior of people at work. This approach had its origin in a series of experiments conducted by Professor Elton Mayo and his associates at the Harvard School of Business at the Western Electric Company's Hawthorne Works, near Chicago.

Hence, the correct option is (C).

33. As per the budget 2018-19, the Government has exempted the profits of Farmer Producer Companies (FPC) from tax for a period of 5 years.

On the recommendations of an expert panel led by Y.K. Alagh, Centre had amended the Indian Companies Act, 1956, in 2002-03 to provide for "producer companies". A Farmer Producer Company is a hybrid between cooperative societies and private limited companies.

A Farmer Producer Company can be formed by any 10 or more primary producers or by two or more producer institutions, or by a contribution of both. They can undertake activities related to production, harvesting, procurement, grading, pooling, marketing, processing, etc., of agricultural produce.

Hence, the correct option is (C).

34. Business means Industry and commerce. The industry is an economic activity, concerned with the procurement and processing of raw materials into finished products, that reach the customer. Commerce is a business activity, wherein exchange for goods and services for value, is done on a large scale. Capital Required.

Hence, the correct option is (B).

35. The primary aim of co-operative is to serve the members. The main purpose of a Co-operative Society is to provide service to its members. It also provides better-quality goods to its members and the general public.
Hence, the correct option is (B).

Mock Test 10

Comprehension

Ques (1-5):Direction: Read the following passage carefully and answer the question given below it.

Shortly after September 11, 2001, the United States began requesting additional financial information about persons of interest by subpoenaing records located at the SWIFT banking consortium. SWIFT, which routes trillions of dollars a day, faced an ethical dilemma: fight the subpoenas in order to protect member privacy and the group's reputation for the highest level of confidentiality, or, comply and provide information about thousands of financial communications in the hope that lives will be saved. SWIFT decided to comply in secret, but in late June 2006, four major U.S. newspapers disclosed SWIFT's compliance. This sparked a heated public debate over the ethics of SWIFT's decision to reveal ostensibly confidential financial communications.

Analyzing the situation in hindsight, three ethical justifications existed for not complying with the Treasury Department's requests. First, SWIFT needed to uphold its long-standing values of confidentiality, non-disclosure, and institutional trust. The second ethical reason against SWIFT's involvement came with inadequate government oversight as the Treasury Department failed to construct necessary safeguards to ensure the privacy of the data. Third, international law must be upheld and one could argue quite strongly that the government's use of data breached some parts of international law.

Although SWIFT executives undoubtedly considered the aforementioned reasons for rejecting the government's subpoena, three ethical justifications for complying existed. First, it could be argued that the program was legal because the United States government possesses the authority to subpoena records stored within its territory and SWIFT maintained many of its records in Virginia. Second, it is entirely possible that complying with the government's subpoena thwarted another catastrophic terrorist attack that would have cost lives and dollars. Third, cooperating with the government did not explicitly violate any SWIFT policies due to the presence of a valid subpoena. However, the extent of cooperation certainly surprised many financial institutions and sparked some outrage and debate within the financial community.

While SWIFT had compelling arguments both for agreeing and refusing to cooperate with the U.S. government program, even in hindsight, it is impossible to judge with certitude the wisdom and ethics of SWIFT's decision to cooperate as we still lack answers to important questions such as: what information did the government want? What promises did the government make about data confidentially? What, if any, potentially impending threats did the government present to justify its need for data?

Q.1 Which of the following can be inferred from the passage?

A. No clear cut answer as to the legality of SWIFT's cooperation existed.

B. SWIFT failed to adequately consult its legal staff before deciding to cooperate.

C. The volume of money routed through SWIFT declined after its cooperation became public.

D. U.S. authorities threatened criminal charges if SWIFT refused their subpoenas.

Q.2 Inferring from the passage, which of the following constituted an ethical justification for SWIFT complying with the government?

A. The U.S. government can subpoena information that pertains to its citizens.

B. SWIFT failed to adequately consult its legal staff before deciding to cooperate.

C. Providing data to the government based upon a valid subpoena did not explicitly violate SWIFT policy.

D. Despite ostensibly poor oversight, senior Treasury Department officials assured SWIFT that data would be kept confidential.

Q.3 The author suggests which of the following is the most appropriate conclusion of an analysis of the ethics of SWIFT's decision?

A. SWIFT acted inappropriately as it compromised its long-standing values of integrity, privacy, and confidentiality.

B. SWIFT's actions cannot be judged with perspicuity as answers to important questions are still unknown.

C. SWIFT acted properly as it complied with the requests of a sovereign government in an attempt to save lives.

D. SWIFT's actions endangered the flow of commerce by sparking public outrage at an important institution.

Q.4 According to the passage, each of the following describes SWIFT EXCEPT:

A. Had data stored in Virginia

B. Valued confidentiality and non-disclosure

C. Routes trillions of dollars a day

D. After over a month of deliberation, complied with the government's subpoena

Q.5 The author implies that which of the following most likely occurred as a result of the news stories that ran in June 2006:

A. U.S. government officials decried the leaking of classified information.

B. SWIFT executives conducted a thorough internal review to assess the legality of SWIFT's actions.

C. Some foreign members of the SWIFT consortium demanded answers from SWIFT's executives.

D. Many members of the public and financial community debated SWIFT's decision.

Ques (6-10):Direction: Read the following passage carefully and answer the question given below it.

Although websites such as Facebook and MySpace experienced exponential growth during the middle of the first decade of the 21st century, some users remain oblivious to the fact that the information they post online can come back to haunt them. First, employers can monitor employees who maintain a blog, photo diary, or website. Employers can look for controversial employee opinions, sensitive information disclosures, or wildly inappropriate conduct. For example, a North Carolina newspaper fired one of its features writers after she created a blog on which she anonymously wrote about the idiosyncrasies of her job and coworkers.

The second unintended use of information from social networking websites is employers who check on prospective employees. A June 11, 2006 New York Times article reported that many companies recruiting on college campuses use search engines and social networking websites such as MySpace, Xanga, and Facebook to conduct background checks. Although the use of MySpace or Google to scrutinize a student's background is somewhat unsettling to many undergraduates, the Times noted that the utilization of Facebook is especially shocking to students who believe that Facebook is limited to current students and recent alumni.

Corporate recruiters and prospective employers are not the only people interested in college students' lives. The third unintended use of social networking websites is college administrators who monitor the Internet—especially Facebook—for student misconduct. For example, a college in Boston's Back Bay expelled its student Government Association President for joining a Facebook group highly critical of a campus police sergeant. In addition, fifteen students at a state university in North Carolina faced charges in court for underage drinking because of photos that appeared on Facebook.

Although more users of websites such as Facebook are becoming aware of the potential pitfalls of online identities, many regular users still fail to take three basic security precautions. First, only make your information available to a specific list of individuals whom you approve. Second, regularly search for potentially harmful information about yourself that may have been posted by mistake or by a disgruntled former associate. Third, never post blatantly offensive material under your name or on your page as, despite the best precautions, this material will likely make its way to the wider world. By taking these simple steps, members of the digital world can realize the many benefits of e-community without experiencing some of the damaging unintended consequences.

Q.6 Based upon the passage, the author implies which of the following:

A. Information obtained unwillingly from the Internet is permissible in court.

B. It is impossible to protect yourself from unintended uses of information online.

C. Making information available only to people whom you trust compromises your online community.

D. Even if you restrict who can view your data, the government may still access it.

Q.7 Which of the following best describes the author's logical flow in the passage?

A. Define a problem, provide examples of it, offer means of remedying it, and offer a brief evaluation of the issue at hand.

B. Provide examples of a problem, offer a counter point, provide a resolution of the conflicting views, and offer a brief evaluation of the issue at hand.

C. Provide examples of a problem, provide means of remedying it, offer a brief evaluation of the issue at hand, and provide a contrasting evaluation of the issue at hand.

D. Define a problem, provide examples of it, offer a brief evaluation of the issue at hand, and offer suggestions to support that evaluation.

Q.8 The author implies that users should take all of the following actions to protect their online privacy EXCEPT:

A. Know to whom you make your online information available.

B. Actively hunt for misinformation or damaging information posted about you or under your name.

C. Speak with recruiters to inform them of any misinformation published about you.

D. Carefully select and limit who can view your electronic profile.

Q.9 The tone of the passage suggests that the author's view toward e-community and the digital world can best be described as:

A. Largely Pessimistic

B. Frustrated

C. Guardedly Optimistic

D. Distressed

Q.10 According to the passage, all of the following represent a possible threat to privacy or an unintended use of data EXCEPT:

A. Disgruntled past associates posting damaging information online.

B. Colleges or universities disciplining students for expressing politically incorrect or institutionally disowned opinions.

C. Government officials using online information, obtained against one's will, to bring legal proceedings.

D. Malicious users impersonating one's identity to commit identity fraud.

Management Data Interpretation

Ques (11-15):Direction: Study the pie chart given below and answer the question that follows.

The pie chart given here shows the spendings of a country on various sports during a particular year. Study the chart carefully and answer the question given below it.

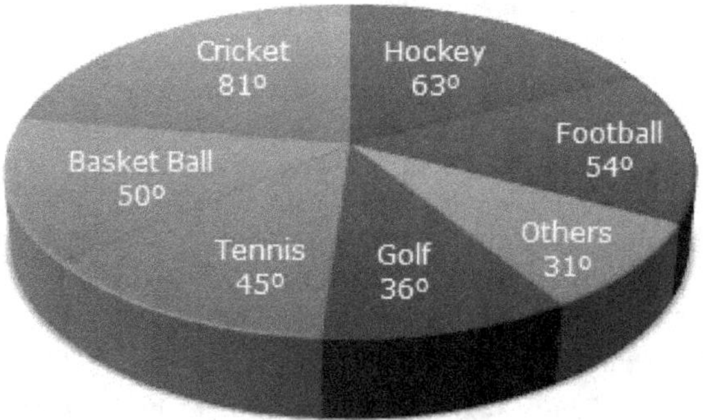

Q.11 What percent of total spending is spent on Tennis?

A. $12\frac{1}{2}\%$ **B.** $22\frac{1}{2}\%$ **C.** 25% **D.** 45%

Q.12 How much percent more is spent on Hockey than that on Golf?

A. 25% **B.** 35% **C.** 37.5% **D.** 75%

Q.13 If the total amount spent on sports during the year be Rs. 1,80,00,000, the amount spent on Basketball exceeds on Tennis by:

A. Rs. 2,50,000 **B.** Rs. 3,60,000
C. Rs. 3,75,000 **D.** Rs. 4,10,000

Q.14 How much percent less is spent on Football than that on Cricket?

A. $22\frac{2}{9}\%$ **B.** 27% **C.** $33\frac{1}{3}\%$ **D.** $37\frac{1}{7}\%$

Q.15 If the total amount spent on sports during the year was Rs. 2 crores, the amount spent on Cricket and Hockey together was:

A. Rs. 8,00,000 **B.** Rs. 80,00,000
C. Rs. 1,20,00,000 **D.** Rs. 1,60,00,000

Ques (16-20):Direction: Study the line graph given below and answer the question that follows.Ratio of Exports to Imports (in terms of money in Rs. crores) of Two Companies Over the Years

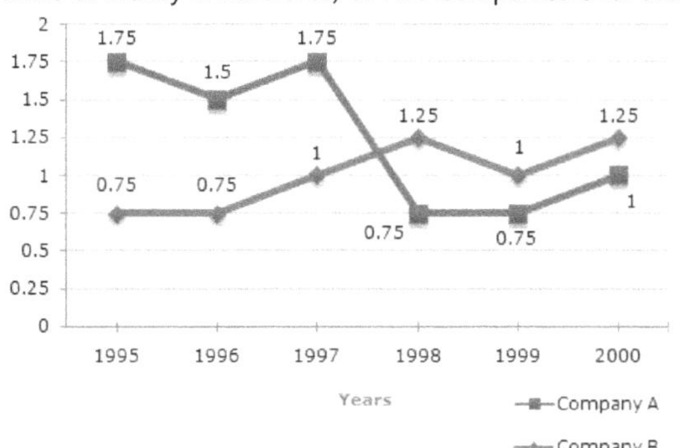

Q.16 In how many of the given years were the exports more than the imports for Company A?

A. 2 **B.** 3 **C.** 4 **D.** 5

Q.17 If the imports of Company A in 1997 were increased by 40 percent, what would be the ratio of exports to the increased imports?

A. 1.20
B. 1.25
C. 1.30
D. Cannot be determined

Q.18 If the exports of Company A in 1998 were Rs. 237 crores, what was the amount of imports in that year?

A. Rs. 189.6 crores **B.** Rs. 243 crores
C. Rs. 281 crores **D.** Rs. 316 crores

Q.19 In 1995, the export of Company A was double that of Company B. If the imports of Company A during the year was Rs. 180 crores, what was the approximate amount of imports of Company B during that year?

A. Rs. 190 crores
B. Rs. 210 crores
C. Rs. 225 crores
D. Cannot be determined

Q.20 In which year(s) was the difference between imports and exports of Company B the maximum?

A. 2000
B. 1996
C. 1998 and 2000
D. Cannot be determined

Ques (21-25):Direction: Study the following table chart carefully and answer the question that follows.The following table shows the number of new employees added to different categories of employees in a company and also the number of employees from these categories who left the company every year since the foundation of the Company in 1995.

Year	Managers		Technicians		Operators		Accountants		Peons	
	New	Left	New	Left	New	Left	New	Left	New	Left
199	760	---	120	---	880	---	116	---	820	---
199	280	120	272	120	256	104	200	100	184	96
199	179	92	240	128	240	120	224	104	152	88
199	148	88	236	96	208	100	248	96	196	80
199	160	72	256	100	192	112	272	88	224	120
200	193	96	288	112	248	144	260	92	200	104

Q.21 What is the difference between the total number of Technicians added to the Company and the total number of Accountants added to the Company during the years 1996 to 2000?

A. 128 **B.** 112 **C.** 96 **D.** 88

Q.22 What was the total number of Peons working in the Company in the year 1999?

A. 1312 **B.** 1192 **C.** 1088 **D.** 968

Q.23 For which of the following categories the percentage increase in the number of employees working in the Company from 1995 to 2000 was the maximum?

A. Managers **B.** Technicians
C. Operators **D.** Accountants

Q.24 What is the pooled average of the total number of employees of all categories in the year 1997?

A. 1325 **B.** 1195 **C.** 1265 **D.** 1235

Q.25 During the period between 1995 and 2000, the total number of Operators who left the Company is what percent of total number of Operators who joined the Company?

A. 19% **B.** 21% **C.** 27% **D.** 29%

Business Awareness

Q.26 Name the first Indian businessman who found place in the cover story of Forbes magazine:

A. Anil Ambani
B. Dr Reddy
C. Azim Hasham Premji
D. Narayan Murthy

Q.27 Which news paper has the motto - Journalism of Courage?

A. The Hindustan Times
B. The Washington Post
C. The Indian Express
D. The Guardian

Q.28 India has lifted the ban of which commodity, that was contracted by importers of Bangladesh?

A. Sugar **B.** Onion **C.** Jute **D.** Cotton

Q.29 Which body has initiated anti-dumping probe against two products imported from China?

A. Directorate General of Trade Remedies
B. Enforcement Directorate
C. Directorate General of Foreign Trade
D. Central Board of Excise and Customs

Q.30 Which is the last state to join the Centre's option for GST compensation shortfall?

A. Kerala **B.** Chhattisgarh
C. Sikkim **D.** Jharkhand

Q.31 What is the name of the new brand identity of Vodafone Idea?

A. Id-fone **B.** Voidea **C.** VI **D.** Mi

Q.32 Which country has recently amended its Procurement rules focussing on Reciprocal Participation?

A. China **B.** USA **C.** India **D.** Russia

Q.33 Harley Davidson announced to stop manufacturing and sales in which Asian country?

A. China **B.** India
C. Pakistan **D.** Sri Lanka

Q.34 As per the World Trade Organization (WTO), what is the growth of World merchandise trade in the year 2020?

A. - 1.2 % **B.** - 5.2 % **C.** - 9.2% **D.** -13.2%

Q.35 The Aditya Birla Fashion and Retail Ltd (ABFRL) has proposed to raise Rs.1500 crore from which company?

A. Reliance India Limited
B. Adani Group
C. Flipkart Group
D. Amazon India

// Smart Answer Sheet //

Correct Indicates percentage of students who answered questions correctly.

Skipped Indicates percentage of students who skipped questions.

Q.	Ans.	Correct / Skipped	Q.	Ans.	Correct / Skipped	Q.	Ans.	Correct / Skipped	Q.	Ans.	Correct / Skipped	Q.	Ans.	Correct / Skipped
1	A	22.29 % / 73.61 %	8	C	87.89 % / 11.88 %	15	B	53.2 % / 32.62 %	22	B	87.03 % / 11.59 %	29	A	28.68 % / 67.81 %
2	C	22.65 % / 75.21 %	9	C	58.61 % / 40.32 %	16	B	80.12 % / 17.66 %	23	A	26.22 % / 69.2 %	30	D	57.7 % / 35.19 %
3	B	43.51 % / 42.71 %	10	D	80.61 % / 12.31 %	17	B	25.22 % / 69.01 %	24	B	44.13 % / 43.32 %	31	C	79.9 % / 14.25 %
4	D	64.72 % / 33.03 %	11	A	88.75 % / 10.35 %	18	D	42.16 % / 57.75 %	25	D	52.87 % / 36.96 %	32	C	50.17 % / 41.23 %
5	D	58.93 % / 32.94 %	12	D	63.4 % / 32.09 %	19	B	24.66 % / 72.79 %	26	C	77.0 % / 12.18 %	33	B	88.85 % / 10.3 %
6	A	57.44 % / 40.28 %	13	A	41.23 % / 38.68 %	20	D	55.68 % / 34.75 %	27	C	50.87 % / 33.05 %	34	C	20.31 % / 70.33 %
7	A	85.58 % / 12.35 %	14	C	48.76 % / 30.15 %	21	D	82.45 % / 11.33 %	28	B	42.4 % / 46.64 %	35	C	61.19 % / 38.38 %

Performance Analysis	
Avg. Score (%)	45.71%
Toppers Score (%)	54.29%
Your Score	

//Hints and Solutions//

1. No clear cut answer as to the legality of SWIFT's cooperation existed can be inferred from the passage.

Option A- The complex and somewhat ambiguous issue of the legality of SWIFT's cooperation can be inferred by the fact that legal reasons exist both for cooperating and for not cooperating. For cooperating: "it could be argued that the program was legal because the United States government possesses the authority to subpoena records stored within its territory and SWIFT maintained many of its records in Virginia." For not cooperating: "international law must be upheld and one could argue quite strongly that the government's use of data breached some parts of international law."

Option B- The passage enables us to infer the contrary by implying that SWIFT considered the legal implications of not cooperating ("SWIFT executives undoubtedly considered the aforementioned reasons for rejecting the government's subpoena").

Option C- The passage never discusses the volume of money (only the number of transactions). Moreover, there is no comparison of money or transactions before and after SWIFT's decision became public.

Option D- There is no information in the passage that allows anything close to this inference. The passage never mentions threats or government efforts to force SWIFT to comply.

Hence, the correct option is (A).

2. Option C- The important quote from the passage is: "cooperating with the government did not explicitly violate any SWIFT policies due to the presence of a valid subpoena" so providing data to the government based upon a valid subpoena did not explicitly violate SWIFT policy constituted an ethical justification for SWIFT complying with the government. So, this is the correct answer.

Option A- An ethical argument for SWIFT complying is that the data are located in Virginia. This does not mean (and it would be wildly improper to conclude) that all the data pertains to U.S. citizens. The article implies that SWIFT deals with the financial information of people in the international community. Further, the article does not explicitly say that the U.S. government wanted information about its citizens.

Option B- The passage states that we cannot answer the following question: "what, if any, potentially impending threats did the government present to justify its need for data?" Given the inability to answer this, there are no grounds to conclude that SWIFT executives believed another attack was imminent.

Option D- The passage states the opposite, noting that one unanswered question was: "What promises did the government make about data confidentially?"

Hence, the correct option is (C).

3. Option B- After stating the ethical pros and cons of SWIFT's decision to cooperate, the author uses the last paragraph to summarize and make an ethical analysis. The conclusion is: "even in hindsight, it is impossible to judge with certitude the wisdom and ethics of SWIFT's decision to cooperate as we still lack answers to important questions." This answer closely mirrors the ethical conclusion the author reaches in the last paragraph.

Option A- The author never concludes that SWIFT acted inappropriately. The author points out that a good case to the contrary could be made.

Option C- The author never concludes that SWIFT acted properly. The author points out that a good case to the contrary could be made.

Option D- There is no mention about the effects of SWIFT's decision on the flow of commerce. For all we know, the traffic volume could have increased.

Hence, the correct option is (B).

4. Option D- The text provides no information about SWIFT's deliberation process or the amount of time that elapsed before it cooperated. The text does not even mention the date that SWIFT decided to cooperate.

Option A- The third paragraph states that "SWIFT maintained many of its records in Virginia".

Option B- The second paragraph states that "SWIFT needed to uphold its long-standing values of confidentiality, non-disclosure, and institutional trust".

Option C- The first paragraph states: "SWIFT, which routes trillions of dollars a day".

Hence, the correct option is (D).

5. Option D- The important quote from the passage is: "in late June 2006, four major U.S. newspapers disclosed SWIFT's compliance. This sparked a heated public debate over the ethics of SWIFT's decision to reveal ostensibly confidential financial communications." This answer closely resembles the information provided in the mentioned sentence.

Option A- The passage makes no mention of the response of government officials nor does it provide any information with which to make an inference.

Option B- The passage makes no mention of the response of SWIFT executives nor does it provide any information with which to make an inference.

Option C- Although the passage indicates that the disclosure of SWIFT's decision sparked "heated debate" and the passage clearly implies that some members of the financial community felt SWIFT crossed the line, there is no indication that questions were posed to SWIFT's executives.

Hence, the correct option is (D).

6. Option A- The portion of text that is of interest is: "In addition, fifteen students at a state university in North Carolina faced charges in court for underage drinking because of photos that appeared on Facebook." The fact that authorities pressed charges "in court" "because of" photos that appeared online strongly implies that these photos were the evidence the police needed and could present in court.

Option B- In the last paragraph, the passage states that the opposite is true. This paragraph elaborates the ways by using whom we can protect ourselves from unintended uses of information online.

Option C- The passage never even approaches discussing this topic.

Option D- The passage never discusses the government's ability to view restricted data. In the case of students in North Carolina, there is no mention that students tried to restrict access to the photos (and the context lends itself to assuming that the students did not take adequate measures to restrict their photos).

Hence, the correct option is (A).

7. Define a problem, provide examples of it, offer means of remedying it, and offer a brief evaluation of the issue at hand describes the author's logical flow in the passage.

The following is an outline of the passage:

Define a problem: "some users remain oblivious to the fact that the information they post online can come back to haunt them."

Provide three examples of the problem: "First, employers can monitor employees who maintain a blog...The second unintended use of information...The third unintended use of social networking websites is..."

Provide Ways to Remedy the Problem: "many regular users still fail to take three basic security precautions. First, only make your information available...Second, regularly search for...Third, never post blatantly offensive"

Evaluate the Issue at Hand: "By taking these simple steps, members of the digital world can realize the many benefits of e-community without experiencing some of the damaging unintended consequences."

Option A- This matches the logical flow of the passage.

Option B- The passage does not begin by offering examples of a problem. Instead, it begins by defining a problem.

Option C- The passage does not begin by offering examples of a problem. Instead, it begins by defining a problem. The passage never provides a contrasting evaluation of the issue at hand.

Option D- The passage does not end by offering suggestions to support an evaluation of the issue at hand (the ending is the final evaluation of the issue by the author).

Hence, the correct option is (A).

8. Option C- The author never discusses or implies this. The closest the passage comes is: "regularly search for potentially harmful information about yourself that may have been posted by mistake or by a disgruntled former associate."

Option A- The author strongly implies this in the last paragraph: "only make your information available to a specific list of individuals whom you approve."

Option B- The author explicitly advises this: "regularly search for potentially harmful information about yourself that may have been posted by mistake or by a disgruntled former associate."

Option D- The author states this in the last paragraph: "only make your information available to a specific list of individuals whom you approve."

Hence, the correct option is (C).

9. Option C- This captures the author's view, which is summarized at the end of the final paragraph. Toward the end of the passage, the author summarizes his view of e-community and the digital world: "By taking these simple steps, members of the digital world can realize the many benefits of e-community without experiencing some of the damaging unintended consequences."

Option A- This does not take into account the author's view as summarized in the last paragraph.

Option B- The author never expresses frustration. The passage is more objective and informative than personal and emotional.

Option D- The author never expresses feeling distressed. The passage is more objective and informative than personal and emotional.

Hence, the correct option is (C).

10. Option D- The passage never mentions malicious users impersonating one's identity to commit identity fraud.

Option A- The passage mentions this. "regularly search for potentially harmful information about yourself that may have been posted by mistake or by a disgruntled former associate."

Option B- The passage mentions this. "a college in Boston's Back Bay expelled its student Government Association President for joining a Facebook group highly critical of a campus police sergeant."

Option C- The passage mentions this. "In addition, fifteen students at a state university in North Carolina faced charges in court for underage drinking because of photos that appeared on Facebook."

Hence, the correct option is (E).

11. Value of Amount spent on Tennis $= 45^\circ$

Percentage of money spend on Tennis $= \left(\frac{45}{360} \times 100\right)\%$

$= 12\frac{1}{2}\%$

Hence, the correct option is (A).

12. Let the total spendings on sports be Rs. x.

Value of Amount spent on Golf $= 36^\circ$

Amount spent on Golf $=$ Rs. $\left(\frac{36}{360} \times x\right)$

$=$ Rs. $\frac{x}{10}$

Value of Amount spent on Hockey $= 63^\circ$

Amount spent on Hockey $=$ Rs $\left(\frac{63}{360} \times x\right)$

$=$ Rs. $\frac{7x}{40}$

Difference $=$ Rs. $\left(\frac{7x}{40} - \frac{x}{10}\right)$

$= \text{Rs } \frac{3x}{40}$

Required % $= \left[\left(\frac{\frac{3x}{40}}{\frac{x}{10}}\right) \times 100\right]\%$

$= 75\%$

Hence, the correct option is (D).

13. Value of Amount spent of Basketball $= 50^\circ$

Value of Amount spent of Tennis $= 45^\circ$

Total amount spent on sports $=$ Rs. $1,80,00,000$

Amount spent on Basketball exceeds that on Tennis by:

Rs. $\left[\frac{(50-45)}{360} \times 1,80,00,000\right]$

$=$ Rs. $2,50,000$

Hence, the correct option is (A).

14. Let the total spendings on sports be Rs. x.

Value of Amount spent on Cricket $= 81^\circ$

Amount spent on Cricket $=$ Rs. $\left(\frac{81}{360} \times x\right)$

$=$ Rs. $\frac{9x}{40}$

Value of Amount spent on Football $= 54^\circ$

Amount spent on Football $=$ Rs. $\left(\frac{54}{360} \times x\right)$

$=$ Rs. $\frac{3x}{20}$

Difference $=$ Rs. $\left(\frac{9x}{40} - \frac{3x}{20}\right)$

$= \text{Rs } \frac{3x}{40}$

Required % $=$ Rs. $\left[\left(\frac{\frac{3x}{40}}{\frac{9x}{40}}\right) \times 100\right]\%$

$= 33\frac{1}{3}\%$

Hence, the correct option is (C).

15. Value of Amount spent on Cricket $= 81^\circ$

Value of Amount spent on Hockey $= 63^\circ$

Total Amount spent on Sports $=$ Rs. 2 crores

Amount spent on Cricket and Hockey together

$=$ Rs. $\left[\frac{(81+63)}{360} \times 2\right]$ crores

$=$ Rs. 0.8 crores

$=$ Rs. $80,00,000$

Hence, the correct option is (B).

16. The exports are more than imports in those years for which the exports to imports ratio are more than 1. For Company A, such years are 1995, 1996 and 1997 where the ratios are 1.75, 1.5 and 1.75 respectively.

Thus, during these 3 years, the exports are more than the imports for Company A.

Hence, the correct option is (B).

17. In 1997 for Company A we have, $\frac{E}{I} = 1.75$ i.e., $E = 1.75I$

Where $E =$ amount of exports and $I =$ amount of imports of Company A in 1997.

Now, the required imports $I_1 = I + 40\%$ of I

$= 1.4I$

$\therefore$ Required ratio $= \frac{E}{I_1}$

$= \frac{1.75I}{1.4I}$

$= 1.25$

Hence, the correct option is (B).

18. Let the amount of imports of Company A in 1998 be Rs. x crores.

Ratio of exports to imports of Company A in $1998 = 0.75$

Then,

$\frac{237}{x} = 0.75$

$\Rightarrow x = \frac{237}{0.75}$

$= 316$

$\therefore$ Amount of imports of Company A in $1998 =$ Rs. 316 crores

Hence, the correct option is (D).

19. In 1995 for Company A we have:

$\frac{E_A}{I_A} = 1.75$ ... (i)

[where $E_A =$ amount of exports, $I_A =$ amount of imports of Company A in 1995]

In 1995 for Company B we have:

$\frac{E_B}{I_B} = 0.75$ ... (ii)

[where $E_B =$ amount of exports, $I_B =$ amount of imports of Company B in 1995]

Also, we have $E_A = 2E_B$ ... (iii)

Substituting $I_A =$ Rs. 180 crores (given) in (i), we get,

$E_A =$ Rs. (180×1.75) crores $=$ Rs. 315 crores

Using $E_A =$ Rs. 315 crores in (iii), we get:

$E_B = \frac{E_A}{2} = \text{Rs. } \left(\frac{315}{2}\right) \text{ crores}$

Substituting $E_B =$ Rs. $\left(\frac{315}{2}\right)$ crores in (ii), we get,

$I_B = \frac{E_B}{0.75} =$ Rs. $\left(\frac{315}{2\times0.75}\right)$ crores

$=$ Rs. 210 crores

So, the amount of imports of Company B in $1995 =$ Rs. 210 crores

Hence, the correct option is (B).

20. We shall try to find the difference between the imports and exports of Company B for various years one by one:

For 1995

We have,

$\frac{E}{I} = 0.75$

Where $E =$ amount of exports, $I =$ amount of imports in 1995.

$\Rightarrow E = 0.75I$

$\therefore I - E = I - 0.75I$

$= 0.25I$

Thus, the difference between the imports and exports of Company B in 1995 is dependent on the amount of imports of Company B in 1995.

Similarly, the difference for other years can be determined only if the amount of imports for these years is known.

Since the imports or exports for various years are not known, the differences between and exports for various years cannot be determined.

Hence, the correct option is (D).

21. Total number of Technicians added to Company from 1996 to $2000 = 272 + 240 + 236 + 256 + 288$

$= 1292$

Total number of Accountants added to Company from 1996 to $2000 = 200 + 224 + 248 + 272 + 260$

$= 1204$

Required difference $= 1292 - 1204$

$= 88$

Hence, the correct option is (D).

22. Total number of peons added to Company from 1995 to $1999 = 820 + 184 + 152 + 196 + 224$

$= 1576$

Total number of peons leaving Company from 1995 to 1999 $= 96 + 88 + 80 + 120$

$= 384$

Total number of Peons working in the Company in $1999 = 1576 - 384$

$= 1192$

Hence, the correct option is (B).

23. Number of Managers working in the Company:

In $1995 = 760$

Total number of Managers added to Company from 1995 to $2000 = 760 + 280 + 179 + 148 + 160 + 193$

$= 1720$

Total number of Managers leaving Company from 1995 to $2000 = 120 + 92 + 88 + 72 + 96$

$= 468$

Total number of Managers in Company in $2000 = 1720 - 468$

$= 1252$

$\therefore$ Percentage increase in the number of Managers

$= \left[\frac{(1252-760)}{760} \times 100\right]\%$

$= 64.74\%$

Number of Technicians working in the Company:

$\ln 1995 = 1200$

Total number of Technicians added to Company from 1995 to $2000 = 1200 + 272 + 240 + 236 + 256 + 288$

$= 2492$

Total number of Technicians leaving Company from 1995 to $2000 = 120 + 128 + 96 + 100 + 112$

$= 556$

Total number of Technicians in Company in $2000 = 2492 - 556$

$= 1936$

$\therefore$ Percentage increase in the number of Technicians

$= \left[\frac{(1936-1200)}{1200} \times 100\right]\%$

$= 61.33\%$

Number of Operators working in the Company:

$\ln 1995 = 880$

Total number of Operators added to Company from 1995 to $2000 = 880 + 256 + 240 + 208 + 192 + 248$

$= 2024$

Total number of Operators leaving Company from 1995 to $2000 = 104 + 120 + 100 + 112 + 144$

$= 580$

Total number of Operators in Company in $2000 = 2024 - 580$

$= 1444$

$\therefore$ Percentage increase in the number of Operators

$= \left[\frac{(1444-880)}{880} \times 100\right]\%$

$= 64.09\%$

Number of Accountants working in the Company:

$\ln 1995 = 1160$

Total number of Accountants added to Company from 1995 to $2000 = 1160 + 200 + 224 + 248 + 272 + 260$

$= 2364$

Total number of Accountants leaving Company from 1995 to $2000 = 100 + 104 + 96 + 88 + 92$

$= 480$

Total number of Accountants in Company in $2000 = 2364 - 480$

$= 1884$

$\therefore$ Percentage increase in the number of Accountants

$= \left[\frac{(1884-1160)}{1160} \times 100\right]\%$

$= 62.41\%$

Number of Peons working in the Company:

$\ln 1995 = 820$

Total number of Peons added to Company from 1995 to $2000 = 820 + 184 + 152 + 196 + 224 + 200$
$= 1776$

Total number of Peons leaving Company from 1995 to 2000
$= 96 + 88 + 80 + 120 + 104$
$= 488$

Total number of Peons in Company in $2000 = 1776 - 488$
$= 1288$

∴ Percentage increase in the number of Peons
$= \left[\frac{(1288-820)}{820} \times 100\right]\%$
$= 57.07\%$

Clearly, the percentage increase is maximum in case of Managers. Hence, the correct option is (A).

24. Total number of employees of various categories working in the Company in 1997 are:

Total number of Managers added to Company from 1995 to $1997 = 760 + 280 + 179$

$= 1219$

Total number of Managers leaving Company from 1995 to $1997 = 120 + 92$

$= 212$

Total number of Managers in Company in $1997 = 1720 - 468$

$= 1007$

Total number of Technicians added to Company from 1995 to $1997 = 1200 + 272 + 240$

$= 1712$

Total number of Technicians leaving Company from 1995 to $1997 = 120 + 128$

$= 248$

Total number of Technicians in Company in $1997 = 1712 - 248$

$= 1464$

Total number of Operators added to Company from 1995 to $1997 = 880 + 256 + 240$

$= 1376$

Total number of Operators leaving Company from 1995 to $1997 = 104 + 120$

$= 224$

Total number of Operators in Company in $1997 = 2024 - 580$

$= 1152$

Total number of Accountants added to Company from 1995 to $1997 = 1160 + 200 + 224$

$= 1584$

Total number of Accountants leaving Company from 1995 to $1997 = 100 + 104$

$= 204$

Total number of Accountants in Company in $1997 = 1584 - 204$

$= 1380$

Total number of Peons added to Company from 1995 to $1997 = 820 + 184 + 152$

$= 1156$

Total number of Peons leaving Company from 1995 to 1997
$= 96 + 88$

$= 184$

Total number of Peons in Company in $1997 = 1776 - 488$

$= 972$

Therefore Pooled average of all the five categories of employees working in the Company in 1997
$= \frac{1}{5} \times (1007 + 1464 + 1152 + 1380 + 972)$
$= \frac{1}{5} \times (5975)$
$= 1195$

Hence, the correct option is (B).

25. Total number of Operators who left the Company during $1995 - 2000 = (104 + 120 + 100 + 112 + 144)$
$= 580$

Total number of Operators who joined the Company during $1995 - 2000$
$= (880 + 256 + 240 + 208 + 192 + 248)$
$= 2024$

∴ Required Percentage $= \left(\frac{580}{2024} \times 100\right)\%$
$= 28.66\% \approx 29\%$

Hence, the correct option is (D).

26. Azim Hasham Premji was the first Indian businessman who found place in the cover story of Forbes magazine.

Azim Hasham Premji (born 24 July 1945) is an Indian business tycoon, investor, engineer, and philanthropist, who was the chairman of Wipro Limited. Premji remains a non-executive member of the board and founder chairman.

Hence, the correct option is (C).

27. The Indian Express has the motto - Journalism of Courage.

The Indian Express is the daily English newspaper published in India. It was founded by Shri Ramnath Goenka in 1932.

Hence, the correct option is (C).

28. Directorate General of Foreign Trade (DGFT) has recently lifted the ban of movement of onion supplies, that were already contracted for by the importers of Bangladesh.

Earlier, the DGFT banned all exports of onion following shortage and sudden increase in prices in the domestic market. After Bangladesh had formally complained about the exports of the commodity, India has lifted the ban.

Hence, the correct option is (B).

29. Directorate General of Trade Remedies (DGTR), Govt. of India has initiated an anti-dumping probe against two products imported from China.

The probe has been initiated against the import of Hydrofluorocarbon (HFC) Blends (used in refrigerators and air conditioners) and Decor Paper. The probe has been initiated by DGRT after SRF Ltd and ITC Ltd have filed applications seeking investigation on dumping of the two products.

Hence, the correct option is (A).

30. Recently, the state Government of Jharkhand has accepted the Union Government's alternative offer to meet the GST compensation shortfall for States. By this, all states and 3 UTs have joined the option 1.

To compensate the shortfall in GST, the central government has proposed two options – First, States can borrow ₹1.1 lakh crore out of the estimated ₹ 2.35 lakh crore shortfall or second, states could borrow the entire compensation shortfall through the issue of market debt.

Hence, the correct option is (D).

31. The Vodafone Idea Limited has revealed its new integrated brand identity "VI" (read as 'We'), using just the initials of both Vodafone and Idea.

The new brand name has been launched after 2 years since the merger of Vodafone and Idea took place. The company has also revealed a reward programme named 'Happy Surprises'. The Supreme Court has given telecom companies 10 years to pay adjusted gross revenue dues (AGR) dues.

Hence, the correct option is (C).

32. India has recently amended its public procurement rules. Under the amended rules, entities of countries which do not allow Indian companies to participate in their government procurement will not be allowed to participate in government procurement in India.

This amendment been notified by the Department for Promotion of Industry and Internal Trade (DPIIT), Ministry of Commerce.

Hence, the correct option is (C).

33. Global automobile manufacturer Harley-Davidson Inc has recently announced that it would discontinue its sales and manufacturing operations in India.

Harley-Davidson has been recently trying to move its dealerships in the country to other cheaper locations. It has also closed its Bawal plant and will incur USD 75 million in restructuring costs. The company made about 17 million bike and scooter sales a year in India.

Hence, the correct option is (B).

34. According to the World Trade Organization's (WTO) revised trade forecast, the World merchandise trade is expected to fall by 9.2 percent in 2020.

However, the WTO also estimated that the world will record a 7.2 percent rise in the year 2021. Earlier in the month of April, WTO had predicted that the volume of world merchandise trade would decline between 13 percent and 32 percent for 2020.

Hence, the correct option is (C).

35. Aditya Birla Fashion and Retail Ltd (ABFRL) has proposed to raise a sum of Rs.1,500 crore from Flipkart Group. This fund rising would be by means of preferential issue of shares.

The capital would be raised at Rs.205 per share. With this capital infusion Flipkart Group will own 7.8% equity stake in ABFRL.

Hence, the correct option is (C).

Mock Test 11

Comprehension

Ques (1-5):Direction: Read the following passage carefully and answer the question given below it.

The most striking feature of Prime Minister Narendra Modi's address to the nation on the decision to scrap Articles 370 and 35A was its temporal focus: the future. This served to both fill the narrative with hope and skirt the messy political discord preceding and accompanying the decision to remove Jammu and Kashmir's special status.

He also held out the promise that J&K would make the transition from Union territory to full statehood, without setting a deadline for that change. He also made it clear that Ladakh's separation from what once was a kingdom of disparate regions would be permanent.

The speech carries forward the project of integrating the troubled state into the Indian mainstream by laying out before them an array of opportunities for building a new future for themselves and for the country as a whole.

The prime minister held out carrots aplenty, juicy ones. Better salaries and service conditions for civil servants and J&K policemen, an immediate flurry of jobs as the government moved to fill all vacancies, new scholarships and educational opportunities, new rights as full-fledged citizens of India and new jobs that Indian enterprises, State-owned and private, would create.

If a leader holds out a carrot, a stick cannot but be part of the package. But if the prime minister wielded one, it was not on display. He did refer to separatism and terror, but implicitly treated them as nothing more than bumps along the road to normalisation and return to statehood.

The detailed list of benefits and legal entitlements that the people of Jammu and Kashmir now stand to gain, governed as they would be by the Constitution and legal system of India, is likely to have the desired impact of shifting the spotlight on the benefits of the political change, from the costs that have been most obvious.

The prime minister did well to announce relaxation, as early as next Monday, when Eid would be celebrated, on the lockdown in place in the state. His call to the rest of India to join in rebuilding the state should rein in lumping temptation to target Kashmiris outside Kashmir.

Q.1 As per the passage, what was the effect of the most striking feature of the Prime Minister's address to the nation regarding the decision to scrap Articles 370 and 35A?

I. Help in having a debate regarding the pros and cons of scrapping the aforementioned articles

II. Help in avoiding the dissonance that was caused due to the scrapping of the said articles

III. Help in painting a picture of hope for the future.

A. Only III **B.** Only I and III
C. Only I **D.** Only II and III

Q.2 "If a leader holds out a carrot, a stick cannot but be part of the package" What is a carrot and stick policy?

A. Offering incentives to increase productivity
B. Offering carrots roasted on a stick to increase strength
C. Offering dieting which is difficult but produces good health
D. Offering reward and threatening with punishment

Q.3 Which of the following can be inferred from the passage?

I. Benefits given to the J&K residents have stolen the limelight from the cost.

II. India is no longer under any threat from Pakistani terrorists.

III. There was a lockdown in Jammu and Kashmir.

A. Only II **B.** Only I
C. Only I and II **D.** Only I and III

Q.4 Which of the following is/are not incentive(s) referred to in the passage?

A. New scholarships and educational opportunities Three-fourth
B. New rights as full-fledged citizens of India
C. Better salaries and service conditions for civil servants
D. Maternity leave for working women

Q.5 Which of the following statements is the author most likely to agree with?

A. Articles 370 and 35 A should not have been scrapped
B. The prime minister made a mistake in addressing the issue.
C. Separatism and terror are acting as invisible sticks.
D. The incentives given out are not enough.

Ques (6-10):Direction: Read the passage and answer the question that follows.

Once upon a time, there lived a farmer who had a little land. His name was Tuan and he was a very kind and good-natured person. He lived in a hut on his land with his wife and children and earned by selling whatever crops he could produce on his small land.

Tuan loved to help others. Whenever someone fell ill or needed something badly, Tuan was there to help that person. If someone died in the village, Tuan assisted the family members of the deceased person in whichever way he could. If anyone fell ill at night, Tuan was right beside the village doctor to help him prepare the medicines and tend to the sick. There seemed to be none who hated this man. He appeared to be loved by one and all.

But there was one person who hated Tuan with all his heart. He was Juan, a neighbour of Tuan, who lived in the land next to him. A lazy person by nature, Juan hardly put in as much effort to cultivate his land as Tuan did to produce crops in his own. So when the harvest season arrived every year, Juan found that he had very few crops to sell. Tuan on the other hand, earned a handsome profit through the selling of his produces.

One year, Juan could no longer contain his jealousy. Just days before Tuan was to reap his harvest, Juan set fire to his crops at night. Tuan was asleep at this time and it was only the alertness of one of his other neighbors that saved much of his crops from being perished in the deadly flames of the fire that Juan had lighted.

When the flames were doused, Tuan saw which direction the fire had started from. Juan's animosity towards him was unknown to Tuan. But he let the matters rest and decided to take action only if he saw Juan repeating his dastardly act once again.

That year, Tuan managed to sell the rest of his crops at a good price but he could not make much profit for a good part of his produces had been burnt. He had a heavy heart but he did not like to tell anyone about it.

Only days later, Tuan was awakened by the sound of lamentations. He went out to find a crowd beside Juan's hut. He rushed to find that Juan's son had fallen ill. He found that the village doctor was unable to provide a cure to his illness. Tuan knew what he had to do. He untied his own horse and rode it. Then he rushed to the town that was ten miles away and fetched a more experienced doctor who lived there.

This doctor was able to guess the disease correctly and provided an exact cure for it. Within hours, the boy was found to sleep soundly and Tuan went with the doctor to take him back to the town.

A day later, Juan went to Tuan's hut and began to weep bitterly. He confessed to his sins but was surprised when Tuan told him that he knew about it all.

"You knew that I had set fire to your crops? And still you fetched the doctor for my son?" asked the astonished Juan. Tuan nodded and said, "I did what I knew was right. Could I do wrong just because you had done so?" Juan stood up and embraced Tuan. Both men were in tears and so were the others who stood by them.

From that day, Juan changed himself. Within a year, he could produce much crops in his land through his hard work. When the others asked him how he had changed so much, he only replied,

"It was the goodness and love of Tuan that transformed me."

Q.6 Which of the following is/are true about Tuan?

I. He was a doctor along with being a farmer.

II. He was a good natured and kind person.

III. He was a wealthy farmer who gave away his wealth to the needy.

A. Only I
B. Only II
C. Only I and III
D. Only II and III

Q.7 Which of the following is/are a/some ways in which Juan transformed himself?

I. He began to work hard on his crops.

II. He became more helpful towards people.

III. He started a small charity in Tuan's name.

A. Only I
B. Only III
C. Only I and II
D. Only II and III

Q.8 Why did Juan hate Tuan with all his heart?

A. Juan wanted attention from people around him but all of them liked Tuan better.
B. Juan wanted to be more good-natured and helpful than Tuan.
C. Juan was jealous of Tuan's harvest which earned him huge profits.
D. Juan did not want Tuan to work as hard as Tuan did.

Q.9 Which among the following is similar in meaning to the word perished as used in the passage?

A. Grew
B. Destroyed
C. Bore
D. Revived

Q.10 What was the result of Juan setting fire to Tuan's crops?

A. Majority of Tuan's harvest was lost in the fire
B. The neighbours came to Tuan's rescue and alerted the police.
C. One of the neighbour's saw Juan setting fire to Tuan's crops and he was arrested.
D. Some of Tuan's crops were damaged but the majority were saved.

Management Data Interpretation

Ques (11-15):Direction : Study the following table chart carefully and answer the question given beside.

The following table gives the information about the number of different models sold by TATA over the years.

(All values are in thousand)

Years/ Model	Nano	Tigor	Zest	Bolt	Hexa	Nexon	Indigo	Sumo	Indica
2011	234	213	456	345	653	98	895	290	543
2012	235	432	542	215	564	431	347	652	128
2013	334	541	874	890	671	341	642	871	52
2014	65	490	431	234	442	653	322	126	322
2015	411	322	621	712	322	124	324	431	322
2016	431	322	561	89	81	111	121	98	751
2017	651	671	125	351	266	265	219	87	781

Q.11 Find the absolute difference between the total number of all the model cars sold by TATA in 2017 and the total number of all the models cars sold by TATA in 2011?

A. 321 thousand **B.** 311 thousand
C. 323 thousand **D.** 302 thousand

Q.12 The total number of Bolt Model sold in 2012 and 2013 together is what percent of the total number of Sumo Model sold in 2014 and 2015 together?

A. 178.28% **B.** 165.25%
C. 198.38% **D.** 204.28%

Q.13 What is the approximate percentage increase in the sales of Nano in 2017 compared to that in 2011?

A. 178.20% **B.** 157.32%
C. 184.68% **D.** 167.47%

Q.14 What is the respective ratio of the Indica model sold in 2015 and 2017 together and the Bolt model sold in 2013 and 2014 together?

A. $1109:1124$ **B.** $1103:1124$
C. $1109:1128$ **D.** $1103:1118$

Q.15 The total number of Nano car sold over the years is how many less than the total number of Indica car sold over the years?

A. 533 thousand **B.** 538 thousand
C. 442 thousand **D.** 446 thousand

Ques (16-20):Direction : Study the following line chart carefully and answer the question given beside.

The following line-graph represents the number of branches of public sector banks in India in different years:

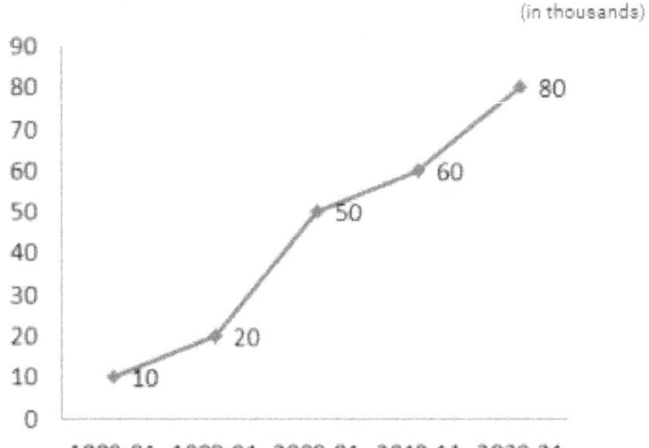

Q.16 Find the percentage increase in the number of branches from $1980-81$ to $2010-11$.

A. 200% **B.** 300% **C.** 400% **D.** 500%

Q.17 If the total number of public sectors banks in $1980-81$ and $2020-21$ were 14 and 28 respectively, then find the ratio of average branches per bank in these two years.

A. $1:3$ **B.** $1:4$ **C.** $1:5$ **D.** $1:7$

Q.18 There is a proposal to merge SBI and its associate banks in $2020-21$ due to which the total number of branches will decrease by 5000. After this SBI has 40% of total branches. Find the percentage change in the total branches of SBI and its associate banks before and after merging.

A. 14% decrease **B.** 15% increase
C. $14\frac{2}{7}\%$ decrease **D.** 16% increase

Q.19 If 40% of the total branches are in rural areas in $1990-91$ and 40% of the total branches are in urban areas in $2020-21$, then find the increase in the number of rural branches in these two years.

A. 30000 **B.** 20000 **C.** 50000 **D.** 40000

Q.20 If there were 10000 branches less in $2000-01$, then between which two decades, is the growth rate in number of branches the lowest?

A. $1980-81$ to $1990-91$
B. $1990-91$ to $2000-01$
C. $2010-11$ to $2020-21$
D. $2000-01$ to $2010-11$

Ques (21-25):Direction: Study the following pie chart and answer the following question.

The following graph shows the percentage of students admitted in various streams in a college in 2018.

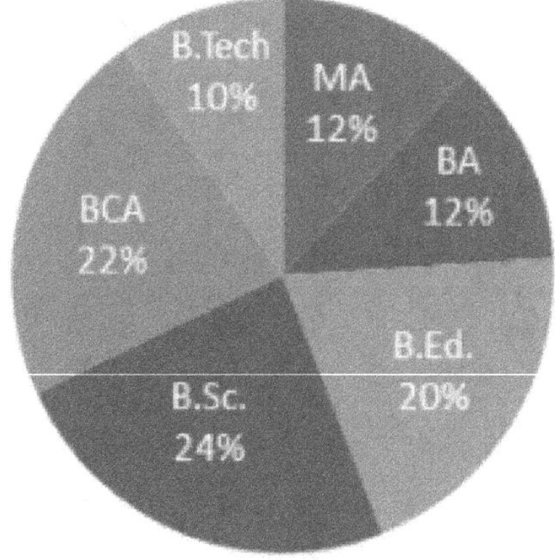

Q.21 If the total number of students taking admission in 2018 in BCA in 660, then number of students taking admission in B.Tech. is what per cent of the number of students taking admission in B.Ed. in the same year?

A. 40% **B.** 25%
C. 45% **D.** None of these

Q.22 The number of students taking admission in B.Sc. is what per cent more than the number of students taking admission in B.Ed. in 2018? The total number of students taking admission in BCA is 550 in 2018.

A. 4% **B.** 20%
C. 12% **D.** None of these

Q.23 The total number of students taking admission in BCA is 770 in 2018. What is the total number of students in MA in the same year?

A. 440 **B.** 520 **C.** 320 **D.** 420

Q.24 In the MA and B.Tech. there are 280 girls and 160 boys admitted respectively in 2018. What is the total number of students taking admission in BA in the same year?

A. 280 **B.** 380
C. 240 **D.** Can't be determined

Q.25 The number of boys and girls in B.Tech. stream is in the ratio of $5:4$, and the total number of students taking admission in B.Sc. is 648 in 2018. Then what is the total number of girls taking admission in B.Tech. in the same year?

A. 150 **B.** 160 **C.** 120 **D.** 180

Business Awareness

Q.26 In strategic human resource management, HR strategies are generally aligned with

A. Business Strategy
B. Marketing Strategies
C. Finance strategy
D. Economic strategy

Q.27 Policy formulation Is the function of

A. top-level managers
B. middle-level managers
C. operational management
D. All of the above

Q.28 The industries which provide support service to other industries are known as _______

A. Primary industries
B. Secondary industries
C. Commericial industries
D. Tertiary industries

Q.29 In a perfectly competitive market

A. Firm is the price giver and industry the price taker
B. Firm is the price taker and industry the price giver
C. Both are price takers
D. None of the above

Q.30 The Fiscal Responsibility and Budget Management Act, 2003 aimed at reducing revenue deficit by _____ % or more of the GDP per annum from the year 2004-05.

A. 2 **B.** 1 **C.** 0.5 **D.** 3

Q.31 According to the Second National Commission on Labour, 'check-off system' must be made compulsory for members of all registered trade unions in establishments employing-

A. 150 workers **B.** 200 workers
C. 250 workers **D.** 300 workers

Q.32 The proportion of women in the workforce is projected to ____

A. increase significantly over the coming decade.
B. decrease as more women decide to stay home with children.
C. stop growing.
D. increase at a decreasing rate.

Q.33 What tactic will employers likely have to take to fill openings left by retiring employees?

A. Instituting flexible work hours
B. Providing eldercare
C. Hiring more women
D. Rehiring retirees

Q.34 The performance of human resource departments is evaluated based on ____.

A. measurable evidence of efficiency
B. measurable evidence of effectiveness
C. anecdotal evidence
D. both (A) and (B)

Q.35 An investor or speculator who subscribes to a new issue with the intention of selling them soon after allotment to realize a quick profit is called?

A. Stag **B.** Tall **C.** Bull **D.** Bear

// Smart Answer Sheet //

Correct — Indicates percentage of students who answered questions correctly.

Skipped — Indicates percentage of students who skipped questions.

Q.	Ans.	Correct	Skipped
1	D	54.18 %	40.84 %
2	D	61.02 %	35.4 %
3	D	50.12 %	36.89 %
4	D	88.63 %	10.33 %
5	C	13.91 %	82.84 %
6	B	69.03 %	30.85 %
7	A	32.74 %	67.12 %
8	C	64.49 %	35.01 %
9	B	18.38 %	70.92 %
10	D	41.96 %	42.22 %
11	B	76.9 %	10.44 %
12	C	45.19 %	53.48 %
13	A	78.26 %	17.06 %
14	B	44.58 %	44.69 %
15	B	77.57 %	17.57 %
16	D	86.07 %	13.85 %
17	B	45.46 %	51.01 %
18	C	46.04 %	47.62 %
19	D	54.28 %	30.92 %
20	C	40.29 %	31.25 %
21	D	86.9 %	10.75 %
22	B	62.83 %	36.31 %
23	D	78.12 %	11.98 %
24	D	84.52 %	11.58 %
25	C	65.47 %	32.74 %
26	A	59.86 %	36.24 %
27	A	53.45 %	35.85 %
28	D	82.53 %	11.54 %
29	B	41.85 %	41.46 %
30	C	76.72 %	22.18 %
31	D	63.24 %	33.4 %
32	C	42.53 %	35.63 %
33	D	44.19 %	48.98 %
34	D	45.22 %	33.63 %
35	A	86.58 %	10.0 %

Performance Analysis	
Avg. Score (%)	57.14%
Toppers Score (%)	68.57%
Your Score	

//Hints and Solutions//

1. The most striking feature of Prime Minister Narendra Modi's address to the nation on the decision to scrap Articles 370 and 35A was its temporal focus: the future. **This served to both fill the narrative with hope and skirt the messy political discord preceding and accompanying the decision to remove Jammu and Kashmir's special status.**

The highlighted portion validates the information given in statements II and III. Thus, statements II and III are correct. However, the address did nothing to encourage further debate regarding the pros and cons of scrapping the articles once the decision had been made. So, the statement I is incorrect.

Hence, the correct option is (D).

2. Carrot and stick (Idiom):

Meaning: A motivational tactic that uses a reward and punishment system to encourage improved performance or behaviour.

Example: Management dangled the carrot of a possible raise before strikers, but at the same time waved the stick of losing their pension benefits.

Hence, the correct option is (D).

3. Statement I: Benefits given to the J&K residents have stolen the limelight from the cost.

Refer to:

The detailed list of benefits and legal entitlements that the people of Jammu and Kashmir now stand to gain, governed as they would be by the Constitution and legal system of India, is likely to have the desired impact of **shifting the spotlight on the benefits of the political change, from the costs that have been most obvious**.

The highlighted part of the passage validates statement I to be correct.

Statement II: India is no longer under any threat from Pakistani terrorists.

Pakistani terrorists have not been mentioned in the passage. Hence, statement II is invalid.

Statement III: There was a lockdown in Jammu and Kashmir.

Refer to:

The prime minister did well to **announce relaxation**, as early as next Monday, when Eid would be celebrated, **on the lockdown in place in the state**.

The highlighted part of the passage validates statement III to be correct.

Hence, the correct option is (D).

4. Refer to:

The prime minister held out carrots aplenty, juicy ones. **Better salaries and service conditions for civil servants and J&K policemen, an immediate flurry of jobs as the government moved to fill all vacancies, new scholarships and educational opportunities, new rights as full-fledged citizens of India and new jobs that Indian enterprises, State-owned and private, would create.**

The highlighted part shows that apart from maternity leave, all other benefits have been mentioned in the passage.

Hence, the correct option is (D).

5. If a leader holds out a carrot, a stick cannot but be part of the package. **But if the prime minister wielded one, it was not on display. He did refer to separatism and terror, but implicitly treated them as nothing more than bumps along the road to normalisation and return to statehood.**

The author believes that the Prime Minister was using a carrot and stick policy but was not showing the stick directly. He just brushed over the threats that were looming by mentioning them briefly. Out of the given option, only option (C) can be a valid point that can be inferred from the passage.

Hence, the correct option is (C).

6. Refer to: 'Once upon a time, there lived a farmer who had a little land. His name was Tuan and he was a very kind and good-natured person.'

As per the passage, Tuan was a simple farmer who was very helpful and good natured. II is correct but I and III are incorrect.

Hence, the correct option is (B).

7. Refer to: 'From that day, Juan changed himself. Within a year, he could produce much crops in his land through his hard work. When the others asked him how he had changed so much, he only replied.'

Clearly, only I is correct while the rest have not been mentioned in the passage.

Hence, the correct option is (A).

8. Refer to: 'A lazy person by nature, Juan hardly put in as much effort to cultivate his land as Tuan did to produce crops in his own. **So when the harvest season arrived every year, Juan found that he had very few crops to sell. Tuan on the other hand, earned a handsome profit through the selling of his produces.'**

As per the highlighted fragment above, only option (C) matches the context.

Hence, the correct option is (C).

9. Perished: Suffered ruin or destruction.

Grew and revived can be used as the antonyms of the given word. Bore is out of context here.

Only destroyed implies the similar meaning to the given word and it can be the synonym of the word.

Hence, the correct option is (B).

10. Refer to: 'Tuan was asleep at this time and it **was only the alertness of one of his other neighbor's that saved much of his crops from being perished in the deadly** flames of the fire that Juan had lighted.'

As per the highlighted fragment above, Option (D) is the best choice here.

Hence, the correct option is (D).

11. The total number of all the model cars sold by TATA in $2017 = 3416$ thousand

The total number of all the model cars sold TATA in $2011 = 3727$ thousand

The required difference $= 3727 - 3416 = 311$ thousand

Hence, the correct option is (B).

12. The total number of Bolt Model sold in 2012 and 2013 together $= 215 + 890 = 1105$ thousand

The total number of Sumo Model sold in 2014 and 2015 together $= 126 + 431 = 557$ thousand

Required $\% = \frac{1105\times100}{557} = 198.38\%$

Hence, the correct option is (C).

13. The sales of Nano in $2011 = 234$ thousand

The sales of Nano in $2017 = 651$ thousand

Required $\% = \frac{(651-234)\times100}{234} = 178.20\%$

Hence, the correct option is (A).

14. The Indica model sold in 2015 and 2017 together $= 322 + 781 = 1103$ thousand

The Bolt model sold in 2013 and 2014 together $= 890 + 234 = 1124$ thousand

Required ratio $= 1103 : 1124$

Hence, the correct option is (B).

15. The total number of Nano car sold over the years $= 2361$ thousand

The total number of Indica car sold over the years $= 2899$ thousand

Required difference $= 2899 - 2361 = 538$ thousand

Hence, the correct option is (B).

16. Number of branches in $1980 - 81$ is 10000 and that in $2010 - 11$ is 60000.

$\%$ Increase $= \frac{60000-10000}{10000} \times 100 = 500\%$

Hence, the correct option is (D).

17. Average branches per bank in $1980 - 81 = \frac{10000}{14}$

Average branches per bank in $2020 - 21 = \frac{80000}{28}$

Ratio $= \frac{10000}{14} : \frac{80000}{28}$

$= \frac{10000}{14} \times \frac{28}{80000} = 1:4$

Hence, the correct option is (B).

18. Total branches of SBI after merging $= 40\%$ of $(80000 - 5000) = 30000$

Total branches of SBI and its associate branches before merging $= 5000 + 30000 = 35000$

Percentage change in SBI and its associate banks after merging $= \frac{5000\times100}{35000}$

$= 14\frac{2}{7}\%$ decrease

Hence, the correct option is (C).

19. Total number of rural branches in $1990 - 91 = 40\%$ of $20000 = 8000$

Total number of rural branches in $2020 - 21 = 60\%$ of $80000 = 48000$

Increase in the number of rural branches $= 48000 - 8000 = 40000$

Hence, the correct option is (D).

20. In $2000 - 01$, total number of branches is 40000.

Percentage increase from $1980 - 81$ to $1990 - 91 = 10k \rightarrow 20k$ i.e., 100%

Percentage increase from $1990 - 91$ to $2000 - 01 = 20k \rightarrow 40k$ i.e., 100%

Percentage increase from $2000 - 01$ to $2010 - 11 = 40k \rightarrow 60k$ i.e., 50%

Percentage increase from $2010 - 11$ to $2020 - 21 = 60k \rightarrow 80k$ i.e., 33%

From $2010 - 11$ to $2020 - 21$, the percentage increase (i.e., growth rate) is the lowest.

Hence, the correct option is (C).

21. Number of students taking admission in B.Tech. $= \frac{660}{22} \times 10 = 300$

Number of students taking admission in B.Ed. $= \frac{660}{22} \times 20 = 600$

Required $\% = \frac{300}{600} \times 100 = 50\%$

Hence, the correct option is (D).

22. Number of students taking admission in B.Sc. $= \frac{550}{22} \times 24 = 600$

Number of students taking admission in B.Ed. $= \frac{550}{22} \times 20 = 500$

Required $\% = \frac{600-500}{500} \times 100 = 20\%$
Hence, the correct option is (B).

23. Given,
The total number of students taking admission in BCA $= 770$
The percentage of students admitted in MA $= 12\%$
The percentage of students admitted in BCA $= 22\%$
Number of students in MA $= \frac{770}{22} \times 12 = 420$
Hence, the correct option is (D).

24. In the Pie Chart the data of students admitted in various streams in a college are given whereas in the question numbers of boys and girls are given for two different streams.

Clearly, in no way we can deduce the number of students taking admissions in BA stream.

The answer is 'Can't be determined'.

Hence, the correct option is (D).

25. Given,

The total number of students taking admission in B.Sc. $= 648$

The percentage of students admitted in B.Tech $= 10\%$

The percentage of students admitted in B.Sc. $= 24\%$

Number of students taking admission in B.Tech. $= \frac{648}{24} \times 10 = 270$

The number of boys and girls in B.Tech. stream is in the ratio $= 5:4$
$\therefore$ Number of girls in B.Tech. $= \frac{4}{9} \times 270 = 120$
Hence, the correct option is (C).

26. In strategic human resource management, HR strategies are generally aligned with Business Strategy. Strategic human resource management can be defined as the linking of human resources with strategic goals and objectives in order to improve business performance and develop organizational culture that foster innovation, flexibility and competitive advantage.
Hence, the correct option is (A).

27. Policy formulation Is the function of top-level managers.

They are the ones, responsible for developing the policies and goals for the organization. On the other hand, middle-level managers interpret these policies in terms of plans and objectives and work towards implementing them with the help of operational management. The operational management as per the instructions of the middle management directly oversees the actual work process.

Hence, the correct option is (A).

28.

- Tertiary activities are based on providing support services to other business.
- Business activity is divided into three categories: primary, secondary and tertiary.
- Primary activities include extracting raw materials. Secondary activities involve manufacturing and construction.
- Commercial industry is an industry that focuses on widespread production with the goal of selling the maximum possible amount of products to consumers.

Hence, the correct option is (D).

29. In a perfectly competitive market, firms are the price taker and the industry the price giver. A perfectly competitive firm would be characterized as a "price taker" due to its inability to influence the market price. In a perfectly competitive market, the price of the products is fixed since each firm is producing just enough to stay in business.

Hence, the correct option is (B).

30. The Fiscal Responsibility and Budget Management Act, 2003 (FRBMA) is an Act of the Parliament of India to institutionalize financial discipline, reduce India's fiscal deficit, improve macroeconomic management and the overall management of the public funds by moving towards a balanced budget. It aimed at reducing the revenue deficit by 0.5 % or more of GDP each year from 2004-05.
Hence, the correct option is (C).

31. The check-off system in an establishment employing 300 or more workers must be made compulsory for members of all registered trade unions.

Hence, the correct option is (D).

32. The proportion of women in the workforce is projected to stop growing.

Since the industrial revolution, the participation of women in the workforce outside of the home has increased in industrialized nations, with particularly large growth seen in the 20th century. Largely seen as a boon for industrial society, women in the workforce contribute to a higher national economic output as the measure in GDP as well as decreasing labor costs by increasing the labor supply in a society.

Hence, the correct option is (C).

33. Employers will likely have rehiring retirees tactics to take to fill openings left by retiring employees. When a position is left open due to a retiring employee, employers identify the easiest way to fill the position. In these cases, rehiring retirees is the simplest method.

Hence, the correct option is (D).

34. The performance of human resource departments is evaluated based on the measurable evidence of efficiency and measurable evidence of effectiveness. Performance Evaluation is defined as a formal and productive procedure to measure an employee's work and results based on their job responsibilities. It is used to gauge the amount of value added by an employee in terms of increased business revenue, in comparison to industry standards and overall employee return on investment (ROI).

Hence, the correct option is (D).

35. An investor or speculator who subscribes to a new issue with the intention of selling them soon after allotment to realize a quick profit is called Stag.

Hence, the correct option is (A).

Mock Test 12

Comprehension

Ques (1-5):Direction: Read the following passage carefully and answer the question given below it.

The catastrophic monsoon floods in Kerala and parts of Karnataka have revived the debate on whether political expediency trumped science. Seven years ago, the Western Ghats Ecology Expert Panel issued recommendations for the preservation of the fragile western peninsular region. Madhav Gadgil, who chaired the Union Environment Ministry's WGEEP, has said the recent havoc in Kerala is a consequence of short-sighted policymaking and warned that Goa may also be in the line of nature's fury. The State governments that are mainly responsible for the Western Ghats — Kerala, Karnataka, Tamil Nadu, Goa and Maharashtra — must go back to the drawing table with the reports of both the Gadgil Committee and the Kasturirangan Committee, which was set up to examine the WGEEP report. The task before them is to initiate correctives to environmental policy decisions. This is not going to be easy, given the need to balance human development pressures with stronger protection of the Western Ghats ecology. The issue of allowing extractive industries such as quarrying and mining to operate is arguably the most contentious. A way out could be to create the regulatory framework that was proposed by the Gadgil panel, in the form of an apex Western Ghats Ecology Authority and the State-level units, under the Environment (Protection) Act, and to adopt the zoning system that it proposed. This can keep incompatible activities out of the Ecologically Sensitive Zones (ESZs).

At issue in the Western Ghats — spread over 1,29,037 sq km according to the WGEEP estimate and 1,64,280 sq km as per the Kasturirangan panel — is the calculation of what constitutes the sensitive core and what activities can be carried out there. The entire system is globally acknowledged as a biodiversity hotspot. But population estimates for the sensitive zones vary greatly, based on interpretations of the ESZs. In Kerala, for instance, one expert assessment says 39 lakh households are in the ESZs outlined by the WGEEP, but the figure drops sharply to four lakh households for a smaller area of zones identified by the Kasturirangan panel. The goal has to be a sustainable development for the Ghats as a whole. The role of big hydroelectric dams, built during an era of rising power demand and deficits, must now be considered afresh and proposals for new ones dropped. Other low-impact forms of green energy led by solar power are available. A moratorium on quarrying and mining in the identified sensitive zones, in Kerala and also other States, is necessary to assess their environmental impact. Kerala's Finance Minister, Thomas Isaac, has acknowledged the need to review decisions affecting the environment, in the wake of the floods. Public consultation on the expert reports that includes people's representatives will find greater resonance now and help chart a sustainable path ahead.

Q.1 Which among the following has been attributed by the experts as a reason of the recent floods in Kerala and Karnataka?

A. The states do not have a proper system in place of drainage and that is why the rainwater always overflows in these two states.

B. The states have no idea how to manage any kind of natural calamity and that is why they cannot tackle any situation however small it may be.

C. The states should be entrusted with the responsibility of protecting the environment in the areas within their jurisdiction.

D. The political decision-making strategy has always taken the upper hand as compared to the real interests of the environment.

Q.2 According to the passage, the states affected by the floods should do which among the following to prevent such incidents in the future?

A. The states should devote more funds towards the reduction of natural calamities in the states.

B. The states should put in place proper warning mechanism so that the government can get to know the possibility of any natural calamity beforehand.

C. The states should plan properly so that they can implement the recommendations of the expert panels regarding the preservation of the Western Ghats Area.

D. The states should not do anything at present and should only focus on the idea of going all out in disaster management operations.

Q.3 Which among the following is the main issue pointed out in the passage in the implementation of the expert panel reports in various states?

A. There is no proper framework depicted in the expert panel reports to regulate the Ecologically Sensitive Zone in the Western Ghat Area.

B. There is no issue pertaining to the Western Ghat area but the main problem is that the governments do not have enough funds.

C. The reservoirs in the vicinity of the area will spell the doom for the area since they will exhaust the groundwater available in the area.

D. The balance between development and preservation should be there in order to develop the area properly.

Q.4 Which among the following should be the objective of all concerned regarding the development of the Western Ghats Area?

A. The development plan should be well supported by money and also manpower by all the states.

B. The development plan must be drawn up correctly at the first place since it will help gain an upper hand in the whole process.

C. The states should take the development of the Western Ghats region seriously so that the area is actually preserved.

D. The Western Ghats Area should be preserved properly so that there is the sustainable development of the area.

Q.5 Which among the following should be the course of action of the government in order to ensure that the Western Ghats Area is preserved properly?

I. There should be the utilization of various clean sources of energy such as solar power in the area

II. There should not be any restriction in mining activities as well as quarrying activities in the area

III. There should not be new construction of hydroelectric dams in the area from now onwards

A. Both I and II **B.** Only II
C. Both I and III **D.** Only I

Ques (6-10):Direction: Read the following passage carefully and answer the question given below it.

It's nothing short of a revolution in how we eat, and it's getting closer every day. Yes, a lot of people are obese, and yes, the definition of "healthy eating" seems to change all the time. But in labs and research centers around the world, scientists are racing to match our genes and our taste buds, creating the perfect diet for each of us, a diet that will fight disease, increase longevity, boost physical and mental performance, and taste great to boot. As a food scientist, J.Bruce German says, "The foods we like the most will be the most healthy for us." Is that going to be a great day, or what?

All this will come to pass, thanks to genomics, the science that maps and describes an individual's genetic code. In the future, personalized DNA chips will allow us to assess our own inherited predispositions for certain diseases, then adjust our diets accordingly. So, if you're at risk for heart disease, you won't just go on a generic low-fat diet. You'll eat foods with just the right amount and type of fat that's best for you. You'll even be able to track your metabolism day-to-day to determine what foods you should eat at any given time, for any given activity. "Since people differ in their genetics and metabolism, one diet won't fit all," says German.

Q.6 What are scientists doing?

A. Racing in labs and research centers around the world.
B. Asking us to start dieting.
C. Creating the perfect diet for us.
D. Try and make us taller.

Q.7 What does J. Bruce German say?

A. The food we like is not healthy for us.
B. In the future, the food we like will be the healthiest one for us.
C. The most healthy food should be liked by us.
D. Food scientists like healthy food.

Q.8 What is genomics?

A. The science which describes maps.
B. The science which describes an individual.
C. The science deals with years.
D. The science that maps and describes an individual's genetic code.

Q.9 Why won't a common diet fit everybody?

A. Because different people eat different food.
B. Because their genes are different.
C. Since they differ in genetics and metabolism.
D. Because of their different moods.

Q.10 What will be possible in the future?

A. Personalized DNA chips for people to assess their own inherited predispositions.
B. You are at great risk for heart disease.
C. You will not be able to determine what food you should eat.
D. You will be unable to adjust your diet.

Management Data Interpretation

Ques (11-15):Direction: Read the following information carefully to answer the questions that follow.

A fruit seller sells boxes of five fruits namely Apple, Mango, Pear, Guava and Orange. The following line charts represent the % marked up on the cost price and the discount % offered on the marked price.

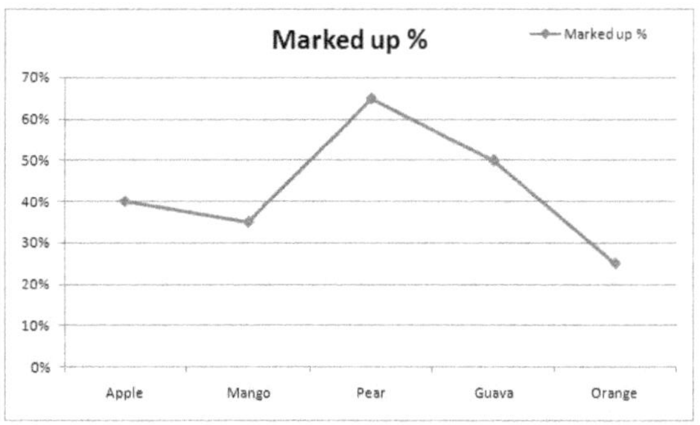

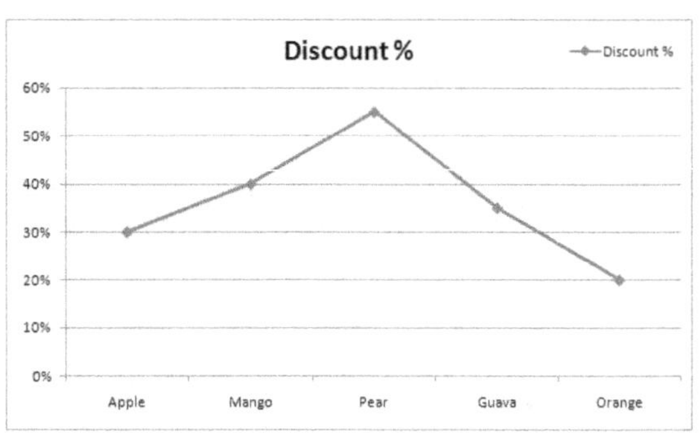

Q.11 If the cost price of one Pear box is $\$120$ and that of Orange is $\$180$, the selling price of one box of Pear is approximately what percent of the selling price of one box of orange?

A. 45% **B.** 50% **C.** 55% **D.** 60%

Q.12 Due to shortage of the stock, the cost price of Mango's is increased by 20% but the marked price and selling price were the same. What will be his profit percentage?

A. -32.5% **B.** 32.5% **C.** -37.5% **D.** 37.5%

Q.13 If the Cost price of each box of any fruit is $\$100$, what is profit % obtained on selling one box each of all the fruits?

A. -7.65% **B.** -11.25%
C. -9.85% **D.** 14%

Q.14 If the Cost price of each box of any fruit is $\$100$ and the shop keeper increased the SP of each box by $x\%$ to break even, what is the nearest integer value of x?

A. 13% **B.** 12% **C.** 11% **D.** 14%

Q.15 If the cost price of each box of Guava and Mango is $\$100$, what is the ratio of the selling price of Mango to the marked price of Guava?

A. $32:57$ **B.** $41:64$ **C.** $38:57$ **D.** $27:50$

Ques (16-20):Direction: Study the table chart carefully and answer the question given below. The table shows the number of cakes sold by the 6 different Bakery on five different days.

Bakery	Days				
	Monday	Tuesday	Thursday	Saturday	Sunday
M	222	255	215	250	266
N	205	275	314	295	260
O	245	266	305	195	235
P	221	230	185	300	280
Q	312	325	298	272	254
R	175	205	255	240	308

Q.16 What is difference between the lowest number of the cake sold by bakery P and the highest number of the cake sold by bakery M out of all the six bakeries?

A. 65 **B.** 71 **C.** 81 **D.** 91

Q.17 If out of the total number of cakes sold by bakery O on Monday, 40% are chocolate cakes and the rest are vanilla cakes. Find out the total number of vanilla cakes sold by the bakery O.

A. 150 **B.** 137 **C.** 135 **D.** 147

Q.18 What is the average number of cakes sold by the bakery R on Monday, Thursday and Sunday?

A. 246 **B.** 320 **C.** 245 **D.** 295

Q.19 What is the approximate percentage of the total number of cakes sold by bakery O on Sunday and Saturday compared to the number of cakes sold by bakery Q on Tuesday?

A. 120% **B.** 121% **C.** 142% **D.** 130%

Q.20 Find the ratio between the number of cakes sold by bakery M on Saturday and the number of cakes sold by bakery N on Tuesday.

A. $13:15$ **B.** $8:9$ **C.** $10:11$ **D.** $12:14$

Ques (21-25):Direction: Study the following pie-charts carefully and answer the question given below.

Pie chart shows the percent of students in five different classes in 2016.

Total Students in all the classes together $= 1000$

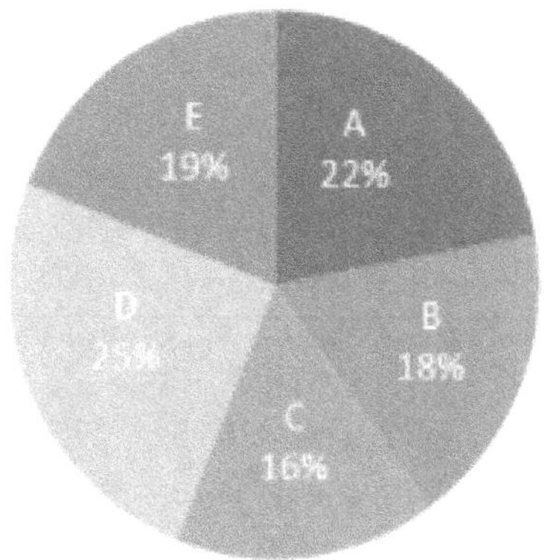

Second pie chart shows the average fee per student of five different classes in 2016.

Total average fee per student of five classes together $=$ Rs. 800

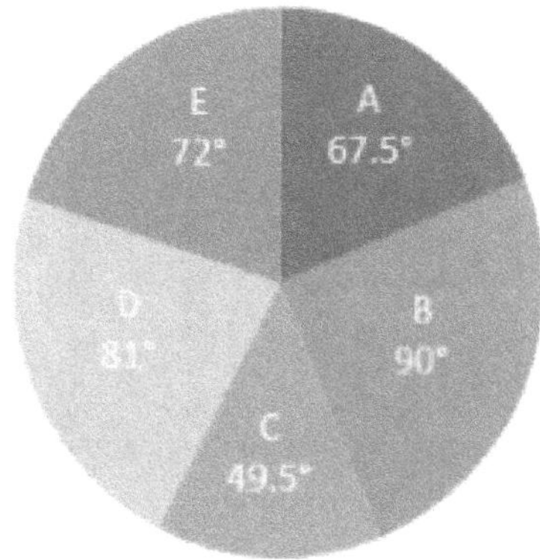

Q.21

If in 2017, the average fee per student as well as the number of students is increased by 20% and 10% respectively from 2016 in class A, then what is the total revenue generated from class A in the year 2017?

A. Rs. 43560 **B.** Rs. 33000
C. Rs. 36300 **D.** Rs. 39600

Q.22

Total revenue generated from class C in 2016 is approximately what percent of the total revenue generated from class E in 2016?

A. 48% **B.** 58% **C.** 68% **D.** 64%

Q.23

What is the ratio of the total revenue generated from class E in 2016 to the total revenue generated from class F in 2016 if number of students in class F is 20 more than the number of students in class B in 2016 and average fee per student in class F is Rs. 50 more than the average fee per student in class B in 2016?

A. 19:20 **B.** 16:25 **C.** 76:125 **D.** 125:76

Q.24
What is the approximate average fee per student of classes C, D and E together in 2016?

A. Rs. 150 **B.** Rs. 145 **C.** Rs. 155 **D.** Rs. 160

Q.25 If in 2015, the number of students in class D was 50% more than the number of students in class D in 2016 and average fee per student of class D was 10% less than the average fee per student of class D in 2016, then what was the total revenue generated from class D in 2015?

A. Rs. 45000 **B.** Rs. 40500
C. Rs. 67500 **D.** Rs. 60750

Business Awareness

Q.26 An association of crane operators in an industrial establishment is an example of:

A. General Union
B. Craft Union
C. Industrial Union
D. Industrial Federation

Q.27 The factor, which does not include the substance of sound industrial relations policy at the macro-level is

A. The business proposition, project development
B. Structure of economy and labour market
C. Structure of union and employers' organizations
D. Policies of the Government

Q.28 The Employee State Insurance Act has enacted on the basis of which committee's report?

A. B. R. Ambedkar Committee
B. B. P. Adarkar Committee
C. Royal Commission on Labour
D. Labour Investigation Committee

Q.29 Demand is determined by

A. Price of the product
B. Relative prices of other goods
C. Tastes and habits
D. All of the above

Q.30 When a firm's average revenue is equal to its average cost, it gets _______.

A. Super profit **B.** Normal profit
C. Sub normal profit **D.** None of the above

Q.31 Managerial economics generally refers to the integration of economic theory with business_______.

A. Ethics **B.** Management
C. Practice **D.** All of the above

Q.32 Match the following:

List-I (Concepts of HRM)	List-II (Factors)
(A) Job satisfaction	1. Achievement
(B) Wage and Salary Administration	2. Halsey Plan
(C) Incentive Plan	3. Halsey Plan
(D) Motivation	4. X-Theory

A. (A) (B) (C) (D) 1 4 3 2
B. (A) (B) (C) (D) 3 4 1 2
C. (A) (B) (C) (D) 1 2 3 4
D. (A) (B) (C) (D) 1 3 4 2

Q.33 _______ is a group of position involving substantially the same duties, skills, knowledge, and responsibilities.

A. Job **B.** HRM
C. Product **D.** Personnel

Q.34 Human Resource Audit System covers

A. By examining the structure and content of the systems to see if the activities are controlling to the fulfillment of objectives.
B. By recording the component of all the systems relating to manpower in the organization and see that all-important activities have been covered by the systems.
C. By examining if the systems are being followed and identifying the bottlenecks.
D. All of the above

Q.35 ______ means reducing the size of the organization. It is the restructuring of the organization whereby non-core activities are disposed off. Where there is surplus staff, trimming will be essential.

A. Downsizing **B.** Exit Policy
C. Golden Handshake **D.** All of these

// Smart Answer Sheet //

Correct Indicates percentage of students who answered questions correctly.

Skipped Indicates percentage of students who skipped questions.

Q.	Ans.	Correct	Skipped
1	D	47.11 %	46.39 %
2	C	78.06 %	16.83 %
3	D	56.27 %	32.91 %
4	D	48.33 %	44.54 %
5	C	80.08 %	10.53 %
6	C	79.26 %	14.14 %
7	B	76.22 %	21.71 %
8	D	29.09 %	68.83 %
9	C	28.02 %	67.54 %
10	A	42.46 %	36.79 %
11	B	50.46 %	45.04 %
12	A	52.58 %	35.45 %
13	C	22.06 %	72.73 %
14	C	29.14 %	69.98 %
15	D	67.48 %	30.36 %
16	C	43.89 %	56.05 %
17	D	54.78 %	38.11 %
18	A	81.3 %	17.15 %
19	D	59.0 %	36.09 %
20	C	65.95 %	31.62 %
21	A	76.94 %	12.16 %
22	B	50.2 %	38.62 %
23	C	19.61 %	79.77 %
24	C	51.09 %	41.94 %
25	D	68.04 %	30.42 %
26	B	80.36 %	17.68 %
27	A	63.52 %	30.46 %
28	B	14.41 %	79.67 %
29	D	80.35 %	17.6 %
30	B	40.18 %	41.05 %
31	C	60.85 %	35.59 %
32	C	68.91 %	30.52 %
33	A	80.32 %	11.49 %
34	D	53.44 %	37.7 %
35	A	23.4 %	68.81 %

Performance Analysis	
Avg. Score (%)	42.86%
Toppers Score (%)	60.0%
Your Score	

//Hints and Solutions//

1. Refer to, "Madhav Gadgil, who chaired the Union Environment Ministry's WGEEP, has said the recent havoc in Kerala is a consequence of short-sighted policymaking and warned that Goa may also be in the line of nature's fury."

It is clear from the above that the experts are of the view that policymaking has been the major reason for such floods in the country as it has not taken into account the environmental considerations of the area.

Hence, the correct option is (D).

2. Refer to, "The State governments that are mainly responsible for the Western Ghats — Kerala, Karnataka, Tamil Nadu, Goa and Maharashtra — must go back to the drawing table with the reports of both the Gadgil Committee and the Kasturirangan Committee, which was set up to examine the WGEEP report. The task before them is to initiate correctives to environmental policy decisions."

It implies from the above lines that the states should ponder over the steps to be taken in order to preserve the ecology of the Western Ghats Area and they should think about the implementation of the expert panel report on this issue.

Hence, the correct option is (C).

3. Refer to, "This is not going to be easy, given the need to balance human development pressures with stronger protection of the Western Ghats ecology."

It is very much clear from the above lines that the objective of sustainable development is very difficult to meet with the political considerations in mind and that is why it becomes very difficult to strike a balance between the political objectives and the environmental requirements of the Western Ghats Area.

Statement A is incorrect since the expert panel has recommended the formation of a committee and authority to oversee the development in the Western Ghats Area. Statements B, C and D are not in sync with the given context though they may sound logical otherwise. Only Option E implies the same as has been depicted in the passage.

Hence, the correct option is (D).

4. Refer to, "The goal has to be sustainable development for the Ghats as a whole."

It is very clear that the main objective of all the activities surrounding the Western Ghats Area should be the overall development of the region and also for all the parties concerned. There should be sustainable development of all the regions in the area.

Except for statement D, all the other options are not related to the given context and that is why they are eliminated. Option D implies the same as referred to in the above reference.

Hence, the correct option is (D).

5. Refer to, "The role of big hydroelectric dams, built during an era of rising power demand and deficits, must now be considered afresh and proposals for new ones dropped. Other low-impact forms of green energy led by solar power are available. A moratorium on quarrying and mining in the identified sensitive zones, in Kerala and also other States, is necessary to assess their environmental impact."

It is clear that in order to preserve the Western Ghats Area, solar energy should be promoted in the area along with a moratorium on the mining and quarrying activities in the area. Apart from that, there should be restrictions on the construction of new hydroelectric power dams in the area. This makes statements I and III true.

Hence, the correct option is (C).

6. Scientists are trying to create diets that taste good as well as have all the health benefits for us. Refer to the following statement of the passage, "But in labs and research centers around the world, scientists are racing to match our genes and our taste buds, creating the perfect diet for each of us, a diet that will fight disease, increase longevity, boost physical and mental performance, and taste great to boot".

Hence, the correct option is (C).

7. According to J. Bruce German, when the perfect diet is created in the future, people will have the option to get the healthiest food according to their genes and have it in the best possible taste as well. Making sure people get the best of both worlds. Refer to the following statement of the passage, "But in labs and research centres around the world, scientists are racing to match our genes and our taste buds, creating the perfect diet for each of us, a diet that will fight disease, increase longevity, boost physical and mental performance, and taste great to boot. As a food scientist, J.Bruce German says, "The foods we like the most will be the most healthy for us."

Hence, the correct option is (B).

8. Genomics is the science that maps and describes an individual's genetic code. Refer to the following statement of the passage, "All this will come to pass, thanks to genomics, the science that maps and describes an individual's genetic code."

Hence, the correct option is (D).

9. People have different tastes and food habits because they differ in genetics and metabolism.

Hence, the correct option is (C).

10. In the future personalized DNA chips will allow people to assess their own inherited predispositions for certain diseases, then adjust their diets accordingly. Refer to the following statement of the passage, "In the future, personalized DNA chips will allow us to assess our own inherited predispositions for certain diseases, then adjust our diets accordingly.

Hence, the correct option is (A).

11. Let us tabulate the data given in the line charts below-

Item	Marked up %	Discount %
Apple	40%	30%
Mango	35%	40%
Pear	65%	55%

Guava	50%	35%
Orange	25%	20%

Given that,

CP of pear $= \$120$

Here, MP is Marked price, SP is Selling price, CP is cost price.

$MP = \left(1 + \frac{\text{PercentageMarkedup}}{100}\right) \times CP$

$SP = \left(1 - \frac{\text{PercentageofDiscount}}{100}\right) \times MP$

MP(marked price) of Pear $= 1.65 \times 120 = \$198$

SP (selling price) of Pear $= 0.45 \times 198 = \$89.1$

CP of Orange $= \$180$

MP (marked price) of Orange $= 1.25 \times 180 = \$225$

SP (selling price) of Orange $= 0.8 \times 225 = \$180$

Required $\% = \frac{89.1 \times 100}{180} = 49.5\% \approx 50\%$

Hence, the correct option is (B).

12. Let us tabulate the data given in the line charts as below.

Item	Marked up %	Discount %
Apple	40%	30%
Mango	35%	40%
Pear	65%	55%
Guava	50%	35%
Orange	25%	20%

Here, MP is Marked price, SP is Selling price, CP is cost price. $MP = \left(1 + \frac{\text{Percentage Marked up}}{100}\right) \times CP$

$SP = \left(1 - \frac{\text{Percentage of Discount}}{100}\right) \times MP$

Let us assume that the initial CP of mango as $\$100$

$MP = 1.35 \times 100 = \$135$

$SP = 0.6 \times 135 = \$81$

His final CP due to shortage $= 1.2 \times (100) = \$120$

His profit $\% = \frac{(81-120)(100)}{120} = -32.5\%$

Hence, the correct option is (A).

13. Let us tabulate the data given in the line charts below.

Item	Marked up %	Discount %
Apple	40%	30%
Mango	35%	40%
Pear	65%	55%
Guava	50%	35%
Orange	25%	20%

Given that Here, MP is Marked price, SP is Selling price, CP is cost price. $MP = \left(1 + \frac{\text{PercentageMarkedup}}{100}\right) \times CP$

$SP = \left(1 - \frac{\text{PercentageofDiscount}}{100}\right) \times MP$

Now let us find the SP of the Apple using the above two tables

SP of apple $= 100 \times 1.4 \times 0.7 = \$98$

In the same way we can calculate and tabulate the data for all the fruits

Caliber	CP in \$	Marked up %	Discount %	SP in \$
Apple	\$100.00	40%	30%	\$98.00
Mango	\$100.00	35%	40%	\$81.00
Pear	\$100.00	35%	55%	\$74.25
Guava	\$100.00	50%	35%	\$97.50
Orange	\$100.00	25%	20%	\$100.00
Total	\$500.00			\$450.75

Sum of CP of all the five boxes $= \$500$

Sum of SP of all the five boxes $= \$450.75$

% of Profit $= \frac{(450.75-500) \times 100}{500} = -9.85\%$

Hence, the correct option is (C).

14. Let us tabulate the data given in the line charts as below.

Item	Marked up %	Discount %
Apple	40%	30%
Mango	35%	40%
Pear	65%	55%
Guava	50%	35%
Orange	25%	20%

Given that Now let us find the SP of the Apple using the above two tables Here, MP is Marked price, SP is Selling price, CP is cost price. $MP = \left(1 + \frac{\text{PercentageMarkedup}}{100}\right) \times CP$

$SP = \left(1 - \frac{\text{PercentageofDiscount}}{100}\right) \times MP$

SP of apple $= 100 \times 1.4 \times 0.7 = \$98$

In the same way we can calculate and tabulate the data for all the fruits.

Caliber	CP in \$	Marked up %	Discount %	SP in \$
Apple	\$100.00	40%	30%	\$98.00
Mango	\$100.00	35%	40%	\$81.00
Pear	\$100.00	35%	55%	\$74.25
Guava	\$100.00	50%	35%	\$97.50
Orange	\$100.00	25%	20%	\$100.00
Total	\$500.00			\$450.75

Sum of CP of all the five boxes $= \$500$
Sum of SP of all the five boxes $= \$450.75$
Here, the required increase in the SP to break even $=$
$\frac{(500-450.75)\times 100}{450.75} = 10.92\%$ (approx)
Hence, the correct option is (C).

15. Let us tabulate the data given in the line charts below.

Item	Marked up %	Discount %
Apple	40%	30%
Mango	35%	40%
Pear	65%	55%
Guava	50%	35%
Orange	25%	20%

Here, MP is Marked price, SP is Selling price, CP is cost price. $MP = \left(1 + \frac{\text{Percentage Marked up}}{100}\right) \times CP$
$SP = \left(1 - \frac{\text{Percentage of Discount}}{100}\right) \times MP$
Given that CP of Guava $= \$100$ MP of Guava $=$
$1.5 \times 100 = \$150$
CP of Mango $= \$100$
MP of Mango $= 1.35 \times 100 = \$135$
SP of Mango $= 0.6 \times 135 = \$81$
Required ratio $= 81:150 = 27:50$
Hence, the correct option is (D).

16. The lowest number of cake sold by bakery $P = 185$
The highest number of cake sold by bakery $M = 266$
Difference $= 266 - 185 = 81$
Hence, the correct option is (C).

17. Given,

40% are chocolate cakes

Rest are vanilla cakes $= 60\%$

Total cakes sold by bakery O in Monday $= 245$

Number of Vanilla cakes $= 60\%$ of $245 = 147$

Hence, the correct option is (D).

18. Total number of cake sold by bakery R on Monday, Thursday and Sunday $= 175 + 255 + 308 = 738$
Average $= \frac{738}{3} = 246$
Hence, the correct option is (A).

19. Total number of cake sold by bakery O on Sunday and Saturday $= 235 + 195$
And the number of cake sold by bakery Q on Tuesday $= 325$
Required $\% = \frac{(235+195)}{325} \times 100$
$= \frac{430}{325} \times 100 = 132.30 \approx 130\%$
Hence, the correct option is (D).

20. The number of cake sold by bakery M on Saturday $= 250$
And the number of cake sold by bakery N on Tuesday $= 275$
Required ratio $= 250:275 = 10:11$
Hence, the correct option is (C).

21. Number of students in class A in $2016 = 22\%$ of $1000 = 220$

Average fee per student in class A in 2016

$= 800 \times \frac{67.5}{360} =$ Rs. 150

Number of students in class A in $2017 = 110\%$ of $220 = 242$

Average fee per student in class A in $2017 = 120\%$ of $150 =$ Rs. 180

Total revenue generated from class A in the year $2017 =$ Number of students $\times$ Average fee per students $=$
$242 \times 180 =$ Rs. 43560

Hence, the correct option is (A).

22. Total revenue generated from class C in $2016 =$ Number of students $\times$ Average fee per students

$\Rightarrow (16\%$ of $1000) \times \frac{800\times 49.5}{360} =$Rs. (160×110)

Total revenue generated from class E in $2016 =$ Number of students $\times$ Average fee per students

$\Rightarrow (19\%$ of $1000\ ) \times \frac{800\times 72}{360} = Rs. (190 \times 160)$

Required $\% = \frac{160\times 110}{190\times 160} \times 100 = 57.89 = 58\%$ (Approx)

Hence, the correct option is (B).

23. Total revenue generated from class E in $2016 =$ Number of students $\times$ Average fee per students

$\Rightarrow (19\%$ of $1000) \times \frac{800\times 72}{360} =$Rs. (190×160)

Number of students in class $F = (18\%$ of $1000) + 20 = 180 + 20 = 200$

Average fee per student in class $= 800 \times \frac{90}{360} + 50 = 200 + 50 =$Rs. 250

Total revenue generated from class F $=$ Rs. (200×250)

Required ratio $= (190 \times 160):(200 \times 250) = 76:125$

Hence, the correct option is (C).

24. Average fee per student $= \frac{\text{Total fee}}{\text{Total students}}$

Total fee of class C $= (16\%$ of 1000 $) \times \left[800 \times \frac{49.5}{360}\right]$

$= 160 \times 110 =$ Rs. 17600

Total fee of class D $= (25\%$ of 1000 $) \times \left[800 \times \frac{81}{360}\right]$

$= 250 \times 180 =$ Rs. 45000

Total fee of class E $= (19\%$ of 1000 $) \times \left[800 \times \frac{72}{360}\right]$

$= 190 \times 160 =$ Rs. 30400

Total fee of classes C,D and E together $=$ Rs. $(17600 + 45000 + 30400) =$ Rs. 93000

Total students in classes C, D and E together $= 160 + 250 + 190 = 600$

Required average $=$ Rs. $\frac{93000}{600} =$ Rs. 155

Hence, the correct option is (C).

25. Number of students in class D in $2015 = 150\%$ of 25% of $1000 = 375$

Average fee per student of class D in 2015

$= 90\%$ of $\left[800 \times \frac{81}{360}\right] =$ Rs. 162

Total revenue generated from class D in $2015 = 375 \times 162 =$ Rs. 60750

Hence, the correct option is (D).

26. An association of crane operators in an industrial establishment is an example of Craft Union. The basic logic behind the formation of such unions is that the workers belonging to the same craft do face similar problems-mostly non-managerial personnel form such unions.

Hence, the correct option is (B).

27. The factor, which does not include the substance of sound industrial relations policy at the macro-level is a Business proposition, project development.

Hence, the correct option is (A).

28. The Employee State Insurance Act has enacted on the basis of the B. P. Adarkar Committee. B.P. Adarkar was appointed by the Government of India to create a report on the health insurance scheme for industrial workers. The report became the basis for the Employment State Insurance (ESI) Act of 1948.

Hence, the correct option is (B).

29. Demand is determined by the Price of the product, Relative prices of other goods, tastes, and habits of the customer.

Hence, the correct option is (D).

30. When a firm's average revenue is equal to its average cost, it gets Normal profit.

- The average cost being equal to average revenue is when the firm wanting to sell their products at no profits.
- They want to maximize the longer-term gains. A new that enters the market would use this method to familiarize the end-users with their products.
- When the product gets established in the market and the people are familiar with it they can slowly remove these promotional methods and the organizations can then move towards profits.

Hence, the correct option is (B).

31. Managerial economics generally refers to the integration of economic theory with business practice. Economics provides tools managerial economics applies these tools to the management of the business.

Hence, the correct option is (C).

32. The correct match will be: (A) (B) (C) (D) 1 2 3 4

(A) Job satisfaction	1. Achievement
(B) Wage and Salary Administration	2. Halsey Plan
(C) Incentive Plan	3. Halsey Plan
(D) Motivation	4. X-Theory

Hence, the correct option is (C).

33. A job is a group of positions involving substantially the same duties, skills, knowledge, and responsibilities. Job is impersonal but the position is personnel. Every job has a title based on standardized Trades specifications.

Hence, the correct option is (A).

34. The human Resource Audit System covers all the above statements. The process involves a systematic review of all aspects of the HR function, typically with a checklist, in order to ensure that regulations and corporate policies are adhered to.

Hence, the correct option is (D).

35. Downsizing means reducing the size of the organization. It is the restructuring of the organization whereby non-core activities are disposed off. Where there is surplus staff, trimming will be essential. Downsizing is a reduction in organizational size and operating costs implemented by management in order to improve organizational efficiency, productivity and/or the competitiveness of the organization.

Hence, the correct option is (A).

Mock Test 13

Comprehension

Ques (1-5):Direction: Read the following passage carefully and answer the question given below it.

Youths, who are skilled and unable to find jobs, are unemployed. India has been fearing this problem of rising unemployment since independence. Many youths, mainly belonging to the village, face this problem. The government tries to overcome this problem by launching many schemes such as NREGA (2005), PMRY, and many others. But this problem is faced by many youths. The interesting thing is that corruption is done by the government. Officers create this problem and they also try to prevent the country from this. It is just like the situation that, those who manufacture the disease-causing things open the hospital for treatment. Corruption in this sector (job sector) creates this problem. To counter this problem of unemployment, first of all, the government should remove the corruption. People who are unskilled get jobs on behalf of money but skilled people fail to get jobs due to lack of money.

Q.1 India has been facing the problem of unemployment since ______

A. 1945 **B.** 1947 **C.** 1949 **D.** 2005

Q.2 How does the government try to overcome this problem of unemployment?

A. By opening hospitals
B. By providing money
C. By launching many schemes
D. By creating corruption

Q.3 What is the thing created by the government and still they try to prevent the country from this?

A. Corruption **B.** Unemployment
C. Many schemes **D.** Money

Q.4 Corruption created by the government is compared to which situation?

A. The one who paints the picture, open the gallery to sell the pictures
B. The one who molds the clay, open the shop to sell the models
C. The one who bakes the cake, open the bakery to sell the cakes
D. The one who manufactures the disease, open the hospital for treatment

Q.5 Why does a skilled person not able to get the appropriate jobs?

A. Lack of talent **B.** Lack of money
C. Lack of jobs **D.** Lack of confidence

Ques (6-10):Direction: Read the following passage carefully and answer the question that follow.

The Madras High Court on Friday granted 30 days of ordinary leave to S. Nalini, 52, a life convict in the former Prime Minister Rajiv Gandhi's assassination case. The order was passed after she argued her case in person and made a fervent plea to the judges in a choked voice that she may be allowed to step out of prison for some days to make arrangements for the marriage of her daughter, who is residing in London.

Nalini had many years ago come out on short paroles of a day each to attend her brother Bhagyanathan's wedding and her father's last rites.

Justices M.M. Sundresh and M. Nirmal Kumar took judicial notice that the State Cabinet itself had on September 9 last year made a recommendation to the Governor to release all seven convicts in the Rajiv Gandhi assassination case. "If, in the view of the government, the petitioner can be allowed to lead a normal life and she would not be a hindrance to the society, the request for leave can never be objected to," they said.

The judges also directed the State government to bear the expenses of providing escort to her during the period of leave since she expressed difficulty in paying the charges.

"There is no material to hold that she is a woman of means. Admittedly, she and her husband are in incarceration for decades. Asking the petitioner to pay the cost would in a way take away the very order passed by us when it is impossible of compliance," they said.

Q.6 Why was S. Nalini sentenced to lifetime imprisonment by the judiciary of the country?

A. She murdered a lot of people during her school days and that came out in the open later.
B. She murdered her family out of mercy though her husband had left her for another woman before that.
C. She did not do anything but the court was of the view that she could do something if left to fend for herself within the society.
D. She was involved in the assassination of the former Prime Minister of India.

Q.7 Which among the following is correct regarding the attitude of the State Government towards the sentence of life imprisonment given to S Nalini?

A. The state government has nothing to say in the whole issue since the case was dealt with by the central government.
B. The state government could not understand the fact that there was nothing wrong done by S Nalini many years ago.
C. The State government is of the opinion that the sentence given to S Nalini can be remitted at once.
D. The state government wants the convict to continue with the given sentence by the court for the crime committed by her.

Q.8 Which among the following is/ are NOT correct, as per the given passage?

I. This is the first time that S Nalini has been given permission to come out on parole.

II. S. Nalini has been granted the right to come out on parole to perform the last rites of her husband.

III. S Nalini has no child and that is why she is not at all happy with the sentence.

A. Both I and II **B.** Both II and III
C. Both I and III **D.** All I, II and III

Q.9 Which among the following is/are correct regarding the observations of the Madras High Court regarding S Nalini?

I. S Nalini is a very rich woman and that is why no monetary support is required to be given to her.

II. S Nalini is a dreaded criminal and that is why she should be put behind the bars for life with no chance at any kind of reformation.

III. S Nalini has intentionally jeopardized her relationship with her husband and that is why she should be punished for that.

A. Both I and II **B.** Both II and III
C. Only III **D.** None of I, II and III

Q.10 Which among the following would be similar in meaning to the word Fervent as used in the passage?

A. Ardent **B.** Vehement
C. Feeling **D.** Pragmatic

Management Data Interpretation

Ques (11-15):Direction: Study the following table carefully and answer the questions that follow. A few data are assigned alphabetically:

(Sales of shirts and jeans sold by Co. x in various years, Rs. Crores)

Year	Shirt (x)	Jeans (y)	$\frac{y}{x}$
2000	56	70	1.25
2001	60	A	1.2
2002	B	160	C
2003	100	140	D
2004	E	160	1.33
2005	200	F	G

Q.11 The percent increase in the shirts' sale between years 2002 and 2004 is:

A. 40% **B.** 50%
C. 45% **D.** Can't be determined

Q.12 The percent increase in the jeans' sale between 2001 and 2005 is:

A. 75% **B.** 37.5%
C. 375% **D.** Can't be determined

Q.13 If $G = 1.5$, what percent is sales of jeans in 2005 of sales of jeans in 2002?

A. 150 **B.** 175 **C.** 187.5 **D.** 160

Q.14 If $C:D = 1:2$ then $7B = ?$

A. 1500 **B.** 1250 **C.** 1600 **D.** 1800

Q.15 The value of $A:E$ is:

A. 0.6 **B.** 0.8 **C.** 1.0 **D.** 1.2

Ques (16-20):Direction: A cosmetic company provides five different products. The sales of these five products (in lakh number of packs) during 2006 and 2011 are shown in the following bar graph.

Sales (in lakh number of packs) of five different products of Cosmetic Company during 2006 and 2011.

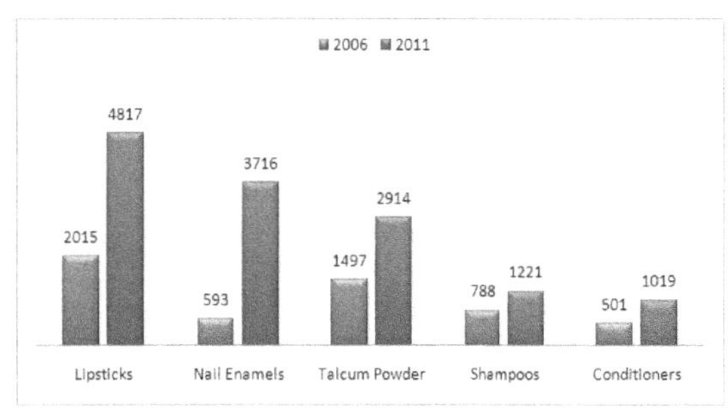

Q.16 The sales of lipsticks in 2011 was by what percent more than the sales of nail enamels in 2011? (rounded off to nearest integer)

A. 33% **B.** 31% **C.** 30% **D.** 22%

Q.17 During the period $2006 - 2011$, the minimum rate of increase in sales is in the case of?

A. Shampoos **B.** Nail enamels
C. Talcum powders **D.** Lipsticks

Q.18 What is the approximate ratio of the sales of nail enamels in 2011 to the sales of Talcum powders in 2006?

A. 7:2 **B.** 5:2 **C.** 4:3 **D.** 2:1

Q.19 The sales have increased by nearly 55% from 2006 to 2011 in the case of?

A. Lipsticks **B.** Nail enamels
C. Talcum powders **D.** Shampoos

Q.20 The sales of conditioners in 2006 was by what percent less than the sales of shampoos in 2006? (rounded off to nearest integer).

A. 57% **B.** 36% **C.** 29% **D.** 25%

Ques (21-25):Direction: The number of soldiers in the army of a country is $10,00,000$. Total females in the army are $2,80,000$. There are 6 divisions within the army namely A, B, C, D, E and F. In the meeting of the Defence Minister with the Chief of Army Staff, the number of soldiers and their status within each division in terms of the male and female population was discussed. Chief of Army Staff gave the following pie charts to Defence Minister.The population of each division in terms of percentage has been given in pie chart -1, and pie chart -2 gives the number of males in those divisions in terms of degrees within the pie chart of the total male population in the army.

Pie Chart - 1

Distribution of Population

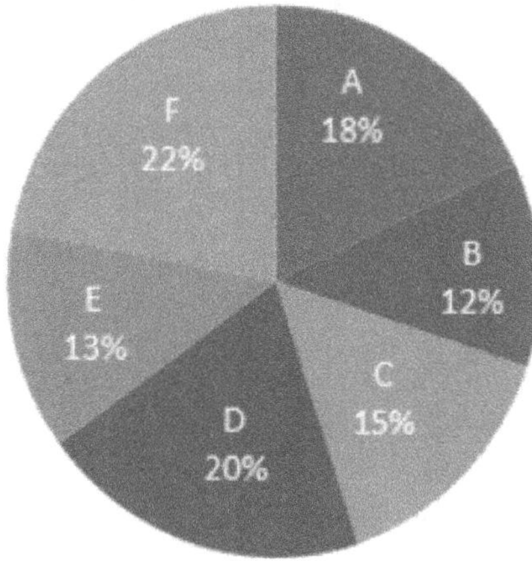

Pie Chart - 2

Number of Males

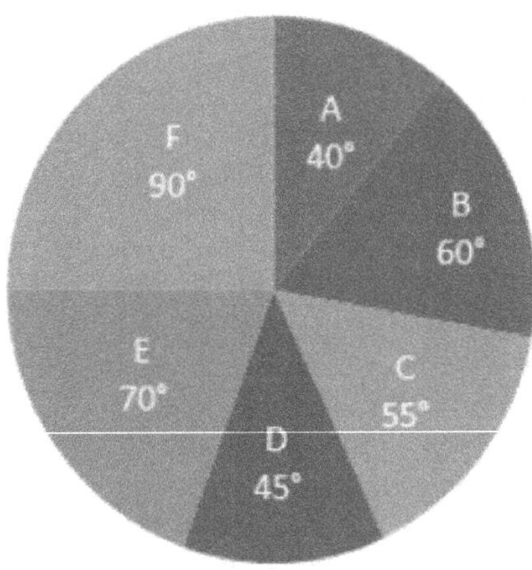

Q.21 In pie chart -2, the secretary of Chief of Army Staff made a discrepancy. Which division has a discrepancy in terms of the number of males and female soldiers in each division?

A. F **B.** E **C.** D **D.** B

Q.22 Find the average number of males in divisions B, D and F together is what $\%$ of the total population of division B?

A. 110.33% **B.** 108.66%
C. 110.66% **D.** 108.33%

Q.23 Half of the females from division A, one-fourth from division C and one-fifth from D were sent for special training. If the number of females on this training are represented on a pie chart then what corresponding angle the females of division C will make? (approximately)

A. 40° **B.** 42° **C.** 44° **D.** 46°

Q.24 After a year from this meeting, in the division A, $20,000$ more soldiers were admitted and in $B, 80,000$ more were admitted and the number of soldiers in all other divisions was not changed. If the pie chart -1 is again prepared, what percentage would division D get in the pie chart -1?

A. 18.18 **B.** 12.5 **C.** 16.66 **D.** 17.66

Q.25 It is known that $15\%, 10\%$ and 5% of males in division $A, C,$ and F respectively are married, while 10% and 20% from B and D respectively are married. In B and D how many more/less men are married with respect to $A, C,$ and F?

A. 5% **B.** 5.25% **C.** 6% **D.** 6.25%

Business Awareness

Q.26 The Reserve Bank of India has directed which bank to stop its digital launches temporarily?

A. ICICI Bank **B.** HDFC Bank
C. Axis Bank **D.** Yes Bank

Q.27 Who had formulated the Employees Provident Fund Scheme?

A. Medical Benefit Council
B. ESIC
C. The State Government
D. The Central Government

Q.28 India's Largest tractor manufacture Mahindra & Mahindra had recently made a takeover bid on a European company, Universal Tractors. The Company is based in:

A. Norway **B.** England **C.** Romania **D.** Finland

Q.29 Business transaction is recorded:

A. In chronological order
B. At the end of the month
C. Weekly
D. Any of the above

Q.30 Australia - based core banking software, Financial Network Services (FNS) has been acquired by an Indian company. Identify the company from the choices given below.

A. Infosys **B.** TCS
C. Mindtree **D.** Wipro Technologies

Q.31 In economics, desire backed by purchasing power is known as:

A. Utility **B.** Demand
C. Consumption **D.** Scarcity

Q.32 Car and petrol are

A. Complimentary goods
B. Substitute goods
C. Supplementary goods
D. Reserve goods

Q.33 Human Resource departments are____________.

A. Line departments
B. Authority department
C. Service department
D. Functional department

Q.34 Asian Hotels Ltd owns and operates the world's one of the leading hotel brands in India. Identify the brand.

A. Hilton **B.** Hyatt Regency
C. Welcome **D.** Le Meridien

Q.35 'Skycar' , a light aerial multi-purpose vehicle, is set to make its world debut in the US. Name the company which has developed the model?

A. Rolls Royce **B.** Moller International
C. Audi **D.** Ford

// Smart Answer Sheet //

Correct Indicates percentage of students who answered questions correctly.

Skipped Indicates percentage of students who skipped questions.

Q.	Ans.	Correct	Skipped
1	B	63.63 %	33.75 %
2	C	85.66 %	12.55 %
3	A	85.29 %	11.34 %
4	D	63.13 %	31.38 %
5	B	48.64 %	38.94 %
6	D	22.17 %	69.98 %
7	C	78.0 %	20.53 %

Q.	Ans.	Correct	Skipped
8	D	23.06 %	76.44 %
9	D	61.97 %	31.91 %
10	A	78.99 %	13.27 %
11	D	56.33 %	30.51 %
12	D	69.34 %	30.28 %
13	C	65.32 %	32.28 %
14	C	55.4 %	43.67 %

Q.	Ans.	Correct	Skipped
15	A	64.24 %	33.21 %
16	C	42.31 %	56.48 %
17	A	12.78 %	79.66 %
18	B	28.56 %	70.57 %
19	D	17.95 %	71.63 %
20	B	32.87 %	67.04 %
21	B	11.87 %	78.92 %

Q.	Ans.	Correct	Skipped
22	D	60.25 %	30.8 %
23	C	56.96 %	32.87 %
24	A	41.14 %	31.41 %
25	D	55.74 %	40.9 %
26	B	50.73 %	46.34 %
27	D	85.01 %	10.54 %
28	C	62.21 %	31.31 %

Q.	Ans.	Correct	Skipped
29	A	47.17 %	49.46 %
30	B	23.7 %	70.15 %
31	B	31.97 %	67.67 %
32	A	76.61 %	23.28 %
33	C	56.87 %	39.52 %
34	B	10.13 %	74.9 %
35	B	15.11 %	67.46 %

Performance Analysis	
Avg. Score (%)	48.57%
Toppers Score (%)	54.29%
Your Score	

//Hints and Solutions//

1. As mentioned in the first few lines of the passage, India has been fearing this problem of rising unemployment since independence. India got its independence in 1947.

Hence, the correct option is (B).

2. As mentioned in the passage, the government tries to overcome this problem by launching many schemes such as NREGA, PMRY, etc.

Hence, the correct option is (C).

3. According to the passage, "Corruption is done by the government and they also try to prevent the country from this".

Hence, the correct option is (A).

4. The situation given in the above passage is, "Those who manufacture the disease-causing things, open the hospital for treatment".

Hence, the correct option is (D).

5. As given in the last few lines of the passage, "Person who is unskilled get jobs on behalf of money but skilled person fails to get jobs due to lack of money".

Hence, the correct option is (B).

6. Refer to, "The Madras High Court on Friday granted 30 days of ordinary leave to S. Nalini, 52, a life convict in the former Prime Minister Rajiv Gandhi's assassination case."

Among the given options, we can see that our answer is described in Option (D) whereas all the other options are incorrect as per the given information in the passage.

Hence, the correct option is (D).

7. Refer to, "Justices M.M. Sundresh and M. Nirmal Kumar took judicial notice that the State Cabinet itself had on September 9 last year made a recommendation to the Governor to release all seven convicts in the Rajiv Gandhi assassination case."

It is the case that the state government already moved a petition to free all the seven prisoners in the Rajiv Gandhi assassination case implying that they have no issue with the rest of the sentence getting remitted by the competent authority. Among the given options, we can see that Option (C) is our pick whereas others are not correct as per the given information given in the passage.

Hence, the correct option is (C).

8. Statement I is not correct for the fact that S Nalini has been given the permission to come out on parole for the third time as she was given the permission twice before also. Refer to, "Nalini had many years ago come out on short paroles of a day each to attend her brother Bhagyanathan's wedding and her father's last rites."

Statement II is also not correct for the fact that S Nalini has been released on parole in order to attend her daughter's wedding and to make arrangements for the marriage. Her daughter is staying in London. Refer to, "The order was passed after she argued her case in person and made a fervent plea to the judges in a choked voice that she may be allowed to step out of prison for some days to make arrangements for the marriage of her daughter, who is residing in London."

Statement III is also not correct for the fact that it is already said that S Nalini has a daughter and that easily makes this particular statement incorrect.

Hence, the correct option is (D).

9. Statement I is not correct because the Madras HC has observed that S Nalini is a woman of no means since she does not have any regular source of income. That is why the court has asked the state to bear the expenses of her security during the parole. Refer to, "The judges also directed the State government to bear the expenses of providing escort to her during the period of leave since she expressed difficulty in paying the charges. "There is no material to hold that she is a woman of means......." they said.

Statement II is not correct for the fact that the first part seems to be correct since S Nalini was sentenced to life imprisonment by the courts for the assassination of our former PM Rajiv Gandhi but it is nowhere referred to in the passage that she should not be given any chance to reform herself.

Statement III is also not correct because the court has held that there is no relation between S Nalini and her husband but there is no reference that she is the reason behind it.

Hence, the correct option is (D).

10. The word fervent has been used in the passage in the sense that S Nalini made a very passionate plea that she wanted to attend the marriage of her daughter staying in London. The plea was heartfelt and obviously, an emotional one and the court granted her permission to come out on parole for the preparations of the wedding. Among the given options, ardent can be used as the word similar in meaning for the given word as used in the passage. The other words vehement and feeling can also be used as similar in meaning but they are not fitting in this context. Pragmatic implies a practical and sensible approach to something.

Hence, the correct option is (A).

11. Since B cannot be found from given data.

Hence, the correct option is (D).

12. Since F cannot be found from given data.

Hence, the correct option is (D).

13. Given,

Sales of Jeans in $2002 = 160$

Sales of Jeans in 2005 be F.

Required percentage $= \frac{F}{200} = 1.5$

$F = 1.5 \times 200 = 300$

Percentage of sales of jeans in 2005 of sales of jeans in 2002

$= \frac{300}{160} \times 100$

$= 187.5$
Hence, the correct option is (A).

14. Given,

$\frac{C}{D} = \frac{1}{2}$
$\Rightarrow C = 0.7$
$\frac{160}{B} = 0.7$
Given,

$B = \frac{1600}{7}$
$\Rightarrow 7B = 1600$
Hence, the correct option is (C).

15. Given,
$\frac{y}{x} = \frac{A}{60}$
$\Rightarrow 1.2 = \frac{A}{60}$
$\Rightarrow A = 72$
Given,
$\frac{y}{x} = \frac{160}{E}$
$\Rightarrow 1.33 = \frac{160}{E}$
$\Rightarrow E = \frac{160}{1.33}$
$= 120$
$\therefore A{:}E = \frac{A}{E} = \frac{72}{120} = 0.6$
Hence, the correct option is (A).

16. Given,

The sales of lipsticks in $2011 = 4817$
The sales of nail enamels in $2011 = 3716$
$\therefore$Required percentage $= \frac{4817-3716}{3716} \times 100 = 29.62 = 30\%$(approx)
Hence, the correct option is (C).

17. From the observation, the increase was less than 100% for only shampoos and talcum powder.

Percentage increase in shampoo $= \frac{1221-788}{788} \times 100 = 54.9\%$

Percentage increase in Talcum powder $= \frac{2914-1497}{1497} \times 100 = 94.6\%$

Percentage increase in Nail enamels $= \frac{3716-593}{593} \times 100 = 526.64\%$

Percentage increase in Lipsticks $= \frac{4187-2015}{2015} \times 100 = 107.79\%$.
So percentage increase was minimum for Shampoos.
Hence, the correct option is (A).

18. Given,
$\frac{\text{Sales of nail enamels in (2011)}}{\text{Sales of Talcum powders in (2006)}}$
$= \frac{3716}{1497} = \frac{5}{2}$
$= 5{:}2$
Hence, the correct option is (B).

19. The percentage increase from 2006 to 2011 for various products are:
Lipsticks $= \left[\frac{(48.17-20.15)}{20.15} \times 100\right]\% = 139.06\%$
Nail enamels $= \left[\frac{(37.76-5.93)}{5.93} \times 100\right]\% = 536.76\%$
Talcum powders $= \left[\frac{(29.14-14.97)}{14.97} \times 100\right]\% = 94.66\%$
Shampoos $= \left[\frac{(12.21-7.88)}{7.88} \times 100\right]\% = 54.95\% \approx 55\%$
Conditioners $= \left[\frac{(10.19-5.01)}{5.01} \times 100\right]\% = 103.39\%$
The increase was 55% for shampoos.
Hence, the correct option is (D).

20. Given,

The sales of conditioners in $2006 = 788$

The sales of shampoos in $2006 = 501$

$\therefore$ Required percentage $= \frac{788-501}{788} \times 100$
$= 36\%$ (approx)
Hence, the correct option is (B).

21. For the solution to this question, we need to find the number of male and female soldiers in each division.
In the common explanation below we see that division E has a discrepancy that the number of female soldiers is negative.
Since the population of the city is $10{,}00{,}000$ we first calculate what population different divisions of the city have:
$A = 18\%$ of $10{,}00{,}000 = 1{,}80{,}000$
$B = 12\%$ of $10{,}00{,}000 = 1{,}20{,}000$
$C = 15\%$ of $10{,}00{,}000 = 1{,}50{,}000$
$D = 20\%$ of $10{,}00{,}000 = 2{,}00{,}000$
$E = 13\%$ of $10{,}00{,}000 = 1{,}30{,}000$
$F = 22\%$ of $10{,}00{,}000 = 2{,}20{,}000$

Total male $=$ Total no. of soldier $-$ Total female

$= 10{,}00{,}000 - 2{,}80{,}000$

$= 7{,}20{,}000$
Total Male-Female population in each of divisions:
A: Male $= 7{,}20{,}000 \times \frac{40}{360}$
$= 7{,}20{,}000 \times \frac{1}{9} = 80{,}000$
A: Female = total population in $A -$ total males in $A = 1{,}80{,}000 - 80{,}000 = 1{,}00{,}000$
B: Male $= 7{,}20{,}000 \times \frac{60}{360}$

$= 7,20,000 \times \frac{1}{6} = 120,000$

B: Female = total population in B − total males in B = $1,20,000 - 1,20,000 = 0$

C: Male $= 7,20,000 \times \frac{55}{360}$

$= 7,20,000 \times \frac{11}{72} = 1,10,000$

C:Female = total population in C − total males in C = $1,50,000 - 1,10,000 = 40,000$

D: Male $= 7,20,000 \times \frac{45}{360}$

$= 7,20,000 \times \frac{1}{8} = 90,000$

D: Female = total population in D − total males in D = $2,00,000 - 90,000 = 1,10,000$

E: Male $= 7,20,000 \times \frac{70}{360}$

$= 7,20,000 \times \frac{7}{36} = 1,40,000$

E: Female = total population $E = 1,30,000 - 1,40,000 = -10,000$ (it has discrepancy)

F: Male $= 7,20,000 \times \frac{90}{360}$

$= 7,20,000 \times \frac{1}{4} = 1,80,000$

F: Female = total population in F − total males in F = $2,20,000 - 1,80,000 = 40,000$

Hence, the correct option is (B).

22. Since the population of the city is $10,00,000$ we first calculate what population different divisions of the city have:

$A = 18\%$ of $10,00,000 = 1,80,000$
$B = 12\%$ of $10,00,000 = 1,20,000$
$C = 15\%$ of $10,00,000 = 1,50,000$
$D = 20\%$ of $10,00,000 = 2,00,000$
$E = 13\%$ of $10,00,000 = 1,30,000$
$F = 22\%$ of $10,00,000 = 2,20,000$

Total male $=$ Total no. of soldier $-$ Total female

$= 10,00,000 - 2,80,000$

$= 7,20,000$

Total Male-Female population in each of divisions:

A: Male $= 7,20,000 \times \frac{40}{360}$

$= 7,20,000 \times \frac{1}{9} = 80,000$

A: Female = total population in A − total males in A = $1,80,000 - 80,000 = 1,00,000$

B: Male $= 7,20,000 \times \frac{60}{360}$

$= 7,20,000 \times \frac{1}{6} = 120,000$

B: Female = total population in B − total males in B = $1,20,000 - 1,20,000 = 0$

C: Male $= 7,20,000 \times \frac{55}{360}$

$= 7,20,000 \times \frac{11}{72} = 1,10,000$

C:Female = total population in C − total males in C = $1,50,000 - 1,10,000 = 40,000$

D: Male $= 7,20,000 \times \frac{45}{360}$

$= 7,20,000 \times \frac{1}{8} = 90,000$

D: Female = total population in D − total males in D = $2,00,000 - 90,000 = 1,10,000$

E: Male $= 7,20,000 \times \frac{70}{360}$

$= 7,20,000 \times \frac{7}{36} = 1,40,000$

E: Female = total population $E = 1,30,000 - 1,40,000 = -10,000$ (it has discrepancy)

F: Male $= 7,20,000 \times \frac{90}{360}$

$= 7,20,000 \times \frac{1}{4} = 1,80,000$

F: Female = total population in F − total males in F = $2,20,000 - 1,80,000 = 40,000$

From the above explanation, we have

Total males would be $M = 10,00,000 - 2,80,000 = 7,20,000$

Number of males in division B would be

$= \frac{60^\circ}{360^\circ} \times M = \frac{M}{6}$

Number of males in division D would be

$= \frac{45^\circ}{360^\circ} \times M = \frac{M}{8}$

Number of males in division F would be

$= \frac{90^\circ}{360^\circ} \times M = \frac{M}{4}$

Total males in these three divisions

$= \frac{M}{M6} + \frac{M}{8} + \frac{M}{4} = \frac{13M}{24}$

Average of this $= \frac{\left(\frac{M}{6}+\frac{M}{8}+\frac{M}{4}\right)}{3}$

$= \frac{\left(\frac{13M}{24}\right)}{3} = \frac{13M}{24\times3}$

$= \frac{13\times7,20,000}{24\times3} = 1,30,000$

Now, population of $B = 1,20,000$

Total males in $B, D,$ and F as a $\%$ of total population of division B $\frac{1,30,000}{1,20,000} \times 100 = 108.33\%$

Hence, the correct option is (D).

23. Since the population of the city is $10,00,000$ we first calculate what population different divisions of the city have:

$A = 18\%$ of $10,00,000 = 1,80,000$
$B = 12\%$ of $10,00,000 = 1,20,000$
$C = 15\%$ of $10,00,000 = 1,50,000$
$D = 20\%$ of $10,00,000 = 2,00,000$
$E = 13\%$ of $10,00,000 = 1,30,000$
$F = 22\%$ of $10,00,000 = 2,20,000$

Total male $=$ Total no. of soldier $-$ Total female

$= 10,00,000 - 2,80,000$

$= 7{,}20{,}000$

Total Male-Female population in each of divisions:

A: Male $= 7{,}20{,}000 \times \frac{40}{360}$

$= 7{,}20{,}000 \times \frac{1}{9} = 80{,}000$

A: Female = total population in A − total males in $A =$ $1{,}80{,}000 - 80{,}000 = 1{,}00{,}000$

B: Male $= 7{,}20{,}000 \times \frac{60}{360}$

$= 7{,}20{,}000 \times \frac{1}{6} = 120{,}000$

B: Female = total population in B − total males in $B =$ $1{,}20{,}000 - 1{,}20{,}000 = 0$

C: Male $= 7{,}20{,}000 \times \frac{55}{360}$

$= 7{,}20{,}000 \times \frac{11}{72} = 1{,}10{,}000$

C:Female = total population in C − total males in $C =$ $1{,}50{,}000 - 1{,}10{,}000 = 40{,}000$

D: Male $= 7{,}20{,}000 \times \frac{45}{360}$

$= 7{,}20{,}000 \times \frac{1}{8} = 90{,}000$

D: Female = total population in D − total males in $D =$ $2{,}00{,}000 - 90{,}000 = 1{,}10{,}000$

E: Male $= 7{,}20{,}000 \times \frac{70}{360}$

$= 7{,}20{,}000 \times \frac{7}{36} = 1{,}40{,}000$

E: Female = total population $E = 1{,}30{,}000 -$ $1{,}40{,}000 = -10{,}000$ (it has discrepancy)

F: Male $= 7{,}20{,}000 \times \frac{90}{360}$

$= 7{,}20{,}000 \times \frac{1}{4} = 1{,}80{,}000$

F: Female = total population in F − total males in $F =$ $2{,}20{,}000 - 1{,}80{,}000 = 40{,}000$

From the above explanation, we have

Females in division $A = 1{,}00{,}000$

Half of it $= \frac{1}{2} \times 1{,}00{,}000 = 50{,}000$

Females in division $C = 40{,}000$

one-fourth of it $= \frac{1}{4} \times 40{,}000 = 10{,}000$

Females in division $D = 1{,}10{,}000$

one-fourth of it $= \frac{1}{5} \times 1{,}10{,}000 = 22{,}000$

Total females on training $= 82{,}000$

On a pie chart we should have,

$82.000 = 360°$

In division C has $10{,}000$ on training,

$10{,}000$ on pie chart $= \frac{10{,}000 \times 360°}{82{,}000}$

$= 43.9 = 44°$ (approximately)

Hence, the correct option is (C).

24. Since the population of the city is $10{,}00{,}000$ we first calculate what population different divisions of the city have:

$A = 18\%$ of $10{,}00{,}000 = 1{,}80{,}000$

$B = 12\%$ of $10{,}00{,}000 = 1{,}20{,}000$

$C = 15\%$ of $10{,}00{,}000 = 1{,}50{,}000$

$D = 20\%$ of $10{,}00{,}000 = 2{,}00{,}000$

$E = 13\%$ of $10{,}00{,}000 = 1{,}30{,}000$

$F = 22\%$ of $10{,}00{,}000 = 2{,}20{,}000$

Total male = Total no. of soldier − Total female

$= 10{,}00{,}000 - 2{,}80{,}000$

$= 7{,}20{,}000$

Total Male-Female population in each of divisions:

A: Male $= 7{,}20{,}000 \times \frac{40}{360}$

$= 7{,}20{,}000 \times \frac{1}{9} = 80{,}000$

A: Female = total population in A − total males in $A =$ $1{,}80{,}000 - 80{,}000 = 1{,}00{,}000$

B: Male $= 7{,}20{,}000 \times \frac{60}{360}$

$= 7{,}20{,}000 \times \frac{1}{6} = 120{,}000$

B: Female = total population in B − total males in $B =$ $1{,}20{,}000 - 1{,}20{,}000 = 0$

C: Male $= 7{,}20{,}000 \times \frac{55}{360}$

$= 7{,}20{,}000 \times \frac{11}{72} = 1{,}10{,}000$

C:Female = total population in C − total males in $C =$ $1{,}50{,}000 - 1{,}10{,}000 = 40{,}000$

D: Male $= 7{,}20{,}000 \times \frac{45}{360}$

$= 7{,}20{,}000 \times \frac{1}{8} = 90{,}000$

D: Female = total population in D − total males in $D =$ $2{,}00{,}000 - 90{,}000 = 1{,}10{,}000$

E: Male $= 7{,}20{,}000 \times \frac{70}{360}$

$= 7{,}20{,}000 \times \frac{7}{36} = 1{,}40{,}000$

E: Female = total population $E = 1{,}30{,}000 -$ $1{,}40{,}000 = -10{,}000$ (it has discrepancy)

F: Male $= 7{,}20{,}000 \times \frac{90}{360}$

$= 7{,}20{,}000 \times \frac{1}{4} = 1{,}80{,}000$

F: Female = total population in F − total males in $F =$ $2{,}20{,}000 - 1{,}80{,}000 = 40{,}000$

From the above explanation, we have

In A, initially there were $1{,}80{,}000$ soldiers, but now $1{,}80{,}000 + 20{,}000 = 2{,}00{,}000$

In B, initially there were $1{,}20{,}000$ soldiers, but now $1{,}20{,}000 + 80{,}000 = 2{,}00{,}000$

Other divisions have same number of soldiers. Increase in overall soldiers in the country $= 10{,}00{,}000 + (20{,}000 + 80{,}000)$ $= 11{,}00{,}000$

D division still has $2{,}00{,}000$ soldiers as we calculated in common explanation.

So, the percentage that D would get

$= \frac{2,00,000}{11,00,000} \times 100 = 18.18\%$

Hence, the correct option is (A).

25. Since the population of the city is $10,00,000$ we first calculate what population different divisions of the city have:

$A = 18\%$ of $10,00,000 = 1,80,000$
$B = 12\%$ of $10,00,000 = 1,20,000$
$C = 15\%$ of $10,00,000 = 1,50,000$
$D = 20\%$ of $10,00,000 = 2,00,000$
$E = 13\%$ of $10,00,000 = 1,30,000$
$F = 22\%$ of $10,00,000 = 2,20,000$

Total male $=$ Total no. of soldier $-$ Total female

$= 10,00,000 - 2,80,000$

$= 7,20,000$

Total Male-Female population in each of divisions:

A: Male $= 7,20,000 \times \frac{40}{360}$
$= 7,20,000 \times \frac{1}{9} = 80,000$

A: Female = total population in $A -$ total males in $A =$
$1,80,000 - 80,000 = 1,00,000$

B: Male $= 7,20,000 \times \frac{60}{360}$
$= 7,20,000 \times \frac{1}{6} = 120,000$

B: Female = total population in $B -$ total males in $B =$
$1,20,000 - 1,20,000 = 0$

C: Male $= 7,20,000 \times \frac{55}{360}$
$= 7,20,000 \times \frac{11}{72} = 1,10,000$

C:Female = total population in $C -$ total males in $C =$
$1,50,000 - 1,10,000 = 40,000$

D: Male $= 7,20,000 \times \frac{45}{360}$
$= 7,20,000 \times \frac{1}{8} = 90,000$

D: Female = total population in $D -$ total males in $D =$
$2,00,000 - 90,000 = 1,10,000$

E: Male $= 7,20,000 \times \frac{70}{360}$
$= 7,20,000 \times \frac{7}{36} = 1,40,000$

E: Female = total population $E = 1,30,000 -$
$1,40,000 = -10,000$ (it has discrepancy)

F: Male $= 7,20,000 \times \frac{90}{360}$
$= 7,20,000 \times \frac{1}{4} = 1,80,000$

F: Female = total population in $F -$ total males in $F =$
$2,20,000 - 1,80,000 = 40,000$

From the above explanation, we have

Males in $A = 80,000, 15\%$ are married, thus 15% of 80,000

$= \frac{15 \times 80,000}{100} = 12,000$

Males in $C = 1,10,000, 10\%$ are married, thus 10% of 1,10,000

$= \frac{10 \times 1,10,000}{100} = 11,000$

Males in $F = 1,80,000, 5\%$ are married, thus 5% of 1,80,000

$= \frac{5 \times 1,80,000}{100} = 9,000$

Total married male in A, C and $F = 12,000 + 11,000 + 9,000 = 32,000$

Males in $B = 1,20,000, 10\%$ are married, thus 10% of 1,20,000

$= \frac{12 \times 1,20,000}{100} = 12,000$

Males in $D = 90,000, 20\%$ are married, thus 20% of 90,000

$= \frac{20 \times 90,000}{100} = 18,000$

Total married male in B and $D = 12,000 + 18,000 = 30,000$

Difference $= 32,000 - 30,000 = 2,000$

In B and D how many more/less men are married with respect to $A, C,$ and F

$= \frac{2000}{32000} \times 100 = 6.25\%$

Hence, the correct option is (D).

26. The Reserve Bank of India (RBI) has recently directed HDFC Bank to temporarily halt all its digital launches and new sourcing of credit card customers.

The country's largest private sector lender has been asked to stop the digital launches as the bank had faced technical glitches in the past two years. RBI also asked the bank's board to examine the lapses and fix accountability.

Hence, the correct option is (B).

27. The Employees Provident Fund (EPF) is the main scheme under the Employees' Provident Funds and Miscellaneous Provisions Act, 1952 formulated by the Central Government. The scheme is managed by the Employees' Provident Fund Organisation (EPFO). It covers every office which has 20 or more employees.

Hence, the correct option is (D).

28. India's Largest tractor manufacture Mahindra & Mahindra had recently made a takeover bid on a European company, Universal Tractors. The Company is based in Romania.

Mahindra & Mahindra Limited is an Indian multinational automotive manufacturing corporation headquartered in Mumbai, Maharashtra, India. It was established in 1945 as Muhammad & Mahindra and later renamed as Mahindra and Mahindra. It is one of the largest vehicle manufacturers by production in India and the largest manufacturer of tractors in the world.

Hence, the correct option is (C).

29. Business transactions are recorded in chronological order.

A business transaction is an economic event with a third party that is recorded in an organization's accounting system.

Hence, the correct option is (A).

30. Australia - based core banking software, Financial Network Services (FNS) has been acquired by TCS.

TCS BaNCS is a core banking software suite developed by Tata Consultancy Services for use by retail banks.

Prior to the corporate takeover by TCS, BaNCS was developed at the headquarters of Financial Network Services (FNS).

Hence, the correct option is (B).

31. In economics, desire backed by purchasing power is known as demand.

Demand is an economic principle referring to a consumer's desire to purchase goods and services and willingness to pay a price for a specific good or service. Holding all other factors constant, an increase in the price of a good or service will decrease the quantity demanded, and vice versa.

Hence, the correct option is (B).

32. Car and petrol are Complimentary goods.

A complementary good or service is an item used in conjunction with another good or service.

Hence, the correct option is (A).

33. Human Resource departments are service departments.

A service department is a cost center that provides services to the rest of a company. The manager of a service department is responsible for keeping costs down or meeting the costs stated in a budget.

Hence, the correct option is (C).

34. Asian Hotels Ltd owns and operates Hyatt Regency.

The Hyatt Regency brand is the oldest brand in the company, with the Grand Hyatt and Park Hyatt brands being introduced in 1980.

Hence, the correct option is (B).

35. 'Skycar', a light aerial multi-purpose vehicle, is set to make its world debut in the US developed by Moller International.

The Moller Skycar is a prototype personal VTOL (vertical take-off and landing) aircraft – a "the flying car" – a concept invented by Paul Moller who has been attempting to develop such a vehicle type for more than fifty years.

Hence, the correct option is (B).

Mock Test 14

Comprehension

Ques (1-5):Direction: Read the following passage carefully and answer the following question.

In the end, the hoped-for knight-in-shining armour never arrived and Jet Airways is now in insolvency court. This marks the last act in a long-winded saga that saw the beleaguered airline and its stakeholders lurch from despondency to hope to gloom once again. The debt-laden airline's troubles began when it defaulted on a loan last December. Hectic salvage attempts at the airline since then have come to naught. Thousands of employees and many operational creditors may end up being the biggest losers in the fiasco.

Among the many factors that led to this state of affairs was the promoter Naresh Goyal's intransigence on valuation and not ceding majority control — till he was eventually forced out in end-March. Then came the volte-face by the SBI-led lender consortium on its emergency funding commitment of Rs. 1,500 crore, which scuttled the bidding process. The airline's already truncated operations rapidly unravelled and it stopped flying mid-April. Jet's assets — prized airport slots, valuable fleet, trained employees — were up for grabs and the competition has since moved in for the kill. Not surprisingly, most potential suitors for Jet Airways backed off and just one conditional bid was received for a minority stake from strategic partner Etihad Airways. Later, the Hinduja Group also threw its hat into the ring. But lenders seem to have found these offers unappealing and have now decided to refer Jet to the National Company Law Tribunal (NCLT) for insolvency proceedings.

Higher value could have been salvaged for all of Jet's stakeholders, had the lenders acted sooner and more decisively. The saga as it has played out has been beset with avoidable delays and wrong signals. First, Naresh Goyal was given an inordinately long rope by the lenders which worked to the detriment of everyone else. Thankfully the prospect of a backdoor entry by the promoter was thwarted. But the lenders' decision to put off the IBC route in favour of a majority equity stake for themselves is difficult to explain. This leads one to wonder whether the need to avoid the bad optics of job losses and fare hikes in the election season was at play. Debt restructuring was a more pragmatic course if they were worried about long delays under IBC but that required lenders to follow through of their emergency funding commitment. It isn't clear what really changed in a fortnight that the lenders backtracked on that commitment. In the bargain, almost everyone except Jet's rivals has lost value. While the creative destruction cycle in businesses should be allowed to play out, the process should be fair, transparent and above reproach. The lenders now say that under the IBC, it is possible to give potential investors the exemptions they seek from SEBI norms. This offers a glimmer of hope that some resolution, even if sub-optimal, may be possible. But stakeholders should keep expectations low, given that the resolution of cases so far referred under IBC have been fraught with long delays and disputes.

Q.1 Which among the following is implied by the phrase "hoped-for-knight-in-shining-armour" as used in the given passage?

A. A very good swordsman who can fight against all odds

B. A very efficient person who can take care of all the troubles in one's own life

C. A person or organization with very deep pockets

D. None of the above

Q.2 Which among the following gives us the correct picture regarding the opinion of the author about the IBC proceedings?

A. The author is very much optimistic regarding the IBC proceedings since they are very efficient in handling such situations.

B. The author is very much disappointed with the Jet management since they have not controlled the airline in the proper way.

C. The author is not sure about the way the Jet saga should have been handled given the fact that all took place too quickly.

D. The author is not at all optimistic about the IBC proceedings in the country since it takes a lot of time and is not always free from disputes.

Q.3 Which among the following has / have been attributed to the failure of the Jet Airways, as per the given passage?

A. The management of the company could have been handled in a better manner by the lenders without any valid reason.

B. The lenders could not take decisions when required since they have not applied their best minds to solve the crisis.

C. SEBI has not given Jet Airways the right to go ahead and file for funding proposal from the market.

D. Both (A) and (B)

Q.4 Which among the following is the reason that the lenders have not accepted the bids received to acquire Jet Airways?

A. The lenders wanted to refer the case to Jet Airways anyways making it an inevitable case and they wanted to buy some time.

B. The lenders have not found the bids accepted in line with their expectations and that is why they decided against accepting the same.

C. The lenders have decided to refer the case to the bidders once the NCLT proceedings are done with.

D. The lenders want to know the real value of the company and that is why it has referred the case to the National Company Law Tribunal.

Q.5 Which among the following has been identified as the main culprit in the Jet Airways saga as it has played out, as described by the author?

A. The promoters of Jet Airways

B. The lenders

C. The bidders who submitted the bids to acquire the company

D. SEBI

Ques (6-10):Direction: Read the passage and answer the question that follow:

Business news does not repeat itself but it sometimes rhymes. In 2007 Walmart, America's biggest grocer, crowed that it would crack the coveted Indian market by being the first global retailer to set up shop there, pipping envious rivals in the process. On May 9th it announced much the same thing: its time in India has come, this time by virtue of paying $16bn for a majority stake in Flipkart, India's largest ecommerce outfit, which had also been coveted by its vast online rival, Amazon. The sense of déjà vu owes to the fact that its original foray proved a disappointment. Walmart's hopes of somehow circumventing rules to protect local shopkeepers, which have long prevented most foreign retailers from opening stores, have been repeatedly dashed. A decade on it has a meagre 21 wholesale stores in India, generating just 0.1% of its $500bn in global revenues and a small loss to boot. Somehow that has not dissuaded the beast of Bentonville from undertaking the biggest foreign acquisition in Indian history.

The Indian e-commerce market is as different from America's brick-and-mortar retail landscape as Walmart's Arkansas home is from Bangalore. Walmart probably has too many stores in its mature home market. Flipkart operates online and in quasi-virgin commercial territory: 95% of Americans shop at Walmart at least once a year, but only 5-10% of Indians have ever bought anything online. The deal is a departure in other ways, too. Walmart has already swooped on companies it thinks will help it grow its ecommerce presence. In 2016 it paid out $3bn for Jet.com, a putative rival to Amazon in America; it has also bagged Bonobos, a purveyor of tailored trousers. But Flipkart, which was founded in 2007 by two former Amazon employees, is in a different league in terms of price tag.

Walmart will own around 77% of the company, which is valued at over $20bn in total. Even for Walmart, that is a lot of money: $20bn is roughly the cash it generates every year net of capital expenditure, say, or 8% of its market capitalisation. Connoisseurs of the Indian tech scene have raised eyebrows at the price tag, given that Flipkart raised money at a valuation of under $12bn just a year ago. SoftBank, a Japanese telecoms and internet giant which became its biggest shareholder after investing $2.5bn just nine months ago, stands to walk away with $4bn. Walmart's new acquisition will not produce quick returns. Analysts reckon Flipkart loses money on each shipment. Margins are unlikely to improve soon given Amazon's incursion into the market (having committed $5bn to India, it probably ranks a close second to Flipkart, which is thought to account for just under half of India's online sales). Paytm Mall, a newish rival backed by Alibaba of China, is also ambitious.

Q.6 How would Wamart's business in America be different from its Indian venture?

I. The business is America is mostly brick and mortar while it is online in nature in India.

II. Walmart owns about 88% of the market share in America but hardly any in the Indian market.

III. The market is vastly under penetrated in India.

A. Only II | **B.** Only I and II
C. Only II and III | **D.** Only I and III

Q.7 Which of the following is/are true about Walmart's performance in India before it bought stake in Flipkart?

I. Its revenues from India form a very minuscule proportion of its total revenues.

II. It has been successful in establishing a small number of retail and wholesale stores.

III. Its brick and mortar business model was running in losses from the past 3 years in India.

A. Only I | **B.** Only I and II
C. Only II and III | **D.** Only II

Q.8 What does the line- 'Business news does not repeat itself but it sometimes rhymes' refer to?

A. It refers to Walmart beating rivals in the e-commerce space.

B. It refers to Walmart entering India via e-commerce to avoid getting caught up in the huge number of regulations India has imposed on retailers.

C. It refers to Walmart's entry in India via a majority stake buyout in Flipkart in 2018 after being unsuccessful in 2007.

D. It refers to Walmart being the first global retailer to set up shop in India.

Q.9 Which of the following is/are true as per the passage?

I. Softbank is the largest shareholder of Flipkart.

II. India's e-commerce market as a whole is worth about $15bn only.

III. Indian regulations dictate that e-commerce sites must sell stuff mainly from third-parties rather than from their own inventory.

A. Only II | **B.** Only I
C. Only I and III | **D.** Only II and III

Q.10 As per your understanding of the passage, which of the following shows that the decision by Walmart to enter Indian e-commerce may not be as lucrative as it appears to be?

I. Analysts reckon Flipkart loses money on each shipment and at one point it was thought to guzzle $2m a day subsidising shipping and using discounts to lure buyers.

II. Venture capitalists in India complain about the lack of exits from dozens of investments in the Indian e-commerce industry.

III. The entire sector was flat in 2016 and grew at perhaps only 10% last year.

A. Only II | **B.** Only I and II
C. Only I and III | **D.** All of the above

Management Data Interpretation

Ques (11-15):Direction: Study the table below to answer these question.
Rate of Interest, Dividend Payout Ratio and the Retained Earnings of Five Companies.

Company	Interest	Rate of Interest (%)	Dividend Payout Ratio (%)	Retained Earnings (₹Lakh)
A	234	18	22.50	155
B	576	24	19.60	402
C	129.6	16	8.75	365
D	144	9	32.50	270
E	180	15	28.00	216

Profit earned is either paid out as a dividend or ploughed back into business as retained earnings. Interest is paid on borrowings.

Q.11 By how much do the borrowings of Company B exceed that of Company A?

A. Rs. 1,210,000 **B.** Rs. 1,320,000
C. Rs. 1,000,000 **D.** Rs. 1,100,000

Q.12 By how much does the dividend paid by Company D exceed the dividend paid by Company B?

A. Rs. 23 lakh **B.** Rs. 32 lakh
C. Rs. 320 lakh **D.** Rs. 230 lakh

Q.13

The profit of E is more/less than that of C by ____ %

A. 33.3% less **B.** 33.3% more
C. 25% less **D.** 25% more

Q.14 What is the sum of profits made by Companies A and B?

A. Rs. 500 lakh **B.** Rs. 600 lakh
C. Rs. 700 lakh **D.** Rs. 800 lakh

Q.15 What is the sum of the borrowings of all five companies?

A. Rs. 146 lakh **B.** Rs. 14.6 lakh
C. Rs. 14.6 crore **D.** None of these

Ques (16-20):Direction: The following line graph gives the ratio of the amounts of imports by a company to the amount of exports from that company over the period from 1995 to 2001.

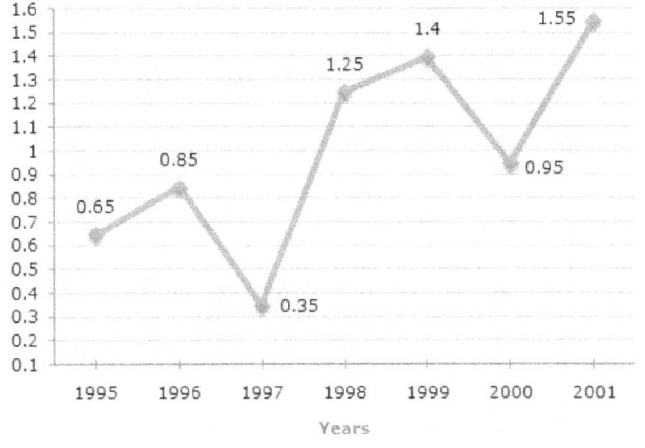

Q.16 If the imports in 1998 was Rs. 250 crores and the total exports in the years 1998 and 1999 together was Rs. 500 crores, then the imports in 1999 was?

A. Rs. 250 crores **B.** Rs. 300 crores
C. Rs. 357 crores **D.** Rs. 420 crores

Q.17 The imports were minimum proportionate to the exports of the company in the year?

A. 1995 **B.** 1996 **C.** 1997 **D.** 2000

Q.18 What was the percentage increase in imports from 1997 to 1998?

A. 72 **B.** 56
C. 28 **D.** Data Inadequate

Q.19 If the imports of the company in 1996 was Rs. 272 crores, the exports from the company in 1996 was?

A. Rs. 370 crores **B.** Rs. 320 crores
C. Rs. 280 crores **D.** Rs. 275 crores

Q.20 In how many of the given years were the exports more than the imports?

A. 1 **B.** 2 **C.** 3 **D.** 4

Ques (21-25):Direction: The following pie chart shows the number of subscriptions generated for India Bonds from different categories of investors.

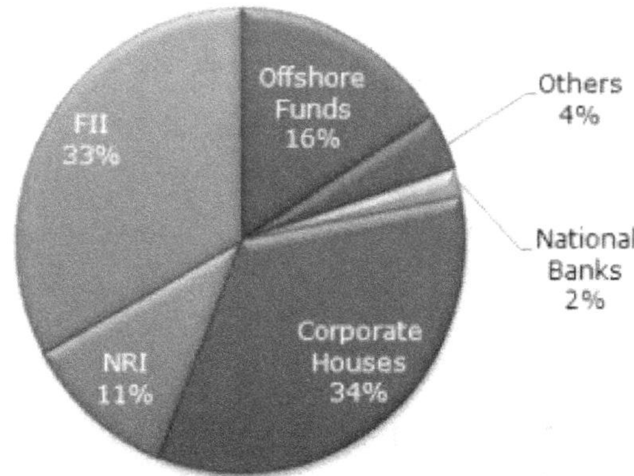

Q.21 In the corporate sector, approximately how many degrees should be there in the central angle?

A. 120 **B.** 121 **C.** 122 **D.** 123

Q.22 If the investment by NRI's is Rs 4,000 crore, then the investments by corporate houses and FII's together is:

A. 24,000 crore **B.** 24,363 crore
C. 25,423 crore **D.** 25,643 crore

Q.23

What percentage of the total investment is coming from FII's and NRI's?

A. 33% **B.** 11% **C.** 44% **D.** 22%

Q.24 If the total investment other than by FII and corporate houses is Rs 335,000 crore, then the investment by NRI's and Offshore funds will be (approximately) ?

A. 274,100
B. 285,600
C. 293,000
D. Cannot be determined

Q.25 If the total investment flows from FII's were to be doubled in the next year and the investment flows from all other sources had remained constant at their existing levels for this year, then what would be the proportion of FII investment in the total investment into India Bonds next year (in US $ millions)?

A. 40% **B.** 50% **C.** 60% **D.** 70%

Business Awareness

Q.26 A Joint Stock Company is managed by the Board of Directors elected by ____ .

A. Top management
B. Shareholders
C. Employees of company
D. None of the above

Q.27 The 'Diamond water' controversy is explained by

A. Total utility **B.** Marginal utility
C. Price offered **D.** Quantity supplied

Q.28 In the case of two perfect substitutes, the indifference curve will be

A. Straight line **B.** L-shaped
C. U-shaped **D.** C-shaped

Q.29 The short-run Average Cost curve is _____ shaped.

A. V **B.** U
C. L **D.** None of the above

Q.30 Which of the following is a source of formulating Human Resource Management Policies?

A. Organizational policies
B. Existing practices and experiences in other organizations of the same nature or in the same geographical area or in the entire nation
C. Past experience of the organization
D. All of the above

Q.31 Which of the following need is not fall under needs of Training and Development?

1. Technological advances
2. Organizational complexity
3. Organizational tenure
4. Performance evaluation
5. Human relation movement

A. 2 and 3 **B.** 2, 3, 4 and 5
C. 1, 2, 3 and 4 **D.** 1, 2, 3, 4 and 5

Q.32 The technique that has been used to evaluate an employee in comparison with other employees

A. Ranking
B. Forced choice
C. Essay evaluation
D. Critical incident technique

Q.33 Which of the following is not a peculiarity of labour market?

A. Labour market is normally local in nature.
B. The number of buyers is less than the number of sellers.
C. Labour is less mobile.
D. Worker can sell not only his own labour but also the labour of his fellow workers.

Q.34 The amount sufficient to enable a worker to live in reasonable comfort, having regard to all obligations to which an average worker would ordinarily be subject to

A. Minimum Wage **B.** Fair Wage
C. Living Wage **D.** Nominal Wage

Q.35 Workers' facilitation centres shall be set up by the facilitating agency under the

A. Payment of Bonus Act, 1965
B. Equal Remuneration Act, 1976
C. Factories Act, 1948
D. The unorganized sector workers' Social Security Act, 2005

// Smart Answer Sheet //

Correct Indicates percentage of students who answered questions correctly.

Skipped Indicates percentage of students who skipped questions.

Q.	Ans.	Correct	Skipped
1	D	58.81 %	40.64 %
2	D	56.07 %	32.01 %
3	D	26.55 %	70.33 %
4	B	77.89 %	20.21 %
5	B	58.2 %	32.26 %
6	D	84.88 %	14.79 %
7	A	64.88 %	32.79 %
8	C	87.93 %	10.36 %
9	B	61.08 %	34.85 %
10	D	78.87 %	18.21 %
11	D	60.43 %	38.67 %
12	C	64.97 %	31.96 %
13	C	82.02 %	12.68 %
14	C	18.0 %	77.74 %
15	D	49.91 %	47.54 %
16	D	76.53 %	16.75 %
17	C	58.36 %	31.43 %
18	D	80.7 %	10.06 %
19	B	41.13 %	57.58 %
20	D	67.17 %	32.71 %
21	C	65.87 %	31.35 %
22	B	52.92 %	40.2 %
23	C	41.25 %	37.18 %
24	A	80.38 %	13.07 %
25	B	59.02 %	33.43 %
26	B	61.39 %	34.42 %
27	B	60.92 %	30.95 %
28	A	65.65 %	30.14 %
29	B	59.37 %	35.97 %
30	D	50.3 %	37.48 %
31	C	47.6 %	49.85 %
32	A	63.28 %	36.36 %
33	D	86.17 %	10.01 %
34	A	51.03 %	35.13 %
35	D	81.34 %	16.96 %

Performance Analysis	
Avg. Score (%)	54.29%
Toppers Score (%)	62.86%
Your Score	

//Hints and Solutions//

1. If we take the connotation of the phrase in the given passage we can find out that we are talking about a chivalrous person who comes to the rescue of a woman in danger but here it can be used in a slightly different manner such as somebody who comes to rescue of a company which is in danger. None of the given options explains this meaning of the given phrase and that is why all these options can be eliminated from consideration.

Hence, the correct option is (D).

2. Refer to, "But stakeholders should keep expectations low, given that the resolution of cases so far referred under IBC have been fraught with long delays and disputes."

It is clear from the above lines that the author is not very hopeful regarding the IBC proceedings in India since most of the times such proceedings have taken too much time to complete and also most of the times they have not been free from the disputes regarding the awards pronounced through such proceedings. All the parties have not agreed to such awards ultimately.

Among the given options, we can see that there is only Option (D) that explains the correct opinion of the author regarding the IBC proceedings in India whereas all the other statements can be eliminated due to the fact that they do not follow from the given passage.

Hence, the correct option is (D).

3. Statement (A) is correct since it is stated in the passage that the owner of Jet Airways has been given a lot of chances to revive the airline but it is hard to explain on what basis the person has been given so many opportunities. The lenders should have handled the situation in a better manner. Refer to, "First, Naresh Goyal was given an inordinately long rope by the lenders which worked to the detriment of everyone else. Thankfully the prospect of a backdoor entry by the promoter was thwarted."

Statement (B) is also correct due to the fact that it is hard to explain why the lenders delayed in referring the case to the National Company Law Tribunal and also they decided to take majority stake without any valid reason. Therefore it has been the case that the lenders have shown lack of judgment in the whole episode. Refer to, "But the lenders' decision to put off the IBC route in favour of a majority equity stake for themselves is difficult to explain."

Statement (C) is not correct since it is not correct as per the information given in the passage that SEBI has barred Jet Airways to tap the market for raising funds for the company. Hence this cannot be considered as a reason for the failure of Jet Airways.

Hence, the correct option is (D).

4. Refer to, "Not surprisingly, most potential suitors for Jet Airways backed off and just one conditional bid was received for a minority stake from strategic partner Etihad Airways. Later, the Hinduja Group also threw its hat into the ring. But lenders seem to have found these offers unappealing and have now decided to refer Jet to the National Company Law Tribunal (NCLT) for insolvency proceedings."

It is very much clear from the above lines that the lenders have not found the bids submitted by Etihard Airways and Hinduja Group as acceptable and that is why they have rejected the bids altogether and have referred the case to the National Company Law Tribunal.

Among the given options, there is Option (B) that explains the actual reason why the lenders have not accepted the bids submitted by the parties in the Jet Airways case whereas the others can be eliminated for the fact that they do not follow from the information given in the passage.

Hence, the correct option is (B).

5. Here we can see that the author is mainly disappointed with the lenders for the way in which they have handled the case. They have only given a long rope to the promoter group and also they have not taken appropriate decisions when required making it difficult to do something for the company. Refer to, "Higher value could have been salvaged for all of Jet's stakeholders, had the lenders acted sooner and more decisively. The saga as it has played out has been beset with avoidable delays and wrong signals."

Therefore, we can see that Option (B) points out the main culprit as per the author in the given passage whereas all the others can be eliminated from consideration.

Hence, the correct option is (B).

6. Refer to: 'The Indian e-commerce market is as different from America's brick-and-mortar retail landscape as Walmart's Arkansas home is from Bangalore. **Walmart probably has too many stores in its mature home market. Flipkart operates online and in quasi-virgin commercial territory: 95% of Americans shop at Walmart at least once a year, but only 5-10% of Indians have ever bought anything online.'**

As per the highlighted fragments, I and III are correct while II has not been specified anywhere.

Hence, the correct option is (D).

7. Refer to: 'A decade on it has a meagre 21 wholesale stores in India, generating just 0.1% of its $500bn in global revenues and a small loss to boot. Somehow that has not dissuaded the beast of Bentonville from undertaking the biggest foreign acquisition in Indian history.'

Statement III is incorrect as this has not been mentioned in the passage.

Statement II is incorrect as only wholesale stores are functional in India.

Statement I is correct.

Hence, the correct option is (A).

8. This line refers to the fact that Walmart had plans to enter the Indian retail space n 2007 which did not see light of the day. However, it has fulfilled its ambition of foraying into India's e-commerce space via a majority stake buyout of Flipkart in 2018.

Options (A) and (D) are incorrect as per the meaning of the statement.

Option (B) is absurd and nowhere mentioned in the passage.

Statement (C) is true.

Hence, the correct option is (C).

9. 'SoftBank, a Japanese telecoms and internet giant which became its biggest shareholder after investing $2.5bn just nine months ago, stands to walk away with $4bn.'

I is correct.

Both II and III have not been mentioned and are incorrect.

Hence, the correct option is (B).

10. All of the statements showcase the negative side of the e-commerce sector and are correct.

Hence, the correct option is (D).

11. Let the borrowing of Company $A = x$
Interest of Company $A = 234000$
Rate of Interest $= 18\%$
$\therefore x \times \frac{18}{100} = 234000$
$\Rightarrow x = 1300000$
Let the borrowing of Company $B = y$
Interest of Company $B = 576000$
Rate of interest $= 24\%$
$\therefore y \times \frac{24}{100} = 576000$
$\Rightarrow y = 2400000$
Required difference $= y - x = 2400000 - 1300000 =$ Rs. 1100000
Hence, the correct option is (D).

12. Let the profit of Company $C = 100\%$
Dividend payout ratio of $C = 8.75\%$
Remaining percentage i.e, retained earning $= 100 - 8.75 = 91.25$
According to question,
$91.25\% =$ Rs. 365 lakh
$\Rightarrow 100\% =$ Rs. 400 lakh
Therefore, Profit of $C =$ Rs. 400 lakh
Let the profit of company $E = 100\%$
Dividend payout ratio of $E = 28\%$
Remaining percentage i.e retained earning $= 100 - 28 = 72\%$
According to question,
$72\% =$Rs. 216 lakh
$\Rightarrow 100\% =$ Rs. 300 lakh
Therefore, Profit of $E =$Rs. 300 lakh
Required percentage $= \frac{100}{400} \times 100 = 25\%$ less
Hence, the correct option is (C).

13. Let the profit of Company $C = 100\%$
Dividend payout ratio of $C = 8.75\%$
Remaining percentage i.e, retained earning $= 100 - 8.75 = 91.25$
According to question,
$91.25\% =$ Rs. 365 lakh
$\Rightarrow 100\% =$ Rs. 400 lakh
Therefore, Profit of $C =$ Rs. 400 lakh
Let the profit of company $E = 100\%$
Dividend payout ratio of $E = 28\%$
Remaining percentage i.e retained earning $= 100 - 28 = 72\%$
According to question,
$72\% =$ Rs. 216 lakh
$\Rightarrow 100\% =$ Rs. 400 lakh
Therefore, Profit of $E =$ Rs. 300 lakh
Required percentage $= \frac{100}{400} \times 100 = 25\%$ less
Hence, the correct option is (C).

14. Profit made by company $A =$ Rs. 200 lakh
Profit made by company $B =$ Rs. 500 lakh
Required Sum $= 200 + 500 =$ Rs. 700 lakh
Hence, the correct option is (C).

15. Required Sum
$= 1300000 + 2400000 + 810000 + 1600000 + 1200000 = 7310000 =$ Rs. 73.1 lakh
Hence, the correct option is (D).

16. The ratio of imports to exports for the years 1998 and 1999 are 1.25 and 1.40 respectively.
Let the exports in the year $1999 =$ Rs x crores.
Then, the exports in the year $1998 =$Rs. $(500 - x)$ crores.
$\therefore 1.25 = \frac{250}{x}$
$\Rightarrow x = \frac{250}{1.25} = 200$ [Using ratio for 1998]
Thus, the exports in the year $1999 =$ Rs. 300 crores.
Let the imports in the year $1999 =$ Rs. y crores.
Then, Imports in the year $1999 = \frac{y}{300} = 1.4$
$\Rightarrow y = 420 =$ Rs. 420 crores.
Hence, the correct option is (D).

17. The imports are minimum proportionate to the exports implies that the ratio of the value of imports to exports has the minimum value.
Now, this ratio has a minimum value 0.35 in 1997, i.e., the imports are minimum proportionate to the exports in 1997.
Hence, the correct option is (C).

18. The graph gives only the ratio of imports to exports for different years. To find the percentage increase in imports from 1997 to 1998, we require more details such as the value of imports or exports during these years.
Therefore, the data is inadequate to answer this question.
Hence, the correct option is (D).

19. The ratio of imports to exports in the year $1996 = 0.85$.
Let the exports in $1996 =$ Rs. x crores.
Then, $\frac{272}{x} = 0.85$
$\Rightarrow x = 320$
Exports in $1996 =$ Rs. 320 crores.
Hence, the correct option is (B).

20. The exports are more than the imports imply that the ratio of the value of imports to exports is less than 1. Now, this ratio is less than 1 in years $1995, 1996, 1997$ and 2000.
Thus, there are four such years.
Hence, the correct option is (D).

21. According to the given data
Corporate sector $= 34\%$
As we know,
$1\% = 36$ degree
$\therefore 34 \times 3.6 = 122.4$
Hence, the correct option is (C).

22. Given,
Investment by NRI's $=$ Rs. $4{,}000$ crore
Investment by corporate house and FII's together $= 34\% + 33\% = 67\%$
$\therefore \frac{67}{11} \times 4000 = 24363.63$ crore
Hence, the correct option is (B).

23. Given,
Investment coming from FII's $= 33\%$
Investment coming from NRI's $= 11\%$
$\therefore$ Total investment coming from FII's and NRI's $= 33\% + 11\%$
$= 44\%$
Hence, the correct option is (C).

24. Investment other than NRI and corporate houses is $33\% = 335{,}000$.
Also, investment by offshore funds and NRI's $= 27\%$.
$\therefore 27 \times \frac{335000}{33} = 274090.909 \approx 274{,}100$
Hence, the correct option is (A).

25. FII's currently account for 33 out of 100.
If their value is doubled and all other investments are kept constant then,
Their new value would be 66 out of $133 =$ approximately equal to 50%
Hence, the correct option is (D).

26. A joint stock company is managed by the board of directors who are elected by the shareholders. All the shareholders are entitled to vote in the decision making process. Board of directors have powers in the management of the business.

Hence, the correct option is (B).

27. The 'Diamond water' controversy is explained by marginal utility. Marginal utility is the additional satisfaction or gains someone gets from using or purchasing an additional unit of a particular good or service. People are willing to pay a higher price for goods with greater marginal utility.

So, let's go back to water and diamonds. There is plenty of water in most parts of the world (not scarce), which means that, as consumers, we usually have a low marginal utility for water. In a typical situation, we aren't willing to pay a lot of money for one more drink of water. Diamonds, however, are scarce. Because they are harder to find and attain, our marginal utility (additional satisfaction), for adding a diamond to our collection is much higher than someone offering us one more drink of water. If one is dying of thirst, then this paradox might not make sense, and the marginal utility from another drink of water would be much higher than the additional satisfaction of owning a diamond.

Hence, the correct option is (B).

28. In the case of two perfect substitutes, the indifference curve will be a Straight line. This is because perfect substitutes have a fixed ratio of substitution. An indifference curve is usually concave towards the origin because the two goods are usually not perfect substitutes. This means that the exchange rate varies hence the slope of the line tangent to the curve (exchange rate) varies.

Hence, the correct option is (A).

29. The U shape of the short-run Average Cost curve is directly due to the law of variable proportions since in the short run some factors are fixed and some are variable. Initially, the average cost falls up to the optimum capacity level of output due to increasing returns to variable factors and it increases thereafter due to diminishing returns to the variable factor.

Hence, the correct option is (B).

30. Source of formulating Human Resource Management Policies-

- Organizational policies
- Existing practices and experiences in other organizations of the same nature or in the same geographical area or in the entire nation
- Past experience of the organization

Hence, the correct option is (D).

31. Training and development involves improving the effectiveness of organizations and the individuals and teams within them. Training may be viewed as related to immediate changes in organizational effectiveness via organized instruction, while development is related to the progress of longer-term organizational and employee goals. While training and development technically have differing definitions, the two are oftentimes used interchangeably and/or together. Training and development has historically been a topic within applied psychology but has within the last two decades become closely associated with human resources management, talent management, human resources development, instructional design, human factors, and knowledge management.

Hence, the correct option is (C).

32. The Ranking technique has been used to evaluate an employee in comparison with other employees. The ranking method is one of the simplest performance evaluation methods. In this method, employees are ranked from best to worst in a group. The simplicity of this method is overshadowed by the negative impact of assigning a 'worst' and a 'best' rating to an employee.

Hence, the correct option is (A).

33. In labour market the relationship between employers and employees is highly impersonal and unbiased. So, workers cannot sell the labour of his fellow workers.

Hence, the correct option is (D).

34. The amount sufficient to enable a worker to live in reasonable comfort, having regard to all obligations to which an average worker would ordinarily be subject to minimum wage. Minimum Wages in India is expected to reach 178.00 INR/Day by the end of 2020, according to Trading Economics global macro models and analysts' expectations.

Hence, the correct option is (A).

35. Workers' facilitation centers shall be set up by the facilitating agency under the unorganized sector workers' Social Security Act, 2005. An act to provide for the general welfare by establishing a system of Federal old-age benefits, and by enabling the several States to make more adequate provision for aged persons, blind persons, dependent and crippled children, maternal and child welfare, public health, and the administration of their unemployment

Hence, the correct option is (D).

Mock Test 15

Comprehension

Ques (1-5):Direction: Read the passage and answer the question that follow.

In a recent discussion paper, NITI Aayog has chalked out an ambitious strategy for India to become an artificial intelligence (AI) powerhouse. AI is the use of computers to make decisions that are normally made by humans. Many forms of AI surround Indians already, including chatbots on retail websites and programs that flag fraudulent bank activity. But NITI Aayog envisions AI solutions for India on a scale not seen anywhere in the world today, especially in five key sectors — agriculture, healthcare, education, smart cities and infrastructure, and transport. In agriculture, for example, machines will provide information to farmers on the quality of soil, when to sow, where to spray herbicide, and when to expect pest infestations. It's an idea with great potential: India has 30 million farmers with smartphones, but poor extension services. If computers help agricultural universities advise farmers on best practices, India could see a farming revolution.

However, there are formidable obstacles. AI start-ups already offer some solutions, but the challenge lies in scaling these to cover the entire value chain, as NITI Aayog envisions. The first problem is data. Machine learning, the set of technologies used to create AI, is a data-guzzling monster. It takes reams of historical data as input, identifies the relationships among data elements, and makes predictions. More sophisticated forms of machine learning, like "deep learning", attempt to mimic the human brain. And even though they promise greater accuracy, they also need more data than what is required by traditional machine learning. Unfortunately, India has sparse data in sectors like agriculture, and this is already hampering AI-based businesses today.

In fact, the lack of data means that deep learning doesn't work for all companies in India. One example is Climate-Connect, a Delhi-based firm, which uses AI to predict the amount of power a solar plant will generate every 15 minutes. This is critical because solar electricity generation can change dramatically every hour depending on weather conditions and the position of the sun. When this happens, the plant must communicate expected changes to power distributors, which will then switch to alternative sources. With India planning to install 100 GW of solar power by 2022, such AI will play a central role in power planning.

But to generate such data, Climate-Connect needs historical inputs like the time of sunrise and sunset, and cloud cover where the plant is located. Unfortunately, since most Indian solar plants are recent, data are available only for a couple of years, whereas deep learning needs data over many years to predict generation. Today, the firm uses traditional machine learning technologies such as regression analysis that work with less data. These methods have an accuracy of around 95%. While deep learning can boost accuracy for operations such as Climate-Connect, it hasn't worked very well in the Indian scenario, says Nitin Tanwar, cofounder of the firm.

Another problem for AI firms today is finding the right people. NITI Aayog's report has bleak news: only about 50 Indian scientists carry out "serious research" and they are concentrated in elite institutions such as the Indian Institutes of Technology and the Indian Institutes of Science. Meanwhile, only about 4% of AI professionals have worked in emerging technologies like deep learning. A survey of LinkedIn found 386 out of the 22,000 people with PhDs in AI across the world to be Indians. How does this skill gap impact companies? To some extent, open libraries of machine learning code, which can be customised to solve Indian problems, help. This means that companies need not write code from scratch, and even computer science graduates can carry out the customisation.

Q.1 Which of the following is/are synonym/s of the word bleak?

I. Depressing

II. Dismal

III. Congenial

IV. Stark

A. Only III **B.** Only I and III

C. Only I, II and IV **D.** Only II, III and IV

Q.2 Which of the following is/are antonym/s of the word sparse?

I. Scant

II. Few

III. Sporadic

IV. Abundant

A. Only II **B.** Only IV

C. Only I, II and IV **D.** Only I, II and III

Q.3 What can be some steps that can be taken by India to improve its AI capabilities?

I. The government must collect and digitize data it has access to due to running numerous schemes.

II. Set up institutes to churn out more skilled people in this field.

III. There should be adequate funding and also fixed deadlines to gauge performance.

A. Only I **B.** Only III

C. Only I and II **D.** All of the above

Q.4 Which of the following weakens the argument for using more of AI powered tools in the future in India?

I. The AI sector uses a tremendous amount of electricity so as to process huge amounts of data which is not sustainable.

II. It is tough to collect, validate, standardize, correlate, archive and distribute AI-relevant data and make it accessible to organizations, people and systems.

III. Although AI will create more jobs than it would destroy.

A. Only I
B. Only II
C. Only I and II
D. Only II and III

Q.5 Which of the following statements weakens the argument about using 'Open Libraries' of machine learning code?

A. They contain material that can be used to solve issues.
B. Using such libraries is not a difficult job and does not need a higher level of understanding of coding.
C. It is possible to do a respectable amount of machine learning without mathematics.
D. These are not helpful in cases where there is neither a fixed algorithm nor a standard procedure.

Ques (6-10):Direction: Read the passage carefully and answer the question given beside.

As the 23rd conference of the UN Framework Convention on Climate Change in Bonn shifts into high gear, developing countries including India are focussing on the imperatives of ensuring adequate financing for mitigation and adaptation. They are moving ahead with specific instruments for loss and damage they suffer due to destructive climate-linked events. India's progress in reducing the intensity of its greenhouse gas emissions per unit of GDP by 20-25% from 2005 levels by 2020, based on the commitment made in Copenhagen in 2009, has been positive. Early studies also suggest that it is on track to achieve the national pledge under the 2015 Paris Agreement for a 33-35% cut in emissions intensity per unit of growth from the same base year by 2030, and thus heed the 2°C warming goal. Since this performance is predicated on a growth rate of just over 7%, and the parallel target for 40% share of renewable energy by that year, the national road map is clear. What is not, however, is the impact of extreme weather events such as droughts and floods that would have a bearing on economic growth. It is in this context that the rich countries must give up their rigid approach towards the demands of low and middle income countries, and come to an early resolution on the question of financing of mitigation, adaptation and compensation. Of course, India could further raise its ambition in the use of green technologies and emissions cuts, which would give it the mantle of global climate leadership.

The climate question presents a leapfrog era for India's development paradigm. Already, the country has chalked out an ambitious policy on renewable energy, hoping to generate 175 gigawatts of power from green sources by 2022. This has to be resolutely pursued, breaking down the barriers to wider adoption of rooftop solar energy at every level and implementing net metering systems for all categories of consumers. At the Bonn conference, a new Transport Decarbonisation Alliance has been declared. It is aimed at achieving a shift to sustainable fuels, getting cities to commit to eco-friendly mobility and delivering more walkable communities, all of which will improve the quality of urban life. This presents a good template for India, building on its existing plans to introduce electric mobility through buses first, and cars by 2030. Such measures will have a beneficial effect not just on transport choices, but on public health through pollution abatement.

Q.6 What does the author wants to convey by saying that- "The country has chalked out an ambitious policy on renewable energy."

I. The country has planned a policy on renewable energy.

II. The country is emphasizing on renewable energy.

III. The country has shifted it's focus from renewable energy to electric mobility.

A. Only I and II
B. Only III
C. Only I
D. Only II

Q.7 Which of the following ensure(s) India to be a leader of global climate change campaign?

I. Use of green technologies.

II. Initiatives for deteriorating emissions.

III. Faster economic growth rate.

A. Only II and III
B. Only II
C. Only I
D. Only I and II

Q.8 Which of the following is true in the context of passage?

I. India has achieved a 33-35% cut in emissions intensity per unit of growth.

II. The transport carbonization alliance will improve quality of life.

III. India is focusing on importance of ensuring adequate financing.

A. Only I and II
B. Only III
C. Only II
D. All of the above

Q.9 What is/are the factor(s) affecting economic growth of the country as per the passage?

A. Climatic conditions of the country
B. Policy framework of the country
C. Both (A) and (B)
D. None of these

Q.10 Which of the following is not true regarding the passage?

I. India's efforts to reduce greenhouse gas emissions by 2020 is based on the commitment made in Paris in 2014.

II. India has shown a drastic improvement as far as efforts on climate change is concerned.

III. 22nd conference on climate change was held at Bonn.

A. Only I
B. Only I and III
C. Only II
D. Only II and III

Management Data Interpretation

Ques (11-15):Direction: Study the following table chart carefully and answer the question given below.

The table below shows the number of cases of various crimes reported at police stations in different states in $2015-16$.

State	Domestic Violance	Dowry	Rape	Molestation	Trafficking
UP	354	496	263	132	342
MP	376	225	216	125	117
HP	87	125	53	56	57

Keral a	535	352	226	364	126
Gujar at	455	225	252	175	144
Bihar	475	576	675	764	852
Punja b	245	256	259	261	263
Assa m	278	274	276	252	363

Q.11 How many cases have been reported from Gujarat in all?

A. 1751 **B.** 1331 **C.** 1251 **D.** 1221

Q.12 The Domestic violance and Dowry cases reported in Bihar are what percent more/less than the Rape and Trafficking cases reported in Punjab?

A. 98.7% less **B.** 101.3% more
C. 101.3% less **D.** 98.7% more

Q.13 Based on the average number of Rape and Molestation cases reported per state, Molestation is approximately how many times as prevalent as Rape?

A. 1.04 **B.** 0.96 **C.** 0.92 **D.** 0.86

Q.14 The total number of Dowry and Molestation cases reported in UP is approximate what percent of the total cases reported in that state, across all crimes?

A. 40% **B.** 45% **C.** 37% **D.** 47%

Q.15 In which state are the least number of cases reported?

A. UP **B.** Punjab **C.** MP **D.** HP

Ques (16-20):Direction: Study the following pie-charts carefully and answer the question given beside.
A tank contains 2400 litres mixture of milk and water in the ratio $2:1$ respectively. The mixture is distributed in five vessels. Percentage-wise distribution of a quantity of milk and percentage-wise distribution of water in five vessels is given in the following pie charts.

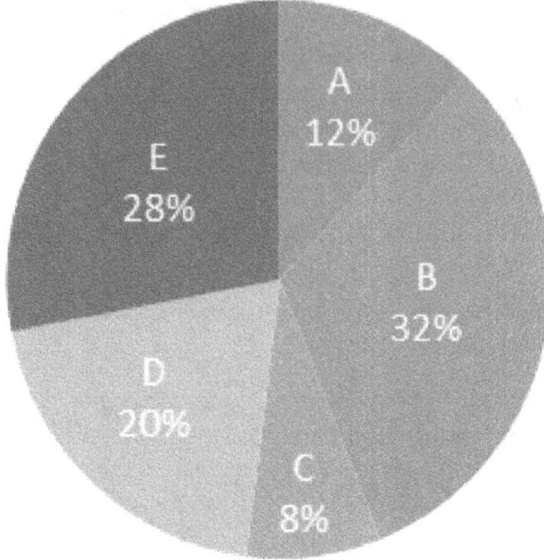

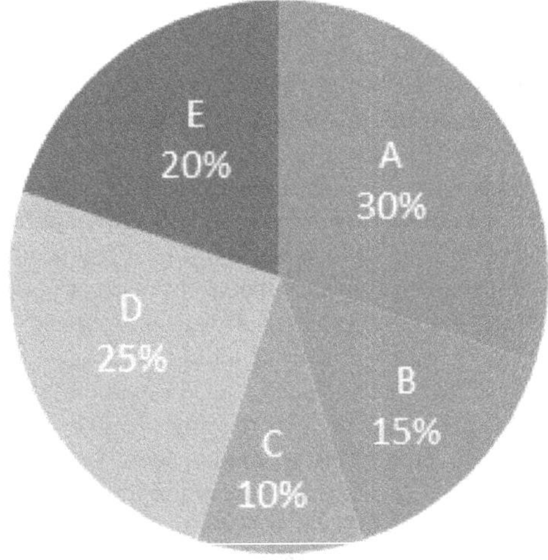

Q.16 Quantity of milk in vessels A and E together is what percent of the quantity of water in vessel D?

A. 410% **B.** 350% **C.** 320% **D.** 280%

Q.17 Find the respective ratio of the quantity of water in vessels B and C together and the quantity of milk in vessel D.

A. 5:8 **B.** 4:9 **C.** 8:5 **D.** 9:4

Q.18 Another vessel F also contains a mixture of milk and water. The quantity of milk in vessel F is 20% more than the quantity of milk in vessel C and quantity of water in vessel F is 20% less than the quantity of water in vessel C. Find the respective ratio of milk and water in vessel F.

A. 5:4 **B.** 12:5 **C.** 4:5 **D.** 5:12

Q.19 Find the sum of the quantity of milk in vessels B and D together and the quantity of water in vessels D and E together.

A. 1542 litres **B.** 1192 litres
C. 1232 litres **D.** 1058 litres

Q.20 Quantity of mixture in vessel C is what percent more/less than the quantity of mixture in vessel E ?

A. 65.78% more **B.** 54.26% less
C. 65.78% less **D.** 52.68% more

Ques (21-25):Direction: Study the following line chart carefully and answer the question given beside.

Distance (in km) travelled by three different buses in seven different days of a week.

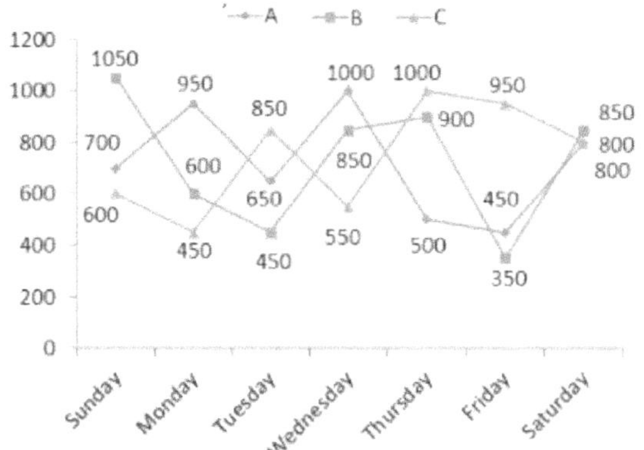

Q.21 Total distance travelled by all the buses on Monday is what percent of total distance travelled by all the buses on Wednesday.

A. 75.56% **B.** 83.33% **C.** 67.78% **D.** 88.88%

Q.22 Find the total distance travelled by bus B throughout the week.

A. 9650 km **B.** 7560 km **C.** 5050 km **D.** 6050 km

Q.23 Find the respective ratio of the distance travelled by bus A on Sunday and Monday together and the distance travelled by bus B on Friday and Saturday together.

A. 13: 12 **B.** 8: 11 **C.** 12: 13 **D.** 11: 8

Q.24 Find the difference between the distance travelled by bus A throughout the week and the distance travelled by bus C throughout the week.

A. 150 km **B.** 200 km **C.** 250 km **D.** 100 km

Q.25 The distance travelled by bus B on Sunday is what percent more than the distance travelled by bus C on Saturday?

A. 36.31% **B.** 31.25% **C.** 21.32% **D.** 18.56%

Business Awareness

Q.26 Which among the following is a most suitable example of double counting in national income ?

A. Wages of bus and train drivers
B. Cotton output and cotton cloth output
C. Electricity output and water output
D. Tax receipts and earnings of inland revenue officials

Q.27 Income tax in India was introduced by:

A. William Jones **B.** James Wilson
C. Nicholas Kaldor **D.** Mahavir Tyagi

Q.28 Planning commission had constituted a high level committee for financial sector reforms in August 2007 under the Chairmanship of:

A. K.V. Kamath **B.** Raghuram G. Rajan
C. Bimal Jalan **D.** None of these

Q.29 During which five year plan was a phase of heavy industrialization initiated?

A. Second five year plan
B. First five year plan
C. Third five year plan
D. Fourth five year plan

Q.30 The meaning of the acronym HRM is

A. Human Relations Management
B. Humanistic Resource Management
C. Human Resource Management
D. Human Resourceful Management

Q.31 HRM is _________

A. a staff functions
B. a line function
C. a staff function, line function and accounting function
D. All of the above

Q.32 Finding ways to reduce ______ is a key responsibility of management

A. dissatisfaction **B.** uncertainty
C. stress **D.** None of the above

Q.33 The minimum number of members required for registration of a co- operative society is_________

A. 2 **B.** 7 **C.** 10 **D.** 20

Q.34 Membership of a co-operative is______.

A. compulsory **B.** voluntary
C. not essential **D.** not compulsory

Q.35 The liability of members of a co-operative society is ________

A. limited to the amount of nominal value of capital held
B. limited to the amount of paid up value of the capital held
C. unlimited
D. limited or unlimited depending upon what the society has opted for it

// Smart Answer Sheet //

Correct — Indicates percentage of students who answered questions correctly.

Skipped — Indicates percentage of students who skipped questions.

Q.	Ans.	Correct	Skipped
1	C	89.89 %	10.06 %
2	B	53.21 %	35.16 %
3	D	80.13 %	13.55 %
4	A	65.37 %	32.27 %
5	D	47.17 %	50.66 %
6	C	81.42 %	16.56 %
7	D	61.19 %	30.65 %
8	B	61.3 %	36.08 %
9	A	14.09 %	71.02 %
10	B	69.27 %	30.42 %
11	C	86.34 %	13.28 %
12	B	63.57 %	36.09 %
13	B	84.54 %	14.8 %
14	A	57.09 %	39.66 %
15	D	82.25 %	12.78 %
16	C	55.03 %	40.1 %
17	A	66.1 %	32.56 %
18	B	64.35 %	35.28 %
19	B	64.33 %	33.38 %
20	C	65.46 %	34.2 %
21	B	53.7 %	38.61 %
22	C	89.89 %	10.01 %
23	D	85.72 %	13.69 %
24	A	51.32 %	37.61 %
25	B	84.69 %	11.58 %
26	B	86.0 %	11.39 %
27	B	47.91 %	44.66 %
28	B	89.02 %	10.29 %
29	A	43.04 %	34.72 %
30	C	88.5 %	10.12 %
31	A	82.34 %	13.21 %
32	B	81.44 %	10.69 %
33	C	89.73 %	10.11 %
34	B	81.77 %	18.09 %
35	D	48.67 %	48.75 %

Performance Analysis	
Avg. Score (%)	51.43%
Toppers Score (%)	54.29%
Your Score	

//Hints and Solutions//

1. Bleak means barren/depressing.

I, II and IV are synonyms.

Congenial means friendly and is the antonym.

So, I, II and IV are correct.

Hence, the correct option is (C).

2. Sparse means scanty or in short supply.

I, II, and III are synonyms and incorrect.

Only IV- abundant is the antonym here and means plenty.

Hence, the correct option is (B).

3. According to the passage, all of the statements are correct as all state valid ways of improving India's AI capabilities.

Hence, the correct option is (D).

4. Statement II is incorrect as it may be tough but not impossible. With proper planning and a scientific approach, this issue can be resolved.

Statement III is incorrect as it strengthens the argument for AI.

Statement I is correct. It weakens the argument as using a huge amount of electricity is not sustainable in the long run.

Hence, the correct option is (A).

5. Options (A) and (B) talk about advantages of open libraries and are incorrect.

Option (C) is incorrect as it simply states that it is possible to understand machine learning without needing mathematics.

Only option (D) fits in. If true, this weakens the point of using Open Libraries.

Hence, the correct option is (D).

6. According to the passage, already, the country has chalked out an ambitious policy on renewable energy, hoping to generate 175 gigawatts of power from green sources by 2022.
If the country has hoped to generate power through renewable energy then there is no point to shift focus from it. Thus statement III is absurd.
The phrase 'chalked out' means to outline or to plan.
This makes statement II wrong as it is about focusing only and not shaping that focus. In this scenario, a statement I gives the correct connotation as it implies that the country has planned to do so.
Thus statement I is true only.
Hence, the correct option is (C).

7. According to the passage, of course, **India could further raise its ambition in the use of green technologies and emissions cuts, which would give it the mantle of global climate leadership.**

With the highlighted text it is clear that statements I and II are the only factors that contribute India to be a global leader.

Statement III is not mentioned in the passage in the context of ensuring India is a global leader of climate change.

Hence, the correct option is (D).

8. According to the passage, early studies also suggest that it is on track to achieve the national pledge under the 2015 Paris Agreement for a 33-35% cut in emissions intensity per unit of growth from the same base year by 2030.
This shows that India is to achieve a 33-35% cut in emissions intensity by 2030. It has not achieved yet.
Thus statement I is false.
According to the passage, **the transport decarbonization alliance has been declared. It is aimed at achieving a shift to sustainable fuels, getting cities to commit to eco-friendly mobility, and delivering more walkable communities, all of which will improve the quality of urban life.**
It is clear from the above-highlighted text that it's Transport Decarbonisation Alliance.
Thus statement II is false.
According to the passage, developing countries including India are focussing on the imperatives of ensuring adequate financing for mitigation and adaptation.
Thus statement III is true.
Hence, the correct option is (B).

9. According to the passage, **what is not, however, is the impact of extreme weather events such as droughts and floods that would have a bearing on economic growth.**
With the highlighted text it is clear that Weather condition is the only factor that could affect the economic growth of a country.
The policy framework is not mentioned anywhere in the passage.
Thus will not be treated as the desired factor.
Hence, the correct option is (A).

10. According to the passage, India's progress in reducing the intensity of its greenhouse gas emissions per unit of GDP by 20-25% from 2005 levels by 2020, based on the commitment made in Copenhagen in 2009.
This makes the statement I to be false.
According to the passage, the climate question presents a leapfrog era for India's development paradigm.
This makes statement II to be true.
According to the passage, the 23rd conference of the UN Framework Convention on Climate Change in Bonn shifts into high gear.
Thus statement III is to be false.
Since statements, I and III are not true.
Hence, the correct option is (B).

11. From the given data,

Total cases reported from Gujarat $= 455 + 225 + 252 + 175 + 144 = 1251$
Hence, the correct option is (C).

12. Domestic Violance and Dowry in Bihar $= 475 + 576 = 1051$

Rape and Trafficking in Punjab $= 259 + 263 = 522$

Difference $= 1051 - 522 = 529$

$\therefore$ Required $\% = \frac{529}{522} \times 100 = 101.3\%$ more

Hence, the correct option is (B).

13. Total cases reported on Molestation
$= 132 + 125 + 56 + 364 + 175 + 764 + 261 + 252 = 2129$

Total cases reported on Rape
$= 263 + 216 + 53 + 226 + 252 + 675 + 259 + 276 = 2220$

$\therefore$ Required ratio $= 2129 : 2220 = 0.96$

Hence, the correct option is (B).

14. Total number of Dowry and Molestation cases reported in UP $= 496 + 132 = 628$

Total cases reported in UP $= 354 + +496 + 263 + 132 + 342 = 1587$

$\therefore$ Required $\% = \frac{628}{1587} \times 100 = 39.57\% \approx 40\%$

The closest value in the options is 40%.

Hence, the correct option is (A).

15. This question can be solved very quickly by observation.
HP has the lowest reported cases for each crime. So, it will have the least number of cases across all crimes.
Hence, the correct option is (D).

16. Total quantity of milk $= \frac{2}{3} \times 2400 = 1600$ litres
Total quantity of water $= 2400 - 1600 = 800$ litres
Quantity of milk in vessels A and E together $= \frac{12+28}{100} \times 1600 = 640$ litres
Quantity of water in vessel $D = \frac{25}{100} \times 800 = 200$ litres
Required $\% = \frac{640}{200} \times 100 = 320\%$
Hence, the correct option is (C).

17. Total quantity of milk $= \frac{2}{3} \times 2400 = 1600$ litres
Total quantity of water $= 2400 - 1600 = 800$ litres
Quantity of water in vessels B and C together $= \frac{15+10}{100} \times 800 = 200$ litres
Quantity of milk in vessel $D = \frac{20}{100} \times 1600 = 320$ litres
Required ratio $= 200 : 320 = 5 : 8$
Hence, the correct option is (A).

18. Total quantity of milk $= \frac{2}{3} \times 2400 = 1600$ litres
Total quantity of water $= 2400 - 1600 = 800$ litres
Quantity of milk in vessel $C = \frac{8}{100} \times 1600 = 128$ litres
Quantity of milk in vessel $F = 128 \times \frac{120}{100} = 153.6$ litres
Quantity of water in vessel $C = \frac{10}{100} \times 800 = 80$ litres
Quantity of water in vessel $F = 80 \times \frac{80}{100} = 64$ litres
Required ratio $= 153.6 : 64 = 12 : 5$
Hence, the correct option is (B).

19. Total quantity of milk $= \frac{2}{3} \times 2400 = 1600$ litres
Total quantity of water $= 2400 - 1600 = 800$ litres
Quantity of milk in vessels B and D together $= \frac{32+20}{100} \times 1600 = 832$ litres
Quantity of water in vessels D and E together $= \frac{25+20}{100} \times 800 = 360$ litres
Required sum $= 832 + 360 = 1192$ litres
Hence, the correct option is (B).

20. Total quantity of milk $= \frac{2}{3} \times 2400 = 1600$ litres
Total quantity of water $= 2400 - 1600 = 800$ litres
Quantity of milk in vessel $C = \frac{8}{100} \times 1600 = 128$ litres
Quantity of water in vessel $C = \frac{10}{100} \times 800 = 80$ litres
Quantity of mixture in vessel $C = 128 + 80 = 208$ litres
Quantity of milk in vessel $E = \frac{28}{100} \times 1600 = 448$ litres
Quantity of water in vessel $E = \frac{20}{100} \times 800 = 160$ litres
Quantity of mixture in vessel $E = 448 + 160 = 608$ litres
Required $\% = \frac{608-208}{608} \times 100$
$= \frac{400}{608} \times 100 = 65.78\%$ less
Hence, the correct option is (C).

21. Total distance travelled by all the buses on Monday $= 950 + 600 + 450 = 2000\ km$

Total distance travelled by all the buses on Wednesday $= 1000 + 850 + 550 = 2400\ km$

Required $\% = \frac{2000}{2400} \times 100 = 83.33\%$

Hence, the correct option is (B).

22. From the given graph,
Total distance travelled by bus B throughout the week $= (1050 + 600 + 450 + 850 + 900 + 350 + 850)$ km $= 5050$ km
Hence, the correct option is (C).

23. Distance travelled by bus A on Sunday and Monday together $= (700 + 950)km = 1650\ km$

Distance travelled by bus B on Friday and Saturday together $= (350 + 850)km = 1200\ km$

Required ratio $= 1650 : 1200 = 11 : 8$

Hence, the correct option is (A).

24. Distance travelled by bus A throughout the week $= 700 + 950 + 650 + 1000 + 500 + 450 + 800 = 5050$ km

Distance travelled by bus C throughout the week $= 600 + 450 + 850 + 550 + 1000 + 950 + 800 = 5200$ km

Required difference $= (5200 - 5050)$ km $= 150$ km
Hence, the correct option is (A).

25. Given,
The distance travelled by bus B on Sunday $= 1050$
The distance travelled by bus C on Saturday $= 800$
Required $\% = \frac{1050-800}{800} \times 100$
$= \frac{250}{800} \times 100 = 31.25\%$
Hence, the correct option is (B).

26. Cotton output and cotton cloth output is a most suitable example of double counting in national income. Double counting means counting of the value of the same product (or expenditure) more than once. In this way certain items are counted more than once resulting in over-estimation of national product to the extent of the value of intermediate goods included.

Hence, the correct option is (B).

27. The 19th century saw the establishment of British rule in India. Following the Mutiny of 1857, the British government faced an acute financial crisis. To fill up the treasury, the first Income-tax Act was introduced in February 1860 by James Wilson, who became British-India's first Finance Minister.

Hence, the correct option is (B).

28. Planning Commission had constituted a high level committee on financial sector reforms under the Chairmanship of Shri Raghuram G. Rajan, Professor, Graduate School of Business, University of Chicago in August, 2007. The Committee submitted the report in September, 2008.

Hence, the correct option is (B).

29. The second five year plan accorded the highest priority to Industrialisation. The plan was based on the famous Mahalanobis Model. Mahalanobis model set out the task of establishing basic and capital goods industries on a large scale to create a strong base for the industrial development.

Hence, the correct option is (A).

30. The meaning of the acronym HRM is Human Resource Management. Human resource management (HRM) is the practice of recruiting, hiring, deploying and managing an organization's employees. HRM is really employee management with an emphasis on those employees as assets of the business.

Hence, the correct option is (C).

31. HRM is a staff functions. A "staff function" supports the organization with specialized advisory and support functions. For example, human resources, accounting, public relations and the legal department are generally considered to be staff functions.

Hence, the correct option is (A).

32. Finding ways to reduce uncertainty is a key responsibility of management. The primary role of a manager is to ensure the daily functioning of a department or group of employees.

Hence, the correct option is (B).

33. A minimum of 10 members are required to form a cooperative society. The Co operative societies Act do not specify the maximum number of members for any co-operative society. However, after the formation of the society, the member may specify the maximum number of members.

Hence, the correct option is (C).

34. Membership of a co-operative is voluntary. "Cooperatives are voluntary organizations, open to all persons able to use their services and willing to accept the responsibilities of membership, without gender, social, political, racial, or religious discrimination."

Hence, the correct option is (B).

35. The liability of members of a co-operative society is limited or unlimited depending upon what the society has opted for it. The liability of members of a co-operative society is limited to the extent of capital contributed by them. Unlike sole proprietors and partners the personal properties of members of the co-operative societies are free from any kind of risk because of business liabilities. An unlimited liability company involves general partners and sole proprietors who are equally responsible for all debt and liabilities accrued by the business. Most companies opt to form limited partnerships, where a partner's liability cannot exceed their investment in the company.

Hence, the correct option is (D).

Mock Test 16

Comprehension

Ques (1-5):Direction: Read the passage and answer the question given below.

Member nations of the United Nations body charged with regulating shipping on the high seas adopted a first-ever strategy to blunt the sector's large contribution to climate change bringing another major constituency on board in the international quest to cap the planet's warming well below an increase of 2 degrees Celsius (3.6 degrees Fahrenheit). The strategy embraced by a committee of the International Maritime Organization would lower emissions from container ships, oil tankers, bulk carriers and other vessels by at least 50 percent by the year 2050 vs. where they stood in 2008. The group also said that emissions from shipping should reach a peak, and begin to decline, as soon as possible.

But the United States "reserved" its position on the strategy, with Coast Guard official Jeffrey Lantz, who headed the delegation to the London deliberations, saying that the country views "the establishment of an absolute reduction target as premature." The United States also objected to how responsibilities would be divided between developed and developing countries, and expressed "serious concern about how this document was developed and finalized." Shipping in recent years has been responsible for about 800 million tons annually of carbon dioxide emissions, according to Dan Rutherford, the marine and aviation program director of the International Council on Clean Transportation, who was in attendance for the deliberations in London. That means shipping's emissions are 2.3 percent of the global total. "If you counted it as a country, it would be the sixth-largest source of CO2 emissions," said Rutherford, noting that 800 million tons of annual emissions is comparable to emissions from Germany.

Moreover, if nothing is done to halt emissions growth in the industry, emissions are projected to continue to grow, and shipping would burn up a significant share of the remaining global carbon emissions allowable under the Paris climate agreement releasing as much as 101 billion tons of carbon-dioxide-equivalent emissions between now and 2075, according to an analysis by Rutherford's organization. Shipping and aviation are two major greenhouse-gas-producing sectors that have sat rather uncomfortably in the context of the global push to cut emissions under the Paris climate agreement.

Both sectors are very difficult to decarbonize, since they rely on energy-dense fuels to allow ships or planes to travel great distances without stopping. Meanwhile, since the sectors have major international components, they are not the responsibility of any single country to regulate as part of a domestic climate-change strategy. Instead, addressing their role in climate change has fallen to United Nations bodies such as the IMO and the International Civil Aviation Organization. Yet despite the ambition of the current strategy for shipping, Rutherford's group's analysis shows that it may not be strong enough. The group says that to be consistent with the Paris agreement, shipping should emit no more than 17 billion tons of carbon-dioxide-equivalent emissions from 2015 onward but that the current agreement implies emissions between 28 billion and 43 billion tons.

The group says that to be consistent with the Paris agreement, shipping should emit no more than 17 billion tons of carbon-dioxide-equivalent emissions from 2015 onward but that the current agreement implies emissions between 28 billion and 43 billion tons. For shipping and aviation to decarbonize, current fuel oils would have to be replaced by biofuels or, perhaps ultimately, hydrogen or batteries. But such innovations so far are being tested only in smaller ships and planes. Rutherford said."The largest container ships and airplanes use a tremendous amount of energy. They're going to be harder to electrify or put hydrogen in," he said.

Q.1 What is the primary purpose of the author of the passage?

I. To highlight the significance of the strategy adopted by IMO to reduce the emissions by shipping industry which would help tackle climate change

II. To highlight the contribution of shipping and aviation industry in the total volume of emissions and its impact on climate.

III. To study the impact of climate change on low lying island nations and address their concerns of emissions from the shipping industry

A. Only I **B.** Only II

C. Only I and III **D.** Only II and III

Q.2 Which out of the following can be inferred from the passage?

A. Shipping and Aviation is regulated individually by the member counties of the UN which has made it difficult to set a target for emission control.

B. Shipping industry is the largest contributor of carbon-dioxide emissions among other industries.

C. The Paris Climate agreement aims to reduce the average global temperature by 1.5 Celsius or 2.7 degrees Fahrenheit.

D. It would be difficult to switch to energy source with low carbon footprint for container ships.

Q.3 Out of the given statements, which one is Dan Rutherford likely to agree with?

I. Shipping emissions annually are equivalent to the emissions of Germany.

II. If the shipping industry emissions continue to grow at the current rate then they would eat into the global carbon budget.

III. The current strategy to curtail shipping industry emissions is not strong enough and the proposed limits are way lower than the required emission levels.

A. Only I **B.** Only II

C. Only I and III **D.** All of the above

Q.4 Which of the following statement highlight the objective of the strategy made by the committee of the International Maritime Organization?

A. It aims to lower the emissions by heavy industries and cargo ships by 50% by the year 2050.

B. It aims to lower the emissions by the transportation sector and food processing sector by 50% by the year 2050.

C. It aims to lower the emissions by the container ships, oil tankers, bulk carriers and other vessels by 50% by the year 2050.

D. It aims to lower the emissions by the energy sector including coal and natural gas and increase the investments in renewable energy.

Q.5 As per the passage, what are the problems which are common to both shipping and aviation industry?

A. Both aviation and shipping industry require intensive investments.

B. Both aviation and shipping industry are vulnerable to automation.

C. Both aviation and shipping industry are difficult to decarbonize as it is not commercially viable to do so.

D. Both aviation and shipping industry are difficult to decarbonize as it is difficult to power large vessels and planes through renewable energy.

Ques (6-10):Direction: Read the passage carefully and answer the question given beside.

The oceans are so vast and deep that until fairly recently, it was widely assumed that no matter how much trash and chemicals humans dumped into them, the effects would be negligible. Proponents of dumping in the oceans even had a catchphrase: "The solution to pollution is dilution."

Today, we need look no further than the New Jersey-size dead zone that forms each summer in the Mississippi River Delta, or the thousand-mile-wide swath of decomposing plastic in the northern Pacific Ocean to see that this "dilution" policy has helped place a once flourishing ocean ecosystem on the brink of collapse.

There is evidence that the oceans have suffered at the hands of mankind for millennia, as far back as Roman times. But recent studies show that degradation, particularly of shoreline areas, has accelerated dramatically in the past three centuries as industrial discharge and runoff from farms and coastal cities has increased.

Pollution is the introduction of harmful contaminants that are outside the norm for a given ecosystem. Common man-made pollutants that reach the ocean include pesticides, herbicides, chemical fertilizers, detergents, oil, sewage, plastics, and other solids. Many of these pollutants collect at the ocean's depths, where they are consumed by small marine organisms and introduced into the global food chain. Scientists are even discovering that pharmaceuticals ingested by humans but not fully processed by our bodies are eventually ending up in the fish we eat.

Many ocean pollutants are released into the environment far upstream from coastlines. Nitrogen-rich fertilizers applied by farmers inland, for example, end up in local streams, rivers, and groundwater and are eventually deposited in estuaries, bays, and deltas. These excess nutrients can spawn massive blooms of algae that rob the water of oxygen, leaving areas where little or no marine life can exist. Scientists have counted some 400 such dead zones around the world.

Solid wastes like bags, foam, and other items dumped into the oceans from land or by ships at sea are frequently consumed, with often fatal effects, by marine mammals, fish, and birds that mistake it for food. Discarded fishing nets drift for years, ensnaring fish and mammals. In certain regions, ocean currents corral trillions of decomposing plastic items and other trash into gigantic, swirling garbage patches.

Pollution is not always physical. In large bodies of water, sound waves can carry undiminished for miles. The increased presence of loud or persistent sounds from ships, sonar devices, oil rigs, and even from natural sources like earthquakes can disrupt the migration, communication, hunting, and reproduction patterns of many marine animals, particularly aquatic mammals like whales and dolphins.

Q.6 Which of the following is the reason for degradation of shore lines of oceans as per the passage?

I. Industrial waste

II. Migration from coastal cities

III. Hunting of Aquatic animals

A. Only I **B.** Only I and II

C. Only III **D.** Only II and III

Q.7 Which of the following statement/s is/are not true in the context of passage?

I. Marine pollution is the resultant of physical pollution only.

II. Plastic bags, foams etc. are rarely consumed by aquatic animals.

III. The earthquakes can disturb lifestyle and behavior pattern of aquatic mammals.

A. Only I and III **B.** Only III

C. Only II and III **D.** Only I and II

Q.8 Which of the following is/are a source of solid waste?

A. Pesticides **B.** Plastics

C. Organic fertilizers **D.** Only (A) and (B)

Q.9 As per the passage, how do nitrogen-rich fertilizers contribute to marine pollution?

A. By releasing chemicals in the water.

B. By absorbing all the oxygen from water, making it near impossible for any marine life to dwell.

C. By raising nitrogen levels in the sea.

D. All of the above

Q.10 Which of the following is/are true as per the passage?

I. Dilution is the key to control pollution.

II. Pollution can make changes in the hunting, migration and communication pattern of dolphins.

III. Solid wastes have fatal effects on marine animals.

A. Only I **B.** Only II

C. Only II and III **D.** All of the above

Management Data Interpretation

Ques (11-15):Direction: Study the following pie-charts carefully and answer the question given beside.

The pie chart 1 given below gives information about the percentage distribution of the funds received from various sources by XYZ college. The pie chart 2 given below gives information about the percentage distribution of the expenditures of the college.

Total funds collection = Total expenditures

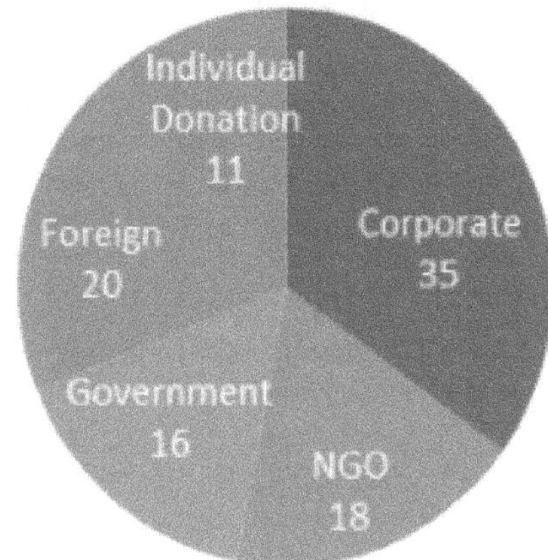

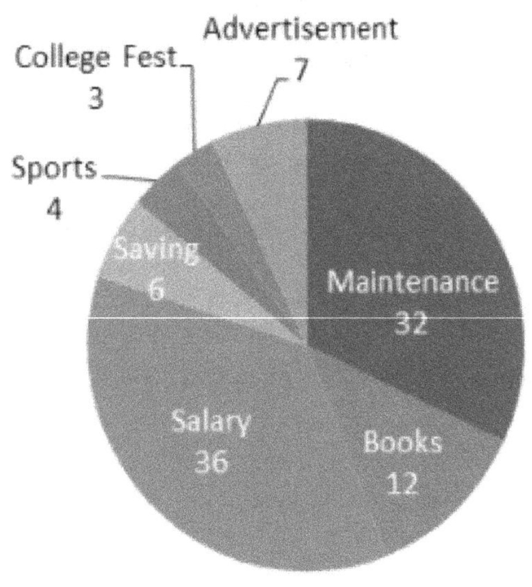

Q.11 Only foreign donation was spent on sports, college fest and advertisements then what percent of foreign donation was spent on other parts?

A. 30% **B.** 25% **C.** 40% **D.** 35%

Q.12 The expenditures on college fest was Rs. 12000 less than that on sports then corporate funds was how much more than that of foreign funds?

A. Rs. 1.75 lakhs **B.** Rs. 2.4 lakhs
C. Rs. 1.8 lakhs **D.** Rs. 1.6 lakhs

Q.13 The total individual donation was Rs. 1.32 lakhs then what was the expenditures of the college on the salary payment?

A. Rs. 3.85 lakhs **B.** Rs. 3.96 lakhs
C. Rs. 4.32 lakhs **D.** Rs. 4.68 lakhs

Q.14 If the college had saved Rs. 30 thousand then what was the funds received from NGO and government together?

A. Rs. 185 thousand **B.** Rs. 170 thousand
C. Rs. 145 thousand **D.** Rs. 175 thousand

Q.15 What was the ratio between the funds collected from NGO to the expenditures of the college on books?

A. 4:3 **B.** 6:4 **C.** 8:5 **D.** 9:7

Ques (16-20):Direction: Study the following information carefully and answer the following question as beside.

The following table gives the information about the number of marks obtained by five students in five subjects in an examination (the total marks in every subject are 300 each).

Student	Subject				
	English	Maths	Physics	Biology	Hindi
A	180	290	215	190	192
B	210	230	264	228	102
C	285	175	176	186	132
D	185	165	188	136	144
E	225	230	162	98	156

Q.16 The total marks obtained by D and E together in Biology and Hindi together was approximately what percent of the marks obtained by A alone in Maths?

A. 187.32% **B.** 192.21%
C. 181.24% **D.** 184.14%

Q.17 If the minimum passing marks of any subject was 30% of the total marks of all the subjects together then the marks obtained by B in all the subjects together was how much more than the minimum passing marks of all the subjects together?

A. 584 **B.** 534 **C.** 564 **D.** 575

Q.18 What was the highest total percentage of the marks of all the subjects together secured by any of the given students? (approximately)

A. 56.64% **B.** 68.93% **C.** 71.13% **D.** 58.34%

Q.19 Find the difference between the marks obtained by A and B in all the subjects together and the marks obtained by C and D in all the subjects together?

A. 349 **B.** 347
C. 345 **D.** None of these

Q.20 The marks obtained in English by all the students together is approximately what percent of the marks obtained in Maths by all the students together?

A. 99.13% **B.** 99.17% **C.** 99.34% **D.** 99.54%

Ques (21-25):Direction: Study the following line chart carefully and answer the question given beside.

The line graph represents the total number of students registered and appeared in five different exams from the city.

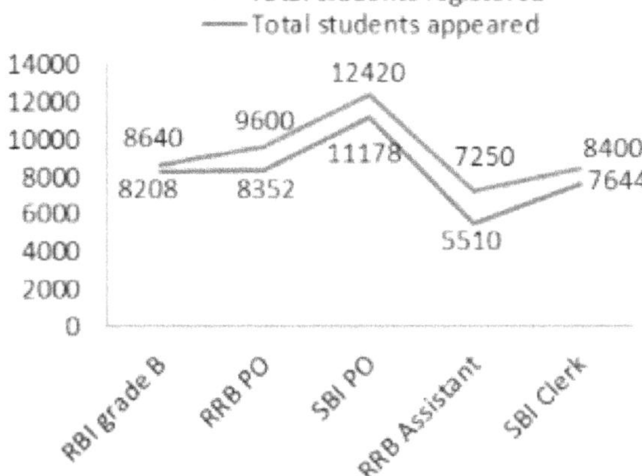

Q.21 The total number of students who did not appeared in RBI grade B is approximately what percentage of the total number of students who did not appeared in SBI PO exam?

A. 39% **B.** 44% **C.** 32% **D.** 35%

Q.22 How many students from the given five exams had not appeared in the exam?

A. 5418 **B.** 6218 **C.** 5118 **D.** 5618

Q.23 80% and 75% of the students who appeared for RRB assistant exam and RRB PO exam respectively had qualified for the tier II exam. If 25% of the students who qualified for tier II from both the exams, had qualified for interview then find the difference between the number of students who qualified for interview from RRB PO and from RRB assistant.

A. 554 **B.** 434 **C.** 464 **D.** 274

Q.24 For which exam, the percentage of the number of students who did not appeared in the exam is second lowest?

A. RBI Grade B **B.** RRB PO
C. SBI PO **D.** SBI Clerk

Q.25 The registration of $\left(\frac{4}{55}\right)$th of total number of students of the given five exams had been cancelled. Find the number of students whose registration was cancelled.

A. 3478 **B.** 3368 **C.** 3648 **D.** 3538

Business Awareness

Q.26 Which of the following is not a part of the 10 C's of Human Resource Management?

A. Coherence **B.** Competence
C. Change **D.** Correctness

Q.27 Which of the following is part of the managerial functions of Human Resource Management?

A. Development **B.** Staffing
C. Procurement **D.** Compensation

Q.28 Which of the following best defines the controlling functions of human resource management?

A. Ability to decide what is to be done and avoided with employees.
B. Establish standards against which the actual performance to be measured.
C. Enforcement of legal and statutory regulations.
D. Gather more data on the job to be done by each employee.

Q.29 Which of the following is not an ownership security?

A. Equity shares **B.** Preference shares
C. Debentures **D.** Both (B) and (C)

Q.30 A bearer of a share warrant of a company is________

A. a creditor of the company
B. a member of the company
C. a member subject to certain conditions
D. not a member of the company

Q.31 Which of the following are components of organized sector of stock exchange?

A. Commercial banks
B. Investors in securities
C. Financial institutions like LFC, IDBI
D. Other financial institutions

Q.32 Leader-Member relations, task structure, and position power are attributes of which leadership theory?

A. Trait Theory
B. Behavioural Theory
C. Situational Theory
D. Contingency Theory

Q.33 Devaluation of currency leads to

A. Fall in domestic prices
B. Increase in domestic prices
C. No impact on domestic prices
D. Erratic fluctuations in domestic prices

Q.34 Since 1983, the RBI's responsibility with respect to regional rural banks was transferred to

A. ARDC **B.** SBI
C. NABARD **D.** PACs

Q.35 One rupee currency note in India bears the signature of

A. The president of India
B. Finance minister of India
C. Governor (RBI)
D. Finance Secretary of Government of India

// Smart Answer Sheet //

Correct Indicates percentage of students who answered questions correctly.

Skipped Indicates percentage of students who skipped questions.

Q.	Ans.	Correct	Skipped
1	A	85.58 %	13.54 %
2	D	89.23 %	10.65 %
3	D	55.65 %	38.51 %
4	C	56.09 %	30.45 %
5	D	40.5 %	58.64 %
6	B	78.27 %	18.95 %
7	D	54.01 %	30.31 %

Q.	Ans.	Correct	Skipped
8	D	55.93 %	36.67 %
9	B	81.84 %	13.36 %
10	C	54.15 %	30.38 %
11	A	70.0 %	30.0 %
12	C	59.05 %	39.27 %
13	C	54.61 %	40.14 %
14	B	77.55 %	20.35 %

Q.	Ans.	Correct	Skipped
15	B	40.48 %	30.78 %
16	D	87.73 %	10.57 %
17	A	87.42 %	10.18 %
18	C	65.14 %	30.82 %
19	D	79.78 %	17.9 %
20	D	80.72 %	11.54 %
21	D	88.41 %	10.68 %

Q.	Ans.	Correct	Skipped
22	A	79.77 %	11.18 %
23	C	54.16 %	38.72 %
24	D	62.77 %	31.96 %
25	B	80.32 %	11.96 %
26	D	48.13 %	31.46 %
27	B	52.48 %	46.22 %
28	B	50.88 %	39.48 %

Q.	Ans.	Correct	Skipped
29	C	67.39 %	31.01 %
30	D	78.75 %	14.23 %
31	B	43.89 %	46.92 %
32	D	66.37 %	33.36 %
33	B	60.57 %	31.43 %
34	C	50.64 %	44.61 %
35	D	89.35 %	10.1 %

Performance Analysis	
Avg. Score (%)	48.57%
Toppers Score (%)	54.29%
Your Score	

//Hints and Solutions//

1. Statement I is correct.
According to the passage, member nations of the United Nations body charged with regulating shipping on the high seas adopted a first-ever strategy to blunt the sector's large contribution to climate change bringing another major constituency on board in the international quest to cap the planet's warming well below an increase of 2 degrees Celsius (3.6 degrees Fahrenheit).
Statements I and II do not cover the entire scope of the passage.
Hence, the correct option is (A).

2. Option (D) is correct. According to the passage, for shipping to decarbonize, current fuel oils would have to be replaced by biofuels or, perhaps ultimately, hydrogen or batteries. But such innovations so far are being tested only in smaller ships, rather than the largest vessels, Rutherford said."The largest container ships use a tremendous amount of energy. They're going to be harder to electrify or put hydrogen in," he said.

Option (A) is incorrect. According to the passage, both sectors are very difficult to decarbonize, since they rely on energy-dense fuels to allow ships or planes to travel great distances without stopping. Meanwhile, since the sectors have major international components, they are not the responsibility of any single country to regulate as part of a domestic climate-change strategy. Instead, addressing their role in climate change has fallen to United Nations bodies such as the IMO and the International Civil Aviation Organization.

Option (B) is incorrect. The passage does not explicitly state that shipping is the largest contributor of carbon-dioxide among other industries.

Option (C) is incorrect. According to the passage, member nations of the United Nations body charged with regulating shipping on the high seas adopted a first-ever strategy to blunt the sector's large contribution to climate change bringing another major constituency on board in the international quest to cap the planet's warming well below an increase of 2 degrees Celsius (3.6 degrees Fahrenheit).

Hence, the correct option is (D).

3. Statement I is correct. According to the passage,"if you counted it as a country, it would be the sixth-largest source of CO_2 emissions," said Rutherford, noting that 800 million tons of annual emissions is comparable to emissions from Germany.

Statement II is correct. According to the passage, moreover, if nothing is done to halt emissions growth in the industry, emissions are projected to continue to grow, and shipping would burn up a significant share of the remaining global carbon emissions allowable under the Paris climate agreement releasing as much as 101 billion tons of carbon-dioxide-equivalent emissions between now and 2075, according to an analysis by Rutherford's organization.

Statement III is correct. According to the passage, yet despite the ambition of the current strategy for shipping, Rutherford's group's analysis shows that it may not be strong enough. The group says that to be consistent with the Paris agreement, shipping should emit no more than 17 billion tons of carbon-dioxide-equivalent emissions from 2015 onward but that the current agreement implies emissions between 28 billion and 43 billion tons.

Hence, the correct option is (D).

4. Option (C) is correct. According to the passage, the strategy embraced by a committee of the International Maritime Organization would lower emissions from container ships, oil tankers, bulk carriers and other vessels by at least 50 percent by the year 2050 vs. where they stood in 2008. The group also said that emissions from shipping should reach a peak, and begin to decline, as soon as possible.

Option (A) is incorrect. The passage does not talk about heavy industries.

Option (B) is incorrect. The passage does not talks about transportation and food processing sector.

Option (D) is incorrect as the passage does not talk about coal and natural gas.

Hence, the correct option is (C).

5. Option (D) is correct. According to the passage, both sectors are very difficult to decarbonize, since they rely on energy-dense fuels to allow ships or planes to travel great distances without stopping.

Rutherford said."The largest container ships and airplanes use a tremendous amount of energy. They're going to be harder to electrify or put hydrogen in," he said.

Option (A) is incorrect. The passage does not talk about intensive investments being required by aviation and shipping industry.

Option (B) is incorrect. The passage does not talk about automation.

Option (C) is incorrect. The passage only discusses the technological aspect of decarbonization of shipping and aviation industry. It does not talk about the financial or commercial aspect of it.

Hence, the correct option is (D).

6. According to the passage, there is evidence that the oceans have suffered at the hands of mankind for millennia, as far back as Roman times. But recent studies show **that degradation, particularly of shoreline areas, has accelerated dramatically in the past three centuries as industrial discharge and runoff from farms and coastal cities has increased.**

Statement I and II can clearly inferred from the highlighted text.

Statement III is not mentioned anywhere in the passage and is incorrect.

Hence, the correct option is (B).

7. According to the passage, **pollution is not always physical**. In large bodies of water, sound waves can carry undiminished for miles.

The highlighted text shows that sound waves can also cause pollution. So statement I is not true.

According to the passage, solid wastes like bags, foam, and other items dumped into the oceans from land or by ships at sea are frequently consumed, with often fatal effects, by marine mammals, fish, and birds that mistake it for food.

This shows that such solid wastes are frequently consumed by marine animals. Thus, statement II is not true.

According to the passage, earthquakes can disrupt the migration, communication, hunting, and reproduction patterns of many marine animals, particularly aquatic mammals...

This shows that statement III is true.

So, statements I and II are untrue.

Hence, the correct option is (D).

8. According to the passage, common man-made pollutants that reach the ocean include pesticides, herbicides, chemical fertilizers, detergents, oil, sewage, plastics, and other solids.

This shows that only pesticides and plastics are the sources of pollution in the ocean and organic fertilizers are not one of the reasons, it will not be considered as solid waste.

Hence, the correct option is (D).

9. According to the passage, **nitrogen-rich fertilizers** applied by farmers inland, for example, end up in local streams, rivers, and groundwater and are eventually deposited in estuaries, bays, and deltas. **These excess nutrients can spawn massive blooms of algae that rob the water of oxygen, leaving areas where little or no marine life can exist.**

As per the highlighted text, only option (B) is true.

Hence, the correct option is (B).

10. According to the passage, "the oceans are so vast and deep that until fairly recently, it was widely assumed that no matter how much trash and chemicals humans dumped into them, the effects would be negligible. Proponents of dumping in the oceans even had a catchphrase: "The solution to pollution is dilution."

This line was said by people who thought dumping waste in the oceans would have no negative impact on the environment. This is shown to be an incorrect way of thinking and is wrong.

So, I is not true.

According to the passage, the increased presence of loud or persistent sounds from ships, sonar devices, oil rigs, and even from natural sources like earthquakes can disrupt the migration, communication, hunting, and reproduction patterns of many marine animals, particularly aquatic mammals like whales and dolphins.

Thus statement II is true, as sound pollution is also a form of pollution.

According to the passage, solid wastes like bags, foam, and other items dumped into the oceans from land or by ships at sea are frequently consumed, with often fatal effects, by marine mammals, fish, and birds that mistake it for food.

This proves that such wastes adversely affect marine animals.

Thus statements III is also true, as solid wastes have fatal effects on marine animals.

Thus, Only statements II and III are true.

Hence, the correct option is (C).

11. Let the total funds collection $=$ the total expenditures $= 100x$

The foreign donation $= 20\%$ of $100x = 20x$

The expenditures on sports, college fest and advertisements together $= (4+3+7)\%$ of $100x = 14x$

The required percentage $= \frac{(20x-14x)\times 100}{20x} = \frac{6\times 100}{20} = 30\%$

Hence, the correct option is (A).

12. Let the total expenditures $= 100x$

Then, the expenditures on college fest $-$ that on sports $= 4\%$ of $100x - 3\%$ of $100x = x =$ Rs. 12000

Corporate funds $= 35\%$ of $100x = 35x$

Foreign funds $= 20\%$ of $100x = 20x$

The required difference $= 35x - 20x = 15x = 15 \times 12000 = 180{,}000 =$ Rs. 1.8 lakhs

Hence, the correct option is (C).

13. Let the total funds collection $=$ the total expenditures $= 100x$

The total individual donation $= 11\%$ of $100x = 11x = 1.32$

$\Rightarrow x = 0.12$

The expenditures of college on salary payments $= 36\%$ of $100x = 36x = 36 \times 0.12 =$ Rs. 4.32 lakhs

Hence, the correct option is (C).

14. Let the total funds collection $=$ the total expenditures $= 100x$

Then, saving $= 6\%$ of $100x = 6x =$ Rs. 30 thousand

$\Rightarrow x =$ Rs. 5 thousand

The funds received from NGO and government together $= 18\%$ of $100x + 16\%$ of $100x$

$= 34x = 34 \times 5 =$ Rs. 170 thousand

Hence, the correct option is (B).

15. Let the total funds collection $=$ the total expenditures $= 100x$

The funds collection from NGO $= 18\%$ of $100x = 18x$

The expenditures of college on books $= 12\%$ of $100x = 12x$

The required ratio $= 18x : 12x = 3:2 = 6:4$

Hence, the correct option is (B).

16. The total marks obtained by D and E together in Biology and Hindi together $= 136 + 98 + 144 + 156 = 534$

The total marks obtained by A alone in maths $= 290$

$\therefore$ Required $\% = 534 \times \frac{100}{290} = 184.14\%$ (approximately)

Hence, the correct option is (D).

17. Total number of subjects $= 5$

The total marks of all the five subjects $= 300 \times 5 = 1500$

Minimum passing marks $= 30\%$ of $1500 = 450$

The marks obtained by B in all the subject together $= (210 + 230 + 264 + 228 + 102) = 1034$

The required difference $= 1034 - 450 = 584$

Hence, the correct option is (A).

18. The marks obtained by A $= 1067$

The marks obtained by B $= 1034$

The marks obtained by C $= 954$

The marks obtained by D $= 818$

The marks obtained by E $= 871$

Since A got the highest marks so the percentage of the marks of all the subject together will be highest for A.

Required $\% = 1067 \times \frac{100}{1500} = 71.13\%$ (approximately)

Hence, the correct option is (C).

19. The marks obtained by A and B in all the subjects together $= 1067 + 1034 = 2101$

The marks obtained by C and D in all the subjects together $= 954 + 818 = 1772$

The required difference $= 2101 - 1772 = 329$

Hence, the correct option is (D).

20. The marks obtained in English by all the students together $= 1085$

The marks obtained in Maths by all the students together $= 1090$

Required $\% = \frac{1085}{1090} \times 100 = 99.54\%$

Hence, the correct option is (D).

21. Total number of students who did not appeared in RBI grade B exam $= 8640 - 8208 = 432$

Total number of students who did not appeared in SBI PO exam $= 12420 - 11178 = 1242$

Required $\% = \frac{432}{1242} \times 100 = 34.78\% \approx 35\%$

Hence, the correct option is (D).

22. Total number of students who did not appeared in RBI grade B exam $= 8640 - 8208 = 432$

Total number of students who did not appeared in RRB PO exam $= 9600 - 8352 = 1248$

Total number of students who did not appeared in SBI PO exam $= 12420 - 11178 = 1242$

Total number of students who did not appeared in RRB assistant exam $= 7250 - 5510 = 1740$

Total number of students who did not appeared in SBI clerk exam $= 8400 - 7644 = 756$

Required number of students $= 432 + 1248 + 1242 + 1740 + 756 = 5418$

Hence, the correct option is (A).

23. Total number of students qualified for tier II from RRB assistant $= 80\%$ of $5510 = 4408$

Total number of students qualified for tier II from RRB PO $= 75\%$ of $8352 = 6264$

Total number of students qualified for interview from RRB assistant $= 25\%$ of $4408 = 1102$

Total number of students qualified for interview from RRB PO $= 25\%$ of $6264 = 1566$

Required difference $= 1566 - 1102 = 464$

Hence, the correct option is (C).

24. Total number of students who did not appeared in RBI grade B exam $= 8640 - 8208 = 432$

Total number of students who did not appeared in RRB PO exam $= 9600 - 8352 = 1248$

Total number of students who did not appeared in SBI PO exam $= 12420 - 11178 = 1242$

Total number of students who did not appeared in RRB assistant exam $= 7250 - 5510 = 1740$

Total number of students who did not appeared in SBI clerk exam $= 8400 - 7644 = 756$

Percentage of students who did not appeared in RBI grade B exam $= \frac{432}{8640} \times 100 = 5\%$

Percentage of students who did not appeared in RRB PO exam $= \frac{1248}{9600} \times 100 = 13\%$

Percentage of students who did not appeared in SBI PO exam $= \frac{1242}{12420} \times 100 = 10\%$

Percentage of students who did not appeared in RRB assistant exam $= \frac{1740}{4250} \times 100 = 24\%$

Percentage of students who did not appeared in SBI clerk exam $= \frac{765}{8400} \times 100 = 9\%$

Hence, the correct option is (D).

25. Total number of students registered in the given five exams $= (8640 + 9600 + 12420 + 7250 + 8400) = 46310$

Number of students whose registration was cancelled $= \frac{4}{55} \times 46310 = 3368$

Hence, the correct option is (B).

26. The 10 C's of human resources management are cost-effectiveness, competitiveness, coherence, credibility, communication, creativity, competitive advantage, competence, change, and commitment. This framework was developed by Alan Price.

Hence, the correct option is (D).

27.

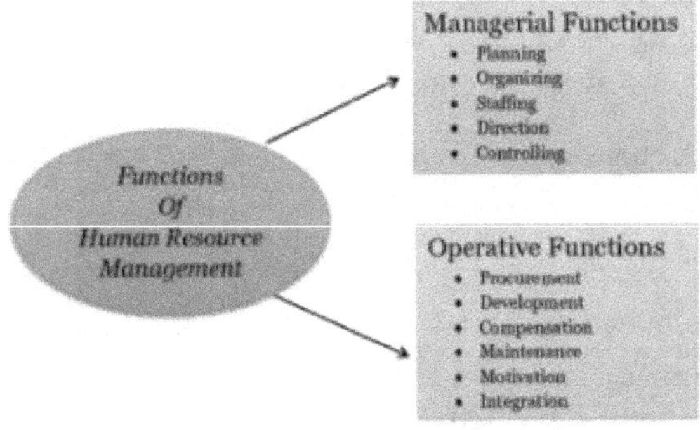

As per the figure, it is clear that staffing is part of the managerial functions of Human Resource Management.

Hence, the correct option is (B).

28. The objectives of the controlling function of human resource management are –

1. Establishment of standard performance so as to measure the actual performance of the employees.

2. Measurement of actual performance with the established performance standards of employees for finding out gaps in employee performance.

3. Comparison of actual performance with the standard one to find the deviation for initiation of corrective actions, if there are any deviations.

Out of the various options, option (B) is the best fit as per the explanation given above and is the correct answer.

Hence, the correct option is (B).

29. Debentures is not an ownership security. A debenture is a type of debt instrument that is not secured by collateral and usually has a term greater than 10 years. Debentures are backed only by the creditworthiness and reputation of the issuer. Both corporations and governments frequently issue debentures to raise capital or funds.

Hence, the correct option is (C).

30. A bearer of a share warrant of a company is not a member of the company. But if the articles of association of the company provide it, then the bearer is deemed to be the member of the company.

Hence, the correct option is (D).

31. Investors in securities are components of the organized sector of the stock exchange. The organized sector of the capital market comprises all the term-lending financial institutions (or development banks or non-banking financial institutions, like IDBI, ICICI, etc.), banks with their medium-term and their merchant banking divisions or subsidiaries, LIC, GIC, UTI and the stock exchanges (an essential component of the capital market).

Hence, the correct option is (B).

32. Leader-Member relations, task structure, and position power are attributes of Contingency Theory. A contingency theory is an organizational theory that claims that there is no best way to organize a corporation, to lead a company, or to make decisions. Instead, the optimal course of action is contingent (dependent) upon the internal and external situation.

Hence, the correct option is (D).

33. Devaluation is the decision to reduce the value of a currency at a fixed exchange rate. A devaluation means that the value of the currency falls. Domestic residents will find imports and foreign travel more expensive. However domestic exports will benefit from their exports becoming cheaper. Thus, the devaluation of currency leads to an increase in domestic prices.

Hence, the correct option is (B).

34. Since 1983, the RBI's responsibility with respect to regional rural banks was transferred to NABARD. NABARD was established on 12 July 1982 to implement the National Bank for Agriculture and Rural Development Act 1981. It replaced the Agricultural Credit Department (ACD) and Rural Planning and Credit Cell (RPCC) of Reserve Bank of India, and Agricultural Refinance and Development Corporation (ARDC). It is one of the premier agencies providing developmental credit in rural areas. NABARD is India's specialised bank for Agriculture and Rural Development in India.

Hence, the correct option is (C).

35. All the paper currency of India except one rupee note bears the signature of the RBI Governor as these are issued by RBI, but the one rupee note bears the signature of the Finance Secretary of the Government of India.

Hence, the correct option is (D).

Mock Test 17

Comprehension

Ques (1-4):Direction: Read the given passage carefully and answer the question that follows.

The first systems of writing developed and used by the Germanic peoples were runic alphabets. The runes functioned as letters, but they were much more than just letters in the sense in which we today understand the term. Each rune was an ideographic or pictographic symbol of some cosmological principle or power, and to write a rune was to invoke and direct the force for which it stood. Indeed, in every Germanic language, the word "rune" (from Proto-Germanic *runo) means both "letter" and "secret" or "mystery," and its original meaning, which likely predated the adoption of the runic alphabet, may have been simply "(hushed) message."

Each rune had a name that hinted at the philosophical and magical significance of its visual form and the sound for which it stands, which was almost always the first sound of the rune's name. For example, the T-rune, called *Tiwaz in the Proto-Germanic language, is named after the god Tiwaz (known as Tyr in the Viking Age). Tiwaz was perceived to dwell within the daytime sky, and, accordingly, the visual form of the T-rune is an arrow pointed upward (which surely also hints at the god's martial role). The T-rune was often carved as a standalone ideograph, apart from the writing of any particular word, as part of spells cast to ensure victory in battle.The runic alphabets are called "futharks" after the first six runes (Fehu, Uruz, Thurisaz, Ansuz, Raidho, Kaunan), in much the same way that the word "alphabet" comes from the names of the first two Hebrew letters (Aleph, Beth). There are three principal futharks: the 24-character Elder Futhark, the first fully-formed runic alphabet, whose development had begun by the first century CE and had been completed before the year 400; the 16-character Younger Futhark, which began to diverge from the Elder Futhark around the beginning of the Viking Age (c. 750 CE) and eventually replaced that older alphabet in Scandinavia; and the 33-character Anglo-Saxon Futhorc, which gradually altered and added to the Elder Futhark in England. On some inscriptions, the twenty-four runes of the Elder Futhark were divided into three ættir (Old Norse, "families") of eight runes each, but the significance of this division is unfortunately unknown.

Runes were traditionally carved onto stone, wood, bone, metal, or some similarly hard surface rather than drawn with ink and pen on parchment. This explains their sharp, angular form, which was well-suited to the medium.

Much of our current knowledge of the meanings the ancient Germanic peoples attributed to the runes comes from the three "Rune Poems," documents from Iceland, Norway, and England that provide a short stanza about each rune in their respective futharks (the Younger Futhark is treated in the Icelandic and Norwegian Rune Poems, while the Anglo-Saxon Futhorc is discussed in the Old English Rune Poem).

While runologists argue over many of the details of the historical origins of runic writing, there is widespread agreement on a general outline. The runes are presumed to have been derived from one of the many Old Italic alphabets in use among the Mediterranean peoples of the first century CE, who lived to the south of the Germanic tribes. Earlier Germanic sacred symbols, such as those preserved in northern European petroglyphs, were also likely influential in the development of the script.

The earliest possibly runic inscription is found on the Meldorf brooch, which was manufactured in the north of modern-day Germany around 50 CE. The inscription is highly ambiguous, however, and scholars are divided over whether its letters are runic or Roman. The earliest unambiguous runic inscriptions are found on the Vimose comb from Vimose, Denmark and the Øvre Stabu spearhead from southern Norway, both of which date to approximately 160 CE. The earliest known carving of the entire futhark, in order, is that on the Kylver stone from Gotland, Sweden, which dates to roughly 400 CE.

The transmission of writing from southern Europe to northern Europe likely took place via Germanic warbands, the dominant northern European military institution of the period, who would have encountered Italic writing firsthand during campaigns amongst their southerly neighbors. This hypothesis is supported by the association that runes have always had with the god Odin, who, in the Proto-Germanic period, under his original name *Woðanaz, was the divine model of the human warband leader and the invisible patron of the warband's activities. The Roman historian Tacitus tells us that Odin ("Mercury" in the interpretatio romana) was already established as the dominant god in the pantheons of many of the Germanic tribes by the first century.

From the perspective of the ancient Germanic peoples themselves, however, the runes came from no source as mundane as an Old Italic alphabet. The runes were never "invented," but are instead eternal, pre-existent forces that Odin himself discovered by undergoing a tremendous ordeal.

Q.1 The word "pantheon" in the passage refers to:

A. A temple of all the gods
B. All the gods collectively of a religion
C. All the gods collectively of a religion
D. A domed circular temple at Rome, erected a.d. 120–124 by Hadrian

Q.2 Which of the following cannot be reasonably inferred with regard to the beliefs of the Proto-Germanic people?

A. Odin came upon the runes after going through a lot of torment
B. The name of a rune was almost always the first sound of a God's name
C. The cosmological power represented by a rune was invoked by writing it
D. Proto-German Gods were modeled on humans

Q.3 Which of the following can be inferred from the passage?
i. Runic script was most likely derived from Old Italic script.

ii. Runes were not used so much as a simple writing system, but rather as magical signs to be used for charms.
iii. In the Proto-Germanic period, the god Tiwaz was associated with war, victory, marriage and the diurnal sky.
iv. The knowledge of the meanings attributed to the runes of the Younger Futhark is derived from the three Rune poems.

A. All of the above **B.** ii and iv
C. i, ii and iv **D.** i and iii

Q.4 Which of the following statements is incorrect?

A. Unlike the Latin alphabet, which is an essentially utilitarian script, the runes are symbols of some of the most powerful forces in the cosmos
B. Runic writing was probably first used in southern Europe and was carried north by Germanic tribes
C. The word "rune" and its meaning was derived from the runic alphabet
D. The first runic alphabets date back to the 1st century CE

Ques (5-10):Direction: Read the following passage carefully and answer the question that follows.

The victory of the small Greek democracy of Athens over the mighty Persian Empire in 490 B.C. is one of the most famous events in history. Darius, king of the Persian Empire, was furious because Athens had interceded for the other Greek city-states in revolt against Persian domination. In anger, the king sent an enormous army to defeat Athens. He thought it would take drastic steps to pacify the rebellious part of the empire.

Persia was ruled by one man. In Athens, however, all citizens helped to rule. Ennobled by this participation, Athenians were prepared to die for their city-state. Perhaps this was the secret of the remarkable victory at Marathon, which freed them from Persian rule. On their way to Marathon, the Persians tried to fool some Greek city-states by claiming to have come in peace. The frightened citizens of Delos refused to believe this. Not wanting to abet the conquest of Greece, they fled from their city and did not return until the Persians had left. They were wise, for the Persians next conquered the city of Eritrea and captured its people.

Tiny Athens stood alone against Persia. The Athenian people went to their sanctuaries. There they prayed for deliverance. They asked their gods to expedite their victory. The Athenians refurbished their weapons and moved to the plain of Marathon, where their little band would meet the Persians. At the last moment, soldiers from Plataea reinforced the Athenian troops.

The Athenian army attacked, and Greek citizens fought bravely. The power of the mighty Persians was offset by the love that the Athenians had for their city. Athenians defeated the Persians in both archery and hand combat. Greek soldiers seized Persian ships and burned them, and the Persians fled in terror. Herodotus, a famous historian, reports that 6,400 Persians died, compared to only 192 Athenians.

Q.5 Who has given an account of the battle between Athens and Persia?

A. Darius **B.** Herodotus
C. Plataea **D.** None of the above

Q.6 Fill in the blanks with the synonym of the word used in the passage:

Darius took drastic steps to _______ the rebellious Athenians.

A. weaken **B.** destroy **C.** calm **D.** irritate

Q.7 Fill in the blanks with the synonym of the word used in the passage:

Their participation ________ to the Athenians.

A. gave comfort **B.** gave honour
C. gave strength **D.** gave fear

Q.8 Fill in the blanks with the synonym of the word used in the passage:

The people of Delos did not want to _____ the conquest of Greece.

A. end **B.** encourage
C. think about **D.** daydream about

Q.9 Fill in the blanks with the synonym of the word used in the passage:

The Athenians were ________ by some soldiers who arrived from Plataea.

A. welcomed **B.** strengthened
C. held **D.** captured

Q.10 Fill in the blanks with the synonym of the word used in the passage:

Athens had ________ the other Greek city-states against the Persians.

A. refused help to
B. intervened on behalf of
C. wanted to fight
D. given orders for all to fight

Management Data Interpretation

Ques (11-15):Direction: Study the following table chart carefully and answer the question given below.

The following table represents marks obtained by five students in five different subjects. The maximum marks for each subject is 100.

Students	Mathematics	Science	English	Hindi	Social Science
Reena	56	94	85	80	86
Tina	98	56	66	70	48
Meena	75	72	78	64	84
Geeta	92	88	86	82	52
Sita	68	90	94	92	54

Q.11 What is the total marks obtained by all the students in English?

A. 420 **B.** 409 **C.** 305 **D.** 506

Q.12 Marks obtained by Reena in all the subjects together is what percent more/less than the marks obtained by Meena in all the subjects together?

A. 7.506% less **B.** 8.504% less
C. 7.506% more **D.** 8.504% more

Q.13 Find the percentage of marks obtained by Geeta in all the subjects together.
A. 55% **B.** 60% **C.** 75% **D.** 80%

Q.14 Find the respective ratio of marks obtained by Meena in Mathematics and Science together and marks obtained by Sita in English and Hindi together.
A. 52:39 **B.** 49:62 **C.** 39:52 **D.** 62:49

Q.15 Marks obtained by all the students in English is what percent of the marks obtained by all the students in Social Science?
A. 126.23% **B.** 134.35%
C. 154.32% **D.** 168.45%

Ques (16-20):Direction: Study the following bar graph carefully and answer the question given below.

The given graph represents the number of users of three Telecom services Jio, Vodafone, and Airtel across 5 cities Mumbai, Delhi, Kolkata, Punjab, and Patna.

Number of users (in thousands)

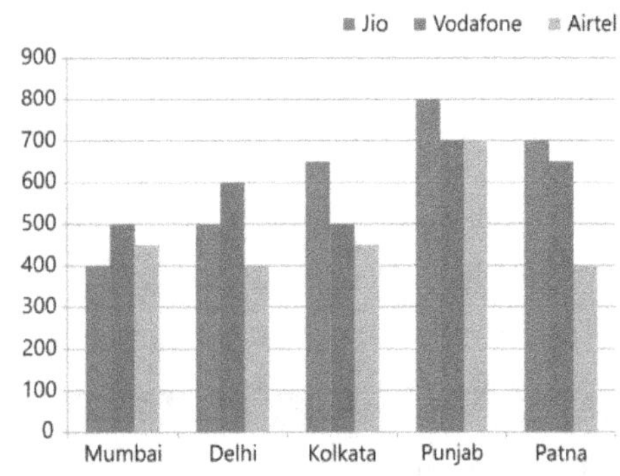

Q.16 What is the total number of users of Vodafone and Airtel across all five cities together?
A. 5350 **B.** 5800 **C.** 5750 **D.** 5700

Q.17 The number of users of Jio and Vodafone together in Patna is what percent of the number of users of Vodafone and Airtel together in Delhi?
A. 120% **B.** 130% **C.** 135% **D.** 140%

Q.18 What is the average number of users of Jio and Airtel across all five cities together?
A. 535 **B.** 540 **C.** 545 **D.** 550

Q.19 What is the difference between the total number of users of Jio, Vodafone, and Airtel together in Kolkata and the total number of users of Jio, Vodafone, and Airtel together in Mumbai?
A. 250 **B.** 200 **C.** 150 **D.** 100

Q.20 What is the ratio of the number users of Jio, Vodafone, and Airtel together in Patna to the number of users of Vodafone and Airtel together in Punjab?
A. 4:3 **B.** 3:4 **C.** 4:5 **D.** 5:4

Ques (21-25):Directions: Study the following pie chart carefully and answer the question given below.

A student scored a total of 542 marks out of 600 in a public examination. Look at the Pie Diagram and answer the following questions:

Marks Scored by a student in various subjects

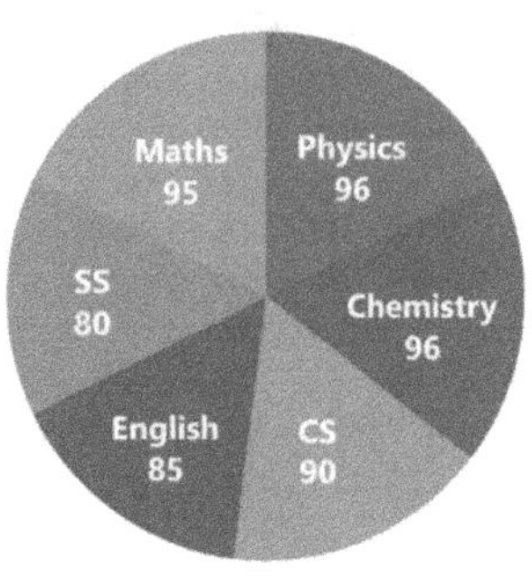

Q.21 The marks scored in Physics, Chemistry, Maths when added together represent approximate what percentage of the total marks obtained?
A. 53 **B.** 49 **C.** 55 **D.** 45

Q.22 The marks scored in CS and Mathematics together is approximately what percent more than the marks scored in SS and English together?
A. 10 **B.** 12 **C.** 8 **D.** 16

Q.23 The difference of marks between Physics and SS is approximate what percent of 600?
A. 5 **B.** 7 **C.** 1 **D.** 3

Q.24 Approximate percentage obtained by the student from the total score is?
A. 86 **B.** 90 **C.** 95 **D.** 98

Q.25 The difference of marks between Mathematics and SS is what percent of 600?
A. 2.5% **B.** 3% **C.** 3.2% **D.** 3.1%

Business Awareness

Q.26 Which organisation has estimated that India needs 6.2% additional spending of GDP to achieve 2030 SDGs?
A. Reserve Bank of India
B. NITI Aayog
C. Ministry of Statistics and Program Implementation
D. National Development Council

Q.27 A written statement of policies and principles that guides the behavior of all employees is called:
A. Code of ethics **B.** Word of ethics
C. Ethics/ Dilemma **D.** Training Manual

Q.28 The term procurement stands for:
A. Recruitment and selection
B. Training and development

C. Pay and benefits
D. Health and safety

Q.29 Strategic human resource management involves:
A. Financing project marketing related programming
B. Setting employment standards and policies
C. Linking human resources with strategic objectives to improve performance
D. Project planning

Q.30 Which organization is to procure 250 electric vehicles from Tata Motors and Hyundai Motors?
A. BEE **B.** EESL **C.** NTPC **D.** ONGC

Q.31 The unstructured interview is:
A. Infrequently conducted
B. Typically unbiased
C. Typically related to future
D. Typically biased job performance

Q.32 Tests that measure traits, temperament, or disposition are example of:
A. Manual dexterity tests
B. Personality tests
C. Intelligence tests
D. Work sample tests

Q.33 The best hiring occurs when the goals of which of the following should be consistent to each other?
A. HR managers, Finance managers
B. Head office, Brand
C. Organisation, Individual
D. Lower managers, Top managers

Q.34 Government has directed Food Corporation of India to provide food grains to NGOs at OMSS rates. What does OMSS stand for?
A. Open Market Sale Scheme
B. Out Market Sale Scheme
C. Open Market State Scheme
D. Out Market Sale Scheme

Q.35 Which of the following role a manager performs as a Resource allocator?
A. Interpersonal role **B.** Decisional role
C. Informational role **D.** Supportive role

// Smart Answer Sheet //

Correct Indicates percentage of students who answered questions correctly.

Skipped Indicates percentage of students who skipped questions.

Q.	Ans.	Correct / Skipped	Q.	Ans.	Correct / Skipped	Q.	Ans.	Correct / Skipped	Q.	Ans.	Correct / Skipped	Q.	Ans.	Correct / Skipped
1	B	81.24 % / 12.01 %	8	B	50.73 % / 47.23 %	15	A	65.91 % / 32.52 %	22	B	53.16 % / 46.68 %	29	C	44.36 % / 51.18 %
2	B	58.35 % / 39.47 %	9	B	80.75 % / 10.95 %	16	A	78.19 % / 16.35 %	23	D	69.5 % / 30.09 %	30	B	31.74 % / 67.1 %
3	D	26.76 % / 68.66 %	10	B	83.85 % / 11.31 %	17	C	55.45 % / 30.94 %	24	B	79.23 % / 11.26 %	31	D	89.65 % / 10.2 %
4	C	25.03 % / 70.46 %	11	B	86.32 % / 11.03 %	18	C	41.81 % / 51.23 %	25	A	46.51 % / 33.94 %	32	B	49.39 % / 49.31 %
5	B	78.46 % / 15.29 %	12	C	64.72 % / 35.26 %	19	A	44.73 % / 31.77 %	26	B	42.22 % / 34.6 %	33	C	85.93 % / 10.1 %
6	C	55.01 % / 39.6 %	13	D	42.72 % / 47.09 %	20	D	44.76 % / 31.01 %	27	A	45.37 % / 43.76 %	34	A	49.33 % / 47.0 %
7	B	68.28 % / 31.42 %	14	B	43.95 % / 31.54 %	21	A	60.88 % / 38.26 %	28	A	80.87 % / 10.39 %	35	B	61.41 % / 38.1 %

Performance Analysis	
Avg. Score (%)	57.14%
Toppers Score (%)	62.86%
Your Score	

//Hints and Solutions//

1. 'Pantheon' refers to All the gods collectively of a religion.

We find the word "pantheon" in the following line of the passage: "The Roman historian Tacitus tells us that Odin ("Mercury" in the interpretatio romana) was already established as the dominant god in the pantheons of many of the Germanic tribes by the first century."
Here, clearly, it refers to Odin being the dominant god amongst all gods of the Germanic tribes.

Hence, the correct option is (B).

2. Option B cannot be reasonably inferred with regard to the beliefs of the Proto-Germanic people

Let us consider the statements in order.
Option A - Odin came upon the runes after going through a lot of torment. True, stated in 'The runes were never "invented," but are instead eternal, pre-existent forces that Odin himself discovered by undergoing a tremendous ordeal'.

Option B - The name of a rune was almost always the first sound of a God's name. It is false. Each rune had a name which was almost always the first sound of the rune's name. Though the example of the T-rune and Tiwaz is given in the passage, it is not stated as a general rule that the name of a rune is the first sound of a God's name. It is the first sound of the rune's name.

Option C - The cosmological power represented by a rune was invoked by writing it. It is true as stated in 'Each rune was an ideographic or pictographic symbol of some cosmological principle or power, and to write a rune was to invoke and direct the force for which it stood'.

Option D- Proto-German Gods were modeled on humans.
It is true. The passage gives the example of Woðanaz, the divine model of the human warband leader in the lines 'Woðanaz, was the divine model of the human warband leader and the invisible patron of the warband's activities'.

Hence, the correct option is (B).

3. Of the four statements above only i and iii can be inferred from the passage.

Let's consider all the statements individually.

Statement i - Runic script was most likely derived from Italic script. True.

As mentioned in 'The runes are presumed to have been derived from one of the many Old Italic alphabets in use among the Mediterranean peoples of the first century CE, who lived to the south of the Germanic tribes'.

Statement ii - Runes were not used so much as a simple writing system, but rather as magical signs to be used for charms. False.

Runes were used as a writing system. They were also used as magical signs. They were more than letters as we understand them today, not just magical signs.

Statement iii - In the Proto-Germanic period, the god Tiwaz was associated with war, victory, marriage and the diurnal sky. True.

We understand from the passage that Tiwaz was perceived to dwell within the daytime sky, had martial role and was associated with victory in battle as mentioned in 'Tiwaz was perceived to dwell within the daytime sky, and, accordingly, the visual form of the T-rune is an arrow pointed upward (which surely also hints at the god's martial role)'.

Statement iv - The knowledge of the meanings attributed to the runes of the Younger Futhark is derived from the three Rune poems. False.

The Younger Futhark is treated in the Icelandic and Norwegian Rune Poems only, not all three rune poems as suggested in the statement above as mentioned in 'the Younger Futhark is treated in the Icelandic and Norwegian Rune Poems'.

Hence, the correct option is (D).

4. The word "rune" and its meaning was derived from the runic alphabet is incorrect.

Let us consider the statements in order.
A - Unlike the Latin alphabet, which is an essentially utilitarian script, the runes are symbols of some of the most powerful forces in the cosmos.
From the passage, we know this to be true. It is mentioned in 'Runes functioned as letters, but they were much more than just letters. Each rune was an ideographic or pictographic symbol of some cosmological power'.

B - Runic writing was probably first used in southern Europe and was carried north by Germanic tribes.
Again, this is stated in the passage and is correct. It is mentioned in lines 'The earliest possibly runic inscription is found on the Meldorf brooch, which was manufactured in the north of modern-day Germany around 50 CE' and 'The transmission of writing from southern Europe to northern Europe likely took place via Germanic warbands'.

C - The word "rune" and its meaning was derived from the runic alphabet.
The word "rune" means both "letter" and "secret" and its original meaning predated the adoption of the runic alphabet as mentioned in 'in every Germanic language, the word "rune" (from Proto-Germanic *runo) means both "letter" and "secret" or "mystery," and its original meaning, which likely predated the adoption of the runic alphabet'. So, statement 3 is incorrect.

D - The first runic alphabets date back to the 1st century CE. Indeed, according to the passage, the development of the Elder Futhark had begun by the first century as mentioned in 'the 24-character Elder Futhark, the first fully-formed runic alphabet, whose development had begun by the first century CE'. So this statement is correct.

Hence, the correct option is (C).

5. Herodotus has given an account of the battle between Athens and Persia.

This can be derived from the line 'Herodotus, a famous historian, reports that 6400 Persians died, compared with only 192 Athenians'.

Hence, the correct option is (B).

6. "Pacify" means to calm or make peaceful. It does not mean to make weaker (A), to destroy (B), or to irritate (D), i.e. annoy or provoke.
Hence, the correct option is (C).

7. "Ennobled" means gave honor to or made noble. It does not mean gave comfort (A) or solace, gave strength (C), i.e. fortified or reinforced, gave fear (D).
Hence, the correct option is (B).

8. To "abet" means to enable, support, or encourage, usually in a crime or doing something wrong. It does not mean to end (A), think about (C), or daydream about (D) something.
Hence, the correct option is (B).

9. "Reinforced" means strengthened, not welcomed (A), held (C), or captured (D).
Hence, the correct option is (B).

10. "Interceded for" means intervened on behalf of, not refused help to (A), wanted to fight (C), given orders for all to fight (D).

Hence, the correct option is (B).

11. Total marks obtained by all the students in English

$= 85 + 66 + 78 + 86 + 94$
$= 409$
Hence, the correct option is (B).

12. Marks obtained by Reena in all the subjects together

$= 56 + 94 + 85 + 80 + 86$
$= 401$
Marks obtained by Meena in all the subjects together

$= 75 + 72 + 78 + 64 + 84$
$= 373$
Required $\% = \frac{401-373}{373} \times 100$
$= \frac{28}{373} \times 100$
$= 7.506\%$ more.
Hence, the correct option is (C).

13. Total marks $= 5 \times 100$
$= 500$
Total marks obtained by Geeta in all the subjects together $=$
$92 + 88 + 86 + 82 + 52$
$= 400$
Required $\% = \frac{400}{500} \times 100$
$= 80\%$
Hence, the correct option is (D).

14. Marks obtained by Meena in Mathematics and Science together

$= 75 + 72$
$= 147$
Marks obtained by Sita in English and Hindi together

$= 94 + 92$
$= 186$

Required ratio $= 147 : 186$
$= 49 : 62$
Hence, the correct option is (B).

15. Marks obtained by all the students in English

$= 85 + 66 + 78 + 86 + 94$
$= 409$
Marks obtained by all the students in Social Science

$= 86 + 48 + 84 + 52 + 54$
$= 324$
Required $\% = \frac{409}{324} \times 100$
$= 126.23\%$
Hence, the correct option is (A).

16. Number of users of Vodafone in Mumbai $= 500$

Number of users of Vodafone in Delhi $= 600$

Number of users of Vodafone in Kolkata $= 500$

Number of users of Vodafone in Punjab $= 700$

Number of users of Vodafone in Patna $= 650$

Number of users of Airtel in Mumbai $= 450$

Number of users of Airtel in Delhi $= 400$

Number of users of Airtel in Kolkata $= 450$

Number of users of Airtel in Punjab $= 700$

Number of users of Airtel in Patna $= 400$

Therefore, Total number of users of Vodafone and Airtel across all five cities
$= (500 + 600 + 500 + 700 + 650 + 450 + 400 + 450 + 700 + 400)$

$= 5350$

Hence, the correct option is (A).

17. Number of users of Jio in Patna $= 700$
Numbers of users of Vodafone in Patna $= 650$
Number of users of Jio and Vodafone together in Patna $=$
$700 + 650$
$= 1350$
Numbers of users of Vodafone in Delhi $= 600$
Numbers of users of Airtel in Delhi $= 400$
Number of users of Vodafone and Airtel together in Delhi $=$
$600 + 400$
$= 1000$
Therefore, the required percentage
$= \frac{1350}{1000} \times 100$
$= 135\%$
Hene, the correct option is (C).

18. Number of users of Jio in Mumbai $= 400$
Number of users of Jio in Delhi $= 500$
Number of users of Jio in Kolkata $= 650$
Number of users of Jio in Punjab $= 800$
Number of users of Jio in Patna $= 700$
Number of users of Airtel in Mumbai $= 450$
Number of users of Airtel in Delhi $= 400$
Number of users of Airtel in Kolkata $= 450$
Number of users of Airtel in Punjab $= 700$
Number of users of Airtel in Patna $= 400$
So, the total number value of users of Jio and Airtel across all five cities together
$= 400 + 500 + 650 + 800 + 700 + 450 + 400 + 450 + 700 + 400$
$= 5450$
Therefore, the average number of users of Jio and Airtel across all five cities together
$= \frac{5450}{10}$
$= 545$
Hence, the correct option is (C).

19. Number of users of Jio in Kolkata $= 650$
Number of users of Vodafone in Kolkata $= 500$
Number of users of Airtel in Kolkata $= 450$
Total number of users of Jio, Vodafone and Airtel together in Kolkata
$= 650 + 500 + 450$
$= 1600$
Number of users of Jio in Mumbai $= 400$
Number of users of Vodafone in Mumbai $= 500$
Number of users of Airtel in Mumbai $= 450$
Total number of users of Jio, Vodafone and Airtel together in Mumbai
$= 400 + 500 + 450$
$= 1350$
Therefore, the required difference $= 1600 - 1350$
$= 250$
Hence, the correct option is (A).

20. Number of users of Jio in Patna $= 700$
Number of users of Vodafone in Patna $= 650$
Number of users of Airtel in Patna $= 400$
Total number of users of Jio, Vodafone and Airtel together in Patna $= 700 + 650 + 400$
$= 1750$
Number of users of Vodafone in Punjab $= 700$
Number of users of Airtel in Punjab $= 700$
Total number of users of Vodafone and Airtel together in Punjab
$= 700 + 700$
$= 1400$
Therefore, required ratio $= \frac{1750}{1400}$
$= 5:4$
Hence, the correct option is (D).

21. Total marks scored in Physics, Chemistry and Maths
$= 95 + 96 + 96$
$= 287$
Total marks obtained $= 542$
∴ Percentage of the marks of PCM out of the total marks obtained
$= \frac{287}{542} \times 100$
$= 52.952 \approx 53\%$
Hence, the correct option is (A).

22. Marks in CS and Mathematics $= 90 + 95$
$= 185$
Marks in SS and English $= 80 + 85$
$= 165$
∴ Required $\% = \frac{185-165}{165} \times 100$
$= 12.1212 \approx 12\%$
Hence, the correct option is (B).

23. Difference in marks between Physics and SS
$\Rightarrow 96 - 80 = 16$
∴ $\%$ out of $600 = \frac{16}{600} \times 100$
$= 2.6666 \approx 3\%$
Hence, the correct option is (D).

24. Total score of the student
$= 90 + 95 + 80 + 85 + 96 + 96$
$= 542$
∴ $\%$ scored $= \frac{542}{600} \times 100$
$= 90.3333 \approx 90\%$
Hence, the correct option is (B).

25. Difference in marks between Mathematics and SS
$\Rightarrow 95 - 80 = 15$
∴ $\%$ out of $600 = \frac{15}{600} \times 100$
$= 2.5\%$
Hence, the correct option is (A).

26. NITI Aayog has estimated that India needs 6.2% additional spending of GDP to achieve 2030 Sustainable Development Goals.

The country's think tank said this in its second Voluntary National Review (VNR) at the UN high-level political forum (HLPF) on sustainable development, 2020. India needs to upgrade its statistical system, improve its monitoring mechanism and capacity building of all stakeholders. It also advised that the Budget should be aligned with SDGs.

Hence, the correct option is (B).

27. A written statement of policies and principles that guides the behavior of all employees is called code of ethics.

Ethics in HRM basically deals with the affirmative moral obligations of the employer towards employees to maintain equality and equity justice. Areas of HRM ethics are Basic human rights, civil and employment fight.

Hence, the correct option is (A).

28. The term procurement stands for recruitment and selection.

Recruitment and Selection is an important operation in HRM, designed to maximize employee strength in order to meet the employer's strategic goals and objectives. It is a process of sourcing, screening, shortlisting and selecting the right candidates for the required vacant positions.

Hence, the correct option is (A).

29. Strategic human resource management involves linking human resources with strategic objectives to improve performance.

Strategic human resource management is the practice of attracting, developing, rewarding, and retaining employees for the benefit of both the employees as individuals and the organization as a whole. As a result, the goals of a human resource department reflect and support the goals of the rest of the organization.

Hence, the correct option is (C).

30. The Ministry of Power's Energy Efficiency Services Limited (EESL) is set to procure 250 electric vehicles from Tata Motors and Hyundai Motors.

The government's electric vehicles procurement arm, will procure 150 units of Tata Nexon EV and 100 units of Hyundai Kona EV. The companies were selected by way of an international competitive bidding.

Hence, the correct option is (B).

31. The unstructured interview is typically biased job performance.

An unstructured interview is an interview in which there is no specific set of predetermined questions, although the interviewers usually have certain topics in mind that they wish to cover during the interview.

Hence, the correct option is (D).

32. Tests that measure traits, temperament, or disposition are examples of Personality tests.

A personality test is a method of assessing human personality constructs. Most personality assessment instruments are in fact introspective self-report questionnaire measures or reports from life records such as rating scales.

Hence, the correct option is (B).

33. The best hiring occurs when the goals of Organisation and individual should be consistent to each other.

Employee relations specialists in HR help the organization achieve high performance, morale and satisfaction levels throughout the workforce, by creating ways to strengthen the employer-employee relationship.

Hence, the correct option is (C).

34. OMSS stands for Open Market Sale Scheme.

Open Market Sale Scheme (OMSS) refers to selling of food grains by Government / Government agencies at predetermined prices in the open market from time to time to enhance the supply of grains especially during the lean season and thereby to moderate the general open market prices especially in the deficit regions.

Hence, the correct option is (A).

35. A manager performs decisional role as a Resource allocator.

The resource allocator role is one of the four decisional managerial roles because its primary focus is on making and implementing decisions. Familiarity with the resource allocator and other managerial roles allows both new and seasoned supervisors to understand a manager's job.

Hence, the correct option is (B).

Mock Test 18

Comprehension

Ques (1-5):Direction : Read the passage and answer the question that follows:

More than three lakh workers will be employed in the solar and wind energy sectors to meet the country's target of generating 175 gigawatts of electricity from renewable sources by 2022, an International Labour Organization (ILO) report said. The report titled, World Employment and Social Outlook (WESO) 2018: Greening with Jobs, quoted from a study conducted by the Council on Energy, Environment, and Water (CEEW) and the Natural Resources Defense Council (NRDC), on the changes in sectoral employment that will occur in order to meet India's target. The study was based on surveys of solar and wind companies, developers, and manufacturers.

"India is rapidly increasing its share of renewable energy sources, but still relies on coal, oil, natural gas, and the related carbon emissions for 80% of its electricity," the report released on Tuesday said. This formed a small part of the report, which focused on the trajectory of the labour market in the backdrop of environmentally sustainable production practices. Tackling the misconception that green economies pave the way for economically undesirable outcomes, the report said rather than a trade-off between the two, their development goes hand in hand. According to the ILO report, there will be a net increase of 18 million jobs across the globe as a result of environmentally sustainable measures taken in the production and use of energy. This net figure is based on the estimation that the resultant job losses of six million will eventually lead to an increase of 24 million jobs as greener practices are adopted. Of this, 14 million jobs created will be in Asia and the Pacific.

"The transition to a green economy will inevitably cause job losses in certain sectors as carbon and resource-intensive industries are scaled-down, but they will be offset by new job opportunities," the report said. However, the report emphasized that the net increase of 18 million jobs is dependent on a supportive policy framework to aid displaced workers and skill development programs to help ease them into jobs that require new skills. It mentioned that although India does have a specific body or council to address the skills development for green transition, it has no existing institutional mechanism to anticipate skills needs and adapt training provision. Of the 27 countries surveyed, India and seven others fall under this category. "Developing and emerging economies have relatively weaker institutional capacity for integrating skills and environmental sustainability," the report said.

The report stressed the urgency of economies adopting sustainable practices, adding, in 2013, humanity used 1.7 times the amount of resources and waste that the biosphere was able to regenerate and absorb. The report reads, "It is striking that in a context of scarce resources and limited ability to absorb waste, current patterns of economic growth rely largely on the extraction of resources, manufacturing, consumption, and waste." It explained this urgency from the perspective of the job market by connecting labour productivity to climate change."Looking ahead, projected temperature increases will make heat stress more common, reducing the total number of working hours by 2% globally by 2030 and affecting workers in agriculture, and developing countries," the report said.

Q.1 What can be some steps that can be taken by India to improve its institutional capacity for integrating skills and environmental sustainability?

I. The government must improve the quality of skill development programs.

II. Set up institutes to produce more skilled people in this domain.

III. There should be adequate funding to support the shift of displaced workers into jobs that require new skills.

A. Only I
B. Only I and II
C. Only II and III
D. All of the above

Q.2 Which of the following weakens the argument of increasing the share of renewable energy in the energy sector?

I. The environmental impacts associated with renewable energy include habitat loss, water use, and the use of hazardous materials in manufacturing, they cause more harm than good in the long run.

II. It is easy to harness and store renewable energy than the traditional sources of energy.

III. The shift to renewable energy source would create jobs.

A. Only I
B. Only II
C. Only I and II
D. All of the above

Q.3 Which of the following statements weakens the argument about the urgency of economies in adopting sustainable practices?

A. The increase in temperature because of climate change would reduce the number of working hours hence productivity will suffer.

B. The resource available to us is limited and nature's ability to replenish them is limited.

C. Developing countries are dependent on agriculture which would be adversely affected because of climate change.

D. The impact of sustainable solutions for energy needs would be limited because for it to be effective all the countries need to participate which is not the case.

Q.4 As per the passage, which of the following could be a/some reason/s for the misconceptions surrounding green economies.

I. There is a belief that adopting a green economy would lead to loss of jobs which could severely impact the economy.

II. The shift from traditional energy sources to renewable energy would be expensive.

III. The technological capability required to transform into a green economy is still in the elementary phase.

A. Only I
B. Only II

C. Only III **D.** Only II and III

Q.5 As per your understanding of the passage, which of the following can be said to be example/s of steps that contribute towards a green economy.

I. The government announces tax incentives for those using public transport.

II. The government provides subsidy on diesel cars so that it becomes affordable

III. The government supports start-ups working on the development of electric cars.

A. Only I **B.** Only II
C. Only I and III **D.** Only II and III

Ques (6-10):Direction : Read the passage and answer the question that follows:

Development is about expanding the capabilities of the disadvantaged, thereby improving their overall quality of life. Based on this understanding, Maharashtra, one of India's richest States, is a classic case of a lack of development which is seen in its unacceptably high level of malnutrition among children in the tribal belts. While the State's per capita income has doubled since 2004, its nutritional status has not made commensurate progress.

Poor nutrition security disproportionately affects the poorest segment of the population. According to NFHS 2015-16, every second tribal child suffers from growth restricting malnutrition due to chronic hunger. In 2005, child malnutrition claimed as many as 718 lives in Maharashtra's Palghar district alone. Even after a decade of double-digit economic growth (2004-05 to 2014-15), Palghar's malnutrition status has barely improved.

In September 2016, the National Human Rights Commission issued notice to the Maharashtra government over reports of 600 children dying due to malnutrition in Palghar. The government responded, promising to properly implement schemes such as Jaccha Baccha and Integrated Child Development Services to check malnutrition. Our independent survey conducted in Vikramgad block of the district last year found that 57%, 21%, and 53% of children in this block were stunted, wasted, and underweight, respectively; 27% were severely stunted. Our data challenges what Maharashtra's Women and Child Development Minister said in the Legislative Council in March — that "malnutrition in Palghar had come down in the past few months, owing to various interventions made by the government."

Stunting is caused by an insufficient intake of macro- and micro-nutrients. It is generally accepted that recovery from growth retardation after two years is only possible if the affected child is put on a diet that is adequate in nutrient requirements. A critical aspect of nutrient adequacy is diet diversity, calculated by different groupings of foods consumed with the reference period ranging from one to 15 days. We calculated a 24-hour dietary diversity score by counting the number of food groups the child received in the last 24 hours. The eight food groups include cereals, roots, and tubers; legumes and nuts; dairy products; flesh foods; eggs; fish; dark green leafy vegetables; and other fruits and vegetables.

In most households, it was rice and dal which was cooked most often and eaten thrice a day. These were even served at teatime to the children if they felt hungry. There was no milk, milk product, or fruit in their daily diets. Even the adults drank black tea as milk was unaffordable. Only 17% of the children achieved a minimum level of diet diversity — they received four or more of the eight food groups. This low dietary diversity is a proxy indicator for the household's food security too as the children ate the same food cooked for adult members.

Q.6 Which of the following is/are true as per the passage?

I. India's situation is worse than in some of the world's poorest countries — Bangladesh, Afghanistan, or Mozambique.

II. Development is more than just economic growth.

III. On average, the nutrition expenditure as a percentage of the Budget has drastically declined from 1.68% in 2012-13 to 0.94% in 2018-19.

A. Only II **B.** Only I and II
C. Only II and III **D.** Only I and III

Q.7 What could possibly be a/some possible reason/s for such extreme food insecurity among tribal households?

I. Loss of their traditional dependence on forest livelihood.

II. Weak implementation of public nutrition schemes.

III. A worsening agriculture situation.

A. Only I **B.** Only II
C. Only III **D.** All of the above

Q.8 Which of the following strengthens the claim that the nutrition indicators fare poorly in India?

I. Stunting declined from 46.3% in 2005 to 34.4% in 2016.

II. As per an NHFS survey, wasting rates have increased from 16.5% to 25.6% over a period of 10 years.

III. The underweight rate (36%) has remained static in the last 10 years.

A. Only I **B.** Only I and II
C. Only III **D.** Only II and III

Q.9 What is ironical about the situation mentioned in paragraph 1?

A. States do not have adequate resources to feed the poor even when there are enough resources with the Centre.

B. Even though states may be classified as rich with a high per capita income, they may not really be developed.

C. Development of states depends on sustained economic growth which in turn leads to high per capita income.

D. The level of malnutrition is abnormally high in states which have a high growth level and better than average per capita income.

Q.10 As per the passage, which of the following is/are needed for an adequate meal?

I. Macro and micro nutrients

II. Multiple food groups

III. High level of Intermittent fasting

A. Only II **B.** Only I and III
C. Only I and II **D.** Only II and III

Management Data Interpretation

Ques (11-15):Direction : Study the following table to answer the question that given below.

The table given below shows expenditure of a Company on various items (in Lakhs).

Item of Expenditure/Year	Salary	Fuel and transport	Bonus	Interest on Loans	Taxes
1998	288	98	3.00	23.4	83
1999	342	112	2.52	32.5	108
2000	324	101	3.84	41.6	74
2001	336	133	3.38	36.4	88
2002	420	142	3.96	49.4	98

Q.11 The ratio between the total expenditure on taxes for all the years and the total expenditure on Fuel and Transport for all the years respectively is approximately:

A. $4:7$ **B.** $10:13$ **C.** $15:18$ **D.** $5:8$

Q.12 The total expenditure of the Company over these items during the year 2000 is:

A. Rs. 544.44 Lakhs **B.** Rs. 501.11 Lakhs
C. Rs. 446.46 Lakhs **D.** Rs. 478.87 Lakhs

Q.13 What is the average amount of interest per year which the Company had to pay during this period?

A. Rs. 32.43 Lakhs **B.** Rs. 33.72 Lakhs
C. Rs. 34.18 Lakhs **D.** Rs. 36.66 Lakhs

Q.14 Total expenditure on all these items in 1998 was approximately what percent of the total expenditure in 2002?

A. 62% **B.** 66% **C.** 69% **D.** 71%

Q.15 The total amount of bonus paid by the Company during the given period is approximately what percent of the total amount of salary paid during this period?

A. 0.1% **B.** 0.5% **C.** 1% **D.** 1.25%

Ques (16-20):Direction: Study the following pie chart and answer the following questions.

Percentage of work done by A, B, C, D and E

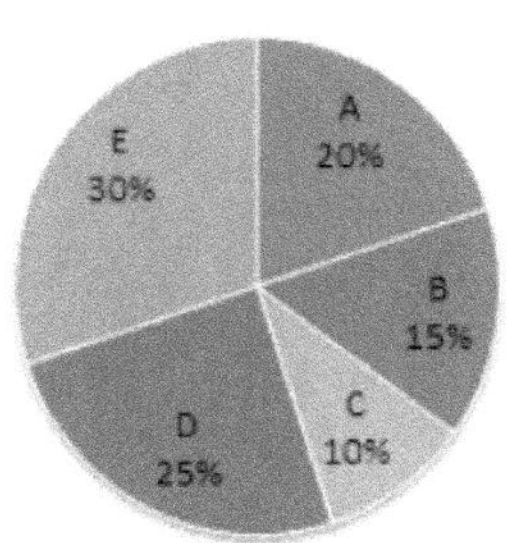

Total 1800 shirts were given to A, B, C, D and E for doing embroidery work on them. The pie chart shows the $\%$ of shirts embroidered by A, B, C, D and E respectively.

Q.16 If it is known that A and B working alone can embroider 1800 shirts in 200 hours and 300 hours respectively. Find the ratio of time taken by A and B to embroider the shirts which were given to them.

A. $5:6$ **B.** $8:9$ **C.** $3:4$ **D.** $2:3$

Q.17 If B falls sick in between, and till then he had done only 40% of the work given to him, the rest work of B was given to D to complete it. Find the total number of shirts embroidered by D.

A. 212 shirts **B.** 340 shirts
C. 612 shirts **D.** 412 shirts

Q.18 If the ratio of the efficiencies of C and D is $4:5$. Find the ratio of the time taken by C and D to do their respective work.

A. $2:5$ **B.** $1:2$ **C.** $2:1$ **D.** $4:5$

Q.19 If 30% of the shirts embroidered by B and 35% of the shirts embroidered by E is Zardozi embroidery. Find the total number of shirts on which Zardozi embroidery was done.

A. 112 shirts **B.** 200 shirts
C. 270 shirts **D.** 250 shirts

Q.20 Find the pair of persons for which the difference between the shirts embroidered is not 90.

A. A and B **B.** B and C **C.** E and D **D.** B and D

Ques (21-25):Direction: Read the following graph carefully and answer the question given below.
In the bar chart, the total numbers of students enrolled in different years from 2015 to 2019 in Sunshine and Aryan Summer camps are given.

Q.21 If in the year 2020 there is 30% increase in total number of students enrolled as compared to 2019, find the total number of students enrolled in 2020?

A. 286 **B.** 245 **C.** 292 **D.** 234

Q.22 What is the ratio between total students in 2016 to the total students in 2019 of both summer camps?

A. $25:21$ **B.** $27:22$ **C.** $29:12$ **D.** $30:13$

Q.23 The number of students of Sunshine in 2015 is what percentage of the number of students of Aryan in 2017?

A. 101.25% **B.** 111.25%
C. 106.25% **D.** 124.25%

Q.24 The total number of students enrolled in Sunshine from 2016 to 2019 is what percentage more than the total number of students enrolled in Aryan in 2018 and 2019?

A. 10.51% **B.** 15.51% **C.** 11.51 **D.** 20.51%

Q.25 Total students enrolled in Aryan in 2018 and 2019 together is what percentage more than students enrolled in Sunshine in 2015 and 2019 together?

A. 61.5% **B.** 65% **C.** 60% **D.** 62.5%

Business Awareness

Q.26 In which year, the International Institute of Labour studies was established?

A. 1919 **B.** 1926 **C.** 1950 **D.** 1960

Q.27 What is the lock in period for ELSS Investments currently?

A. 2 years **B.** 3 years **C.** 4 years **D.** 5 years

Q.28 National Housing Bank is the wholly subsidiary of RBI. In which year, NHB was established?

A. 1985 **B.** 1986 **C.** 1987 **D.** 1988

Q.29 Tata Airlines was renamed as Air India in which year?

A. 1946 **B.** 1947 **C.** 1948 **D.** 1945

Q.30 Which is India's first airport to be built under Public Private Partnership (PPP) model?

A. Rajiv Gandhi International Airport
B. Cochin International Airport
C. Kempegowda International Airport
D. Chatrapati Shivaji International Airport

Q.31 In which year was Apollo Hospitals established?

A. 1983 **B.** 1989
C. 1980 **D.** None of the above

Q.32 When was Tata Iron and Steel Company formed?

A. 1903 **B.** 1910 **C.** 1907 **D.** 1900

Q.33 Which state is the largest e-waste producer in India?

A. Telangana **B.** Maharashtra
C. Tamil Nadu **D.** Karnataka

Q.34 In Factor Comparison method, each factor is ascribed a:

A. Money value **B.** Ranking
C. Scale **D.** None of the above

Q.35 The technique that have been used to evaluate an employee in comparison with other employees:

A. Ranking
B. Forced choice
C. Essay evaluation
D. Critical incident technique

// Smart Answer Sheet //

Correct — Indicates percentage of students who answered questions correctly.

Skipped — Indicates percentage of students who skipped questions.

Q.	Ans.	Correct	Skipped
1	D	53.13 %	43.56 %
2	A	61.46 %	35.86 %
3	D	47.04 %	42.01 %
4	A	45.14 %	43.39 %
5	C	26.71 %	72.85 %
6	A	68.59 %	30.58 %
7	D	15.41 %	83.48 %
8	D	64.85 %	30.21 %
9	B	79.2 %	18.88 %
10	C	49.47 %	35.81 %
11	B	47.9 %	43.52 %
12	A	84.21 %	12.42 %
13	D	55.13 %	33.95 %
14	C	48.62 %	45.68 %
15	C	41.78 %	52.76 %
16	B	21.72 %	72.59 %
17	B	59.78 %	36.81 %
18	B	22.99 %	72.25 %
19	C	48.79 %	39.76 %
20	D	20.5 %	77.61 %
21	A	63.43 %	31.3 %
22	B	87.87 %	10.73 %
23	C	79.73 %	19.14 %
24	D	62.8 %	36.91 %
25	D	50.06 %	32.87 %
26	D	12.13 %	67.3 %
27	B	61.11 %	32.06 %
28	D	26.49 %	71.98 %
29	A	45.54 %	43.69 %
30	C	42.34 %	33.61 %
31	A	30.79 %	67.72 %
32	C	47.95 %	43.59 %
33	B	55.15 %	35.42 %
34	A	42.61 %	34.49 %
35	A	55.08 %	31.26 %

Performance Analysis	
Avg. Score (%)	60.0%
Toppers Score (%)	60.0%
Your Score	

//Hints and Solutions//

1. All of the statements are correct as all state valid ways of improving India's institutional capacity for integrating skills and environmental sustainability.

Hence, the correct option is (D).

2. Statement I is correct. It weakens the argument as the whole point of increasing the share of renewable energy in the energy sector is to reduce environmental degradation in the long run.

Statement II and Statement III strengthen the argument for renewable energy.

Hence, the correct option is (A).

3. Only option D fits in. If true, this weakens the point of adopting sustainable practices.

Options A, B, and C talk about the reasons for adopting sustainable practices.

Hence, the correct option is (D).

4. Only Statement I can be a reason for the misconceptions surrounding green economies.

Refer to: "The transition to a green economy will inevitably cause job losses in certain sectors as carbon and resource-intensive industries are scaled-down"

Statement II and Statement III have not been mentioned in the passage.

Hence, the correct option is (A).

5. Statements I and III are both correct. Both steps would help in reducing fossil fuel consumption.

Statement II is incorrect. The subsidy on diesel would not help in tackling environmental degradation in any way and would actually lead to more pollution.

Hence, the correct option is (C).

6. Statement II is correct as can be seen from the first paragraph of the passage.

Refer to: "Development is about expanding the capabilities of the disadvantaged, thereby improving their overall quality of life."

Statements I and III have not been mentioned in the passage and are incorrect.

Hence, the correct option is (A).

7. All the statements are valid as all give probable reasons for the prevailing condition of food insecurity.

Hence, the correct option is (D).

8. Statement I is positive and weakens the claim.

Statements II and III are negative and show the poor state of nutrition in India.

Hence, the correct option is (D).

9. "Even though states may be classified as rich with a high per capita income, they may not really be developed" is ironical about the situation mentioned in paragraph 1.

The passage gives the example of Maharashtra and states that even though its growth is high and it has a high per capita income, yet its development is low due to the prevalence of malnutrition. It is mentioned in line " Based on this understanding, Maharashtra, one of India's richest States, is a classic case of a lack of development which is seen in its unacceptably high level of malnutrition among children in the tribal belts".

Only option B makes sense. The irony specified above is portrayed well here.

Option A is incorrect as this is clearly untrue.

Option C is incorrect as this may be correct factually but does not represent the irony.

Option D is incorrect as this cannot be concluded from the information given in the paragraph.

Hence, the correct option is (B).

10. Statements I and II are needed for an adequate meal.

Refer to:

'Stunting is caused by an insufficient intake of macro- and micro-nutrients. It is generally accepted that recovery from growth retardation after two years is only possible if the affected child is put on a diet that is adequate in nutrient requirements. A critical aspect of nutrient adequacy is diet diversity, calculated by different groupings of foods consumed with the reference period ranging from one to 15 days.'

III has not been mentioned in the passage.

Hence, the correct option is (C).

11. Total expenditure on taxes for all the years $= 83 + 108 + 74 + 88 + 98$

$=$ Rs. 451 Lakhs

Total expenditure on fuel and transport for all the years $= 98 + 112 + 101 + 133 + 142$

$=$ Rs. 586 Lakhs

Required Ratio $= \frac{451}{586} \approx \frac{1}{1.3}$

$= \frac{10}{13}$

Hence, the correct option is (B).

12. Total expenditure of the Company during 2000 $=$ Rs. $(324 + 101 + 3.84 + 41.6 + 74)$ Lakhs

$=$ Rs. 544.44 Lakhs

Hence, the correct option is (A).

13. Average amount of interest paid by the Company during the given period

$=$ Rs. $[\frac{(23.4+32.5+41.6+36.4+49.4)}{5}]$ lakhs

$= \text{Rs. } \left(\frac{183.3}{5}\right)$ lakhs

$=$ Rs. 36.66 lakhs

Hence, the correct option is (D).

14. Required percentage $= \left[\frac{(288+98+3.00+23.4+83)}{(420+142+3.96+49.4+98)} \times 100\right]\%$

$= \left[\frac{495.4}{713.36} \times 100\right]\%$

$\approx 69.45\%$

Hence, the correct option is (C).

15. Total amount of bonus paid by the Company $= 3.00 + 2.52 + 3.84 + 3.38 + 3.96$

$= 16.7\% \approx 17\%$

Total amount of salary paid by the Company $= 288 + 342 + 324 + 336 + 420$

$= 1710$

Required percentage

$= \left(\frac{17}{1710} \times 100\right)\%$

$= 0.99\% \approx 1\%$

Hence, the correct option is (C).

16. Calculations for A:

A alone can embroider 1800 shirts in $= 200$ hours

A can embroider 1 shirt in $= \frac{200}{1800}$ hour

$= \frac{1}{9}$ hour

Number of shirts given to A to embroider $= 20\%$ of 1800

$= 360$

Time taken to embroider 360 shirts by $A = 360 \times \frac{1}{9}$ hours

$= 40$ hours

Calculations For B:

B alone can embroider 1800 shirts in $= 300$ hours

B can embroider 1 shirt in $= \frac{300}{1800}$ hour

$= \frac{1}{6}$ hour

Number of shirts given to B to embroider $= 15\%$ of 1800

$= 270$

Time taken to embroider 270 shirts by $B = 270 \times \frac{1}{6}$ hours

$= 45$ hours

$\therefore$ Ratio of time taken by A and $B = 40:45$

$= 8:9$

Hence, the correct option is (B).

17. Calculations for B:

Shirts given to $B = 15\%$ of 1800

$= 270$

But he could only complete 40% of 270 shirts $= 108$

So, Remaining shirts $= 270 - 108$

$= 162$

Calculations for D:

D was given shirts initially $= 25\%$ of 1800

$= 450$

Extra shirts given to $D = 162$ shirts

$\therefore$ Total number of shirts given to $D = 450 + 162$

$= 612$

Hence, the correct option is (C).

18. Given:

Ratio of the efficiencies of C and $D = 4:5$

C has to embroider $= 10\%$ of $1800 = 180$ shirts.

D has to embroider $= 25\%$ of $1800 = 450$ shirts

Ratio of work to be done by C and $D = 180:450 = 2:5$

Total work done $=$ Time taken $\times$ Efficiency

$\Rightarrow \frac{2}{5} = \left[\frac{\text{Time taken by C}}{\text{Time taken by D}}\right] \times \frac{4}{5}$

$\therefore \frac{\text{Time taken by C}}{\text{Time taken by D}} = \frac{1}{2} = 1:2$

Hence, the correct option is (B).

19. Calculations For B:

Shirts embroidered by $B = 15\%$ of 1800

$= 270$

Shirts on which Zardozi embroidery was done by $B = 30\%$ of 270

$= 81$

Calculations For E:

Shirts embroidered by $E = 30\%$ of 1800

$= 540$

Shirts on which Zardozi embroidery was done by $E = 35\%$ of 540

$= 189$

$\therefore$ Total Shirts $= 81 + 189$

$= 270$

Hence, the correct option is (C).

20. Given:

If the difference between the shirts embroidered $= 90$ shirts

Therefore, Percentage $= \frac{90}{1800} \times 100 = 5\%$

The difference between the number of shirts embroidered must be 5%

The percentage of shirts embroidered by $A = 20\%$

The percentage of shirts embroidered by $B = 15\%$

The percentage of shirts embroidered by $C = 10\%$

The percentage of shirts embroidered by $D = 25\%$

The percentage of shirts embroidered by $E = 30\%$

$\therefore$ The difference is 5%, between A and B, B and C and E and D.

The only pair which does not has a difference of 5% i.e. 90 embroidered shirts is B and D.

Hence, the correct option is (D).

21. Number of students enrolled in 2019 in both camps

$= 70 + 150$

$= 220$

Total number of students enrolled in 2020 in both camps

$= \frac{130}{100} \times 220$

$= 286$

Hence, the correct option is (A).

22. In 2016, total students in both camps

$= 60 + 210$

$= 270$

In 2019, total students in both camps

$= 70 + 150$

$= 220$

Required ratio $= 27:22$

Hence, the correct option is (B).

23. In 2015, the number of students in Sunshine $= 170$

In 2017, the number of students in Aryan $= 160$

Required $\% \Rightarrow \frac{170}{160} \times 100$

$= 106.25\%$

Hence, the correct option is (C).

24. Total number of students enrolled in Sunshine from 2016 to 2019

$= 60 + 140 + 200 + 70$

$= 470$

Total number of students enrolled in Aryan in 2018 and 2019

$= 240 + 150$

$= 390$

Difference in total number of students enrolled in Aryan in 2018 and 2019 and Sunshine from 2016 to 2019

$= 470 - 390$

$= 80$

Required $\% = \frac{80}{390} \times 100$

$= 20.51\%$

Hence, the correct option is (D).

25. Total students enrolled in Aryan in 2018 and 2019 together $= 240 + 150$

$= 390$

Total students enrolled in Sunshine in 2015 and 2019 together $= 170 + 70$

$= 240$

Difference between total students enrolled in Aryan in 2018 and 2019 and Sunshine in 2015 and 2019

$= 390 - 240$

$= 150$

Required $\% = \frac{150}{240} \times 100$

$= 62.5\%$

Hence, the correct option is (D).

26. "The International Institute for Labour Studies (IILS) was established by the International Labour Organization in 1960 as a centre for advanced studies in the social and labour fields. It produces the annual "World of Work Report".

Hence, the correct option is (D).

27. Every investment permitted under Section 80C comes with a mandatory lock-in period. ELSS investments come with a lock-in period of 3 years which is lowest among Section 80C investments. Public Provident Fund (PPF) and National Savings Certificate (NSC), traditional favourites, come with longer lock-in period. PPF is essentially a 15-year product, whereas NSC has a lock-in period of five years.

Hence, the correct option is (B).

28. National Housing Bank was set up on July 9, 1988 under the National Housing Bank Act, 1987 as a wholly-owned subsidiary of the Reserve Bank to act as an apex level institution for housing.

Hence, the correct option is (D).

29. Tata Airlines became a public limited company in 1946, and it was renamed as Air India.

Hence, the correct option is (A).

30. Kempegowda International Airport Bengaluru has the distinction of being the first airport in India, to be constructed through a public-private partnership (PPP).

Hence, the correct option is (C).

31. Apollo Hospital established its first branch in Chennai in 1983. It is the first hospital to be registered as a publicly listed company in India.

Hence, the correct option is (A).

32. TISCO- Tata Iron and Steel Company was formed in 1907. It was founded at Sakchi, Jamshedpur by Jamshedji Tata.

Hence, the correct option is (C).

33. Maharashtra is the largest e-waste Producer. It produces about 19.8% of e-waste produced in India. Out of the produced amount, it recycles only about 47,810 tons per annum (TPA).

Hence, the correct option is (B).

34. In Factor Comparison method, each factor is ascribed a Money value. Factor comparison is systematic and scientific method designed to carry out job evaluation which instead of ranking job as a whole, ranks according to a series of factors. The aim of factor comparison is to assign financial value to the relative parts of each job role.

Hence, the correct option is (A).

35. The Ranking technique have been used to evaluate an employee in comparison with other employees. Ranking method is one of the simplest performance evaluation methods. In this method, employees are ranked from best to worst in a group. The simplicity of this method is overshadowed by the negative impact of assigning a 'worst' and a 'best' rating to an employee.

Hence, the correct option is (A).

Mock Test 19

Comprehension

Ques (1-4):Direction: Read the following passage carefully and answer the question that follows.

Prior to the fall of the Union of Soviet Socialist Republics (USSR), Mikhail Gorbachev, seeing a country falling behind its Western rival and a people increasingly clamoring for change, addressed the growing internal unrest in the summer of 1987 by introducing a series of reforms known as perestroika (literally, restructuring). In Perestroika: New Thinking for Our Country and the World, Mikhail Gorbachev discussed his analysis of the problems facing the USSR and his plans to solve them.

Perhaps the most pressing and visible problem facing the USSR in the last 1980s came in the form of the country's consistently mediocre economic performance, despite its vast natural resource wealth and large labor force. Gorbachev flatly admitted that economic failures were increasing and current policies were failing to offer a sustainable remedy. Failing to take advantage of the numerous scientific and technological advancements available, the USSR relied on inefficient and outdated business models. As a result, Gorbachev said, "in the last fifteen years the national income growth rates had declined by more than a half and by the beginning of the eighties had fallen to a level close to economic stagnation." With business executives focused on using more resources (in order to employ more people) instead of becoming more efficient, the country produced poor quality products unable to compete in a global economy. Further, this inefficiency led to shortages: "the Soviet Union, the world's biggest producer of steel, raw materials, fuel and energy, has shortfalls in them due to wasteful or inefficient use."

The decrepit economy engendered social unrest and woe that only compounded economic difficulties and societal misery. Gorbachev wrote of "a gradual erosion of the ideological and moral values of our people" and noted the considerable growth in "alcoholism, drug addiction and crime." Accentuating these difficulties, the Communist government often ignored the needs of the average citizen, causing distrust and resentment. Perhaps the most destructive element of the social unraveling and inadequate government response was the mediocre education system. Gorbachev said, "Creative thinking was driven out from the social sciences, and superfluous and voluntarist assessments and judgments were declared indisputable truths."

Although Gorbachev also opined about the growing public disbelief in the content of the immense government propaganda campaigns, the extent to which economic underdevelopment and social deviance gripped Soviet culture made the collapse of the USSR virtually inevitable in the minds of many observers. When combined with glasnost (literally, openness), Gorbachev's plan that allowed greater transparency, perestroika actually served to hasten the collapse of the USSR. Contrary to its purpose, perestroika ensured that the fall of the USSR would occur sooner rather than later. Only a few years after Gorbachev implemented changes that would have been unthinkable and antithetical to the philosophy of previous leaders like Lenin, Stalin, and Khrushchev, the USSR fell.

Q.1 Which of the following best describes the primary objective of the passage?

A. Argue that the implementation of perestroika caused the fall of the Soviet Union

B. Explain perestroika along with its roots and consequences

C. Analyse the pros and cons of Mikhail Gorbachev's decision to implement perestroika

D. Explain the short-falls of a communist system and offer remedies

Q.2 The passage implies that which of the following was most true of the Soviet economy prior to perestroika:

A. Suffered from under performance due to excessive government regulation and micro-management

B. Failed to meet its potential as a result of corruption and bureaucratic overhead

C. Lacked adequate natural resources to grow efficiently, regardless of business management

D. Focused on achieving high-employment rather than export-capable products

Q.3 Based upon the passage, the author would likely agree most with which of the following characterizations of the impact of the USSR's troubled economy during the days leading up to perestroika?

A. Cause for renewed determination in communist philosophy

B. Reason that natives looked increasingly to the West and capitalism

C. Source of frustration and discomfort among citizens that fueled social friction

D. Justification for the USSR's neglect of the needs of many citizens

Q.4 According to the passage, which of the following best describes the relationship between perestroika and the fall of the USSR?

A. Perestroika mildly delayed the fall of the USSR, although the decline of the Soviet Republic was inevitable

B. Perestroika hastened the decline of the USSR

C. Perestroika enabled the USSR to pursue much needed restructuring

D. Perestroika softened the impact from the collapse of the USSR

Ques (5-10):Direction: Read the following passage carefully and answer the question that follows.

The Sun, while going on his daily rounds saw a princess and fell in love with her. Whenever he could slip away from the heavens he would take human form and go down to the princess to spend some time with her. The princess too became quite fond of him and would wait for him to come. One day the Sun decided to send her a blood-red ruby as a token of his love for her. He put the gem in a silk bag, and calling a crow that was flying past, asked the bird to deliver the gem to his beloved. Crows had milky white feathers in those days and it was considered auspicious if a crow came anywhere near you. So the Sun was pleased that he had found a crow to deliver the gem. As the crow sped through the sky with the silken bag, the aroma of food lured him. Looking down, the crow saw that a wedding feast was in progress, and immediately it was distracted from its mission. Food was one thing it could never resist.

Alighting on a tree nearby, it hung the bag on a twig and went off to find some food. While the crow was feasting, a merchant passing by saw the bag on the tree and knocked it down with a pole. When he opened the bag and saw its contents he almost swooned in joy. Quickly pocketing the ruby, he filled the bag with dry cow dung that was lying there, and then deftly returned the bag to the branch. It was all done so quickly that the crow missed all the action. After having its fill, it flew up to the tree, and picking up the bag, and took it to the person it was intended for. The princess was in the garden. When the crow gave her bag, she took it eagerly, knowing that it was from the Sun. But when she saw its contents she reeled back in shock and anger. Believing that it was the Sun's way to telling her that he did not care for her, she flung the bag away, rushed to her palace, and never came out again. When the Sun learned of what had happened he was furious. So great was his anger that when he turned his scorching gaze on the crow, its feathers were burned black. Its feathers have been black ever since. The ruby did not stay with the man who stole it. It fell out of his pocket and rolled into a deep pit. Men have been trying to dig it out ever since. Many precious stones have been found in the process, making Myanmar one of the richest sources of rubies and sapphires, but the ruby that the Sun sent to the princess is yet to be found.

Q.5 What did the Sun send for the princess as a token of his love?

A. He sent her the crow
B. He sent her dry cow dung
C. He sent her a red ruby
D. He gifted her the city of Myanmar

Q.6 Why did the princess fling the gift away?

A. She did not like rubies
B. The crow was known to bring bad luck
C. She had found cow dung in the bag
D. She thought the Sun was playing a cruel joke on her

Q.7 What led to the discovery of precious stones in Myanmar?

A. Humans discovered the stones in their search for the lost ruby
B. The crow spread the news of the lost ruby
C. The princess went in search of the lost ruby and discovered other precious stones
D. The merchant went in search of the ruby that fell off his pocket

Q.8 While on its way to the princess, the crow was distracted by:

A. The merchant calling out to him
B. The wedding that was taking place below
C. The ruby that the Sun sent for the princess
D. The temptation of the smell of the food

Q.9 Why did the Sun send his gift for the princess along with the crow?

A. The princess loved crows
B. The crow was the only bird available at the time
C. The crow was considered to be an auspicious bird
D. The crow knew where the princess lived

Q.10 Choose the word that is most OPPOSITE in meaning to : FURIOUS

A. Beaming **B.** Angry
C. Forgiving **D.** Calm

Management Data Interpretation

Ques (11-15):Direction: Study the following table carefully and answer the question given beside:

Number of accounts opened (in hundred) in four banks in various months

Bank	May	June	July	Aug	Sept	Oct	Nov	Dec
SBI	25	28	35	65	55	62	80	90
BOB	22	18	32	30	45	55	50	60
Canara	30	45	50	35	40	48	72	85
PNB	35	42	45	50	60	65	75	78

Q.11 In which of the following months is the average of the number of opened accounts the maximum?

A. November **B.** October
C. August **D.** July

Q.12 The number of accounts opened in September is approximately what percent more or less than the number of accounts opened in May?

A. 44% **B.** 42%
C. 40% **D.** None of these

Q.13 What is the ratio of the number of accounts opened in SBI to that opened in BOB from May to December?

A. 29:55 **B.** 37:41 **C.** 55:39 **D.** 39:50

Q.14 In which bank is the average number of accounts opened the maximum?

A. SBI and BOB **B.** BOB
C. BOB and PNB **D.** PNB

Q.15 The average number of accounts opened in Canara is what percent more or less than the average number of accounts opened in BOB? (approximation)

A. 19% **B.** 17% **C.** 20% **D.** 23%

Ques (16-20):Direction : Study the following bar chart carefully and answer the questions given beside.

This chart gives information about the number of Foreigners and Indians who visited five different places Goa, Shimla, Manali, Agra, and Pondicherry in India during the year 2017.

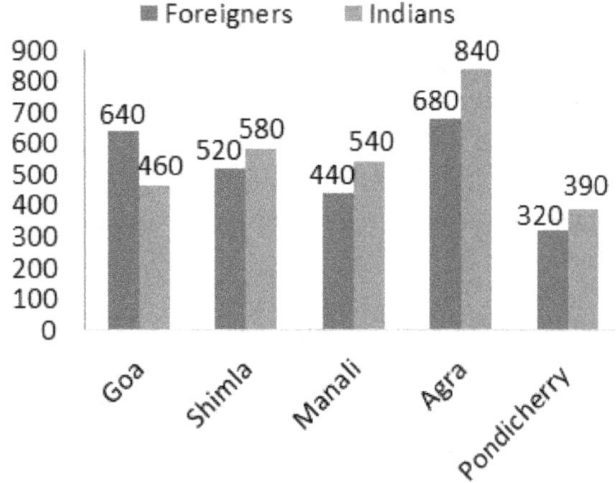

Q.16 The number of foreigner tourists visited in Goa during the year 2017 is approximately what percentage more than the number of foreigner tourists visited in Pondicherry during the year 2017?

A. 100% **B.** 200% **C.** 125% **D.** 150%

Q.17 What is the difference between the number of foreigners who visited in the given five places during the year 2017 and the number of Indians who visited in the given five places during the year 2017?

A. 240 **B.** 280 **C.** 210 **D.** 270

Q.18 By what percentage the number of Indians who visited Shimla during the year 2017 is less than the number of Indians who visited Agra during the year 2017?

A. 31% **B.** 34% **C.** 27% **D.** 24%

Q.19 What percentage of total people who visited Goa during the year 2017 were Indians?

A. 43.33% **B.** 44.67% **C.** 41.82% **D.** 48.88%

Q.20 The number of Foreigners who visited Agra during the year 2017 was approximately what percentage of the sum of the total number of Foreigners who visited the given five states during the year 2017?

A. 24.25% **B.** 28.34% **C.** 16.15% **D.** 26.15%

Ques (21-25):Directions: Study the following information carefully and answer the questions that follow:

Percentage distribution of teachers who teach six different subjects

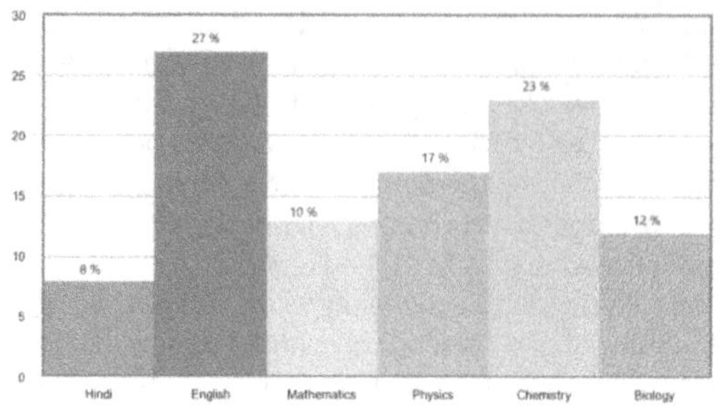

Q.21 If two-ninths of the teachers who teach Physics are females, then the number of male Physics teachers is approximately what per cent of the total number of teachers who teach Chemistry?

A. 57% **B.** 42% **C.** 63% **D.** 69%

Q.22 What is the total numbers of teachers who teach Chemistry, English and Biology?

A. 1226 **B.** 1116 **C.** 1176 **D.** 998

Q.23 What is the difference between the total number of employees teacher who teaches English and Physics together and total number of teacher who teaches Mathematics and Biology together?

A. 352 **B.** 342 **C.** 643 **D.** 653

Q.24 What is the ratio of the teachers who teach mathematics to the number of teachers who teach Hindi?

A. 13:7 **B.** 7:13 **C.** 7:26 **D.** 13:8

Q.25 If the percentage of Mathematics teachers is increased by 50% and the percentage of Hindi teachers is decreased by 25%, what will be the total number of Mathematics and Hindi teachers together?

A. 390 **B.** 379 **C.** 459 **D.** 480

Business Awareness

Q.26 The organization's ___ must be conducive to productivity and quality improvement.

A. Culture **B.** Development
C. Policy **D.** Environment

Q.27 In which evaluation method, the evaluator is asked to describe the strong and weak aspects of the employee's behavior?

A. Graphic rating scale
B. Forced choice
C. Essay evaluation
D. Management by Objective

Q.28 The following technique is used to evaluate an employee individually:

A. Graphic scale rating **B.** Ranking
C. Paired comparison **D.** Forced distribution

Q.29 During which of the following stage, the firm plans the proposed changes into practice.

A. Clarification **B.** Monitoring

C. Assessment **D.** Design

Q.30 Which authority has approved the draft of Banking Regulations in International Financial Services Centers (IFSC)?

A. Reserve Bank of India
B. International Financial Services Centres Authority
C. Securities and Exchange Board of India
D. Indian Banking Association

Q.31 Human Resource Management (HRM) is:

A. Employee oriented **B.** Employer oriented
C. Legally oriented **D.** None of the above

Q.32 Which of the following department is responsible for handling the safety & health issues of employees?

A. HR department
B. Procurement department
C. Finance department
D. Marketing department

Q.33 The term Human Resource Development was coined by whom of the following?

A. Leonard Nadler, 1969
B. Patricia Mclagan, 1983
C. T V Rao, 1974
D. Udai Pareek, 1988

Q.34 The Smithsonian Agreement of 1971 is related to:

A. Widening the permissible band of the exchange rates to 2.5 percent above or below the new 'central rates'
B. Tackle a shortage of liquidity during the Great Depression
C. Moving from fixed to floating exchange rate
D. Bop crisis faced by countries after the fall of the Bretton Woods System

Q.35 Which company has signed a non-exclusive term sheet to acquire rival FreeCharge?

A. MChek **B.** Obopay **C.** Paytm **D.** Paymate

// Smart Answer Sheet //

Correct — Indicates percentage of students who answered questions correctly.

Skipped — Indicates percentage of students who skipped questions.

Q.	Ans.	Correct	Skipped
1	B	64.79 %	34.09 %
2	D	53.16 %	42.85 %
3	C	44.82 %	35.58 %
4	B	45.92 %	40.19 %
5	C	80.88 %	15.78 %
6	C	57.57 %	42.0 %
7	A	67.46 %	32.3 %
8	D	64.15 %	35.35 %
9	C	45.72 %	41.85 %
10	D	84.55 %	14.23 %
11	A	14.86 %	68.91 %
12	D	44.19 %	44.35 %
13	C	47.1 %	51.01 %
14	D	26.81 %	70.13 %
15	D	55.11 %	34.83 %
16	A	76.58 %	20.82 %
17	C	85.1 %	12.27 %
18	A	80.86 %	11.86 %
19	C	87.4 %	12.14 %
20	D	81.63 %	13.74 %
21	A	22.18 %	70.3 %
22	B	46.27 %	42.72 %
23	B	68.05 %	31.13 %
24	D	49.08 %	34.01 %
25	C	11.93 %	80.26 %
26	A	81.27 %	10.69 %
27	C	41.24 %	45.47 %
28	A	22.07 %	77.17 %
29	D	53.86 %	32.44 %
30	B	28.51 %	68.82 %
31	A	67.22 %	30.95 %
32	A	53.99 %	43.09 %
33	A	23.74 %	72.18 %
34	A	30.31 %	69.06 %
35	C	40.14 %	39.59 %

Performance Analysis	
Avg. Score (%)	62.86%
Toppers Score (%)	65.71%
Your Score	

//Hints and Solutions//

1. "Explain perestroika along with its roots and consequences" best describes the primary objective of the passage.

In order to ascertain the primary objective of a passage, it is important to consider the logical flow and conclusion of the passage.

1st Paragraph - Introduction: What is perestroika?

2nd Paragraph - Why Perestroika: Explaining the business and economic problems facing the USSR?

3rd Paragraph - Why Perestroika: Explaining the social and cultural problems facing the USSR?

4th Paragraph - Conclusion: The consequences and effects of perestroika.

"When combined with glasnost (literally, openness), Gorbachev's plan that allowed greater transparency, perestroika actually served to hasten the collapse of the USSR. Contrary to its purpose, perestroika ensured that the fall of the USSR would occur sooner rather than later."

Option B. This encapsulates the outline, logical flow, and argument of the passage.

Option A. The passage makes no mention of the implementation of perestroika as the problem, saying instead: "perestroika actually served to hasten the collapse of the USSR"

Option C. The passage explains why Gorbachev implemented perestroika and notes the negative consequences of this decision. However, no attention is paid to elucidating the pros of perestroika.

Option D. The passage does not discuss the problems of the communist system in general and philosophical terms, focusing instead on the situation in the USSR and how perestroika sought to address this situation.

Hence, the correct option is (B).

2. "Focused on achieving high-employment rather than export-capable products" was most true of the Soviet economy prior to perestroika.

Option D. The passage strongly implies this: "With business executives focused on using more resources (in order to employ more people) ['high-employment' part of answer] instead of becoming more efficient, the country produced poor quality products unable to compete in a global economy ['export-capable' part of the answer]."

A. The passage never explicitly mentions government regulation, taxation, fiscal policy, etc.

B. The passage never mentions corruption or bureaucratic overhead. Instead, the passage provides another explanation for failure to reach potential: employers focused on employing people instead of becoming efficient. The closest the passage comes to discussing government regulation is: "executives focused on using more resources (in order to employ more people)". One would have to take this example and infer from it that excessive government regulation and micro-management existed across the economy.

C. The passage contradicts this: "the Soviet Union, the world's biggest producer of steel, raw materials, fuel and energy, has shortfalls in them due to wasteful or inefficient use."

Hence, the correct option is (D).

3. The characterizations of the impact of the USSR on which the author would likely agree most which troubled economy during the days leading up to perestroika is "Source of frustration and discomfort among citizens that fueled social friction".

Option C. This is reflected toward the beginning of the third paragraph: "The decrepit economy engendered social unrest and woe that only compounded economic difficulties and societal misery."

Option A. The passage implies that economic difficulties drove Gorbachev to undertake policies "antithetical to previous leaders like Lenin, Stalin, and Khrushchev." These leaders defined classical communist philosophy.

Option B. The passage cites not the economy but lack of government concern as the source of social unrest: "the Communist government often ignored the needs of the average citizen, causing distrust and resentment." Further, the passage never states that citizens of the USSR were demanding Western philosophy and capitalism. Instead, the passage simply notes that they were "clamoring for change."

Option D. Although the passage cites the USSR's neglect of its citizens, it offers no explanation for why nor does it imply that the government lacked the economic resources to provide these services. Instead, the passage intimates that the government simply did not care.

Hence, the correct option is (C).

4. "Perestroika hastened the decline of the USSR" best describes the relationship between perestroika and the fall of the USSR.

The relevant portion of the text is:

"When combined with glasnost (literally, openness), Gorbachev's plan that allowed greater transparency, perestroika actually served to hasten the collapse of the USSR. Contrary to its purpose, perestroika ensured that the fall of the USSR would occur sooner rather than later."

Hence, the correct option is (B).

5. The sun sent a red ruby for the princess as a token of his love.

Kindly refer to the 4th sentence of the 1st paragraph.

"One day the Sun decided to send her a blood-red ruby as a token of his love for her."

Hence, the correct option is (C).

6. The princess flung the gift away because she had found cow dung in the bag.

The answer can be inferred from the 8th sentence of the 2nd paragraph.

"But when she saw its contents she reeled back in shock and anger. Believing that it was the Sun's way to telling her that he did not care for her, she flung the bag away, rushed to her palace, and never came out again."

Hence, the correct option is (C).

7. Humans discovered the precious stones in Myanmar in their search for the lost ruby.

The answer can be inferred from the last sentence of the 2nd paragraph.

"Men have been trying to dig it out ever since. Many precious stones have been found in the process, making Myanmar one of the richest sources of rubies and sapphires, but the ruby that the Sun sent to the princess is yet to be found."

Hence, the correct option is (A).

8. While on its way to the princess, the crow was distracted by the temptation of the smell of the food.

Kindly refer to the last 2 sentences of the 1st paragraph.

"So the Sun was pleased that he had found a crow to deliver the gem. As the crow sped through the sky with the silken bag, the aroma of food lured him. Looking down, the crow saw that a wedding feast was in progress, and immediately it was distracted from its mission. Food was one thing it could never resist."

Hence, the correct option is (D).

9. The Sun send his gift for the princess along with the crow because the crow was considered to be an auspicious bird.

The answer can be inferred from the 5th sentence of the 1st paragraph.

"Crows had milky white feathers in those days and it was considered auspicious if a crow came anywhere near you. So the Sun was pleased that he had found a crow to deliver the gem."

Hence, the correct option is (C).

10. In the given context, the most opposite word of 'Furious' is 'Calm' or 'Composed'.

Furious: Very angry

Calm: Not excited, worried or angry; quiet

Angry: Feeling or showing anger

Beaming: Smiling Happily

Forgiving: Ready and able to forgive

Hence, the correct option is (D).

11. The average number of accounts in November

$= \frac{80+50+72+75}{4}$

$= \frac{277}{4}$

$= 69.25$

The average number of accounts in October

$= \frac{62+55+48+65}{4}$

$= \frac{230}{4}$

$= 57.5$

The average number of accounts in August

$= \frac{65+30+35+50}{4}$

$= \frac{180}{4}$

$= 45$

The average number of accounts in July

$= \frac{35+32+50+45}{4}$

$= \frac{162}{4}$

$= 40.5$

Therefore, in November the average number of accounts opened is the maximum.

Hence, the correct option is (A).

12. The total number of accounts opened in September

$= 55 + 45 + 40 + 60$

$= 200$

The total number of accounts opened in May

$= 25 + 22 + 30 + 35$

$= 112$

∴ Required %

$= \frac{200-112}{112} \times 100$

$= \frac{88}{112} \times 100$

$= 78.57 \approx 79\%$

Hence, the correct option is (D).

13. Number of accounts opened in SBI from May to December

$= 25 + 28 + 35 + 65 + 55 + 62 + 80 + 90$

$= 440$

Number of accounts opened in BOB from May to December

$= 22 + 18 + 32 + 30 + 45 + 55 + 50 + 60$

$= 312$

Required ratio $= \frac{440}{312} = 55:39$

Hence, the correct option is (C).

14. Total number of accounts opened in SBI

$= 25 + 28 + 35 + 65 + 55 + 62 + 80 + 90$

$= 440$

∴ Average number of accounts in SBI

$= \frac{440}{8} = 55$

Total number of accounts opened in BOB

$= 22 + 18 + 32 + 30 + 45 + 55 + 50 + 60$

$= 312$

∴ Average number of accounts in BOB

$= \frac{312}{8} = 39$

Total number of accounts opened in Canara

$= 30 + 45 + 50 + 35 + 40 + 48 + 72 + 85$

$= 405$

∴ Average number of accounts in Canara

$= \frac{405}{8} = 50.625$

Total number of accounts opened in PNB

$= 35 + 42 + 45 + 50 + 60 + 65 + 75 + 78$

$= 450$

∴ Average number of accounts in PNB

$= \frac{450}{8} = 56.25$

Therefore, in PNB the average number of accounts opened is the maximum.

Hence, the correct option is (D).

15. Total number of accounts opened in Canara

$= 30 + 45 + 50 + 35 + 40 + 48 + 72 + 85$

$= 405$

∴ Average number of accounts in Canara

$= \frac{405}{8} = 50.625$

Total number of accounts opened in BOB

$= 22 + 18 + 32 + 30 + 45 + 55 + 50 + 60$

$= 312$

∴ Avg no. of accounts in BOB

$= \frac{312}{8} = 39$

Required $\%$

$= \frac{50.625-39}{50.625} \times 100$

$= \frac{11.625}{50.625} \times 100$

$= 22.96 \approx 23\%$

Hence, the correct option is (D).

16. Foreigner tourists in Goa in $2017 = 640$

Foreigner tourists in Pondicherry in $2017 = 320$

The required $\% = \frac{(640-320)\times 100}{320}$

$= \frac{320\times 100}{320}$

$= 100\%$

Hence, the correct option is (A).

17. The number of foreigners who visited in the given five places during the year $2017 = (640 + 520 + 440 + 680 + 320)$

$= 2600$

The number of Indians who visited in the given five places during the year $2017 = (460 + 580 + 540 + 840 + 390)$

$= 2810$

The required difference $= 2810 - 2600$

$= 210$

Hence, the correct option is (C).

18. The number of Indians who visited Shimla during the year $2017 = 580$

The number of Indians who visited Agra during the year $2017 = 840$

The required $\% = \frac{(840-580)}{840} \times 100$

$= \frac{260}{840} \times 100$

$= 30.95\% \approx 31\%$

Hence, the correct option is (A).

19. Total number of tourists visited Goa during the year $2017 = 640 + 460$

$= 1100$

The Indian tourists $= 460$

The required $\% = \frac{460}{1100} \times 100$

$= 41.82\%$

Hence, the correct option is (C).

20. The number of foreigners who visited Agra during the year $2017 = 680$

The sum of the total number of foreigners who visited the given five states during the year $2017 = 460 + 520 + 440 + 680 + 320$

$= 2600$

The required $\% = \frac{680}{2600} \times 100$

$= 26.15\%$

Hence, the correct option is (D).

21. If $\frac{2}{9}$th of physics are female teachers, then

Male teachers = $1 - \frac{2}{9} = \frac{7}{9}$th of physics

Let's take x% of male physics teacher equal to Chemistry teachers, then

⇒ x% of Chemistry teacher = $\frac{7}{9}$th of physics

⇒ x% of (23% of 1800) = $\frac{7}{9}$th (17% of 1800)

⇒ x% of 23 = $\frac{7}{9}$th of 17

⇒ x = $\frac{7}{9} \times \frac{17}{23} \times 100$ = 57.4% ≈ 57%

Hence, the correct option is (A).

22. Total teachers who teach Chemistry, English and Biology

$= (23 + 27 + 12)\%$ of 1800

$= 62\%$ of 1800

$= \frac{62}{100} \times 1800$

$= 1116$

Hence, the correct option is (B).

23. Required difference $=$ [(English + Physics) $-$ (Mathematics + Biology)] $\%$ of 1800

$\Rightarrow [(27 + 17) - (13 + 12)]\%$ of 1800

$\Rightarrow (44 - 25)\%$ of 1800

$\Rightarrow 19\%$ of 1800

$\Rightarrow \frac{19}{100} \times 1800$

$\Rightarrow 342$

Hence, the correct option is (B).

24. Ratio Ratio = Number of teachers who teach Mathematics : Number of teachers who teaches Hindi

$\Rightarrow 13\%$ of $1800: 8\%$ of 1800

$\Rightarrow 13: 8$

Hence, the correct option is (D).

25. Percentage of Mathematics teacher $= 13\%$

After increasing by 50%,

Percentage of Mathematics teacher $= 13 + 13 \times \frac{50}{100}$

$= (13 + 6.5)\%$

$= 19.5\%$

Similarly,

Percentage of Hindi teacher $= 8\%$

After decreasing by 25%,

Percentage of Hindi teacher $= 8 - 8 \times \frac{25}{100}$

$= (8 - 2)\%$

$= 6\%$

Now, the percentage of total teachers becomes,

$(19.5 + 6)\%$

$= 25.5\%$

Therefore, 25.5% of 1800

$\Rightarrow \frac{25.5}{100} \times 1800$

$= 25.5 \times 18$

$= 459$

Hence, the correct option is (C).

26. The organization's Culture must be conducive to productivity and quality improvement.

The ways the employees interact amongst themselves and with others outside the organization contribute to the culture of the workplace. The culture gives an identity to the organization and makes it distinct from others. Communication and relationship play an important role in a healthy organization culture.
Hence, the correct option is (A).

27. In essay evaluation method, the evaluator is asked to describe the strong and weak aspects of the employee's behavior.

In the essay evaluation method, the appraiser prepares a written statement about the employee being appraised. The statement usually concentrates on describing specific strengths and weaknesses in job performance.
Hence, the correct option is (C).

28. Graphic scale rating technique is used to evaluate an employee individually.

A graphic rating scale lists the traits that each employee should have and rates workers on a numbered scale for each trait. The scores are meant to separate employees into tiers of performers, which can play a role in determining promotions and salary adjustments.
Hence, the correct option is (A).

29. During design stage, the firm plans the proposed changes into practice. These projects are designed with the aim of efficient management.
Hence, the correct option is (D).

30. The International Financial Services Centers Authority (IFSCA) has approved the draft of the International Financial Services Centers Authority (Banking) Regulations, 2020.

This was to enable setting up of banking units in the International Financial Services Centre. The regulation would be notified by the Government of India soon, which will contain what kind of banking activities that would be permitted in the IFSC.

Hence, the correct option is (B).

31. Human Resource Management (HRM) is Employee oriented.

Employee orientation is the process of introducing new hires to their jobs, co-workers, responsibilities, and workplace. Effective employee orientation answers any questions or concerns a new colleague may have, makes them aware of company policies and expectations, and eases them comfortably into their new positions.
Hence, the correct option is (A).

32. The HR department is responsible for handling the safety & health issues of employees.

Human resources professionals play an important role in ensuring employee health and safety, as they know the workplace, the employees, and their job demands. While human resources professionals are not expected to know the technical aspects of workplace health and safety, they should know when and how to use existing resources to respond to employee concerns.
Hence, the correct option is (A).

33. Leonard Nadler introduced and coined the term Human Resource Development in 1969. He described it as a learning experience that takes place for a specific time period and is aimed at bringing about a behavioral change.

TV Rao is known as the father of Indian Human Resource Development.

Hence, the correct option is (A).

34. The 'Smithsonian Agreement' in 1971, which widened the permissible band of movements of the exchange rates to 2.5 percent above or below the new 'central rates' with the hope of reducing pressure on deficit countries, lasted only 14 months. The developed market economies led by the United Kingdom and soon followed by Switzerland and then Japan began to adopt floating exchange rates in the early 1970s.

In 1976, the revision of IMF Articles allowed countries to choose whether to float their currencies or to peg them (to a single currency, a basket of currencies, or to the SDR). There are no rules governing pegged rates and no de facto supervision of floating exchange rates.

Hence, the correct option is (A).

35. Alibaba Group-backed Paytm has signed a non-exclusive term sheet to acquire rival FreeCharge, the digital payments platform owned and operated by beleaguered online marketplace Snapdeal, in what is expected to be an all-cash deal. The deal, estimated at between $45 million and $90 million, could be finalized in a month once the deal is successful.

Hence, the correct option is (C).

Mock Test 20

Comprehension

Ques (1-5):Direction: Read the following passage carefully and answer the question that follows.

The passage of a statutory resolution and a Bill in Parliament — "abrogating" Article 370 which confers special political status on Jammu and Kashmir, and bifurcating the State into two Union Territories — has robbed the Kashmir Valley of its political autonomy, or whatever remains of it after all these years. It may deepen the State's trust deficit vis-a-vis the Centre. The "abrogation" of Article 370, being hailed as a "glorious" move, is itself a misnomer. "Amending" or "abrogating" Article 370 is a Constitutional improbability; the amending provision of Article 368 says no Constitutional amendments have effect in relation to J&K unless applied by Order of the President under Article 370 that requires the concurrence of the State's legislature and ratification by its Constituent Assembly. The moves on Monday can be seen as an exercise in political optics, pandering to a certain majoritarian sentiment. What the Centre has done is to shred even the garb of democracy and spirit of dialogue that successive governments felt was important to engage the people of Kashmir. Through as many as 45 Presidential Orders, the most critical being the Order of 1954, Article 370 has already been divested of its spirit. Secessionist elements and some Indian Constitutional experts have cited this gradual advance of the Union as the conquest of the Valley by stealth.

What even this controversial process of assimilation, with Article 370 in place, has done is to achieve the growth of local political engagement. It legitimises a pan-Indian sentiment in the Valley where the secessionists would like to portray India as a mere occupational force. Indeed, there are several other provisions in the Constitution such as Article 371(A), 371(G), 371(B), 371(C) that validate indigenous political forces in States like Nagaland, Mizoram, Assam, Manipur et al. This asymmetric form of federalism has its global parallels in the substantial autonomy enjoyed by Scotland and Wales and Northern Ireland within Great Britain. The protests in Hong Kong affirm the relevance of democratic processes inherent in the one country-two systems followed even by China.

By robbing Article 370 of its special provisions, the BJP has undermined these nuanced and extremely critical democratic processes. Simultaneously, the State has been carved up into two Union Territories with J&K having a legislature and Ladakh without it. The unprecedented step of reorganizing a State and divesting it of its legislative authority without even a semblance of consultation with the stakeholders sets a dangerous precedent underlined by several regional groups and political parties, particularly the DMK and the MDMK. It is possible that the BJP would reap rich political dividends for this muscular policy. But the Centre would be responsible for escalation of violence in the Valley where all doors for political engagement and democratic exchange seem to have been closed down for good. Without meaningful participation of the people, any such unilateral integration can remain at best territorial.

Q.1 Which among the following is correct regarding the Article 368 in the Constitution of India, as stated in the passage?

A. It should not go unattended if there is something within the purview of the state and the centre.

B. It should be noted that there are so many issues in the offing so that the central government can come.

C. Any law can be implemented in Jammu and Kashmir only if there is support from the state legislature.

D. The state of Jammu and Kashmir should note that India will not remain spectators in the whole thing.

Q.2 Which among the following is correct regarding Scotland and Wales as stated in the passage?

A. The area comes under the supervision of India whereas the rest of the country does not come here.

B. The area is within suspension by the international territory though other areas are also accepting it.

C. The area enjoys similar status just like Jammu and Kashmir in India and there are several other areas also like this.

D. This area has been in the storm of dispute between various countries because there are so many problems.

Q.3 Which among the following is correct regarding the possible consequence of the decision taken by the centre to abrogate Section 370?

A. The people of the area will not understand the importance of autonomy and they will come to India.

B. The people of the area will have more trust deficit with the mainland government of India since they will feel things are not being in their interests.

C. The people in the area will not be within the jurisdiction of the police and the army of the central government.

D. It will have no impact on the population of Jammu and Kashmir though they are yet to know the fact.

Q.4 Which among the following is/are correct regarding the decision taken by the Government of India to revoke Article 370 of the Indian Constitution?

I. Jammu and Kashmir will be a Union Territory with a legislature whereas Ladakh will not have the same.

II. This decision will help the separatists in the valley to portray India as a force working against the interests of the valley people.

III. This decision will not stand in the court of law and there has already been petition in the Supreme Court against it.

A. Both I and II **B.** Both II and III

C. Both I and III **D.** Only III

Q.5 Which among the following is SIMILAR in meaning to the word Misnomer as used in the passage?

A. Understanding

B. Utilization

C. Misleading statement

D. Mutual

Ques (6-10):Direction: Read the following passage carefully and answer the question given beside.

Remote sensing and GIS are promising tools for handling spatial and temporal data and help in integrating them for successful planning of natural resources. It is the science of measuring the earth using sensors mounted on high-flying aircrafts or satellites. These sensors collect data in the form of images and provide insights for manipulating, analyzing and visualizing those images. Since natural resources are not uniformly distributed and are spatially varied, it is challenging to capture the correct picture. Management of natural resources calls for scientific tools for timely and accurate dissemination of information. In natural resource management, remote sensing and GIS are mainly used in the mapping process. These techniques are useful in management of land, soil, coastal, watershed, urban and many more.

In India, the agriculture sector alone sustains the livelihood of around 50 percent of the population. Therefore, increase in crop productivity has been a major concern. Since, the scope for increasing area under agriculture is limited, advanced crop production forecasting is required for better policymaking. Indian Space Research Agency (ISRO) and Indian Council of Agricultural Research (ICAR) successful experiment-Agricultural Resource Inventory and Survey Experiment (ARISE) used aerial color photographs to estimate crop acreage in many states of India. Other Important uses of remote sensing include crop identification, stress detection, and crop yield modeling, drought monitoring, land degradation mapping and more. Urbanization is important and inevitable for development, but its proper planning and management is crucial for sustenance. One of the important features of GIS is multilayered mapping. This kind of mapping helps municipal corporations, town planning boards to build cities that are better organized. The information systems with socio-economic data overlaid upon satellite data makes urban planning cost-effective and accurate.

Coastal ecosystems have high ecological significance. GIS and remote sensing data are used to study coastal ecosystem and marine living resources which include habitats like mangroves, coral reefs and more. Apart from this, suspended shoreline dynamics can be studied and climatic changes leading to cyclone and sea level rise may be of special interest too. Geospatial data is effective in the analysis and determination of factors that affect the utilization of these resources. The technologies provide a platform through which we can generate information that can be used to make sound decisions for sustainable development of the natural resources of India.

Q.6 What can be the most appropriate title for the passage?

A. GIS and remote sensing in natural resource management.
B. Use of GIS and remote sensing in land management.
C. Use of GIS and remote sensing in urban management.
D. Use of GIS and remote sensing in coastal ecosystem management.

Q.7 What is the tone of the author?

A. Ridiculing **B.** Critical
C. Informative **D.** Pessimistic

Q.8 Why, according to the passage, are GIS and remote sensing considered as promising tools?

I. They collect data in the form of graphs.
II. They provide scope for manipulating, analyzing and visualizing the images.
III. They disseminate data's more accurately.

A. Only I and II **B.** Only II and III
C. Only I and III **D.** Only II

Q.9 In the given context of the passage, why are GIS and remote sensing tools crucial in the agriculture sector?

I. This sector alone sustains the livelihood of around 50 percent of the population.
II. GIS and remote sensing would help in advanced crop production forecasting.
III. Drought monitoring can be done using GIS and remote sensing tools.

A. Only I **B.** Only I and III
C. Only II and III **D.** All I, II and III

Q.10 How effective are remote sensing and GIS in managing urban growth?

I. GIS and remote sensing are helpful in building cities that are better organized.
II. The system makes urban planning cost-effective and accurate.
III. They help the government disseminate people living in extremely densed areas to less populated ones.

A. Only II and III **B.** Only I and II
C. Only III **D.** Only I and III

Management Data Interpretation

Ques (11-15):Direction: Study the following bar graph carefully and answer the question given beside.

The following graph gives the information about calories per day required for different ages of babies in the first six years of their lives.

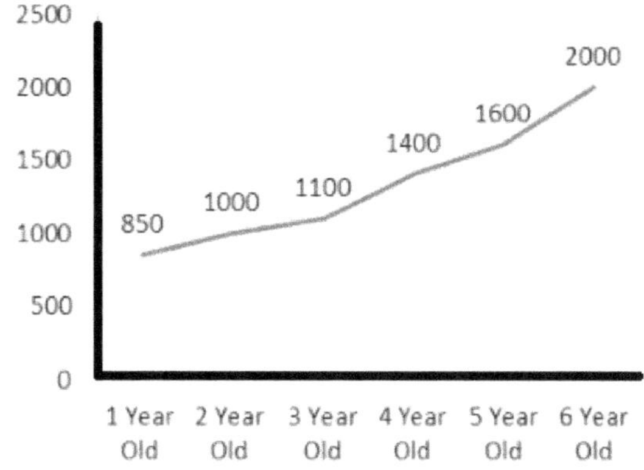

Q.11 In a family, there are 4 babies of 1 - year, 3 - year, 5 - year, and 6 - year old. Total how many calories will be required per day in the family for babies?

A. 5550 **B.** 4850 **C.** 5400 **D.** 5150

Q.12 Calories required per day for 5-year old baby is how much percentage less than that of 6-year-old baby?

A. 25% **B.** 20% **C.** 15% **D.** 10%

Q.13 In the month of January total how much calories will be consumed by a 2 - year old baby?

A. 30000 **B.** 12000 **C.** 1000 **D.** 31000

Q.14 Total calories consumed by a 5 - year old baby in the month of April is what percentage of total calories consumed by a 6 - year old baby in the month of March ? (rounded off two decimal)

A. 67.42% **B.** 78.87% **C.** 76.49% **D.** 77.42%

Q.15 Find the absolute difference between total calories consumed by a 2 - year old baby in the month of December and the total calories consumed by a 3 - year old baby in the month of July?

A. 3100 **B.** 3000 **C.** 2000 **D.** 2100

Ques (16-20):Direction: Study the following table chart carefully and answer the question given beside.

General Election Results analysis for party P1			
Year	**Percentage of population eligible to vote**	**Voters turnout %**	**Percentage of votes casted for party P1**
1962	60	70	45
1967	50	75	40
1971	45	80	48
1977	55	60	50
1980	40	75	60
1984	52	78	50
1989	30	80	35

Q.16 If population of the state in the year 1977 was 800 million, then how many people voted for party $P1$ in the year 1977?

A. 125 million **B.** 132 million
C. 140 million **D.** 148 million

Q.17 Between 1984 and 1989 the number of people eligible to vote increased by 20%. Find the percentage increase in the population?

A. 112% **B.** 201% **C.** 140% **D.** 108%

Q.18 In 1967, if another 5% of the population had been eligible to vote, $24{,}000{,}000$ more people would have voted, assuming the same voters turnout percentage. How many people actually voted in 1967?

A. 200,000,000 **B.** 320,000,000
C. 240,000,000 **D.** 250,000,000

Q.19 If population of the state in 1962 was 500 million and every year population of the state increases by 10 million, what is the average number of people voting for party $P1$ in every election from 1962 to 1977?

A. 89.5505 **B.** 91.5505 **C.** 94.5005 **D.** 96.5505

Q.20 If the voters turnout in 1989 and the number of people who voted for party $P1$ in 1980 were the same, then find the ratio of the population in 1980 to that of population in 1989?

A. $\frac{4}{5}$ **B.** $\frac{4}{3}$ **C.** $\frac{3}{4}$ **D.** $\frac{3}{2}$

Ques (21-25):Direction: Study the following information to answer the given question.

Total number of passengers travelling from Patna Junction to different districts $= 12000$

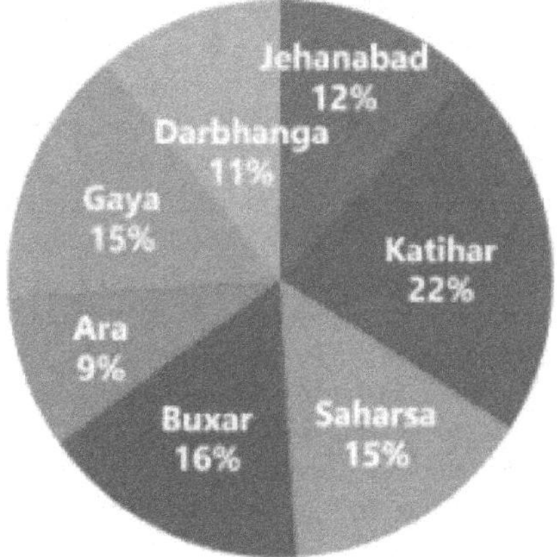

Q.21 The number of passengers travelling from Patna to Buxar is what per cent more than the number of passengers travelling to Jehanabad?

A. 20% **B.** 25% **C.** $33\frac{1}{3}\%$ **D.** $66\frac{2}{3}\%$

Q.22 The number of passengers travelling from Patna to Gaya is what per cent of the total number of passengers travelling from Patna to Darbhanga and Ara together?

A. $133\frac{1}{3}\%$ **B.** 75% **C.** $66\frac{2}{3}\%$ **D.** 33%

Q.23 What is the average number of passengers travelling from Patna to Saharsa, Katihar and Buxar together?

A. 2140 **B.** 2220 **C.** 2020 **D.** 2120

Q.24 What will be the central angle for passengers travelling from Patna to Buxar if it is put in the form of a pie-chart?

A. 57.6° **B.** 67.6° **C.** 45° **D.** 75.6°

Q.25 Among the passengers who are travelling from Patna to Katihar, 42% are female adults and 38% are male adults. What is the number of children? (Transgenders are not to be considered.)

A. 268 **B.** 278
C. 288 **D.** None of these

Business Awareness

Q.26 The Job Characteristics Model is one of the most influential attempts to_________.

A. design jobs with increased motivational properties
B. assign jobs with proper motivational properties
C. analyze jobs with increase and proper motivation
D. describe jobs with increase motivation for proper jobs

Q.27 A firm under perfect competition is

A. Price maker **B.** Price breaker
C. Price taker **D.** Price shaker

Q.28 The scheme pertaining to leadership development of minority women and being implemented by the Ministry of Minority Affairs is named _________.

A. Nai Manzil
B. Nai Roshni
C. Mahila Samriddhi Yojna
D. Nai Udaan

Q.29 The oldest form of business organization is ________.

A. partnership
B. sole proprietorship
C. joint-stock company
D. co-operative undertaking

Q.30 Which of the following securities proves a burden on the finances of the company, when the company is not earning profits?

A. Equity shares
B. Preference shares
C. Redeemable preference shares
D. Debentures

Q.31 Investment in which of the following is most risky?

A. Equity shares **B.** Preference shares
C. Debentures **D.** Land

Q.32 The meaning of the acronym 'SHRM' is

A. Short-term Human Resource Management
B. Strategic Human Resource Management
C. Strategestic Human Resource Management
D. Strategic Human Relations Management

Q.33 Whenever ____________ is greater than average total cost, average total cost is rising.

A. marginal cost **B.** variable cost
C. fixed cost **D.** full cost

Q.34 The marginal revenue equation can be derived from the

A. Demand equation **B.** Supply equation
C. Cost equation **D.** Price equation

Q.35 A dyadic relationship between a manager who is offering help and an employee to whom such help is given. This is known as__________.

A. mentoring **B.** counselling
C. coaching **D.** helping

// Smart Answer Sheet //

Correct — Indicates percentage of students who answered questions correctly.

Skipped — Indicates percentage of students who skipped questions.

Q.	Ans.	Correct	Skipped
1	C	53.61 %	32.27 %
2	C	52.76 %	39.06 %
3	B	55.07 %	37.51 %
4	A	62.75 %	36.53 %
5	C	76.62 %	12.93 %
6	A	82.2 %	10.79 %
7	C	87.3 %	11.76 %
8	B	52.65 %	39.7 %
9	C	60.77 %	37.31 %
10	B	44.04 %	32.65 %
11	A	84.6 %	13.36 %
12	B	85.71 %	13.44 %
13	D	54.95 %	34.31 %
14	D	45.09 %	42.09 %
15	A	41.71 %	37.0 %
16	B	77.53 %	12.8 %
17	D	62.71 %	37.2 %
18	C	47.72 %	32.15 %
19	D	28.94 %	67.44 %
20	B	48.6 %	33.16 %
21	C	78.42 %	19.91 %
22	B	87.99 %	10.76 %
23	D	66.66 %	32.15 %
24	A	83.48 %	16.4 %
25	D	58.06 %	37.4 %
26	D	60.03 %	38.81 %
27	C	65.37 %	33.5 %
28	B	82.78 %	11.6 %
29	B	88.29 %	11.11 %
30	D	40.84 %	50.88 %
31	A	46.76 %	49.29 %
32	B	85.09 %	13.05 %
33	A	89.16 %	10.1 %
34	A	85.52 %	13.43 %
35	B	47.48 %	31.09 %

Performance Analysis	
Avg. Score (%)	42.86%
Toppers Score (%)	65.71%
Your Score	

//Hints and Solutions//

1. According to the passage, **"the amending provision of Article 368 says no Constitutional amendments have effect in relation to J&K unless applied by Order of the President under Article 370 that requires the concurrence of the State's legislature and ratification by its Constituent Assembly."**

It is stated in the passage that Article 368 of the Indian Constitution is regarding the amendment of any law in the country. Any law will only be applicable in Jammu and Kashmir if the state legislature also accepts the same. The Presidential Order should also be in force regarding this. Among the given options, we can see that Option (C) gives us the correct information regarding Article 368 of the Indian Constitution whereas the rest can be eliminated from consideration as they do not follow from the passage.

Hence, the correct option is (C).

2. Refer to, **"This asymmetric form of federalism has its global parallels in the substantial autonomy enjoyed by Scotland and Wales and Northern Ireland within Great Britain."**

It is stated in the passage that the area of Scotland and Wales are within the jurisdiction of Great Britain and the areas are governed by the autonomous bodies. This is actually similar to the status of Jammu and Kashmir in India because till now Jammu and Kashmir also enjoyed similar autonomy in India. Among the given options, we can choose Option (C) since it provides us the correct information regarding similarity between Jammu and Kashmir and Scotland and Wales. Other options can be eliminated since they do not follow from the passage.

Hence, the correct option is (C).

3. It is clear from the passage that the decision by the government to revoke Section 370 without discussing anything with the local political parties will have far reaching impact on the relationship between India and Jammu & Kashmir. Therefore the people in the area will not feel that Indian government is working to fulfill their interests but they are only working in the interests of the mainland country. It will definitely increase the trust deficit between the people in India and the state of Jammu and Kashmir. Among the given options, we can easily choose Option (B) since it provides us the correct information whereas the rest can be eliminated from consideration since they do not follow from the passage.

Hence, the correct option is (B).

4. Statement I is correct since it has been stated in the passage that J & K will not be a state anymore and it will only be a UT. Apart from that, Ladakh will also be a UT but there will not be any legislative assembly there unlike Jammu and Kashmir. Refer to, **"Simultaneously, the State has been carved up into two Union Territories with J&K having a legislature and Ladakh without it."**

Statement II is correct since it has been stated in the passage that the decision taken unilaterally by the Indian government is actually going to hurt the sentiment of the people of Jammu and Kashmir. The separatists there will take this opportunity to brainwash the people there against the interests of the valley people. Refer to, **"It legitimises a pan-Indian sentiment in the Valley where the secessionists would like to portray India as a mere occupational force."**

Statement III is not correct since there are references that the government has not done it in the correct manner but it cannot be said that there have been applications already in the Supreme Court. Therefore it cannot be considered as correct.

Hence, the correct option is (A).

5. The word misnomer has been used in the passage in the sense that the image that is being created of abrogation of Section 370 being a bold decision is actually wrong since the government has not done it in the correct manner. It should have consulted the local political leaders before taking such a decision. This will have long lasting impact on the area and its people. Among the given options, it is easy to point out (C) as the correct meaning of the given word. Other words are not correct and can be eliminated.

Hence, the correct option is (C).

6. According to the passage, in natural resource management, remote sensing and GIS are mainly used in the mapping process. These techniques are useful in the management of land, soil, coastal, watershed, urban, and many more.
The whole passage mentions the uses of remote sensing and GIS in various areas for planning and effective management and this can be inferred from the highlighted part above.
Evidently, option (A) suits best as the title of the passage and therefore is the correct answer.
Hence, the correct option is (A).

7. Option (A) is wrong as the author is not making a mockery of the successful work of GIS and remote sensing.

Option (D) is wrong as the author is optimistic about GIS and supports its usage.

Option (B) is also wrong as the author is nowhere seen criticizing GIS and remote sensing technique.

The author supplements the entire passage with various examples and successful works of ISRO and ICAR. Evidently, the tone of the passage is 'informative'.

Hence, the correct option is (C).

8. Statement I. They collect data in the form of graphs.

Refer to:

These sensors collect data in the form of images and provide insights for manipulating, analyzing and visualizing those images.

From the highlighted sentence above, it's clear that Statement A is wrong as GIS and remote sensing tools collect data in the form of images and not graphs. Statement I is hence invalid

Statement II. They provide scope for manipulating, analyzing and visualizing the images.

From the same sentence as taken above for reference, we can infer that the mentioned tools are indeed helpful for manipulating, analyzing and visualizing the images. Statement III is hence true.

Statement III. They disseminate data's more accurately.

Refer to:

Management of natural resources calls for scientific tools for timely and **accurate dissemination of information**. In natural resource management, remote sensing and GIS are mainly used in the mapping process.

We can infer from the highlighted part above that GIS and remote sensing disseminate data's more accurately.

Statement III is valid too.

Hence, the correct option is (B).

9. Statement I. This sector alone sustains the livelihood of around 50 percent of the population.

The above statement doesn't mention significance of GIS and remote sensing tools with respect to agriculture sector in India. Had the question been "Why is agriculture sector important for India?", the statement would have been correct. So, statement I is invalid.

Statement II. GIS and remote sensing would help in advanced crop production forecasting.

Refer to:

Remote sensing and GIS are promising tools for handling spatial and temporal data and help in integrating them for successful planning of natural resources.

Since, the scope for increasing area under agriculture is limited, advanced crop production forecasting is required for better policymaking.

The highlighted parts above confirm what's been stated in statement II. So, statement II is valid.

Statement III. Drought monitoring can be done using GIS and remote sensing tools.

Refer to:

Other Important uses of remote sensing include crop identification, stress detection, and crop yield modeling, drought monitoring, land degradation mapping and more.

Clearly, the highlighted part above validates what's been stated in statement III. So, statement III is also valid.

Hence, the correct option is (C).

10. Statement I. Helps municipal corporations, town planning boards to build cities that better organized.

Refer to:

One of the important features of GIS is multilayered mapping. This kind of mapping helps municipal corporations, town planning boards to build cities that better organized.

The highlighted parts above confirm what's been stated in statement I. So, statement I is valid

Statement II. The system makes urban planning cost-effective and accurate.

Refer to:

The information systems with socio-economic data overlaid upon satellite data makes urban planning cost-effective and accurate.

From the highlighted part in the sentence above, it's clear that Statement II is true. So, statement II is valid too.

Statement III. They help the government disseminate people living in extremely densed areas to less populated ones.

Nothing about the population is mentioned in the passage. Clearly, statement III is not true.

Hence, the correct option is (B).

11. From the graph,

Calories per day required for 1 - year old baby $= 850$

Calories per day required for 3 - year old baby $= 1100$

Calories per day required for 5 - year old baby $= 1600$

Calories per day required for 6 - year old baby $= 2000$

Therefore, calories per day will be required for 4 babies together $= 850 + 1100 + 1600 + 2000 = 5550$

Hence, the correct option is (A).

12. From the graph,

Calories per day required for 5-year old baby $= 1600$

Calories per day required for 6-year old baby $= 2000$

Required $\% = \frac{(2000-1600)\times 100}{2000} = \frac{400}{20} = 20\%$

Hence, the correct option is (B).

13. Calories per day required for 2 - year old baby $= 1000$

In January, total number of days $= 31$

Total calories will consume in the whole month $=$ $1000 \times 31 = 31000$ calories

Hence, the correct option is (D).

14. Calories per day required for 5 - year old baby $= 1600$

In April, total number of days $= 30$

Total calories will consume in the whole month $=$ $1600 \times 30 = 48000$ calories

Calories per day required for 6 - year old baby $= 2000$

In March, total number of days $= 31$

Total calories will consume in the whole month $=$ $2000 \times 31 = 62000$ calories

Required $\% = \frac{48000\times 100}{62000} = \frac{48000}{62} = 77.42\%$

Hence, the correct option is (D).

15. Calories per day required for 2 - year old baby $= 1000$

In December, total number of days $= 31$

Total calories will consume in the whole month $=$ $1000 \times 31 = 31000$ calories

Calories per day required for 3 - year old baby $= 1100$

In July, total number of days $= 31$

Total calories will consume in the whole month $= 1100 \times 31 = 34100$ calories

The required difference $= 34100 - 31000 = 3100$

Hence, the correct option is (A).

16. Number of people to eligible vote $= 55\%$ of $800 = 440$ million

Voters turnout $= 60\%$ of $440 = 264$ million

Number of people who voted for party $P1 = 50\%$ of $264 = 132$ million

Hence, the correct option is (B).

17. Let, the population in 1984 and 1989 be x and y respectively.

Number of people eligible to vote in $1984 = 0.52x$

Number of people eligible to vote in $1989 = 0.30y$

According to the question,

$$\frac{0.30y - 0.52x}{0.52x} = 0.20$$

$$\Rightarrow 0.30y - 0.52x = 0.20 \times 0.52x$$

$$\Rightarrow 0.30y - 0.52x = 0.104x$$

$$\Rightarrow 0.30y = 0.104x + 0.52x = 0.624x$$

$$\Rightarrow y = \frac{0.624x}{0.30}$$

$$\Rightarrow y = 2.08x$$

$\%$ increase in population $= \frac{y-x}{x} \times 100$

$$= \frac{2.08x - x}{x} \times 100$$

$$= 1.08 \times 100$$

$$= 108\%$$

Hence, the correct option is (D).

18. Let the population of the state be $'x'$ in 1967.

Number of people who voted in $1967 = x(0.5)(0.75)$

According to question,

$$x(0.55)(0.75) - x(0.5)(0.75) = 24{,}000{,}000$$

$$\Rightarrow x = 640{,}000{,}000$$

Number of people who voted in $1967 = 640{,}000{,}000 \times 0.5 \times 0.75 = 240{,}000{,}000$

Hence, the correct option is (C).

19. Population in $1962 = 500$ million

Number of people voting for party $P1$ in $1962 = 60\%$ of 70% of 45% of $500 = 94.5$ million

Population in $1967 = 550$ million

Number of people voting for party $P1$ in $1967 = 50\%$ of 75% of 40% of $550 = 82.5$ million

Population in $1971 = 590$ million

Number of people voting for party $P1$ in $1971 = 45\%$ of 80% of 48% of $590 = 101.952$ million

Population in $1977 = 650$ million

Number of people voting for party $P1$ in $1977 = 55\%$ of 60% of 50% of $650 = 107.25$ million

Therefore, required average $= 96.5505$ million

Hence, the correct option is (D).

20. Let the population in 1980 and 1989 be u and v respectively.

Number of who voted for party $P1$ in $1980 = u \times 0.75 \times 0.40 \times 0.60$

Voters turnout in $1989 = v \times 0.80 \times 0.30$

According to the question,

$$u \times 0.75 \times 0.40 \times 0.60 = v \times 0.80 \times 0.30$$

$$\Rightarrow \frac{u}{v} = \frac{0.80 \times 0.30}{0.75 \times 0.40 \times 0.60}$$

$$\Rightarrow \frac{u}{v} = \frac{100}{75}$$

$$\Rightarrow \frac{u}{v} = \frac{4}{3}$$

Hence, the correct option is (B).

21. The number of passengers from Patna to Buxar $= 16\%$

No. of passengers from Patna to Jehanabad $= 12\%$

Required $\% = \frac{16-12}{12} \times 100 = \frac{4 \times 100}{12} = 33\frac{1}{3}\%$

Hence, the correct option is (C).

22. No. of passengers travelling from Patna to Gaya $= 15\%$

No. of passengers travelling from Patna to Darbhanga and Ara $= 11\% + 9\% = 20\%$

Required $\% = \frac{15}{20} \times 100 = 75\%$

Hence, the correct option is (B).

23. Total percentage of Saharsa, Katihar and Buxar $=$ $(15\% + 22\% + 16\%) = 53\%$

Therefore, 53% of $12000 = (50\%$ of $12000 + 3\%$ of $12000) = 6000 + 360 = 6360$

Required average $= \frac{6360}{3} = 2120$

Hence, the correct option is (D).

24. Given,

Passengers travelling from Patna to Buxar $= 16\%$

Central angle $= \frac{16}{100} \times 360° = 57.6°$

Hence, the correct option is (A).

25. No. of children travelling from Patna to Katihar $=$ $100\% - (42 + 38)\% = 100\% - 80\% = 20\%$

Total no. of children travelling from Patna to Katihar $= 20\%$ of 22% of 12000

$= \frac{20}{100} \times \frac{22}{100} \times 12000 = 528$

Hence, the correct option is (D).

26. The Job Characteristics Model is one of the most influential attempts to describe jobs with increase motivation for proper jobs. The job characteristics model applicable to a business identifies the job characteristics of skill variety, autonomy, task significance, task identity and feedback, and the outcomes of high job performance, high job satisfaction, high intrinsic motivation, and low absenteeism or turnover.
Hence, the correct option is (D).

27. A firm under perfect competition is a price taker. In perfect market conditions (also called perfect competition) a firm is a price taker because other firms can enter the market easily and produce a product that is indistinguishable from every other firm's product. This makes it impossible for any firm to set its own prices.
Hence, the correct option is (C).

28. The Ministry of Minority Affairs has started the implementation of a scheme "Nai Roshni" for Leadership Development of Minority Women from 2012-13.

It has the twin objectives of empowering and instilling confidence in women of minority communities by equipping them with knowledge, tools, and techniques to interact with government systems, banks, and intermediaries. Also, it aims at encouraging minority community women to move out of the home and assume leadership roles within the community.

Hence, the correct option is (B).

29. The oldest form of business organization is a sole proprietorship. When the ownership and management of a business are in control of one individual the form of business is called sole proprietorship.
Hence, the correct option is (B).

30. Debentures prove a burden on the finances of the company when the company is not earning profits. Debenture puts a permanent burden on the earnings of a company. Therefore, there is a greater risk when the earnings of the company fluctuate.
Hence, the correct option is (D).

31. Investment in Equity shares is most risky. The higher the volatility of a stock, or any asset, the higher its risk. Unit trusts that invest only in equities are higher risk than those that invest in other assets. Their prices move further and the chance of loss is higher.

Hence, the correct option is (A).

32. The meaning of the acronym 'SHRM' is Strategic Human Resource Management. Strategic human resource management includes typical human resource components such as hiring, discipline, and payroll, and also involves working with employees in a collaborative manner to boost retention, improve the quality of the work experience, and maximize the mutual benefit of employment for both the employee and the employer.

Hence, the correct option is (B).

33. Whenever the marginal cost is greater than the average total cost, the average total cost is rising.
Marginal cost is the change in the total cost that arises when the quantity produced is incremented by one unit, that is, it is the cost of producing one more unit of a good.
Hence, the correct option is (A).

34. The marginal revenue equation can be derived from the demand equation.

The demand equation is the mathematical expression of the relationship between the quantity of a good demanded and those factors that affect the willingness and ability of a consumer to buy the good.

Hence, the correct option is (A).

35. A dyadic relationship between a manager who is offering help and an employee to whom such help is given. This is known as counselling.

Counselling is a psychological technique and that is used in various forms. The main objective of it is to support the employees by providing them advice, guidance, suggestions to solve the prevailing problems and improve physical and mental conditions, performance and which can take many forms.

Hence, the correct option is (B).

// Notes //

// Notes //

www.ingramcontent.com/pod-product-compliance
Lightning Source LLC
LaVergne TN
LVHW080551200726
843510LV00008B/1075

* 9 7 8 8 1 9 4 8 7 4 7 1 3 *